# STUDIES IN
# IMPERIALISM

General editor: Andrew S. Thompson
Founding editor: John M. MacKenzie

When the 'Studies in Imperialism' series was founded by Professor John M. MacKenzie more than thirty years ago, emphasis was laid upon the conviction that 'imperialism as a cultural phenomenon had as significant an effect on the dominant as on the subordinate societies'. With well over a hundred titles now published, this remains the prime concern of the series. Cross-disciplinary work has indeed appeared covering the full spectrum of cultural phenomena, as well as examining aspects of gender and sex, frontiers and law, science and the environment, language and literature, migration and patriotic societies, and much else. Moreover, the series has always wished to present comparative work on European and American imperialism, and particularly welcomes the submission of books in these areas. The fascination with imperialism, in all its aspects, shows no sign of abating, and this series will continue to lead the way in encouraging the widest possible range of studies in the field. 'Studies in Imperialism' is fully organic in its development, always seeking to be at the cutting edge, responding to the latest interests of scholars and the needs of this ever-expanding area of scholarship.

## Savage worlds

MANCHESTER
1824

Manchester University Press

# Savage worlds

## GERMAN ENCOUNTERS ABROAD, 1798–1914

Edited by Matthew P. Fitzpatrick and Peter Monteath

MANCHESTER
UNIVERSITY PRESS

Copyright © Manchester University Press 2018

While copyright in the volume as a whole is vested in Manchester University Press, copyright in individual chapters belongs to their respective authors, and no chapter may be reproduced wholly or in part without the express permission in writing of both author and publisher.

Published by MANCHESTER UNIVERSITY PRESS
ALTRINCHAM STREET, MANCHESTER M1 7JA
www.manchesteruniversitypress.co.uk

*British Library Cataloguing-in-Publication Data*
A catalogue record for this book is available from the British Library

ISBN 978 1 5261 2340 4 hardback
ISBN 978 1 5261 5165 0 paperback

First published 2018

The publisher has no responsibility for the persistence or accuracy of URLs for any external or third-party internet websites referred to in this book, and does not guarantee that any content on such websites is, or will remain, accurate or appropriate.


Typeset
by Toppan Best-set Premedia Limited

# CONTENTS

CONTENTS

# FIGURES

# NOTES ON CONTRIBUTORS

**Eva Bischoff** is Lecturer in International History at the University of Trier. Her research interests include colonial and imperial history, postcolonial theory, and gender/queer studies. She received her PhD from the Ludwig-Maximilians University in Munich. Her thesis was published in 2011 as a monograph: *Kannibale-Werden. Eine postkoloniale Geschichte deutscher Männlichkeit um 1900*. She recently concluded a book project investigating the history of a group of Quaker families and their roles in the process of settler imperialism in early nineteenth-century Australia.

**Andrew G. Bonnell** is Associate Professor of History at the University of Queensland. He previously taught at the University of Sydney and Griffith University, Australia. His publications include *The People's Stage in Imperial Germany. Social Democracy and Culture, 1890–1914* (1905), *Shylock in Germany: Antisemitism and the German Theatre from the Enlightenment to the Nazis* (2008) and *An American Witness in Nazi Frankfurt: The Diaries of Robert W. Heingartner, 1928–1937* (edited, 2011), as well as numerous book chapters and journal articles on modern German history.

**Matthew P. Fitzpatrick** is Associate Professor in International History at Flinders University, Adelaide. He is the author of *Purging the Empire: Mass Expulsions in Germany, 1871–1914* (2015) and *Liberal Imperialism in Germany: Expansionism and Nationalism, 1848–1884* (2008). He has been a Humboldt Fellow at the Westphalian University of Münster in Germany and is currently working on a monograph on Kaiser Wilhelm II's role in German foreign and colonial policy prior to the First World War.

**Hilary Howes** is Postdoctoral Fellow at The Australian National University (ANU) in Canberra, working on Professor Matthew Spriggs's Laureate Fellowship project 'The Collective Biography of Archaeology in the Pacific: A Hidden History' (CBAP). Her current research, which addresses the German-speaking tradition within Pacific archaeology and ethnology, builds on her doctoral dissertation, published as *The Race Question in Oceania: A.B. Meyer and Otto Finsch between metropolitan theory and field experience, 1865–1914* (2013). From 2011 to 2015 she was employed at the Australian Embassy in Berlin, where her responsibilities included bilateral research collaboration and the repatriation of Australian Indigenous ancestral remains from German collecting institutions.

**Antje Kühnast** is Research Assistant with the research network Race and Ethnicity in the Global South (REGS) in the Department of History at the University of Sydney. She investigates the appropriation and scientific utilisation of Australian Aboriginal ancestral remains by German naturalists and physical anthropologists during the long nineteenth century. Her research interests include the histories of racial and evolutionary theorising, transnational scientific networks and German physical anthropology in the Pacific region. She has published a number of book chapters on these topics.

**Daniel Midena** is Postdoctoral Research Fellow in the Instituted for Advanced Studies in the Humanities at the University of Queensland. His research interests span the histories of science and religion (and their intersection) in German and British colonies in the South Pacific. He is currently preparing a monograph on the history of Lutheran missionary ethnography in German New Guinea.

**Peter Monteath** is Professor of History at Flinders University in Adelaide. He has been a Humboldt Fellow at the Technical University of Berlin. He is the editor and translator of Friedrich Gerstäcker's *Australia: A German Traveller in the Age of Gold* (2016), and he is the co-author, with Valerie Munt, of a biography of the anthropologist Frederick Rose, published under the title *Red Professor: The Cold War Life of Fred Rose* (2015).

**Ulf Morgenstern** is Member of the Research Staff of the Otto-von-Bismarck-Foundation, Friedrichsruh. He is the author of *Bürgergeist und Familientradition. Die liberale Gelehrtenfamilie Schücking im 19. und 20. Jahrhundert* (2012) and the editor of the *Bismarck-Documents of 1886–87 (2017)* and of the *Autobiography of Robert Lucius von Ballhausen* (2017). As a Postdoctoral Research Fellow in Global History at the University of Hamburg he is currently working on a monograph on colonialism in photographs, letters, and book chapters that the German scholar and politician Carl Heinrich Becker produced and reproduced during and after two travels in the Orient, 1900–2 and 1931–2.

**Nicole Perry** is Lecturer in German at the University of Auckland, New Zealand. Her research interests are German/North American indigenous connections and contemporary Austrian literature. She has been a Lise Meitner-Programme Fellow at the University of Vienna for her project 'Performing Germanness, Reclaiming Aboriginality', which examines North American indigenous artistic reactions and reappropria-tions of the German *Indianer* image.

**Stefan Rinke** is Professor and Chair of the Department of History at the Institute of Latin American Studies and the Friedrich-Meinecke-Institute at the Freie Universität Berlin. He has been the recipient of the Premio Alzate from the Mexican Academy of Sciences and the Einstein Research Fellowship. He has also been President of the European Association of Historians of Latin America (AHILA). Rinke has published numerous monographs, collected volumes and articles. His latest book, *Latin America and the First World War*, was published by Cambridge University Press in 2017.

**Hidde van der Wall** is Assistant Professor in the Department of Fine Arts, Ateneo de Manila University, Philippines. Having received his PhD in German Studies from the University of Nottingham for a thesis on East German intellectuals in the 1950s, he is currently interested in postcolonial Philippine culture and historiography as well as German and Dutch observations of the Philippines in the nineteenth and twentieth centuries. He has recently published on the Manila poems of Jan Jacob Slauerhoff and is currently working on articles on the historical writings of Nick Joaquin.

**Judith Wilson** has recently retired from a position as Lecturer in German Studies at the University of Adelaide. Her present research is focused on intercultural and postcolonial approaches to German literature and German–Australian connections in the nineteenth century. She has published a number of articles on the role of Australia as an imaginary space in the works of nineteenth-century German writers.

# CHAPTER ONE

# The savagery of empire

## Matthew P. Fitzpatrick and Peter Monteath

The savage global effects of imperialism have been identified, studied, and in some places mitigated and apologised for; but they have not been undone.[1] As recent works examining attempts to decolonise knowledge and institutions have shown,[2] contemporary social attitudes, structures and practices around the world remain deeply connected with their point of origin in the structures of Europe's global empires.[3] In many places, particularly the settler colonial lands of the Americas, Oceania, the Middle East and Africa, a truly 'post-colonial' moment has never arrived and the colonial order of things has persisted, despite recent calls for a reckoning with colonial institutions and social structures.[4] Even in lands where formal decolonisation did take place, the social and cultural meanings of pre-colonial practices, sometimes revived and positioned as 'authentic' traces of the pre-colonial world, have often revealed how the epistemic violence of empire has rendered their original role and social logic irretrievable.[5] In this environment, definitive forms of postcolonial reconciliation remain elusive, as the descendants of Europe's colonisers and the colonised indigenous peoples of the world wrestle with the meanings of the colonial past. Globally, empire remains an unhealed wound that periodically generates fresh symptoms, such as the present push for reparations made by peoples colonised by Britain, France and Germany.[6] Understanding and coming to terms with Europe's colonial past remains, it seems, an urgent task; not so that a final moment of reconciliation between colonisers and the colonised might be reached but so that honest working relationships and understandings that recognise the ongoing legacies of the colonial past might be generated.

Having lost its colonies at the end of the First World War, Germany is often seen by non-specialists as having been a modest player in

Europe's global imperial endeavours and as having another, more urgent twentieth-century imperial history to confront in the shape of Nazism's genocidal bid for Continental empire.[7] As such, it is not frequently recognised outside of German studies that the German state and the global German diaspora were in fact deeply implicated in nineteenth- and twentieth-century imperial practices and the moral, intellectual and political economy of Europe's age of global empire. For those working in the field of German colonial history, however, this story of Germany's vigorous colonial past is not a revelation. Ever since Horst Drechsler's seminal *Let Us Die Fighting*, a critical historiography attuned to the causes and effects of Germany's colonial interactions has been quietly building.[8]

The different phases of this historiography are well known.[9] However the present volume, dedicated to understanding the nature of German interactions with the non-European world, diverges from earlier, more established lines of inquiry by parenthesising the role of the omnipresent German state, so as to focus on the role of non-state actors. Unlike other earlier works, it does not attempt to tease out what 'Germanness' looked like abroad, or to scrutinise the various strands of national identification within Germany's global diaspora.[10] Nor does it seek to affirm or deny the marginality or pervasiveness of colonialism inside Germany itself.[11] Instead, this volume investigates how Germans moved away from the role thrust upon them by commentators and colonial agitators in the colonial metropole as representatives of and interlocutors for German state power, and explored their extended scope for intellectual and cultural agency, an agency granted by overarching imperial structures that privileged European projects in frontier zones. Without forgetting the historical importance and the indispensable weight of the imperial state, that which Sebastian Conrad and Jürgen Osterhammel have compellingly described as the *'Kaiserreich transnational'*,[12] or the German state's exploitation of the extra-European world for its own ends, this volume focuses on specific frontier entanglements. This is in the hope that the terrain of the debate might shift beyond the state, beyond even the transatlantic transplanting of more or less recognisably German communities – that which H. Glenn Penny calls 'German polycentrism'[13] – to look at the nature and impact of settler and sojourner experiences in the extra-European world, as well as the resonance of reflections on these experiences. By providing microhistories of German frontier entanglements, this volume offers historians an opportunity to capture the heterogeneity of the modes of exchange between Germans and non-European peoples, which ran the full gamut of experiences from eliminatory violence to intermarriage. In this vein, the essays in this book offer a series of case studies of German interactions with the extra-European world that together offer some of the missing texture and finer grain of Germany's colonial-era global reach.

By focusing on microhistories and specific case studies, this book also seeks to reshape productively the contours of the ongoing debate about the nature of German interactions with non-Europeans, a debate perhaps best encapsulated by the line that currently divides historians of German anthropology such as Penny and Andrew Zimmerman. At issue has been the question of whether German liberal humanism exercised a mitigating influence that softened anthropology's racialising tendencies, or whether German anthropology was racialised through and throughout its overseas settler and sojourner contexts. Arguing in favour of the former position in the introduction to their volume *Worldly Provincialism*, Penny and Matti Bunzl characterised nineteenth-century German anthropology as 'a self-consciously liberal endeavour, guided by a broadly humanistic agenda'. They argued that prior to the First World War, 'the majority [of German anthropologists] were not racist, but strongly opposed to biologically based theories of human difference'.[14] It was only with the postwar period, they argued, that German anthropology took a biologically racist turn.

In the same volume and in his book *Anthropology and Antihumanism*, however, Andrew Zimmerman argued against precisely this depiction of German engagement with non-Europeans (which he called the 'liberal to racism historiography in physical anthropology').[15] For Zimmerman, empire-enabling racial theory lay at the heart of German anthropology, irrespective of whether it was evinced in Rudolf Virchow's anti-evolutionist stance or Ernst Haeckel's Darwinism.[16]

This debate, which is in some ways a reworking of positions outlined two decades ago by Susanne Zantop and Russell Berman, hinges on differing interpretations of how the Enlightenment project and 'Humboldtian' ideals translated into German actions in the extra-European world.[17] It has focused on the qualitative nature of German interactions with the extra-European world, and has questioned whether Germans held exceptionally benevolent 'feelings of affinity' or an 'enchantment' with indigenous peoples, which Penny has recently argued was most evident in a subjective affinity with and empathy for the suffering of Native Americans.[18]

While most of the chapters here engage with this debate by offering detailed empirical pictures of what frontier interactions between Germans and colonised peoples looked like, the question of such subjective affinities is taken up explicitly in this volume by Nicole Perry and Judith Wilson, who scrutinise how German interactions with the world were represented to metropolitan audiences. In her contribution, Perry makes clear that, on the one hand, the indigenous peoples of North America were often used metaphorically in both metropolitan and frontier narratives as ciphers for intrinsically European dilemmas surrounding the arrival of a post-*ancien-régime* political and social modernity. On the other hand, even when drawn sympathetically, indigenous peoples were often still represented as ineluctably inhabiting the 'anachronistic space' identified more than twenty years ago by Anne McClintock, appearing as mere non-historical atavisms who would inevitably fall away with the arrival of colonisers serving the *Weltgeist* of European progress.[19]

For Wilson, a closer, contextualist reading of Friedrich Gerstäcker's oeuvre (drawn from his extensive travels) and that of his contemporaries shows exactly the problem with the binary nature of this debate. Wilson illustrates just how a chauvinistic and Eurocentric conceptualisation of alterity which countenanced an acceptance of the inevitability of indigenous decline could co-exist with a fierce critique of the presumptions of those Europeans who considered themselves to be the bearers of civilisation to an extra-European world conceived of as the domain of the savage. Decentring the colonial metropole, Wilson problematises a historiographical binary which has viewed Germans as tendentially either sympathetic or antagonistic towards indigenous peoples. In the process, she suggests that by closely studying actual frontier interactions and episodes historians can uncover the high degree of inconsistency and cognitive dissonance not just amongst Germans but even within the attitudes and actions of a single individual.

As a whole, the contributions in this volume support the view that even the most sympathetic of Germans viewed the demise of some indigenous cultures and populations in Hegelian terms as the price of world historical progress.[20] If the conclusions offered by the research here make it difficult to substantiate Penny's sense of German solidarity with the colonised in the face of frontier violence, it is, however, equally difficult to view the (latently genocidal) assumptions of colonising Germans as somehow uniquely German. The sense that the world was full of dying races who could not meet the rigours of the coming European world was shared by most colonising powers, with British Prime Minister Salisbury perhaps the most prominent advocate of the view that 'the living nations will gradually encroach on the territory of the dying'.[21] Yet, notwithstanding the recent proliferation of studies investigating the record of colonial mass violence and genocide in North America, Australia, the Dutch East Indies and the Belgian Congo (to name but a few),[22] some historians of German colonialism have looked to assert the uniqueness of German imperialism, viewing the Germans as particularly violent in their methods of colonisation, as especially uncompromising in their application of racial theory or as perfecting violent regimes of racialisation that would form the basis for and prehistory of the atrocities of Nazism in later decades.[23]

Given the proliferation of brutal colonial violence around the world at much the same time, this retooling of the *Sonderweg* thesis for colonial purposes seems unjustified.[24] Fighting colonial wars in China, East Africa and most famously South-West Africa,[25] as well as suppressing indigenous resistance in the Pacific,[26] the German state was just as brutal as other European states in its support of the outpost settlements they had grafted on to indigenous territories. Germans, like other Europeans in colonial spaces, were buttressed by the might of armies and navies with a global reach which, if called upon, were capable of unleashing campaigns of overwhelming violence to protect European hegemony. The maintenance of European rule over non-European spaces was a key objective of virtually all settler colonies, not just those hosting Germans, and the violence this imperative engendered in the Americas, Australia, Asia and Africa has been well established.[27] The violence condoned and perpetrated by Germans in the extra-European world, however, was not an expression of a unique German *Sonderweg* that led the Germans 'from Africa to Auschwitz'. Rather, Germany's colonial violence interlocked with the broader, pan-European project of global expansionism that in Europe was portrayed as 'pacification' in the service of a civilising mission, but was experienced in the extra-European world as violence and dispossession. As Stefan Rinke demonstrates in his chapter here devoted to frontier violence in colonial Brazil, Germans were not only just as likely to participate in the genocidal processes of settler colonialism as non-German settlers, they also took part in this frontier violence alongside and in conjunction with other colonists from a range of settler nations who shared their colonising objectives.

To point to the structural violence that lay at the heart of settler colonialism is not, however, to say that colonising states such as Germany were home to a monolithically pro-colonial citizenry, as Andrew Bonnell demonstrates here. In a contribution that demonstrates how essentialising umbrella terms such as 'European imperialism' and 'Western colonialism' can airbrush out the political and structural heterogeneity of the colonial metropole,[28] Bonnell engages constructively with Guettel's work to point out that German Social Democrats remained opposed to colonialism and to wars against indigenous peoples in the German colonies, notwithstanding the enormous pressure brought to bear upon the party in the context of a colonial uprising which had seen the deaths of German colonists and an election campaign in 1907 that sought to wedge the Social Democrats on the 'colonial question'. Crucially, for Bonnell, the Social Democrats' expressions of solidarity with the colonised were not sparked by the kind of subjective affinity that Penny has explored, but rather reflected a firmly articulated matter of principle based on a clear view of the political and economic nature of empire and its effects on the colonised. Rather than seeking to identify personally with non-Europeans (whose experience they manifestly did not share), German Social Democrats simply adhered to a political position of solidarity with indigenous peoples such as the Herero and Nama who had been dispossessed by the violent forces of globalising capitalism that afflicted German workers domestically.

Conversely, while Social Democrats did not have to leave Germany to register their solidarity with colonised peoples they had never met, Ulf Morgenstern's discussion here of Carl Heinrich Becker shows clearly the extent to which a total scholarly immersion in the non-European world was no guarantee of an ability to see past essentialising notions of 'the authentic native' that could be documented, studied and understood by the itinerant scholar. A more contrasting example to that offered by Bonnell's Social Democrats is hard to imagine, with the haughty Becker rubbing shoulders with elite European politicians and industrialists in Egypt before approvingly surveying the wreckage of the Sudan in the wake of Herbert Kitchener's reconquest. Far from Suzanne Marchand's portrait of the dispassionate scholar, Morgenstern makes clear that German orientalists such as Becker blended scholarship with a particularly political, that is imperial, understanding and experience of the extra-European world.[29]

Such metropolitan variations in attitudes towards colonialism and colonised people were, of course, matched by similar forms of differentiation at the local, frontier level. Marked by violence, but also by negotiation, co-operation and intermingling, the different micro-ecologies of empire were given their shape by the interlocking mechanics of, on the one hand, the variegated expressions of agency of those at the colonial interface and, on the other, the macro-structural imperatives of imperial exploitation and dispossession. By locating and studying the dynamics of specific sites of colonial exchange at the micro level, as many of the following chapters do, the well documented macro-level picture of trans-imperial exchanges and structures that has been uncovered by transnational historians of empire is complemented by a firmer grasp of the undergrowth of interpersonal, face-to-face interactions between Europeans and non-Europeans in colonial spaces.[30] Focusing on this individuating terrain yields surprisingly complex pictures, complicating the (at times one-dimensional) macro-level narratives of state actors exercising smoothly functioning forms of power with little friction from below.[31]

Enmeshed in a frontier dynamic of forcible dispossession that similarly faced colonisers from other backgrounds, Germans responded in the same fashion as others in settler colonial situations. In some contexts this meant radical violence, whereas in others it meant less violent forms of domination or even mutual exchange. With this in mind, Penny and Bunzl are certainly correct to caution against totalising, teleologically loaded assumptions about German attitudes towards the extra-European world and (in particular) race that reduce the colonial period to merely an incubator for the racial violence of the metropolis under Nazism or even a genocidal prelude to the Holocaust.[32] This is particularly the case for the interactions studied here, in which Germans were active in colonial sites not controlled by the German state. With Germany only formally acquiring extra-European state colonies after 1884, German colonial entanglements initially occurred in the absence of any formal German colonial structures to guide them. Ignoring these non-state endeavours risks overlooking important examples of Germans' involvement in colonising endeavours. As Sebastian Conrad has argued, 'the bulk of the literature continues to focus on the territorial empire – and neglects the much broader fields of imperial activity Germany was involved in, both before and after 1884'.[33] Examining the experiences of Germans in these non-German colonial spaces offers glimpses into how the transnational mechanics of imperialism looked at the grassroots level. Felicity Jensz's study of Moravian missionaries in colonial Australia is instructive in this regard, demonstrating how an understanding of the colonising efforts of 'influential strangers' like German missionaries and anthropologists in non-German colonies allows for a 'critical examination of colonial politics ... revealing the treatment of indigenous inhabitants as seen through the eyes of a non-English ... organization'.[34] Often overlooked in colonial history, these insider–outsider roles were regularly played by Germans who came into sustained contact with indigenous societies, but with aims that were not necessarily identical with those of the colonising power that hosted them. These multidirectional frontier entanglements between the colonising state, colonised indigenous peoples and German sojourners spanned a range of modalities, including pitiless violence and mutual exchange.

The concept of frontier entanglements has proved to be an important heuristic for researchers seeking ways to describe the full range of modalities of frontier interaction. The term 'entanglements' offers an explanatory mechanism that can encompass both colonial antagonism and co-operation. Coined by the anthropologist Nicholas Thomas in 1991,[35] it has recently been adopted by historians seeking a way out of the impasse presented by monodirectional narratives of colonial relations that focus solely on the (all too prevalent) physical and epistemic violence wrought by the colonisers.[36] Without doubt, frontier violence remains integral to the history of imperialism; particularly the history of settler colonialism, where it is often the most important part of the story.[37] Nonetheless, some of the literature on imperial encounters also points to more complicated frontier interactions in which varying expressions of indigenous agency and cross-cultural intimacies emerged and sometimes flourished underneath the asymmetrical structures of economic, political and military power that supported European imperialism.[38] Similarly, the improvised adaptations made by both colonisers and colonised to the highly charged, socially and culturally fluid frontier situation is also becoming more apparent courtesy of accounts that stress the permeability of the frontier.

This permeability was often a product of existing patterns of cross-cultural interaction in non-European spaces. Although, by its very nature, European imperialism greatly disrupted the economic, political and cultural patterns that characterised polities in the 'pre-contact' era, some of these polities had long been plugged into complex, pre-existing, multidirectional webs of contact – including localised imperial webs within the Afro-Eurasian exchange network that had thrived for hundreds of years before European hegemony.[39] Others, however, had previously experienced only limited contact with more immediate neighbours for equally long periods.[40] In both cases, the irreversible disruption of the pre-colonial order led to the construction of new cultural amalgams marked by new forms of inequality and patterns of hierarchy.[41] Studying the broader dimensions of imperialism's entanglements alongside the frontier violence that accompanied them allows historians to lay bare the textured nature of frontier encounters and to appreciate the complex interconnectedness between its disparate symptoms, without denying the structural inequalities and violence that underwrote it.

With an eye to recovering the heterogeneity of such exchanges between German sojourners and settlers and indigenous peoples in extra-European zones of contact, this volume maps German interactions with African, North and South American, Pacific, Australasian and Asian peoples. It examines the heterogeneous goals and experiences of German explorers, settlers, travellers, merchants, academics and state officials in the extra-European world, and questions how the variety of projects they undertook intersected with indigenous cultural priorities and shaped frontier relationships. Its emphasis on colonial experiences gained on the frontier, and their gradual and uneven repatriation to the metropole, seeks to amplify and augment similar efforts made by scholars in recent years. In 2014, Nina Berman, Klaus Mühlhahn and Patrice Nganang argued for a shift in the terrain of the debate regarding German colonialism, pointing to the need for an approach 'centring on practices of interaction'. This approach, they have correctly suggested, 'sheds new light on local power dynamics'.[42] In a survey of the literature on German interactions with South America, Penny has noted that such studies in the case of Germans in South America have uncovered 'cultural flexibility and a striking degree of agency' in the navigation of 'overlapping cultural spaces'.[43] Admittedly such work continues, however, to be lopsided, given that contemporaneous indigenous attitudes towards these frontier interactions remain difficult to uncover. Despite enormous strides in recovering indigenous agency, Gayatri Chakravorty Spivak's question of the extent to which 'subaltern' perspectives are accessible to historians remains just as relevant now as it was twenty years ago.[44] Confronted with apparent indigenous silences (or rather the silencing of indigenous peoples), most historians, including many contributions here, have approached this problem through attentive, contrapuntal readings of European archival holdings, an approach that Ann Laura Stoler has rightly both championed and urged historians to treat with caution.[45]

As Stoler has pointed out, the archive itself, as well as its contents, are situated, with colonial archives by their very nature most heavily imprinted at points where state power is most fragile. Archival records follow an institutional logic that foregrounds conflicts and problems that required a state or institutional response.[46] Most obviously, for example, revolts against the colonial state generated enormous bodies of archival material that have been of great use for studying the dynamics of imperial power. Historians of German imperialism have fruitfully used such archival material to study colonial revolts in German South-West Africa, the Pacific and East Africa, so as to test their metonymic value for understanding the broader nature of German and European approaches towards controlling an unruly alterity.[47] In this record of frontier colonial warfare, the archival record speaks to indigenous agency; not only amongst those tens of thousands revolting against the metropole but also in the action of the forty to fifty thousand indigenous people who took up arms for the German colonisers rather than against them, a practice held in common with other European empires.[48]

Particularly in regions where independent indigenous written and oral records of frontier encounters have not survived, archival approaches remain important. For all their innate shortcomings, archival records can at least partially reveal the texture of frontier lives and experiences. Certainly, archival approaches can only reconstruct those elements of indigenous culture, politics and life that intersected most heavily with those of their colonisers (and only imperfectly). They can answer only a subset of the questions that historians have about frontier zones and those who inhabited them, while leaving the question of the politics of representation unsatisfactorily answered.[49]

State archives are even less successful at gauging and recording non-state intercommunal interactions, whether unreported instances of low-intensity frontier violence, scholarly or missionary endeavours, or cross-frontier trade or marriage. Here, historians rely, as many of the authors in this collection do, upon sources such as diaries, travelogues, literature, newspaper reports, indigenous traditions and colonial ephemera to offer a sense of the texture of frontier encounters and to attempt to assess the nature and depth of exchanges that took place. Through these sources the subjectivities of Germans who encountered non-Europeans in North America, Africa, the Levant, Asia and the Pacific and who reflected upon these encounters can be accessed and studied. More problematically, these sources also (although frequently poorly and always imperfectly) ventriloquise the positions (or imagined positions) of colonised peoples. Deconstructing these representations of the colonised remains important work, but sensitive microhistorical readings attuned to the specific power constellations revealed by frontier texts can offer imperfect, partial but nonetheless useful reconstructions of the multidimensional nature of the dynamics of colonial frontiers, in the hope that the erasure of indigenous peoples from the history of empire (a history which unfolded on their territories) can be mitigated or even resisted if not entirely alleviated.

By way of example, in this volume, the contribution by Hilary Howes seeks to read the colonial record in ways that bring to light dimensions of both the indigenous experience of imperialism and the European narration of this experience. Focusing on East New Britain in the Bismarck Archipelago, Howes illustrates that the depictions of the Tolai by Otto Finsch served a dual purpose of, on the one hand, asserting his (to his mind under-acknowledged) credentials as the foremost expert on New Guinean affairs but, on the other, of rehabilitating the reputation of the Tolai in Europe and critiquing aspects of European penetration of the region and its effects on local conditions. Although operating within a Eurocentric frame of reference which assumed simple binaries such as civilised and savage, Finsch sought to push beyond them, to demonstrate that behaviours coded by Europeans as either civilised or savage could easily co-exist in the same person, as demonstrated (to his mind) by his young New Guinean protégé, Tapinowanne, who voluntarily visited Europe for a time before returning home. The meaning of Finsch and Tapinowanne's shared experience of global travel remains hard to reconstruct definitively from Tapinowanne's perspective. What is clear, however, is that the interaction between the European and the Melanesian cannot be explained as simply an expression of Finsch's imperial power over a young indigenous man. The presence of Europeans afforded Tapinowanne an opportunity for agency, and he took it.

Travelogues too have an important if ambivalent role to play in reconstructing frontier encounters, as Eva Bischoff's chapter here makes clear. Bischoff illustrates both the usefulness and the difficulties of first-person accounts in her discussion of Meg Gehrts's travelogue *A Camera Actress in the Wilds of Togoland*. Gehrts travelled to Africa to act in *The White Goddess of the Wangora*, a film that centred on the fictional story of a white girl raised as a black one, who discovers her racial identity and escapes her African captors. Whilst travelling, Gehrts kept a diary which not only recorded her perceptions of the Africans she met in Togo but also captured her reimaginings of herself and her position as both white and a woman in Africa. It recounts her sense of her gendered role on the expedition as an *ersatz* domestic homemaker, while highlighting her perceived new freedoms in the extra-European world, a sense of expanded possibilities in Africa that Bischoff suggestively describes as 'imperial feminism'. At the same time, Bischoff argues, Gehrts's account betrays her rudimentary attempts to come to terms with the situatedness of social and cultural encodings of phenotypic difference, as she ponders the significance of the comments of some honest Africans who told her bluntly that her whiteness was in fact a form of ugliness, which they could but only try not to hold against her.

As this and other contributions in this volume show, the forms of exchanges across the frontier defy easy aggregation and differ markedly, depending on the political, geographical and economic nature of the frontier site in question. These variances in the structuring contexts of imperialism demonstrate that, while there might be overarching material foundations that account for imperialism at the macro level, historians must be careful when positing definitive conclusions about the intrinsic nature of the 'colonial experience' that these material foundations generated. The differing material priorities and functions of settler, plantation and mercantile colonies partially structured the range of possibilities for intersubjectival frontier encounters, just as differences in the gender, class and 'race' of those on the frontier also further magnified the scope for individuating colonial experiences. Charting the permutations and intersections of these differences requires a microhistorical approach, something approaching a prosopography of the frontier, focused not on heroic biographies of settlers or explorers but on fine-grained studies of the fragments of concrete sites of exchange, mutual interaction and conflict.

Studying such imperial entanglements reveals that, notwithstand-ing the fact that these encounters took place within the context of dispossession and increasingly pronounced asymmetries of power, frontier entanglements were not uniformly acrimonious (even if many were). It further reveals that the acrimony was most often not a direct translation of an overarching theory of race into a form of ideological praxis, but more often reflected intensely localised economic, political and interpersonal dynamics that approximately shadowed the broader (fundamentally material) struggle unleashed by Europeans attempting to wrest control of non-European societies and their lands.

Despite not being the only productive lens through which colonial encounters can be viewed, the category of race nonetheless informs most of the discussions in this collection. In employing race as an analytical category, however, it is necessary to have a clear understanding of its ontological status as a concept. Post-Foucauldian and Butlerian scholarship has regularly made the strong ontological claim that 'the materiality of the racial body is an effect of discourse'.[50] Under this reading, the raced body appears as a discursively constituted line of demarcation between the colonised and the colonisers, called upon to naturalise the myriad forms of hierarchy required for the creation and maintenance of imperial rule. While the denaturalisation of the essentialist, connotative value judgements accompanying racialisation remains a *sine qua non* of any serious scholarship on race, it does not follow that colonial-era phenotypic difference can be explained away as being intrinsically performative. Understandably, historians who have positioned race as 'being performatively constituted' have rejected the ontological status of embodied difference in an attempt to disarm colonial (and indeed contemporary) racist theoretics that have mobilised phenotypic differences as a means of naturalising imperial hierarchies.[51]

Recent work on race, however, has made clear that this ontological route is not the only way to defuse essentialist colonial racial hierarchies. As Arun Saldanha has argued, 'battling against racism is ... not a question of denying race, but of cultivating its energies against the stickiness of racial segregation'.[52] Toril Moi is similarly instructive here, insisting that, while 'biological facts cannot ground human values', the biological is not entirely absent, a mere empty signifier waiting to be allocated meaning by discourse. With this in mind, Linda Martín Alcoff has similarly argued that, 'race is real' in the phenomenological sense that 'race is constitutive of bodily experience, subjectivity, judgment, and epistemic relationships'. It is, Alcoff makes clear, 'a constitutive element of fundamental, everyday embodied existence, psychic life, and social interaction'.[53] For historians, the consequences of this ontological rethinking are that histories of colonial spaces in which racialised bodies played a dynamic role are histories firmly grounded in materialism, rather than linguistic idealism.[54]

The accounts here offer some of the empirical terrain against which this phenomenological materialist understanding of race might be tested, by making clear that the social encoding of physical differences was a product of both immediate contextual imperatives and available discursive structures. At both levels, the meaning of race was subject to change, wherever and whenever the material and intellectual conditions required for differing conceptualisations of race emerged. At the microhistorical level, however, interpersonal and intersubjectival entanglements show a range of modalities and understandings of racial 'worth' that co-existed with apparently totalising conditions of structural violence. Often, in scrutinising the overarching conditions attending the production of metropolitan racial knowledge in search of an epochal 'episteme' or 'discursive formation' at the macro level,[55] scholars of race have overlooked the subsystemic frontier experiences and exchanges of those on the frontier whose firmest 'knowledge' of racial matters was a product of the conditions of the particular colonial site they inhabited. Focusing too closely on metropolitan discourses of race risks the construction of unreliable chains of causality which fail to recognise that metropolitan understandings and encodings of phenotypic difference were partly aggregations and partly imperfect (mis)readings of the multifarious ways that race functioned in concrete frontier situations.[56]

Many of the contributions here deal with the extra-European experiences of German scholars. While it is clear that their 'knowledge' (more *doxa* than *episteme*) garnered from frontier interracial encounters was repatriated to the colonial metropole, this frontier knowledge was routinely altered, filtered, misunderstood and in many instances simply ignored. Antje Kühnast makes abundantly clear in her offering to this volume that, even in the case of dealing with indigenous skeletal remains in the ostensibly scientific discipline of physical anthropology, the frontier collector's contextual knowledge of the indigenous remains' provenance was often overlooked or altered. This was demonstrably the case when the German naturalist and collector Ludwig Becker stressed to his German anthropological counterparts the unreliability of skulls as a guide to the intellectual or cultural worth of the individuals to whom they had belonged. Kühnast illustrates precisely how even Becker's partial understanding of the complexity of the individual Australian Aborigines whose remains he acquired was overlooked by the recipients of the remains, who then imposed the disciplinary assumptions of German anthropology upon them.

Away from the physical sciences, the travel narratives of Carl Semper and Fedor Jagor, discussed here by Hidde van der Wall, similarly illustrate how essentialist and racialised assumptions based on phenotypical differences were distilled through cultural conditions that pertained to a particular site of colonisation. While still employing a racialised taxonomy of the Filipino population, both travellers blamed what they viewed as a lack of culture not on intrinsic racial traits but rather on the impact of Spanish colonists on the local population. Their conclusions, half racialised, half culturally chauvinist, were malleable enough to be repurposed and reused thereafter by a number of different discourse communities. While they underpinned the arguments of Germans looking for the Philippines to be transferred to German rule, they also met the purposes of Filipino nationalists seeking independence from the Spanish. Ultimately they even supplied justifications for invading North Americans who found the anthropological assumptions of the German writers to be a useful tool for justifying their own turn to empire in the Philippines.

With the imperial penetration of the extra-European world requiring political and economic forms of hierarchy that privileged the colonisers over the colonised, racial knowledge became an anthropological and political shorthand for locally prevailing variants of imperial hierarchy. Regionally specific racial theorising and practice always remained malleable and adaptable enough to be applied in different imperial sites with different imperial dynamics. Phenotypic difference allowed the underlying material status differentials required by empire to be articulated through the language of race, because, outside of Europe, phenotypic differences were an obvious and easy way to discern the privileged coloniser from the colonised. Under these conditions, materially derived, context-specific social distinctions ossified and came to be understood as intrinsic forms of racial inequality. As Patrick Wolfe famously argued, however, 'race is but one among various regimes of difference that have served to distinguish dominant groups from groups whom they initially encountered in colonial contexts'.[57] In imperial sites where phenotypic differences were not as pronounced, or the overlap between racial difference and the needs of power were not great, other forms of difference – some externally apparent, others not – came to the fore. Thus, confession, caste, culture, linguistic difference and not least class differentials played their role in metropolitan imperial sites (such as the Polish East, the French West and the Danish North in the German case), where phenotypic difference could not do the heavy lifting required by empire.

For those (such as missionaries) operating outside of the apparatus of the colonial state, race understood as a question of biology and the body mattered much less than cultural attributes. Accordingly, the difference between a settler pastoralist's and a missionary's conceptualisation of the colonised could at times be immense – as demonstrated by the animosity that pastoralist settlers showed German missionaries during the Herero-Nama Wars, when missionaries were accused of having incited Africans to attack farmers.[58] With missionaries seeking to transplant variants of Europe's Christian cosmology around the globe, their efforts came to hinge not so much on a critique of the indigenous body and its place in a colonial social hierarchy as on an understanding of non-European belief patterns and the capacity of Indigenous peoples' epistemological and conceptual frameworks to accommodate the foreign cultural and religious concepts that were central to Christianity. As Daniel Midena's contribution here makes clear, with conceptual change so important to the missionary task, a theory of indigenous language, semiotics and of the indigenous mind became central to missionary work. In the context of their work in New Guinea, Neuendettelsau missionaries saw the creation of an indigenous vernacular Bible that could convey Christian concepts to the New Guinean mind as a task of foremost importance. An important prelude to this work was undertaking a survey of the existing abstract conceptual repertoire of local languages such as Jabêm. For these missionaries, the chief difficulty they claimed to face was the ostensible conceptual poverty of New Guinean myth, which they judged as too heavily anchored to the immediate, sensory world and therefore incapable of sustaining the weight of a Christian cosmology. In this particular frontier encounter, a major site of struggle was the perceived incommensurability of two radically different systems of meaning. This incommensurability presented itself to the minds of the missionaries as indicative of an indigenous lack – precisely the kind of lack or 'absence' that Dipesh Chakrabarty once argued 'translates into "inadequacy"' by default in the estimation of the colonisers.[59]

As Midena shows, notwithstanding the awareness and seeming sensitivity of some Germans towards the plight of indigenous peoples, many Germans continued to describe, categorise and interact with the peoples they encountered in the global south in ways that sometimes betrayed a strong cultural chauvinism and at other times reinforced the anthropological commitment to racially derived hierarchies of peoples. Given that this sense of the importance of cultural and phenotypic difference offered the discursive terrain for the material dispossession of the world's colonised peoples, it is unsurprising that non-Europeans both feared and sought to resist the sudden and often savage entry of colonial populations newly arrived from Europe.

As settler colonists, Germans were no more prone to genocidal violence than other European settler colonists. Nor were they as anthropologists more often driven to assertions of racial or cultural superiority than other anthropologists. Given, however, the high levels of dispossession and frontier violence in both German and non-German colonies and the broad, pan-European purchase of variously expressed assumptions of cultural and racial superiority, this is by no means a statement that could be read as exculpatory. As the collection of essays presented here demonstrates, Germans were equal, but not exceptional (in the *Sonderweg* sense) partners in the pan-European project of globalising Europe's economies, populations, culture and Christian cosmology. This they did, in common with the settlers and sojourners of other European states, through radical violence, scientific enquiry, economic and territorial dispossession, but also through less overtly confrontational frontier interactions and entanglements that saw some attempts to balance the desires and agency of both the colonisers and the colonised, albeit within the framing logic of disempowerment and dispossession that characterised global imperialism. The new states and societies that emerged from Europe's empires still bear the traces of Europe's attempt to globalise itself. Understanding the finer historical grain, the microhistories of these attempts, is a first step towards addressing the legacies of imperialism. In the German case, this means moving on from the Eurocentric idea that the legacy of colonialism finds its primary meaning as the prehistory of the Holocaust, and recognising instead that, while imperial remnants haunt the metropoles of Europe, the primary impact of colonialism was outside of Europe. Here, it figures as the prehistory of globalised structural inequality, embattled indigenous communities, racialised population politics and ongoing cultural depletion.

## Notes

1  See for example the recent moves towards formal apologies and reparations in Australia, Canada and Germany. Tom Bentley, *Empires of Remorse: Narrative, Postcolonialism and Apologies for Colonial Atrocity* (New York: Routledge, 2016); Sheryl Lightfoot, 'Settler-State Apologies to Indigenous Peoples: A Normative Framework and Comparative Assessment', *Native American and Indigenous Studies* 2:1 (2015), 15–39.

2  Sundhya Pahuja, *Decolonising International Law: Development, Economic Growth and the Politics of Universality* (Cambridge: Cambridge University Press, 2011); Lars Eckstein, 'Some Reflections on Entangled Knowledge and Decolonisation', *Zeitschrift für Religions- und Geistesgeschichte* 65:3 (2013), 283–8; Estelle H. Prinsloo, 'The Role of the Humanities in Decolonising the Academy', *Arts and Humanities in Higher Education* 15:1 (2016), 164–8.

3  Tony Ballantyne and Antoinette Burton, *Empires and the Reach of the Global, 1870–1945* (Cambridge, MA: Harvard University Press, 2012).

4  Lorenzo Veracini, 'Settler Colonialism and Decolonisation', *Borderlands* 6:2 (2007), www.borderlands.net.au/vol6no2_2007/veracini_settler.htm.

5   Maintaining a strategic essentialism in the face of this epistemic violence has been theorised as both a constructive and a reactionary strategy for decolonisation. See Luis Galanes Valledejuli, '"Are We There Yet?" The Tension between Nativism and Humanism in Fanon's Writings', *Human Architecture* 5 (2007), 59–70. For the contours of this debate within a feminist theoretics, see Emily S. Lee 'The Epistemology of the Question of Authenticity, in Place of Strategic Essentialism', *Hypatia* 26:2 (2011), 258–79.

6   Jeremy Sarkin, 'Should Reparations for Massive Human Rights Abuses Perpetrated on African Victims during Colonial Times Be Given?', in Inge Vanfraechem, Antony Pemberton and Felix Mukwiza Ndahinda, *Justice for Victims: Perspectives on Rights, Transition and Reconciliation* (New York: Routledge, 2014), pp. 89–104.

7   This has been explored in Klaus Bachmann, 'On the Margins of German *Vergangenheitsbewältigung*. Germany's Colonial Past Revisited', *Przegląd Zachodni* 1 (2014), 147–50; Volker Langbehn and Mohammed Salama, 'Reconfiguring German Colonialism', in Volker Langbehn and Mohammed Salama (eds), *German Colonialism. Race, the Holocaust and Postwar Germany* (New York: Columbia University Press, 2011), pp. ix–xiii.

8   Horst Drechsler, *'Let Us Die Fighting'* (London: Zed Press, 1980), originally published as *Südwestafrika unter deutscher Kolonialherrschaft* (Berlin: Akademie Verlag, 1966).

9   For a recent summary, see Nina Berman, Klaus Mühlhahn and Alain Patrice Nganang (eds), *German Colonialism Revisited: African, Asian, and Oceanic Experiences* (Ann Arbor: University of Michigan Press, 2014), pp. 3–5.

10  See for example Krista O'Donnell, Renate Bridenthal and Nancy Reagin (eds), *The Heimat Abroad: The Boundaries of Germanness* (Ann Arbor: University of Michigan Press, 2005); Bradley D. Naranch, 'Inventing the Auslandsdeutsche: Emigration, Colonial Fantasy, and German National Identity, 1848–1871', in Eric Ames, Marcia Klotz and Lora Wildenthal (eds), *Germany's Colonial Pasts* (Lincoln: University of Nebraska Press, 2005), pp. 21–40; Alexander Maxwell and Sacha E. Davis, 'Germanness beyond Germany: Collective Identity in German Diaspora Communities', *German Studies Review* 39:1 (2016), 1–15.

11  Geoff Eley, 'Empire by Land or Sea? Germany's Imperial Imaginary, 1840–1945', in Bradley Naranch and Geoff Eley (eds), *German Colonialism in a Global Age* (Durham, NC, and London: Duke University Press, 2014), p. 20; Matthew P. Fitzpatrick, *Liberal Imperialism in Germany: Expansionism and Nationalism, 1848–1884* (New York: Berghahn Books, 2008).

12  Sebastian Conrad and Jürgen Osterhammel (eds), *Das Kaiserreich transnational: Deutschland in der Welt, 1871–1914* (Göttingen: Vandenhoeck and Ruprecht, 2006).

13  H. Glenn Penny, 'German Polycentrism and the Writing of History', *German History* 30:2 (2012), 265–82.

14  Matti Bunzl and H. Glenn Penny, 'Introduction: Rethinking German Anthropology, Colonialism, and Race', in Penny and Bunzl (eds), *Worldly Provincialism* (Ann Arbor: University of Michigan Press, 2010), pp. 1–2.

15  Andrew Zimmerman, 'Adventures in the Skin Trade: German Anthropology and Colonial Corporeality', in Penny and Bunzl (eds), *Worldly Provincialism*, p. 157.

16  On these intra-German debates, see Benoit Massin, 'From Virchow to Fischer: Physical Anthropology and "Modern Race Theories" in Wilhelmine Germany', in George W. Stocking (ed.), *Volksgeist as Method and Ethic: Essays on Boasian Ethnography and the German Anthropological Tradition* (Madison: University of Wisconsin Press, 1998), pp. 79–154.

17  Susanne Zantop, *Colonial Fantasies: Conquest, Family and Nation in Precolonial Germany, 1770–1870* (Durham, NC: Duke University Press, 1997); Russell Berman, *Enlightenment or Empire: Colonial Discourse in German Culture* (Lincoln: University of Nebraska Press, 1998). On the debate, see Nina Berman, *Impossible Missions?: German Economic, Military, and Humanitarian Efforts in Africa* (Lincoln: University of Nebraska Press, 2004), pp. 9–12. Oliver Lubrich and Rex Clark, 'German Studies Go Postcolonial', *Eighteenth-Century Studies* 35:4 (2002), 625–34.

18  See for example Penny's argument that the German press roundly condemned North American frontier atrocities and felt a 'sense of affinity' with the colonised, contradicted by Jens Uwe Guettel who has maintained that pro-colonial Germans 'accepted violence against conquered ethnic groups to open "living space" to whites and, in some cases, forms of what is now called ethnic cleansing'. H. Glenn Penny, "Elusive Authenticity: The Quest for the Authentic Indian in German Public Culture', *Comparative Studies in Society and History* 48:4 (2006), 798–9. H. Glenn Penny, *Kindred by Choice: Germans and American Indians since 1800* (Chapel Hill: University of North Carolina Press, 2013), pp. 69–72; Jens-Uwe Guettel, 'From the Frontier to German South-West Africa: German Colonialism, Indians and American Westward Expansion', *Modern Intellectual History* 7:3 (2010), 523–52.

19  Anne McClintock, *Imperial Leather: Race, Gender and Sexuality in the Colonial Contest* (New York: Routledge, 1995), pp. 36–41.

20  On Hegel's division of the world into historical and non-historical peoples, see Ranajit Guha, *History at the Limit of World History* (New York: Columbia University Press, 2003).

21  Salisbury, quoted in Ronald Hyam, *Understanding the British Empire*, Cambridge: Cambridge University Press, 2010), p. 98.

22  Benjamin Madley, *An American Genocide: The United States and the California Indian Catastrophe* (New Haven: Yale University Press, 2016), A. Dirk Moses (ed.), *Genocide and Settler Society: Frontier Violence and Stolen Indigenous Children in Australian History* (New York: Berghahn, 2004), Bart Luttikhuis and Dirk Moses, 'Mass Violence and the End of the Dutch Colonial Empire in Indonesia'. *Journal of Genocide Research* 14:3–4 (2012), 257–76, Aldwin Roes, 'Towards a History of Mass Violence in the Etat Indépendant du Congo, 1885–1908', *South African Historical Journal* 62:4 (2010), 634–70.

23  Jürgen Zimmerer, *Von Windhuk nach Auschwitz? Beiträge zum Verhältnis von Kolonialismus und Holocaust* (Berlin: LIT Verlag, 2011); Benjamin Madley, 'From Africa to Auschwitz: How German South West Africa Incubated Ideas and Methods Adopted and Developed by the Nazis in Eastern Europe', *European History Quarterly* 35:3 (2005), 429–64. Recently, Volker Berghahn has also suggested a return to the *Sonderweg* when analysing German colonialism. Volker Berghahn, 'German Colonialism and Imperialism from Bismarck to Hitler', *German Studies Review* 40:1 (2017), 157–8.

24  Robert Gerwarth and Stephan Malinowski, 'Hannah Arendt's Ghosts: Reflections on the Disputable Path from Windhoek to Auschwitz', *Central European History* 42:2 (2009), 279–300; Matthew P. Fitzpatrick, 'The Pre-History of the Holocaust? The Sonderweg and Historikerstreit Debates and the Abject Colonial Past', *Central European History* 41:3 (2008), 477–503.

25  Susanne Kuss, trans. Andrew Smith, *German Colonial Wars and the Context of Military Violence* (Cambridge, MA: Harvard University Press, 2017).

26  Thomas Morlang, *Rebellion in der Südsee: Der Aufstand auf Ponape gegen die deutschen Kolonialherren 1910/11* (Berlin: Ch. Links, 2010). With the notable exception of George Steinmetz, Thomas Morlang, and more recently Livia Loosen and Gabriele Förderer, the historiography of German colonialism has predominantly focused on the experience of Germans in Africa and, to a lesser extent South and North America. Where once no lesser historian than Paul Kennedy devoted a full-length monograph to colonial Samoa (albeit one entirely from the perspective of the contest of the 'Great Powers'), the Pacific contact zone has been largely outsourced to Pacific specialists such as Peter J. Hempenstall and Hermann Joseph Hiery. While far from exclusively devoted to the Pacific, this volume seeks to address a lacuna that is only gradually being filled. See George Steinmetz, *The Devil's Handwriting: Precoloniality and the German Colonial State in Qingdao, Samoa and Southwest Africa*, (Chicago: University of Chicago Press, 2007), Thomas Morlang, *Rebellion in der Südsee*, Livia Loosen, *Deutsche Frauen in den Südsee-Kolonien des Kaiserreichs. Alltag und Beziehungen zur indigenen Bevölkerung, 1884–1919* (Bielefeld: Transcript, 2014); Gabriele Förderer, *Koloniale Grüße aus Samoa: Eine Diskursanalyse von deutschen,*

*englischen und US-amerikanischen Reisebeschreibungen aus Samoa von 1860–1916* (Bielefeld: Transcript, 2017); Eugene S. Cassidy, 'Germanness, Civilisation, and Slavery: Southern Brazil as German Colonial Space (1819–1888)' (Unpublished Dissertation, University of Michigan, 2015); Paul M. Kennedy, *The Samoan Triangle: A Study in Anglo-German-American Relations, 1878–1900*. (Dublin: Irish University Press, 1974); Hermann J. Hiery, *The Neglected War: The German South Pacific and the Influence of World War I* (Honolulu: University of Hawai'i Press, 1995); Peter J. Hempenstall, *Pacific Islanders under German Rule: A Study in the Meaning of Colonial Resistance* (Canberra: Australian National University Press, 1978); Stewart Firth, *New Guinea under the Germans* (Melbourne: Melbourne University Press, 1983); Gabrielle Richter, ' "Zake: The Papuan Chief": An Alliance with a German Missionary in Colonial Kaiser-Wilhelmsland (Oceania)', in Nina Berman, Klaus Mühlhahn and Patrice Nganang (eds), *German Colonialism Revisited*, pp. 130–45. See too the special issue 'Narrating Colonial Encounters: Germany in the Pacific Islands' in *Journal of Pacific History* 42:3 (2007).

27   See for example A. Dirk Moses (ed.), *Empire, Colony, Genocide: Conquest, Occupation, and Subaltern Resistance in World History* (New York: Berghahn, 2008).

28   Neil Lazarus, 'What Postcolonial Theory Doesn't Say', *Race and Class* 53:3 (2011), 3–27.

29   Suzanne Marchand, *German Orientalism in the Age of Empire: Religion, Race and Scholarship*. (Cambridge: Cambridge University Press, 2009).

30   Volker Barth and Roland Cvetkovski (eds)., *Imperial Cooperation and Transfer, 1870–1930 Empires and Encounters* (London: Bloomsbury, 2015); Janne Lahti, 'German Colonialism and the Age of Global Empires', *Journal of Colonialism and Colonial History* 17:1 (2016), DOI: 10.1353/cch.2016.0015; Sebastian Conrad, 'Rethinking German Colonialism in a Global Age', *Journal of Imperial and Commonwealth History* 41:4 (2013), 543–66.

31   Microhistorical, local narratives complement and complicate but cannot completely replace overarching structural approaches. See Kerwin Lee Klein, 'In Search of Narrative Mastery: Postmodernism and the People without History', *History and Theory* 34:4 (1995), 275–98.

32   Penny and Bunzl, *Worldly Provincialism*, p. 2. For a concise summary of these debates, see Shelley Baranowski, *Nazi Empire: German Colonialism and Imperialism from Bismarck to Hitler* (Cambridge: Cambridge University Press, 2011), pp. 9–66.

33   Sebastian Conrad, 'Rethinking German Colonialism in a Global Age', p. 545.

34   Felicity Jensz, *German Moravian Missionaries in the British Colony of Victoria, Australia, 1848–1908. Influential Strangers* (Leiden: Brill, 2010), p. 4.

35   Nicholas Thomas, *Entangled Objects: Exchange, Material Culture, and Colonialism in the Pacific* (Cambridge, MA: Harvard University Press, 1991).

36   See for example Tony Ballantyne, *Entanglements of Empire: Missionaries, Maori, and the Question of the Body* (Durham, NC: Duke University Press, 2014): Gail D. MacLeitch, *Imperial Entanglements: Iroquois Change and Persistence on the Frontiers of Empire* (Philadelphia: University of Pennsylvania Press, 2011).

37   Patrick Wolfe, 'Settler Colonialism and the Elimination of the Native', *Journal of Genocide Research* 8:4 (2006), pp. 387–409.

38   Angela Wanhalla, ' "One White Man I Like Very Much" Intermarriage and the Cultural Encounter in Southern New Zealand, 1829–1850', *Journal of Women's History* 20:2 (2008), 34–56; Stephen Janiewicz, 'Orientalists in Love: Intimacy, Empire and Cross-Cultural Knowledge', *Journal of World History* 23:2 (2012), pp. 345–73; Ann McGrath, *Illicit Love: Interracial Sex and Marriage in the United States and Australia* (Lincoln: University of Nebraska Press, 2015).

39   B.K. Gills and A.G. Frank, 'World System Cycles, Crises and Hegemonic Shifts, 1700BC –1700AD', in *The World System: Five Hundred Years or Five Thousand?* (London: Routledge, 1993), pp. 143–99; Janet L. Abu-Lughod. *Before European Hegemony: The World System AD 1250–1350* (New York: Oxford University Press, 1989).

40   For a discussion of technology and commodity exchanges between Indigenous Australians and others in Oceania, see Ian J. McNiven, 'Colonial Diffusionism and

the Archaeology of External Influences on Aboriginal Culture', in Bruno David, Bryce Barker and Ian J. McNiven, *The Social Archaeology of Australian Indigenous Societies* (Canberra: Aboriginal Studies Press, 2006), pp. 85–106.

41 Robin Torrence and Anne Clarke (eds), *The Archaeology of Difference: Negotiating Cross-Cultural Engagements in Oceania* (London: Routledge, 2000).

42 Nina Berman, Klaus Mühlhahn and Patrice Alain Nganang (eds), *German Colonialism Revisited: African, Asian, and Oceanic Experiences* (Ann Arbor: University of Michigan Press, 2014), p. 7.

43 H. Glenn Penny, 'Latin American Connections: Recent Work on German Interactions with Latin America', *Central European History* 46:2 (2013), 393.

44 Gayatri Chakravorty Spivak, *A Critique of Postcolonial Reason: Towards a History of the Vanishing Present* (Cambridge, MA: Harvard University Press, 1999), pp. 269–74.

45 Ann Laura Stoler, *Along the Archival Grain: Epistemic Anxieties and Colonial Common Sense.* (Princeton: Princeton University Press, 2009), pp. 50–1.

46 Ann Laura Stoler, 'Colonial Archives and the Arts of Governance', *Archival Science* 2:1 (2002), 103–9.

47 Jürgen Zimmerer, *Deutsche Herrschaft über Afrikaner. Staatlicher Machtanspruch und Wirklichkeit im kolonialen Namibia.* (Münster: Lit Verlag, 2002); Hull, *Absolute Destruction*; Kuss, *German Colonial Wars*; Thomas Morlang, *Rebellion in der Südsee*; Felicitas Becker and Jigal Beez (eds), *Der Maji Maji-Krieg gegen die deutsche Kolonialherrschaft in Tanzania, 1905–08* (Berlin: Christoph Links Verlag, 2005); James Leonard Giblin and Jamie Monson (eds), *Maji Maji: Lifting the Fog of War* (Leiden: Brill, 2010).

48 Thomas Morlang, *Askari und Fitafita: 'Farbige' Söldner in den deutschen Kolonien.* (Berlin: Ch Links, 2008), pp. 7–8; Michelle Moyd, 'Bomani: African Soldiers as Colonial Intermediaries in German East Africa, 1890–1914', in Nina Berman, Klaus Mühlhahn and Patrice Alain Nganang (eds), *German Colonialism Revisited*, pp. 101–13.

49 This question has been framed by both Edward Said and Spivak via Marx's sardonic comment: 'Sie können sich nicht vertreten, sie müssen vertreten werden.' Edward Said, *Orientalism* (London: Penguin, 2003), p. 21; Gayatri Chakravorty Spivak, *A Critique of Postcolonial Reason*, pp. 257–62.

50 Jonathon Xavier Inda, 'Performativity, Materiality and the Racial Body', *Latino Studies Journal* 11:3 (2000), 74–5.

51 Inda, 'Performativity, Materiality and the Racial Body', pp. 74–5.

52 Arun Saldanha, 'Reontologising Race: The Machinic Geography of Phenotype', *Environment and Planning D: Society and Space* 24 (2006), pp. 9–24.

53 Linda Martín Alcoff, *Visible Identities: Race, Gender, and the Self* (New York: Oxford University Press, 2006), p. 183. On this theme, see Frantz Fanon, 'The Fact of Blackness'.

54 On Judith Butler's linguistic idealism, see Saskia Wendel, 'Feminist Nominalism? A Critique of Feminist Radical Constructionism', in Deborah Orr, Linda Lopez McCalister, Eileen Kahl and Kathleen Earle (eds), *Belief, Bodies, and Being: Feminist Reflections on Embodiment* (Oxford: Rowman & Littlefield, 2006), pp. 187–9.

55 Michel Foucault, *The Order of Things: An Archaeology of the Human Sciences* (New York: Routledge, 2002), pp. xxviii–xxiv; Michel Foucault, *The Archaeology of Knowledge* (Routledge, New York, 2002), pp. 69–75.

56 Matthew P. Fitzpatrick, 'The Samoan Women's Revolt: Race, Intermarriage and Imperial Hierarchy in German Samoa', *German History* 35:2 (2017), 206–28.

57 Patrick Wolfe, 'Land, Labor and Difference: Elementary Structures of Race', *American Historical Review* 106:3 (2001), 867.

58 Nils Ole Oermann, *Mission, Church and State Relations in South West Africa under German Rule (1884–1915)* (Stuttgart: Franz Steiner Verlag, 1999), pp. 102–4.

59 Dipesh Chakrabarty, *Provincializing Europe: Postcolonial Thought and Historical Difference* (Princeton: Princeton University Press, 2007), p. 32.

# CHAPTER TWO

# 'No alternative to extermination': Germans and their 'savages' in southern Brazil at the turn of the nineteenth century

## Stefan Rinke

The present Indians of São Paulo do not represent an element of labour and progress. As in the other parts of Brazil no serious and sustained labour can be expected of the civilised Indians and as the savage Kaingangs are an impediment to the colonization of the backwoods they inhabit, it seems that we have no alternative but to exterminate them.[1]

These words, written by the distinguished ethnologist Hermann von Ihering in 1906, reflect the attitude of most immigrants of German origin in southern Brazil toward their indigenous neighbours at the beginning of the twentieth century. Since Brazilian independence in the 1820s, settlers from the German states had been attracted to that country in steadily growing numbers throughout the nineteenth century. Although these numbers were never quite comparable to the waves of immigrants from other European countries, Germans built important settlement enclaves in the southern states of Brazil. Until the twentieth century, these were frontier regions where settlers encountered the indigenous peoples of the Xokleng and Kaingang nations whom they considered 'savages'.

During the course of the nineteenth century, a typical situation of what historians have called settler imperialism emerged in that region. The historian Norbert Finzsch recently argued about that concept from a vantagepoint of genocide theory. His idea 'of a sliding continuum of genocide that ranges from everyday practices to organised mass murder' is clearly helpful to understand the interactions that are of interest here.[2] Over the course of some sixty years, German immigrants joined other ethnic groups of European origin in a genocidal endeavour against the indigenous population. This was not obvious as a concerted effort at first sight and can be understood only by looking at the micro-constellations and everyday interactions which slowly but surely were destroying the foundations of indigenous life. In a small-scale war with guerrilla tactics both sides learned and adopted techniques from the other. The effect was a 'creeping genocide'.[3]

This chapter will address some of the key questions on the functioning of this settler imperialism.[4] When did cohabitation work and when did it fail? How did German settlers react to challenges by the indigenous in the frontier situation? What role did the Brazilian context play in these interactions? Of course, the Europeans had an advantage due to their sophisticated weaponry, but there was no simple road to extermination of the indigenous peoples, as older studies have implied. In general, the historiography on Germans in Brazil has hardly considered the clash at the frontiers. The older literature was mainly of a celebratory character, and until well into the twentieth century scholarship kept praising the pioneering role of German settlers in an 'empty space' which, paradoxically, at the same time they perceived as a savage world full of danger.[5] Only the new ethno-history produced in southern Brazil itself has lately introduced new dimensions of the German presence in that region. It has shown that the indigenous peoples were actors in their own right, influencing the ways in which the interaction with the Europeans developed.[6]

Drawing on those findings my chapter will first introduce the region of interest and the indigenous populations living there. Then I will turn to German settlement in Brazil, its motives, problems and challenges. The third part discusses the crucial issue of cohabitation and conflict focusing on the later nineteenth and early twentieth centuries. The period under study ends in 1914, when the so-called 'pacification of the Indians' led to a change in the official attitude of the Brazilian government towards the indigenous peoples.

## Indian populations in southern Brazil

In the late nineteenth century, the Xokleng (also Botocudo) of Santa Catarina and the Kaingang (also Coroado) of São Paulo were among the indigenous peoples to offer fierce resistance to Brazil's westward expansion in the south. Traditionally they lived in the lands between the rivers Tietê and Uruguai, which roughly correspond with the limits of the federal states of São Paulo and Rio Grande do Sul, also comprising territories of the states of Paraná and Santa Catarina. Both groups belonged to the family of speakers of the Gê language, living at that group's southernmost extreme. The Kaingang were the larger of the two groups living to the west of the Xokleng in an area roughly from

São Paulo state to the north of Argentina. They comprised about ten thousand individuals in 1900, while the Xokleng at that time numbered probably no more than fifteen hundred in total, splitting up into three major subgroups.[7]

Although contemporary maps often implied this, both groups did not live in clearly limited territories but rather inhabited huge circulating areas. Theirs was a semi-nomadic lifestyle based on hunting, fishing and collecting. This was complemented by subsistence agriculture on a small scale with maize as the most important product. Amongst the Xokleng, men produced weapons and other objects of daily use like baskets, textiles and nets, while women produced clothing, took care of children, cooked and prepared the important alcoholic beverages.[8] In the wintertime, both communities gathered pine nuts from the Araucarian pine trees, which grew beyond 500 m above sea level. They also sought honey and the larvae of beetles, snakes and lizards. In addition, with the help of dogs they hunted birds, tapirs, wild pigs and deer, often using bows and arrows, bolas, clubs and spears as weapons. When the hunt was successful, they observed special hunting rituals. The individual hunter would usually give the meat of his prey to somebody else. The whole group also performed rites before eating. Some animals like the jaguar – and some deer, too – were taboo.[9]

When not on the move, they built large huts of straw, where numerous people lived.[10] They were very skilful tree climbers and stored provisions for the wintertime.[11] Like most indigenous cultures they maintained a very close relationship to their natural surroundings. In the Kaingang imagination, for instance, the land influenced both mythology and cosmology. They considered their origins to be in the land itself.[12] Their way of life was dependent upon nature and the environment. As to their clothing, they generally went naked except for a belt. Both Kaingang and Xokleng removed their body hair and put on body paint for different occasions. The body paintings were also a symbol of distinction between the different groups, which lived together in a community. Indeed, the indigenous people formed small tribes of extended families, which were all united under one chief.

The world that the indigenous people lived in was by no means a peaceful one. In the nineteenth century, both groups looked back to a long history of resistance against Portuguese, later Brazilian expansion. However, there was also constant fighting among different indigenous groups. Groups of Kaingang would attack each other and they were in an almost permanent state of war with the Xokleng. Contemporary observers from Europe characterised them as very warlike peoples.[13] Yet, more often than not, their aggressiveness was due to the contact with the settlers who invaded their living environment, pushing them back and making scarce resources even scarcer.[14] Following rivers like the Rio Doce and the Itajaí inland, they were looking for new bases of subsistence, thereby creating new conflicts with indigenous groups who had been there before them.[15]

Before the second half of the nineteenth century, not a lot of knowledge about these Indians existed. Ironically, the research on these groups done by German ethnologists such as Ihering or Gustav von Koenigswald was fundamental to establishing the knowledge of their existence as independent indigenous groups and in documenting their ways of life.[16] However, in the early years of ethnographic research many misunderstandings prevailed. Even the correct name of the peoples remained in dispute for a long time. The Kaingang went by this name only from 1882, but Europeans also often called them *Coroado* because of their Franciscan-like tonsure. In addition, many, including Ihering, classified them as *botocudos* because of the use of the labret. A common and pejorative label for Kaingang and Xokleng alike was the term *bugre*, derived from the French term *bougre* (rascal). In general, most ethnologists were agreed that these indigenous peoples were about to perish. Koenigswald, for example, wrote in 1908:

> only in Southern Brazil, in a region rich in forests at the border between Paraná and Santa Catarina do the *botocudos* still exist today. Long since encircled by civilization they defend their land with extreme tenacity and live in a constant state of war with the whites, their natural mortal enemies.[17]

### German settlement in southern Brazil

Half a century earlier, until 1850, the Xokleng and the Kaingang of the region between São Paulo and Rio Grande do Sul were the more or less undisputed owners of their lands. To be sure, German settler communities had already come to Brazil since 1822, and they settled in Rio Grande do Sul. Indeed, they were amongst the first European immigrants to come, not the least because of Empress Leopoldine's Austrian roots. The newly independent Brazilian monarchy needed immigration to the southernmost provinces in order to populate that border region and thus establish its sovereignty against the Argentine rivals. In addition, the influx of German settlers would also increase land prices, benefiting the politically influential land speculators. Behind this process was a discourse that emphasised the fear of 'demographic emptiness' in a frontier region. The court in Rio did not consider the indigenous peoples living in the region as citizens but rather trusted in foreign immigrants from Europe, who started the extractive process typical of the colonial situation.[18]

Indeed, historians have pointed out that the immigration from the German-speaking states constituted an important source of population, which deeply changed the ethnic, social and environmental landscapes of southern Brazil.[19] These Germans settled in forested territories which Luso-Brazilian society had not yet occupied. The forests were part of the Mata Atlântica habitat and were not an easy terrain for settlement. Existence was tough and carried risks that the immigrants had not foreseen, making for a life of hardship and fear. In their letters and newspapers settlers express concern about the atmosphere of the unknown and unfamiliar in what they called the *Urwald* becoming tangible.

In Santa Catarina, the coastal town of Itajaí was founded in 1820. In the following decades German immigrants came to settle in the area and the settled area grew fast. In 1850, the scientist and traveller Hermann Blumenau started his own colony with the support of a recruiting agent from Brazil. What started as a very small endeavour after a decade developed into a successful settlement scheme mainly along the valley of the Itajaí river, drawing some ten thousand people from the German states. The centre itself became a city in 1880 named after its founder. The young settlement profited from its connections to other settlements in the region like the Dona Francisca colony founded by the Hamburger Kolonisations-Verein. Not only Germans but also Brazilians of Portuguese stock, Italians, Swiss and English lived in these colonies.[20] Often in scattered settlements, the colonists grew maize and produced milk, turning Itajaí valley into the most productive region of Santa Catarina.[21]

Because of their isolation and relative economic success, the settlers themselves, as well as the increasing number of visitors from the metropole, took great pride in their achievement and in the fact that they did not own slaves and avoided mixing with Africans.[22] In contemporary publications, topoi like 'cleanliness' and 'bright sparkling roofs' reflecting allegedly typical German character traits were regularly repeated.[23] According to their self-perception, the Germans had brought their cultural perfection to the jungle. They portrayed Blumenau especially as an island which in connection with other colonies such as Dona Francisca, São Bento and Brusque boasted a direct connection to the German Reich and its global trade routes. These German colonies were isolated from the Brazilian cities and from the Indians who, it was said, did not want and were not able to contribute to progress.[24]

According to this discourse, the Brazilian state caused the problems that the settlers had to deal with, not keeping its promises due to a

[ 25 ]

constant lack of financial resources. Indeed, German settlement faced many challenges because of a lack of capital and infrastructure even in the southern states. When in the 1850s immigrants were exploited as substitutes for slaves in the coffee plantations of São Paulo, the image of Brazil as a country for German emigration was severely shattered. In 1859, the so-called von der Heydt'sches Reskript even prohibited the active recruitment of emigrants in Prussia. Until 1891 Protestants encountered further difficulties in Brazil. Their marriages were not officially legal, and they attracted the distrust of Brazilians because they received subsidies from a foreign state.[25]

Nevertheless, the Brazilian south remained quite attractive, and chain migration led to constant growth. After the founding of the German Reich, specialised organisations like the Allgemeiner Deutscher Schulverein, the Preußische Landeskirche and the Pan German and Navy Leagues supported emigrants in Brazil. In 1914, around 350,000 to 400,000 people of German descent lived in Brazil and most of them in southern Brazil, although the category 'German' remained notoriously diffuse. This was a small number when compared to the much higher numbers who lived in the United States, but it made for the most densely populated German settlement area outside Europe and North America. In the state of Santa Catarina, for example, twenty per cent of the population had German origins, making for the highest percentage in Brazil.[26] In the end, Germans struggled to adapt to their new surroundings and to new crops. They were, as Soraia Sales Dornelles has argued, as much colonised by the land as they colonised it themselves.[27]

## Cohabitation and conflict

In 1908, the ideal world of German settlers and their admirers was shattered when the Czech ethnologist Alberto Frič testified to the misery of the indigenous peoples living in southern Brazil at the International Congress of Americanists in Vienna. Not only the recently published scandal about Belgian rule in the Congo should draw world attention, Frič claimed, but maltreatment of indigenous peoples at the hands of German settlers, too. According to Frič civilised settlers hired contract killers whom they celebrated as heroes. In the context of an academic congress of high repute, Frič's statements did not fail to cause a scandal.[28] German settlers and their spokespersons in Europe and beyond rushed to blame the Czech of lying. Ihering was at the forefront arguing for settlers' rights to defend themselves against the savages. Who was right?

There were conflicts between the settlers from Germany and the Kaingang and Xokleng from the very start. A first wave of attacks by the Kaingang against the new settlements in their territory occurred from

1829 to 1835. Thereafter, there were fewer reports about fights at that frontier, which, however, had more to do with other conflicts catching the attention of the media than with frontier peace. Nevertheless, the scarce evidence available suggests that the Kaingang had indeed withdrawn to the hinterland. A second wave of attacks started in the mid-1840s, however, when the settlement process intensified again. At that point, military units, the Companhias de Pedestres (founded in 1836 and dissolved in 1879), were supposed to protect the settlers. For example in 1836 a detachment of foot soldiers was stationed at Colonia Itajaí to safeguard the settlements in the valley from Xokleng attacks. In the case of resistance, they had orders to annihilate the indigenous group completely. Yet the Xokleng continued with their assaults, attacking the founder of the colony, Hermann Blumenau himself, in 1852. The demands for state action, including those of the state governor himself, grew louder. Nevertheless, the militia units remained notoriously undermanned, poorly armed and ineffective. The government was not able to guarantee security.[29]

Problems in interethnic relations increased when the Brazilian government started to advertise systematically for European immigration, and when the number of settlers became massive in the second half of the nineteenth century. Tensions were especially stark in the Itajaí valley, which was at the heart of the historic Xokleng territory. The year 1850 was a turning point not just because of the foundation of Blumenau but also because of the new Land Law (*Lei de Terras*) creating the legal foundation for a proactive immigration policy.[30] The government advertised the land for sale to the immigrants as 'virgin land', which, of course, it was not. The new settlers were often unaware that indigenous groups continued to assert their right to live in that space, too. In their fights with the indigenous people, they saw themselves as defending what they held to be their very own land titles from intruders, and they did so by fencing in their lands, thus provoking additional tensions.[31] Later generations, then, began to explore even further west without any pretence of legal title, trying to dispossess the indigenous and absentee property owners who held claims to gigantic tracts of land. The squatters were often individual and isolated farmers especially vulnerable to indigenous attacks.[32]

With the expansion of settlements went the building of roads, and with the roads the transport of the highly valuable pine wood to the coastal settlements became easier.[33] This caused further resistance by the Xokleng, not only because of the rising number of settlers but also because of the destruction of their habitat. From the Xokleng point of view, this was a process aimed at their dispossession. In many regions, the indigenous people fell into destitution as a direct result

[ 27 ]

of the expansion of settlements. Attacks seemed to be the only way out for them.[34] Many indigenous groups continued their semi-nomadic lifestyle and attempted to adapt to the white challenge. They did not go on the offensive frequently, but when they did they prepared their raids carefully and observed their victims for a long time in order to know exactly how they behaved. Assaults were usually carried out at dawn, using clubs and lances as weapons, and surprised the victims. Sometimes they would take women and children with them into the woods. After taking all metal objects, which they later transformed into spearheads and arrowheads and into status symbols, they burned down what they could not carry away.[35] Victory did not make them blind to the dangers of being hunted down, but better knowledge of the wild forests gave them an advantage over their pursuers.[36]

The attacks by the Xokleng were sporadic at most. For the period between 1852 and 1914, José Deeke, a settler of German descent, counted a total number of 61 assaults causing 41 deaths and wounding another 22 people.[37] From the perspective of contemporary German observers, however, these attacks were a constant source of fear. The fact that the Xokleng attacked at dawn and did not usually spare women and children caused hatred and rage and led to their dehumanisation by German colonisers. This was exacerbated by the fact that German settlers considered Brazil's indigenous people to be an 'impediment to the course of history on American soil'.[38] The ethnologist Paul Ehrenreich, for example, who travelled through Brazil extensively in the late nineteenth century and took a deep interest in indigenous cultures, was in no doubt that 'civilisation' would win in the end. He showed understanding for settlers who showed no pity after suffering attacks.[39] The German Brazilian Paul Aldinger wrote in his doctoral thesis in 1910: 'This fight was not without bloodshed on both sides. But it is just a matter of time until the savage will accept the hand of peace directed towards him and be transferred to a sedentary way of life, or until he must perish due to the expansion of culture and colonization if he insists on his savagery.'[40] For Ihering it was a question of progress and culture which could not be 'halted by Indian arrows', he wrote. 'The life of a woodsman and colonist', Ihering emphasised, 'is certainly worth more to us than the life of a savage.' He continued: 'The fate of the Indians is certain. Many of them will accept our culture; the remainder will continue to be our enemies and as such will gradually disappear.'[41] The discourse of progress, which posited that the laws of nature dictated the displacement of indigenous peoples, covered the brutal reality of the normalisation of frontier atrocities.

In the words of the average settler, the rhetorical aggressiveness was more obvious. They did not distinguish between Kaingang and Xokleng.

For them the indigenous were nothing but savage 'bugres'.[42] Their image of their neighbours was that of 'jungle dwellers', whose nakedness was a proof of their inferiority, who fought with stone axes and lived on worms. In the settlers' eyes indigenous life was nothing but a basic animal-like fight for existence, and their own European-style culture separated them by more than a thousand years from the autochthonous peoples they were displacing. From the German perspective, even in comparison to other indigenous populations of the Americas, those of southern Brazil were degraded, completely savage, and weak.[43] The German-Brazilian chronicler Robert Bernhard condemned them as 'unspeakably coward', never daring to fight in the open and overly afraid of the effect of the settlers' shotguns.[44] To be sure, this was not a uniquely German perspective. Italians who settled in the same region held very similar views. The us-and-them dichotomy included the idea of the natural superiority of the colonisers of European stock and of the irresistible expansion of civilisation.[45]

Behind the claims of superiority, however, there was more often than not plain fear. Watchful waiting on both sides characterised frontier life, as German immigrant autobiographies reported. The official advice was always to carry firearms and to be attentive all the time. Travellers were never to stand still in order not to be a target for the vicious arrows coming out of nowhere. In addition, the very negative image of the indigenous people and the rumours about unbelievable atrocities helped create an atmosphere of terror, which in itself seemed to legitimise violent and genocidal attacks.[46] German settlers adopted an extirpative discourse in which seemingly natural causes of the demise of indigenous peoples such as the destruction of the indigenous ecosystem and territorial dispossession needed to be complemented by warfare. In doing so, they attempted the biopolitical destruction not just of individual enemies but of an enemy 'race', as Bernhard argued:

> Next to the German colonist their existence has become impossible, they have to perish. [...] Culture cannot tolerate such unproductive human beings if it does not want to imperil itself and its supporters. Its rise and heyday brings out of natural necessity doom and death to all animals of prey, and it will not spare the human animal embodied in the South Brazilian Indian.[47]

From genocidal discourse, it was only a small step to genocidal warfare, and settlers took this step in the second half of the nineteenth century on a quite regular basis. According to their own accounts, they contracted 'caboclos', mixed breeds of whites and indigenous populations, who knew the woods and the way of life of the indigenous people very well to carry out the attacks. Analysing the last names of participants,

Ritz-Deutch has claimed that the majority of the gang members were not of German origin. However, it can be proved that settlers themselves often did take part in these actions (often to get revenge for the loss of their family members), while those who did not actively participate contributed to paying the killers.[48]

The contemporary term for the contract killers was *bugreiro*. Usually about eight to fifteen *bugreiros* would take part in a raid, adopting the guerrilla tactics of the indigenous people in order to surprise them.[49] Koenigswald has described their actions in vivid terms. One of the *bugreiros* had to climb trees in order to explore the region for campfires. When finding this sign of human presence, the posse would very carefully stalk the indigenous camp. This had to be done with the greatest caution because it was not easy to catch the 'treacherous Indians' by surprise. In the early morning, the killers would attack first, firing a volley into the crowd of sleeping victims and then finishing their bloody work with knives and machetes.[50] Their strategy was to kill all the men but to kidnap some of the women and children in order to prove their success and to sell their prisoners as slaves. Sometimes they would bring cut-off ears or limbs as a proof. Often the kidnapped children ended up in monasteries, where they usually died quickly as a result of disease and desperation.

Officially, some *bugreiros* claimed to be only scaring away the Indians. Yet most people knew what they did and how they did it. The genocidal character of the attacks became obvious when, in 1888, the *bugreiro* Joaquim Bueno boasted about poisoning water wells, thereby killing thousands of Kaingang.[51] Some of these contract killers achieved veritable fame. Marcelino de Jesus Martins, commonly known as Martinho, was perhaps the most notorious hunter of Xokleng in Santa Catarina. Settlers hired him because of his absolute ruthlessness. His employers knew that he would not just capture but kill the highest number of indigenous people possible. While Martinho considered himself above the law, he sometimes accepted commissions to kill from state agents.[52]

Also employed were indigenous client groups who had accepted contact with the settlers. This was the case when in 1855 some hundred Kaingang under their chief Doble came to the village of Lages. The mayor of Lages provided food and clothing in exchange for the Kaingang's support in fighting the Xokleng who were threatening the settlement. From then on, Doble and his men were repeatedly commissioned by provincial governors or settlers to fight against other indigenous groups. The chief was also paid for bringing groups of at least fifty indigenous people to the reservation of Nonoai at the border between Rio Grande do Sul and Santa Catarina where they were 'pacified'. Other chiefs like the cacique Vitorino Condá followed his example, working for pay alongside the *bugreiros*. Settlers often referred to these allies as 'tame Indians' profiting especially from the longstanding rivalry between Kaingang and Xokleng.[53]

For the indigenous people, attacks by the *bugreiros* left survivors shocked but not completely helpless. Similarly, not all of the manhunts ended successfully for the contract killers, and the *bugreiros* themselves suffered many losses. Koenigswald reported that the Xokleng and Kaingang would never give up on their kidnapped children but only wait for an opportunity to get them back.[54] In their retributive actions, they did not differentiate between the settlers but took revenge on all whites who fell into their hands. Reprisal bred reprisal, and whole regions lived through periods of extended low-intensity warfare.[55]

In this tense frontier situation, Christian missions offered only superficial relief. The Kaingang initially welcomed the first Capuchin missionaries from Italy who approached them in the 1840s.[56] However, the missionising attempts failed, not least owing to the distrust that the indigenous people developed against all Europeans because of 'the infamous actions of the white conquerors'.[57]

In addition, the very negative experiences of the kidnapped women and children who ended up in mission stations did not help in building trust. Those children who survived disease usually suffered from the traumatic experience and fell silent. Their teachers treated them as slow-witted and unintelligent, in accordance with the racist discourse of the time, which posited this as an intrinsic quality of indigenous peoples. Often they became the target of ridicule, but their masters also professed to fear their allegedly wild aggressiveness and treacherousness. Rumours about indigenous children burning down the houses of their adoptive parents abounded.[58]

Under such conditions, peaceful co-existence was a utopian dream, and yet there were some elements of interaction. The internecine warfare of chiefs like Doble or Condá was a negative example of co-operation, while other indigenous people served as (often unwilling) intercultural brokers in otherwise tense frontier situations. Indicative of this was the example of a Kaingang child kidnapped by the *bugreiros* and christened Luis Bugre, who lived with the settlers and helped in their negotiations with indigenous people.[59] Phases of repeated and intensive attacks on both sides were regularly followed by quieter periods. In the Xokleng circulating area peace ruled, especially when they were looking for pine nuts in the highlands, thus leaving the more densely settled coastline.[60] Some believed that frontier relationships were highly individualised, with Koenigswald even going so far as to state that 'the "bugres" were able to distinguish between their neighbours. Those who settled peacefully

[ 31 ]

and who did not respond violently to attacks against their cattle and to occasional thefts have nothing to fear and feel safe.'[61]

Irrespective of how accurate this statement was, zones of contact were established, particularly through the attempts to concentrate indigenous peoples in reservation camps like Nonoai, the so-called *aldeamentos*, which were established in 1846. Regional politicians such as the president of Santa Catarina, João José Coutinho, supported this approach to containing indigenous people. In 1856, Coutinho addressed the Assembly with a speech referring to the Xokleng as barbarians and murderers, who had to be caught and put into camps in order to civilise them.[62] Some indigenous groups accepted the camps voluntarily in order to survive. In the *aldeamentos* they got objects they could not produce, as well as protection and food. However, many continued their itinerant lifestyles and practised other everyday forms of resistance such as secret hunting, bad work and fleeing. The camps did not entirely dissipate the threat of violence, either, with the chief Bragas, for example, able to extract more privileges for his group by continuing to threaten the peace through irregular attacks.[63]

Even if the number of *aldeamentos* grew over time, the periods of temporary peace had ended by the turn of the century when atrocities flared up again on both sides. Some historians have argued that the intensity of conflicts remained relatively low until late in the nineteenth century, because enough 'virgin' land was still available where the indigenous people could live without contact. What is certain is that contacts and aggressive acts increased when land became sparse.[64] In the first two decades of the republic, there was an intensification of the expansion toward the hinterland. Geographers, scientists and engineers entered these regions in growing numbers for political, scientific or economic reasons.[65] After the turn of the century, southern Brazil experienced an outburst of violence when indigenous groups resisted the invasion of their lands by colonists. The threat to security on the streets grew to such a degree that in 1905 settlers of German origin organised a major punitive expedition, in which many of them took part personally, while the colony in general raised the necessary funds.[66]

The main reason for this eruption of indigenous violence was the construction of railways. In the young republic, trains were an important symbol of modernisation, and politicians deemed the construction of the line from São Paulo to Rio Grande do Sul between 1894 and 1910 to be necessary to connect the rapidly growing coffee economy with the meat-producing states in the south. The line did in fact help to develop transport in the region; however it was also seen by the government as a means of reinforcing its claim to the border regions of Paraguay, Argentina and Uruguay. Of course, politicians were aware of the effects that this policy would have on the indigenous population, but the Brazilian government invested both money and hope into its settlement and railway policy. Correspondingly, it treated resolutely the indigenous people who threatened it.[67] Indeed, the first constitution of the republic of 1891 worsened the situation of Brazil's indigenous inhabitants by abolishing their official status as an ethnic entity. The allegedly 'unoccupied land' now became property of the states, which had even fewer scruples in dealing with its indigenous owners than the central government. According to the new Civil Code, Indians had the same status as married women or adolescents with restricted access to civil rights. Compounding their difficulties, the separation of church and state brought the termination of protection by the missionaries, however weak that might have been.[68]

As construction got under way, railway workers poured into lands which had hitherto been used as a retreat.[69] The expansion of the railway and of land-hungry coffee estates into the interior where the soil was ideal for growing the plants caused steep increases in land prices and ever more settlers.[70] In addition, because of the introduction of meat refrigeration, cattle ranching grew immensely in the region. Small farmers often had to sell out to big business and looked for new land in even more remote areas on the frontiers. There lawlessness abounded. Dubious speculators sold land titles to squatters who soon found out that indigenous groups lived there and that absentee estate owners held formal claims to it.[71]

In this context, Brazil's indigenous people were forced to retreat even further, as the railways and new settlements cut through the heart of their circulating territory.[72] The spiral of violence and a climate of insecurity returned as both the Kaingang of São Paulo and the Xokleng in Santa Catarina tried to defend their territory. For their part, the Kaingang were the last indigenous group in Brazil to be temporarily successful in stopping the onslaught of the railway and controlling a large territory. They massacred large numbers of rail gang workers and, in at least one incident, even decapitated their victims in an attempt to terrorise and scare off their enemies.[73]

The Europeans, however, retaliated in kind. On 13 October 1908 the *Correio da Manhã*, a leading newspaper in Rio de Janeiro, published a letter to the editor reporting the massacre that railway workers committed against a group of Kaingang:

It is horrible what the workers of the Estrado de Ferro Noroeste do Brasil are doing to the poor *coroado* Indians [Kaingang] of the region between Bahurú and Avanhandava. Here the massacre of Indians is a kind of sport – a highly entertaining form of game hunting for those workers. Several days ago, according to witnesses, the poor *coroados* were celebrating in their

[ 33 ]

own manner the rites of a wedding ceremony, when suddenly they were discovered by railroad workers who slaughtered men, women, old people and children. They spared only one young girl whom they abused in a most barbarous fashion before proceeding to ransack the encampment.[74]

In its introduction to the letter, the editors of the *Correio da Manhã* expressed their disgust at the treatment of those 'poor Indians' in vivid terms. By 1908, when the article appeared, a change in Brazilian public opinion occurred. Until then, Brazilian society had accepted violence against the indigenous as unavoidable for the sake of progress. To be sure, some individuals such as Alfredo d'Escragnolle Taunay who became governor of Santa Catarina in 1877 had criticised the ongoing genocide earlier. Moreover, liberal intellectuals of an indigenist disposition had since the middle of the nineteenth century considered the autochthonous peoples as curiosities of an ancient past idealising the 'noble savage' in a stream of romantic literature.[75] However, Taunay, much like his successor the German Brazilian Felippe Schmidt some twenty-five years later, remained conservative in his search for improvements in dealing with the indigenous population, demanding more money for the missions in order to stop the massacres. From Schmidt's perspective, this act of 'magnanimity of civilised men' would bring the necessary change.[76]

Yet only the dispute between Frič and Ihering in Vienna in 1908 marked a genuine turning point, because from that moment the whole history of European contact with indigenous peoples was brought into question.[77] From the perspective of decision-makers in the central cities, the indigenous peoples in Brazil did not present a major threat any longer because of their decline in numbers. Voices who had long since called for pride in the indigenous roots of Brazil and the 'Brazilian race' as different from the Europeans and especially the Portuguese now gained support. Intellectuals discovered the mixed heritage of the population as a source of national greatness.[78]

In this climate Ihering's more or less open demands for extermination of the aggressive indigenous groups caused an uproar of protest by nationalists, who blamed the 'imported science' of Germans for the misery of 'Brazilian Indians'. This accorded well with the growing attacks against German immigrants, who according to many Luso-Brazilian observers failed to integrate into the national community, clinging to their language and traditions. What started as a local and regional issue developed into a national problem which had international implications, too, because of the alleged role of the German government in supporting separatist movements amongst the settlers. When in 1905 the scandal around the visit of the German gunboat *Panther* to Itajaí caused major diplomatic tensions between Berlin and Rio de Janeiro, word of a 'German danger' (*perigo alemão*) spread in Brazil, causing embarrassment for the Germans of southern Brazil.[79] In this climate, Frič's criticism of German atrocities against the indigenous and German imperialism at large were warmly received, while Ihering became the scapegoat in a nativist discourse.[80]

Criticism of the extermination policies increased also outside Brazil.[81] Frič was not the only German-speaking ethnologist who tried to defend the indigenous people. There was a long tradition of anthropologists from Germany who worked in Brazil and had demanded a better treatment of their objects of study. One of them, the Jesuit Carl Teschauer, argued that the Kaingang whom he studied intensively had originally been peaceful but had been forced into violent actions by the expansion of the white settlers.[82] The ethnologist Curt Unckel Nimuendajú from Jena criticised Ihering sharply in his numerous contributions to the German-language press in southern Brazil.[83] In Germany, a leading intellectual like Eduard Seler disapproved of the extirpative discourse of many German-Brazilians.[84]

Within Brazil, this discursive shift had practical effects. At the beginning of the twentieth century, the military officer Cândido Mariano da Silva Rondon became engaged in protecting southern Brazil's indigenous peoples.[85] In 1910, the Brazilian government created the Indian Protection Service (Serviço de Proteção aos Índios or SPI) in reaction to the scandal of 1908.[86] The creation of the SPI led to the so-called pacification of the Kaingang in 1912 and of the Xokleng in 1914 under the young Eduardo Hoerhan, himself son of an Austrian immigrant. Hoerhan was engaged in keeping the Xokleng from attacking the settlers and vice versa. His principal tool was gift giving, which enabled the Xokleng to decide for themselves on the intensity of the contact. However, when disease spread throughout their reserve at Ibirama until 1932 about two-thirds of the four hundred Xokleng died, and the survivors became dependent on Hoerhan. Brazilian society looked down on these 'tame Indians' living under precarious conditions and in misery even more than on the 'wild Indians' of the forest. The results of 'pacification' were thus deeply ambivalent: far more profitable for the state and the settlers than for the dispossessed indigenes.[87]

Despite this, many German settlers continued to complain that 'pacification' did not go far enough, that the state was being overly generous and that indigenous people were still a danger.[88] The 'German' city of Blumenau and its surroundings were growing rapidly in this period, and modernisation was in full swing. In 1907 railways connected it with the outer world, and two years later water power enabled the generation of electricity. In consequence, there were many who, like the editor of the newspaper *Der Urwaldsbote*, Eugen Fouquet, continued to demand the complete extermination of the area's indigenous people in order that progress might continue. Others, however, like the medical doctor Hugo Gensch, who had adopted a Xokleng girl, objected, claiming that improvement through education was possible. Debates ended only when the First World War created a new and much more formidable threat to the community of German-Brazilians.[89]

## Conclusion

When Germans came to the South of Brazil in the nineteenth century, they became new participants in an ongoing process of genocidal violence against indigenous groups. Violence of German-born settlers against the indigenous Brazilians was in itself not exceptional, because the Portuguese, Brazilians, Italians and other ethnic groups were all part of the same processes of dispossession. Like settler colonists in many other non-European contexts, German settlers in Brazil perceived the indigenous as *'vogelfrei'*, outside of the law and an impediment to civilisation. When the legitimacy of this frontier warfare became a matter of public debate, it was German ethnologists who came to lead it, academics who were neither unified in their views about their objects of study nor contributing to an improvement of the indigenous situation. Although Germans considered themselves to be more civilised than their other European neighbours, this did not mean that their behaviour towards Brazil's indigenous people was any more 'civilised' even if evaluated according to their own standards. Rather, the evidence confirms that, while it was the *bugreiro*, the mixed-blood *caboclo*, who did the dirty work, German settlers professed to remain detached from the killings in a bubble of self-created civilisation – a detachment that was often shattered when one of their own fell victim to the frontier violence. German settlers may have looked at these professional killers with a mixture of disgust and racist arrogance; however, they remained convinced that the *bugreiro* did what had to be done and, of course, they paid him for doing it.

German settlers in Brazil shared a belief in a civilising mission and a preparedness to exterminate those who stood in the way of settler colonialism in southern Brazil. They were reinforced in their acceptance of violent measures by living in a hard and dangerous context and by the experience of other colonisers, who had been there before them and shared their experiences with them. The effect was a low-speed, long-term genocide. In the end, even 'pacification' came to mean little more than simplifying the violent processes of dispossession. Settlers considered indigenous people to be part of nature, with no rights and therefore liable to be killed without punishment. The settlers' legitimation of this view was the 'march of civilisation', a discourse that preceded 'scientific' racism, which gained sway in the second half of the nineteenth century.[90]

In general, the state increasingly supported this expansion of settlement at the expense of the Xokleng and Kaingang. These first nations were systematically dispossessed by violent means and by very heterogeneous groups of actors. This led to retaliatory attacks by the indigenous populations, who stole metal products, destroyed houses and – rarely – killed settlers or kidnapped women and children in return. In a spiral of violence, the state would react with its militia units stalking and massacring whole groups of Indians in their habitat. However, more often than not the Brazilian state was effectively unable to protect German settlers in southern Brazil. Hence, they took matters into their own hands, organising raids and contracting killers. Much like in the Australian case, the killing occurred without pitched battles or major 'Indian Wars' of the North American type.[91] However, in everyday practice and in its discursive assumptions, the genocidal impetus did not differ significantly.

## Notes

1  Hermann von Ihering, *The Anthropology of the State of S. Paulo* (São Paulo: Typography of the 'Diario Official', 1906), p. 12.
2  Norbert Finzsch, ' "[...] Extirpate or remove that vermine": Genocide, Biological Warfare, and Settler Imperialism in the Eighteenth and Early Nineteenth Century', *Journal of Genocide Research* 10:2 (2008), 215–32, here p. 215.
3  Mark Levene, 'The Chittagong Hill Tracts: A Case Study in the Political Economy of "Creeping" Genocide', *Third World Review* 20:2 (1999), 339–69.
4  Lynette Russell, 'Introduction', in Lynette Russell (ed.), *Colonial Frontiers: Indigenous-European Encounters in Settler Societies* (Manchester: Manchester University Press, 2001), pp. 1–17. Norbert Finzsch, ' "The aborigines were never annihilated, and still they are becoming extinct": Settler Imperialism and Genocide in Nineteenth Century America and Australia', in A. Dirk Moses (ed.), *Empire, Colony, Genocide: Conquest, Occupation, and Subaltern Resistance in World History* (New York: Berghahn Books, 2008), pp. 253–70. Lorenzo Veracini, ' "Settler Colonialism": Career of a Concept', *Journal of Imperial and Commonwealth History* 41:2 (2013), 313–33.
5  Carlos Fouquet, *Der deutsche Einwanderer und seine Nachkommen in Brasilien, 1808–1824–1974* (São Paulo: Instituto Hans Staden, 1974), pp. 145–6. Karl H. Oberacker and Karl Ilg, 'Die Deutschen in Brasilien', in Hartmut Fröschle (ed.), *Die Deutschen in Lateinamerika: Schicksal und Leistung* (Tübingen: Erdmann, 1979), p. 198.
6  Luisa Tombini Wittmann, *O vapor e o botoque: Imigrantes alemães e índios Xokleng no Vale do Itajaí/SC (1850–1926)* (Florianópolis: Letras Contemporâneas, 2007), p. 22.
7  For an early description of the Kaingang see Alfredo d'Escragnolle Taunay, 'Os Índios Caingangs', *Revista Trimensal do Instituto Historico e Geographico Brazileiro*, LI (1888), supplement, 251–310. Ute Ritz-Deutch, 'Alberto Vojtěch Frič, the German Diaspora, and Indian Protection in Southern Brazil, 1900–1920: A Transatlantic

Ethno-Historical Case Study' (PhD Dissertation, Binghamton University, 2008), pp. 132–3.

8 Sílvio Coelho dos Santos, *Os índios Xokleng: memoria visual* (Florianópolis: Editora da UFSC, 1997), pp. 15–18.

9 Alfred Métraux, 'The Caingang', in Julian H. Steward (ed.), *Handbook of South American Indians, vol 1., The Marginal Tribes* (Washington: Cooper Square Publishers, 1946), pp. 451–5. See also Telemaco Morocines Borba, 'Die Caingangs-Indianer in der brasilianischen Provinz Paraná', *Globus. Illustrierte Zeitschrift für Länder- und Völkerkunde*, L:15 (1886), 233–6.

10 Métraux, 'The Caingang', pp. 445–75. See also Luis Fernando Laroque, *Lideranças Kaingang no Brasil Meridional (1808–1889)* (São Leopoldo: Instituto Anchietano de Pesquisas, 2000). Marisa Schneider Nonnenmacher, *Aldeamentos Kaingang no Rio Grande do Sul: Século XIX* (Porto Alegre: EDIPUCRS, 2000).

11 Gustav von Koenigswald, 'Die Botokuden in Südbrasilien', *Globus* 93:3 (1908), 40.

12 Sandor Fernando Bringmann, 'Índios, Colones e Fazendeiros: Conflitos Interculturais e Resistência nas Terras Altas do Rio Grande do Sul (1829–1860)' (MA Thesis, Universidade Federal de Santa Catarina, 2010), p. 26.

13 John Hemming, *Amazon Frontier: The Defeat of the Brazilian Indians* (London: Harvard University Press, 1987), p. 449. Simoens da Silva, *A Tribu Caingang* (Rio de Janeiro: Alba, 1930), p. 24.

14 Ítala Irene Basile Becker, *O índio Kaingáng no Rio Grande do Sul* (São Leopoldo: Instituto Anchietano de Pesquisas, Universidade do Vale do Rio dos Sinos, 1995), pp. 47–8.

15 Sonia de Almeida Demarquet, *Os Xokleng de Ibirama, uma comunidade indígena de Santa Catarina, Boletim do Museo do Índio: Documentação*, 3 (1983), 6–7.

16 Hermann von Ihering, 'Os Botocudos de Rio Doce', *Revista do Museu Paulista* 8 (1910), 38–51. Koenigswald, 'Die Botokuden in Südbrasilien', p. 40.

17 Koenigswald, 'Die Botokuden in Südbrasilien', p. 37.

18 Arlene Renk, 'Território e alteridade', in Aneliese Nacke, Arlene Renk, Leonel Piovezana and Neusa Maria Sens Bloemer (eds), *Os kaingang no oeste catarinense: tradição e atualidade* (Chapecó: Argos, 2007), pp. 22 and 30.

19 Silvio Coelho dos Santos, *Indios e brancos no sul do Brasil: a dramática experiência dos Xokleng* (Florianópolis: Movimento, 1973), pp. 50–1.

20 Hemming, *Amazon Frontier*, p. 451.

21 Paul Aldinger, *Das Itajahy-Tal. Deutsche Siedlung im brasilianischen Urwald. Blumenau und Hansa* (Hamburg: H.O. Persiehl, 1910), pp. 6–17. Dos Santos, *Indios e brancos no sul do Brasil*, p. 51.

22 Aldinger, *Das Itajahy-Tal*, p. 7.

23 Robert Bernhard, *Dona Francisca, Hansa und Blumenau, drei deutsche Mustersiedelungen im südbrasilianischen Staate Santa Catharina: Eine Festschrift zur Feier des 50jährigen Bestehens von Dona Francisca und Blumenau* (Breslau: S. Schottlaender, 1901), pp. 200–9. The best new study on German colonial discourse in Brazil is Frederik Schulze, *Auswanderung als nationalistisches Projekt: 'Deutschtum' und Kolonialdiskurse im südlichen Brasilien (1824–1941)* (Cologne: Böhlau, 2016).

24 K.A. Wettstein, 'Die Verkehrsverhältnisse der deutsch-brasilianischen Kolonie Blumenau' (PhD Dissertation, Universität Heidelberg, 1907), p. 4.

25 Schulze, *Auswanderung als nationalistisches Projekt*, pp. 46–63.

26 Rinke, 'Nach Norden oder Süden'.

27 Soraia Sales Dornelles, 'De Coroados a Kaingang. As experiências vividas pelos indígenas no contexto de imigração alemã e italiana no Rio Grande do Sul do século XIX e início do XX' (MA Thesis, Universidade Federal do Rio Grande do Sul, 2011), p. 28.

28 Alberto Frič, 'Völkerwanderungen, Ethnographie und Geschichte der Konquista in Südbrasilien', *Verhandlungen des XVI. Internationalen Amerikanisten-Kongresses, Wien 1908*, 65–6. Already in 1907 the Pole Pedro Trompowsky Taulois had published a pamphlet against German maltreatment of Indians comparing it to the treatment of Poles in the Reich, thereby enraging settlers. Frič had co-operated with Taulois,

[ 38 ]

*As Matanças de Bugres e o 'Urwaldsbote'* (Curitiba: Impressora Paranaense, 1907). For the context see Ritz-Deutch, 'Alberto Vojtěch Frič', pp. 35–80. H. Glenn Penny, 'The Politics of Anthropology in the Age of Empire: German Colonists, Brazilian Indians, and the Case of Alberto Vojtěch Frič', *Comparative Studies in Society and History*, 45:2 (2003), 249–50.

29  Bringmann, 'Índios, Colones e Fazendeiros', pp. 82–90. Dos Santos, *Indios e brancos no sul do Brasil*, p. 66. Hemming, *Amazon Frontier*, p. 451. Jackson Alexsandro Peres, 'Entre as matas de araucárias: cultura e história Xokleng em Santa Catarina (1850–1914)' (MA Thesis, Universidade Federal de Santa Catarina, 2009), p. 16.

30  Peres, 'Entre as matas de araucárias', pp. 12–15.

31  Dornelles, 'De Coroados a Kaingang', p. 14.

32  Dos Santos, *Os Índios Xokleng*, p. 9.

33  Dos Santos, *Indios e brancos no sul do Brasil*, p. 59. Peres, 'Entre as matas de araucárias', p. 18.

34  Itala Irene Basile Becker, 'O índio kaingáng e a colonização alemã', in *Anais do 2o simpósio de historia da imigração e colonização alemã no Rio Grande do Sul, São Leopoldo 1976*, 51–2.

35  Becker, 'O índio kaingáng', pp. 60–1.

36  Koenigswald, 'Die Botokuden in Südbrasilien', pp. 37–9.

37  José Deeke, *Das Munizip Blumenau und seine Entwicklungsgeschichte* (São Leopoldo: Rotermund, 1917), vol. 2, p. 15.

38  Sílvio Marcos de Souza Correa, 'Heterologia das gentes do Brasil meridional por viajantes alemães', in Martin N. Dreher et al. (eds), *Imigração e relações interétnicas: XVII simpósio de história da imigração e colonização* (São Leopoldo, 2008), pp. 992–9 (p. 994).

39  Paul Ehrenreich, 'Ueber die Botocudos der brasilianischen Provinzen Espiritu Santo und Minas Gerais', *Zeitschrift für Ethnologie* 19 (1887), 1–47, here p. 4.

40  Aldinger, *Das Itajahy-Tal*, p. 18.

41  Ihering as quoted in Hemming, *Amazon Frontier*, p. 474. See also Hermann von Ihering, 'A questão dos indios no Brazil', *Revista do Museu Paulista* 8 (1911), 112–40.

42  Borba, 'Die Caingangs-Indianer', p. 233. Becker, *O indio Kaingáng*, p. 47.

43  Karl Alexander Wettstein, *Brasilien und die deutsch-brasilianische Kolonie Blumenau* (Leipzig: F. Engelmann, 1907), pp. 55–6.

44  Bernhard, *Dona Francisca, Hansa und Blumenau*, p. 248.

45  Mauricio da Silva Selau, 'A ocupação do território Xokleng pelos imigrantes italianos no Sul Catarinense (1875–1925): Resistência e Extermínio' (MA Thesis, Universidade Federal de Santa Catarina, 2006).

46  Wittmann, *O vapor e o botoque*, pp. 30 and 36.

47  Bernhard, *Dona Francisca, Hansa und Blumenau*, p. 254.

48  Wittmann, *O vapor e o botoque*, pp. 49–51. Ritz-Deutch, 'Alberto Vojtěch Frič', pp. 159–63.

49  Dos Santos, *Indios e brancos no sul do Brasil*, pp. 81–2.

50  Koenigswald, 'Die Botokuden in Südbrasilien', pp. 37–9.

51  Hemming, *Amazon Frontier*, p. 463.

52  Ritz-Deutch, 'Alberto Vojtěch Frič', pp. 147–63.

53  Becker, *O índio Kaingáng*, p. 48. Hemming, *Amazon Frontier*, pp. 367 and 452–,4. For Nonoai, see Becker, *O índio kaingáng*, pp. 55.

54  Koenigswald, 'Die Botokuden in Südbrasilien', pp. 37–9.

55  Dos Santos, *Indios e brancos no sul do Brasil*, pp. 103–4.

56  Hemming, *Amazon Frontier*, p. 457.

57  Koenigswald, 'Die Botokuden in Südbrasilien', pp. 37–9.

58  Wittmann, *O vapor e o botoque*, pp. 94 and 123.

59  Dornelles, 'De Coroados a Kaingang', pp. 52–4.

60  Darcy Ribeiro, *Os índios e a civilização: a integração das populações indígenas no Brasil moderno* (São Paulo, 1996), pp. 488–9. Peres, 'Entre as matas de araucárias', p. 14.

61  Koenigswald, 'Die Botokuden in Südbrasilien', p. 40

62  Ritz-Deutch, 'Alberto Vojtěch Frič', p. 147.
63  Bringmann, 'Índios, Colones e Fazendeiros', pp. 65, 100 and 108.
64  Wittmann, *O vapor e o botoque*, p. 49.
65  Engineers also send reports: Francisco R. Ewerton Quadros, 'Memoria sobre os trabalhos de exploração e observação efetuada pela secção da comissão militar encarregada da linha telegráfica de Uberaba a Cuiabá, de fevereiro a junho de 1889', *Revista do Instituto Histórico e Geográfico Brasileiro* 55:1 (1892), 233–60.
66  Wittmann, *O vapor e o botoque*, p. 52. See also the report of a contemporary witness: Wettstein, 'Die Verkehrsverhältnisse', pp. 14–15.
67  Wittmann, *O vapor e o botoque*, pp. 64–6.
68  Hemming, *Amazon Frontier*, p. 470.
69  David H. Stauffer, 'Origem e fundação do Serviço de Proteção nos Indios', *Revista de História* (São Paulo), 10:37 (1959), 80–5. Ruy Christovam Wachowicz, 'A imigração e os Botocudos (Xokléng) do Taió', *Anais do IV Simpósio Nacional dos Professores Universitários de História, Porto Alegre 1967*, 474–9.
70  Walmir da Silva Pereira, 'A ferrovia São Paulo-Rio Grande e os índios Xokleng: relações interétnicas e modernidade no Brasil meridional' (MA Thesis, Universidade Federal de Santa Catarina, 1995), pp. 63–70.
71  Hemming, *Amazon Frontier*, p. 471.
72  Ritz-Deutch, 'Alberto Vojtěch Frič', p. 128.
73  Pereira, 'A ferrovia São Paulo-Rio Grande', pp. 71–5. Shelton H. Davis, *Victims of the Miracle: Development and the Indians of Brazil* (Cambridge: Cambridge University Press, 1977), p. 1. Ritz-Deutch, 'Alberto Vojtěch Frič', p. 154.
74  'Revoltante!', *Correio da Manhã* (13 October 1908), p. 1.
75  Hemming, Amazon Frontier, p. 466.
76  Felippe Schmidt, *Mensagem apresentado ao congresso representativo em 1 de septembre de 1902* (Florianópolis, 1902), pp. 20–1.
77  Wittmann, *O vapor e o botoque*, pp. 64–6.
78  Emilia Viotti da Costa, *The Brazilian Empire: Myths and Histories* (Chicago: University of Chicago Press, 1985) pp. 234–46.
79  Ritz-Deutch, 'Alberto Vojtěch Frič', p. 88. For the Panther affair, see Gerhard Brunn, *Deutschland und Brasilien (1889–1914)* (Cologne, 1971), pp. 88–99.
80  Ritz-Deutch, 'Alberto Vojtěch Frič', p. 24.
81  Dos Santos, *Indios e brancos no sul do Brasil*, pp. 116–18.
82  C. Teschauer, ';Die Caingang oder Coroados-Indianer im brasilianischen Staate Rio Grande do Sul', *Anthropos* 9 (1914), 20. Koenigswald attacked the violent land grabbing of German-Brazilians ('Die Botokuden in Südbrasilien', p. 37).
83  Several articles have recently been published in translation. See e.g. Curt Unckel Nimuendajú, 'Quanto à Questão Coroado', *Tellus* 13:24 (2013), 269–74 and 291–7. Elena Welper, 'Apresentação da presente edição dos textos de Nimuendajú publicados no Jornal Deutsche Zeitung', *Tellus* 13:24 (2013), 261–7.
84  Eduard Seler, 'Vorbemerkung', *Zeitschrift für Ethnologie* 40 (1908), 745.
85  Todd A. Diacon, *Stringing Together a Nation: Mariano da Silva Rondon and the Construction of a Modern Brazil, 1906–1930* (Durham, NC: Duke Univversity Press, 2004).
86  Stauffer, 'Origem e fundação do Serviço de Proteção nos Indios', pp. 73–96. Ritz-Deutch, 'Alberto Vojtěch Frič', pp. 178–81.
87  See for example the report of 1916 by contemporary visitors: Geraldo H. de Paula Souza, 'Notas sobre uma visita a acampamentos de Índios Caingangs', *Revista do Museu Paulista* 10 (1918), 739–58. José María de Paula, 'Memoria sobre os botocudos do Paraná e Santa Catharina organisada pelo serviço de protecção aos selvicolas sob a inspecção', *Annaes do XX Congreso Internacional de Americanistas, Rio de Janeiro 1922* 1, 117–37. See also Santos, *Os Índios Xokleng*, p. 22. Rafael Casanova de Lima e Silva Hoerhann, 'O Serviço de Proteção aos Índios e a desintegração cultural dos Xokleng (1927–1954)' (PhD Dissertation, Universidade Federal de Santa Catarina, 2012), pp. 59–186.
88  Wettstein, *Brasilien*, p. 58. Ihering, 'A questão dos indios no Brazil', pp. 124–7.

89  Wittmann, *O vapor e o botoque*, pp. 73–92. See also Greg Urban, 'Interpretations of Inter-Cultural Contact: The Shokleng and Brazilian National Society 1914–1916', *Ethnohistory* 32:3 (1985), 224–44. For the situation today, see Joel João Carini, *Estado, índios e colonos: o conflito na reserve indgena de Serrinha norte do Rio Grande do Sul* (Passo Fundo: University of Passo Fundo, 2005), pp. 31–112. Alexandro Machado Namem, *Indios botocudos: uma reconstituição histórica do contacto* (Florianópolis: Editora da UFSC, 1991), pp. 52–91.
90  Finzsch, ' "[...] Extirpate or remove that vermine" ', p. 225.
91  Finzsch, ' "[...] Extirpate or remove that vermine" ', pp. 221–2.

# CHAPTER THREE

# 'Far better than their reputation': the Tolai of East New Britain in the writings of Otto Finsch[1]

Hilary Howes

In 1907, responding to a call for assistance from the German Colonial Society (DKG), its Braunschweig branch organised a 'colonial festival' to raise funds for the establishment of Elisabeth Haus, a maternity hospital in Windhoek, German South-West Africa (now Namibia).[2] Among the contributions to this festival, which raised an impressive total of 23,000 Reichsmarks, was a booklet titled *Tapinowanne Torondoluan: New Pomerania's first world traveller (1882)*.[3] Two small sepia photographs on the olive-green cover depict the 'world traveller', unclothed, from the waist up. One snap shows him in profile; the other has caught him looking towards the camera, his posture a little hunched, his facial expression difficult to read: is he surprised, resigned, abstracted? His eyes do not meet the viewer's gaze. These two portraits, intimate and inscrutable at the same time, contrast oddly with the bold precision of the Gothic type and the confident symmetry of the German imperial eagle. The tensions symbolised by this contrast – vaulting imperial ambition on the one hand, ambiguous personal encounters on the other – are the focus of this chapter.

In order to comprehend these tensions, I draw particularly on Bronwen Douglas's theory of 'indigenous countersigns'. Written and visual representations of Pacific Islanders produced by European travellers, Douglas suggests, 'should be read not merely as involuntary expressions of dominant metropolitan discourses and conventions but also as personal productions generated in the flux, excitement, stress, and ambiguity of encounters'; 'local initiatives, actions, and demeanours [...] left distorted countersigns in what [European travellers] wrote or drew'. Such countersigns, 'though never transparent', 'can be identified through systematic critical comparison of different media, genres, and

Zum Besten des Elisabeth=Hauses in Windhuk

# Tapinowanne Torondoluan

der erste Weltreisende Neupommerns (1882)

Kolonialfest
⚜ 1907 ⚜

Abteilung Braunschweig der
Deutschen Kolonialgesellschaft

**Figure 3.1** Cover of *Tapinowanne Torondoluan: New Pomerania's first world traveller* (1882)

modes of representation and the language and tone of their utterance'.[4] Accordingly, I critically compare *Tapinowanne Torondoluan: New Pomerania's first world traveller (1882)* with other writings by its author, Otto Finsch, as well as with accounts of local lifeways and cross-cultural encounters in New Pomerania (now New Britain) by other historical and contemporary authors.

In 1907 Otto Finsch was curator of the ethnological collection at Braunschweig's Municipal Museum. This position was the final stage in a long and eventful career which had taken him twice around the world, linking him inextricably with Germany's imperial ambitions in the Pacific and with the development of the nascent sciences of physical anthropology and ethnology in nineteenth-century Europe's metropoles. However, his booklet had an earlier genesis. The text, unaltered except for the title, first appeared in the 1902 anthology *Beneath the Trident: A New Naval and Colonial Book for Young and Old.*[5] Here, 'Tapinowanne Torondoluan. A conversation from pre-colonial New Pomerania' rubbed shoulders with an extraordinary mixture of Boy's Own Adventure-style stories, stirring verse and informative prose. Dramatic accounts of lion hunts, 'native' revolts, shipwrecks and sea-serpents were interspersed with introductions to semaphore, lists of nautical expressions, data-heavy comparisons between Germany's maritime trade, shipping and navy and those of other imperial powers, and verses titled 'To Germany's Youth!', 'The Trident Belongs in Our Fist!' and 'Song of the Fleet'. Contributions were illustrated with black-and-white photographs, sketches and the occasional full-colour plate. The frontispiece, 'His Majesty Kaiser Wilhelm II in Admiral's Uniform', set the tone for the remainder of the volume in no uncertain terms.

In some respects, Finsch's text was an odd fit in this context too. Certainly New Pomerania was a German protectorate at the time *Beneath the Trident* was published; in fact, as leader of an expedition sent out in June 1884 by a small group of influential businessmen to locate land suitable for German appropriation, Finsch himself had been instrumental in its acquisition. However, the events described in 'Tapinowanne Torondoluan' – his stay of almost eight months on Matupit Island in East New Britain, his departure and subsequent travels with the eponymous Tapinowanne in tow – dated to an earlier voyage of exploration, funded not by explicitly colonial but by scientific interests.

In order to understand the ways in which Finsch described the indigenous inhabitants of East New Britain – New Britons, as he called them, or Tolai, as they later began to call themselves – in general, and Tapinowanne in particular, it is necessary first to comprehend his own biography. Born in 1839 in the spa town of Warmbrunn in

Lower Silesia (now Cieplice, south-western Poland), he had little formal education, attending only the local elementary school; however, he began sketching the local landscape, flora and fauna, as well as 'foreign' visitors to the town's public baths, at an early age, foreshadowing what were to be lasting interests in natural history and ethnology. His father, a glass painter and trader, took him on as a commercial apprentice, but Finsch had other ideas. In 1857, while still a teenager, he broke off the apprenticeship and headed south-east, studying briefly at the university in Pest (now Budapest, Hungary), then working as a private tutor in Rustchuk (now Ruse, Bulgaria), at that time part of the Ottoman Empire. In 1861 he relocated to Leiden, Netherlands, to take up a position as assistant to the prominent ornithologist Hermann Schlegel at the Imperial Museum of Natural History. Three years later he moved to Bremen, Germany, to become curator of the local Museum Society's natural history and ethnographic collections; when the City of Bremen assumed responsibility for these collections, Finsch was appointed their director. He held this position for almost fifteen years, during which period he was active as a scientific traveller and author. Destinations included North America, Lapland and western Siberia; major publications ranged from *New Guinea and its Inhabitants* (1865), the first substantive monograph on the topic ever published in German, to the two-volume *Treatise on Parrots* (1867–68), for which he received an honorary doctorate from the University of Bonn.[6]

In 1879, having successfully applied for a Humboldt Foundation travel grant from the Royal Prussian Academy of Sciences, he resigned from his directorship in Bremen; he would have preferred to take extended leave, but the city's government declined this request.[7] His initial proposal was for a year's travel to Micronesia

> to obtain for [Prussia's] scientific institutions and museums as much [material] as possible from the anthropologically and ethnographically interesting populations of Micronesia, which are swiftly nearing extinction, and at the same time to investigate the flora, fauna and geological formation of these islands.[8]

However, the Academy was sufficiently pleased with his progress to approve two requests for additional funding.[9] As a result, Finsch's first Pacific voyage extended from mid-1879 to late 1882, a total of just over three years, and took him not only to Hawai'i, the Marshall, Gilbert, and Caroline Islands and Nauru but also to New Britain, New Zealand, Australia and south-east New Guinea. Prussia's Royal Museums benefited to the tune of 157 crates of specimens, ranging from stuffed birds and animals to preserved plants, fossils, cultural artefacts, and human remains.[10] In Finsch's eyes, Tapinowanne was also (though not only) a specimen, as I discuss in more detail below. But of all that Finsch collected, Tapinowanne alone left and returned to his homeland alive.

In June 1884, only a few months after Tapinowanne's safe homecoming to Matupit Island, Finsch departed for the Pacific again, this time for explicitly colonial purposes. The Prussian diplomat Heinrich von Kusserow, an enthusiastic advocate of colonial policy, had introduced him, shortly after his return, to Adolph von Hansemann, a banking heavyweight with a finger in multiple pies.[11] Hansemann had promptly engaged Finsch to assist him in concocting one particular pie, the Consortium for the Preparation and Establishment of a South Sea Island Company (later the New Guinea Company). Finsch was to lead an expedition tasked with the

> [i]nvestigation of the unknown or little-known coasts of New Britain, as well as the north coast of New Guinea to the 141st meridian, in order to locate harbours, establish friendly communication with the natives, and acquire land to the greatest possible extent.[12]

Starting from Sydney in the steamer *Samoa*, Finsch and his fellow expedition members made six separate voyages between September 1884 and July 1885. To dispel potential Australian suspicions about their intentions, they posed initially as a 'harmless' group of scientists on board a vessel belonging to the German Trading and Plantation Company (DHPG). However, word quickly 'oozed out' that the *Samoa* had been joined in Mioko, New Ireland, by the German warships *Hyäne* and *Elisabeth*, and that the German flag had been hoisted 'over Goko [Mioko], Matupi [Matupit], and over such parts of the north coast of New Britain which are claimed by Germans as their property'.[13] These rumours were confirmed in December 1884 by a statement in the London *Standard*, widely reported in Australia's major newspapers,

> that Germany has notified to the powers the annexation of New Britain, New Ireland, New Hanover, the Marshall Islands, Anderson Island, Duke of York Island, the Admiralty Islands, and the northern part of New Guinea [...] Dr. Finsch [...] will probably be appointed administrator of the annexed territory.[14]

If Finsch had indeed hoped for such an appointment, it did not eventuate. He was offered a contract as Station Director to 'investigate the usefulness of regions previously unexplored, prepare station facilities etc.', but took exception both to the menial nature of the responsibilities involved and to the contract's prescriptive language. The prospect of having all his publications vetted by the New Guinea Company, and any items of ethnographic interest he collected confiscated for their commercial benefit, was distinctly unappealing; their insistence that he observe 'strict moderation in the enjoyment of spirituous liquors' and practise 'friendly and humane treatment of the natives' was unnecessary and insulting.[15] But finding a more congenial position proved exceedingly difficult. Following his return to Germany, Finsch spent the best part of a decade without formal employment, though Ildikó Cazan-Simányi observes that he 'did not remain idle: he compiled inventories of his collections, published, exhibited his collections, sold parts of them, and maintained his contacts with colleagues in local and international museums'.[16] In 1897 he moved to the Netherlands with his wife and daughter to take up a position as Head of the Ornithological Division of the Imperial Museum of Natural History in Leiden, but his correspondence during this period reveals that he was deeply unhappy with virtually every aspect of his situation:

> [W]e live as though in exile, and I am sorriest for my wife and our little daughter [...] who is German with all her soul and cannot understand why her father moved to this country. Well! I did not do it for pleasure, but what else is one to do, when one must provide for one's wife and child? I have also abandoned ethnology, with a heavy heart, and have been compelled to return to ornithology [...] Unfortunately the museum, a large warehouse without any noticeable scientific life, is far from cheery, but of course I do my duty [...] Had I not gone to the Pacific, I would now have a fine position in good old Bremen![17]

Finsch strongly believed that his achievements as a colonial pioneer had been overlooked. His correspondence while in Leiden consistently stressed this, as did publications with the indicative titles 'How I acquired Kaiser Wilhelm's Land' (1902) and 'Kaiser Wilhelm's Land: A peaceful colonial acquisition' (1905). Copies of the former publication accompanied a series of letters he composed in September 1902 to the Prussian Cultural Minister and the current and former Presidents of the German Colonial Society, all seeking recognition of his contribution to realising Germany's colonial ambitions. The eventual decision, in January 1904, to grant him an honorarium of 1,000 Reichsmarks per year can partly be attributed to the intervention of his friend Julius Lohmeyer, who not only published the serials in which Finsch's abovementioned articles appeared but was also the editor of the 1902 anthology *Beneath the Trident*.[18] Seen within this context, *Tapinowanne Torondoluan* can be understood as a further declaration of Finsch's colonial achievements. The following paragraph, highlighting the nature of his personal role as an agent of German colonialism, would not be out of place in a training manual for colonial propagandists:

> In remembering those times of arbitrariness and lawlessness, it often seems to me like a dream that scarcely four years later, on the same island

[...] I witnessed the solemn hoisting of the German imperial flag, a very important event, signifying a new era of peace and civilised behaviour in that region now known as the 'Bismarck Archipelago'. Our warships, with the same solemnity, were then able to proclaim [this new era] in New Guinea [...] where my successful voyages and enterprises in the steamer *Samoa* had secured what is now 'Kaiser Wilhelm's Land' for the New Guinea Company and thus for Germany.[19]

However, there was more to this grandstanding than meets the eye. Importantly, Finsch's accusation of 'arbitrariness and lawlessness' was aimed as much at supposedly 'civilised' Europeans as at New Britain's indigenous inhabitants. His description of the region on his arrival in July 1880 alternated between humanitarian concern and casual arrogance. Although 'German trading stations, that is to say, the beginnings of a "sphere of interest"', already existed in New Britain at the time, 'the land was still masterless' and 'the natives were held in the most evil repute as "naked savages" and "cannibals"'.[20] Although Finsch at no point acknowledged the possibility that 'natives' might legitimately consider themselves masters over their own land, he did argue for a more nuanced understanding of the causes of conflicts in the region:

All this did not deter me from living for more than seven months amongst this infamous society; quite peacefully, in fact, although there was no lack of murder and manslaughter during that time, from both sides of course. For there were, amongst the representatives of civilisation, truly dubious men, with a morality below that of the natives [...] In general these 'savages' proved themselves to be far better than their reputation. For me it was thus a congenial duty to advocate for these natural people, still relatively unspoilt at that time, and to depict them as faithfully as possible in word and image.[21]

Several aspects of Finsch's argument deserve closer examination. His juxtaposition of 'truly dubious men, with a morality below that of the natives', and unjustly vilified 'natural people' in need of his advocacy, recalls what Jane Samson has described as the 'humanitarian interpretation of island conditions', containing 'two interdependent themes: a benevolent, protective view of islanders and the condemnation of white men defined as threats to "Christianization and Civilization"'. However, the similarity is not absolute. Certainly Finsch explained some violent clashes in terms corresponding to those employed by Samson's humanitarians, who were 'determined to put white agency at the center of the story, confining islanders' motives to an easily understood "retaliation theory"'.[22] In his earliest published description of New Britain, which appeared in mid-1881 in the regional newspaper *Hamburger Nachrichten* under the title 'From the Pacific', he denied that the Tolai were 'murderous and bloodthirsty people, as is always assumed of such so-called savages'. Although 'murders committed against whites, of which five took place during my stay here alone', might seem to contradict 'this favourable opinion', in fact 'such cases warrant a judgement as impartial as it is mild; it often becomes apparent that the whites' own behaviour was the cause of their misfortune'.[23] Finsch's essay 'Cannibals in New Britain', published in November 1883 in the popular German weekly *Illustrirte Zeitung*, offered essentially the same explanation for indigenous violence:

> The New Briton [...] knows no absolute trust; he lies, cheats and is perhaps even deceitful towards his white friend, but this may have its basis in the unhappy experiences which he has had from his first acquaintance with the white man. For certainly those whom the desire for profit and the love of adventure first induced to settle in these regions were not the best elements; even today, amongst the relatively small number of whites here, there are notorious individuals who, with the assistance of powder and lead, play [at being] little autocrats. I count amongst these, to give just one example, a trader who buys girls from the natives for a limited time, pays only a minimal portion of the purchase price, and simply resells the unhappy victims for cash. If the native allows such infamous deeds to go unavenged, it is because he recognises his powerlessness; he merely postpones his revenge to a favourable occasion, and it may perhaps strike someone completely innocent.[24]

However, Finsch also acknowledged other motives for indigenous violence that had little to do with revenge. In April 1878, two years before his arrival in New Britain, the Wesleyan Methodist missionary George Brown had responded to the killing of four Fijian teachers in the hinterland of the Gazelle Peninsula 'by organising and leading an armed raid on the villages he believed had either ordered the killings or had accepted the body parts of the slain for consumption'. Helen Gardner notes that Brown was charged with manslaughter by the British High Commissioner for the Western Pacific, but 'the charges were eventually dropped over a conflict in judicial authority', and Brown's narrative of the events involved, though not entirely unchallenged, 'became definitive in the absence of any other versions'.[25] Finsch's description of the raid made his opinion of Brown's conduct very clear, but was ambivalent in its treatment of Tolai participants:

> The New Briton, although belligerent on the whole, is cowardly, like most so-called savages, and will only fight when he believes he has the advantage [...] When the mission, scarcely established, raised the banner of war in 1878 to avenge the death of four teachers, natives of Fiji, who had ventured too far into the interior amongst hostile communities, contrary to the warnings of the coastal dwellers, a great number of the

natives followed that banner against their own brothers. After all, six or eight white or half-white foreigners accepted the responsibility; thirty-odd coloured mission teachers from Fiji or Samoa, armed with rifles, guaranteed their success; and, most importantly, one could count on rich spoils in [the form of] shell money.[26]

Whether the 'native' participants in this raid actually considered its targets 'their own brothers' is open to question. The anthropologist A.L. Epstein, drawing on 'the writings of [...] the first outsiders to have more than fleeting contact with the area', describes '[s]ocial life on the Gazelle Peninsula' during the early contact period as 'characteristically minute in scale'; although the area's inhabitants 'shared a common language [...] and a relatively homogeneous culture', they 'possessed no single common name for themselves as a group' prior to the emergence of the group designation 'Tolai' in the 1930s (I follow Epstein in employing 'Tolai' retrospectively on grounds of convenience). The polity was 'fragmented and highly local' in character; relations between territorial groupings of two to three hundred persons 'were marked by suspicion and hostility, often culminating in raiding and warfare', although marriage links sometimes served to create 'bonds between otherwise hostile communities'.[27] Finsch was probably more accurate in highlighting the appeal of rifles and shell money. According to Epstein, demand for the former 'increased rapidly' following contact with Europeans, as Tolai leaders swiftly realised 'the advantages that firearms gave them over their enemies'; the latter, 'shell money' known locally as *tambu* or *tabu*, was not simply 'a source of influence and power' but 'permeated the entire culture [...] there was not a custom connected with life or death in which this money did not play a great and leading part'. The Tolai historian Jacob L. Simet explains that *tabu* functions as 'a medium of communication about matters which are culturally Tolai'; the ritual presentation of *tabu* enables the expression of 'desires, intents and emotions' which 'cannot be uttered by word of mouth because they are socially disruptive, undesirable, humiliating and even dangerous'.[28]

Although Finsch followed Samson's humanitarians in comparing 'benign islanders' unfavourably with ' "savage" white men', he did not share their view that '[m]issionaries offered civilization's benefits [...] but other white men introduced only civilization's evils'.[29] On the contrary, even when advocating the benefits of colonial intervention, he was distinctly sceptical of Christian influence. His assessments of the relative merits of these two forms of European intervention differ from more recent Tolai understandings. The historian Klaus Neumann, who undertook research in East New Britain in the 1980s, noted that the *lotu* (Christian religion) had become one of three key concepts on which Tolai based their individual lives and society, along with *matanitu*, 'government' (introduced political structures, Western-style education, judiciary and police) and *balanagunan*, 'traditional' Tolai customs. Accordingly, 'stories concerning the coming of the missions [were] widely known throughout the whole Tolai area', whereas '[s]tories about other events of the colonial past' were known to only a few individuals 'outside the areas affected'.[30]

Finsch's disapproval of Christian influence was voiced most strongly and consistently with regard to Brown's armed raid, a 'war of retaliation' which 'could scarcely be condoned from a purely Christian point of view' and had taken the lives of 'more than 200 innocent savages'.[31] More generally, he doubted the efficacy of mission work. As I have argued elsewhere with particular reference to the indigenous inhabitants of Torres Strait, his views on Western influence varied greatly. Generally, after his time in the Pacific, Finsch viewed the influence of commerce as mostly positive, while being uniformly dismissive of missionary activity.[32] He was unimpressed by the endeavours of Wesleyan Methodists in New Britain and surrounding islands:

> Whatever successes the mission may have had during its six-year existence, next to nothing can be seen of them [...] I was told that 34 natives had been baptised to date [...] The missionaries affirm that all of these proselytes are staunch in all fundamental principles and teachings of Christianity [...] but he who knows at least a few of the converts personally may perhaps be permitted [to entertain] mild doubts. The so-called 'King' Tauralome [...] hosted a heathen feast, which I myself attended, only two months before his sudden baptism [...] and continued to lie to me after his baptism as a Christian just as much as he had beforehand as a heathen.[33]

Comparison with Finsch's pre-voyage publications on the subject indicates a marked transformation in his views of missionary endeavour over the course of his first Pacific voyage. In *New Guinea and its Inhabitants* (1865), a compilation based on published accounts from French and Dutch voyages to the region, he acknowledged the efforts of Carl Ottow and Johann Geissler in establishing north-west New Guinea's first mission presence, an outpost of the Utrecht Mission Society in Doreh Bay; they deserved 'the fullest respect' for the 'fearful privations and toils' they had endured, and although 'seven years' labour' had not yet produced any 'results [...] to speak of', their eventual success 'must be of incalculable value for the entire future of New Guinea'.[34] 'Sketches from New Guinea' (1866) congratulated the missionaries in Doreh Bay on their 'most notable' contribution to expanding European knowledge of 'New Guinea, namely [...] its inhabitants', mentioning in particular their studies of 'the manners and customs, even the language', of local indigenous people.[35] But by the time Finsch was in a position to write about New Britain from personal experience, his accounts suggest that he had abandoned any expectation of benefit from the presence of missionaries there. Instead, he looked to eventual imperial intervention to lessen social violence:

> Let us hope that with the greater expansion of trade in these regions, the powers concerned may also undertake more towards the energetic protection of whites and natives; bloody scenes between whites and natives will then cease gradually as a matter of course [...] But it will probably be a long time yet before a great power assumes responsibility for the protectorate.[36]

Although it is not evident from this particular quotation, Finsch was in fact deeply divided between his enthusiasm for the civilising effects of imperial rule and his regret for the transformations in Pacific Island societies following European contact. As an ethnologist, he shared the views of many of his contemporaries in interpreting such transformations as a loss of cultural originality, a tainting of purity, even a corruption of Edenic innocence: *Tapinowanne Torondoluan* spoke of the Tolai as 'unclothed, as though in Paradise'.[37] Finsch used similar language when discussing his progress on the manuscript of his monograph *Ethnological Experiences and Specimens from the South Seas* (1893), writing of 'working on the difficult chapter "Micronesia", a book of which only a few pages remain, as the original has for the most part been tattered, stained and spoilt by civilisation and Christianity [...] one can only collect the shards and attempt to glue them together, as [the archaeologist Heinrich] Schliemann does his pots'.[38] In contrast, Finsch considered the Tolai 'relatively unspoilt', though he was aware of prior contact between Tolai and Europeans, noting (with some understatement) that 'whites had been seen now and then since the days of the whalers', and that pidgin, introduced by whalers, 'constituted the lingua franca' of the Blanche Bay region at the time of his visit.[39]

Finsch's descriptions of the Tolai as 'unspoilt', 'natural people' suggest a worldview in which the supposedly positive process of civilisation in fact represented a regrettable, if inevitable, falling-away from an original, ideal condition. In short, this view cast New Britain's indigenous inhabitants as noble savages, as a number of statements in *Tapinowanne Torondoluan*, as well as elements of Finsch's other writings, make clear. For example, he followed his affectionate description of the children on Matupit Island – 'dear little creatures' with 'great dark eyes', 'always merry and cheerful', who 'scarcely differ from our children in their harmless games of various kinds' – with the wistful comment: 'At all events, these black children, free from schooling and every other kind of compulsion, could enjoy their youth far more, even though they had to assist [the adults] from time to time and in general become independent at an earlier age'.[40] Other observers' accounts of Tolai society simultaneously confirm and challenge elements of this curiously contradictory description. According to Richard Parkinson, a plantation manager and ethnographic collector who lived and worked in the Bismarck Archipelago from 1882 until his death in 1909,[41] boys in the Gazelle Peninsula would relocate at the age of six or eight from their parents' house to that of an uncle. From then on, they

> help the uncle in his plantations, practise the various dances, and are proud when they are admitted to the *duk-duk* society or the *ingiet* association. From their youth, they studiously imitate the expressions, gestures and behaviour of their elders, and childish glee or childish exuberance is for the most part foreign to them. In appearance and behaviour, a boy of fourteen or fifteen years is already a fully adult man.[42]

Such difficulties are legion in Finsch's works. In 'Cannibals in New Britain', he first argued for the necessity of getting to know other 'human races' personally before forming any judgements – 'Everywhere, where I made the acquaintance of South Seas natives in their own country, I found them to be quite different than I had imagined [...] and most descriptions in compilatory works turned out to be incorrect on many points' – before launching into an extended panegyric that suggested his time amongst the Tolai had not helped him move beyond the noble savage mythology of the armchair ethnologist:

> The longer one lives amongst these savages, the more one finds that they are in fact very happy people, in some respects much happier than us. They know no care, no conventionality, no burdensome constraint, they know nothing of politics, subservience, dependency, they need not contend with daily anxieties to win their bread and do not consider themselves superior to others by virtue either of physical or of spiritual merits.[43]

It is difficult to believe that Finsch could have remained, after almost eight months' close engagement with Tolai society, so completely ignorant of it as this rhapsody suggests.[44] In fact, 'From the Pacific' described several practices directly contradicting the idea of a non-hierarchical society whose members knew 'nothing of politics [or] subservience', noting that women were 'not permitted to participate at all in some festivals' and that certain areas could 'only be entered by men [...] [who] belong to the "Dugdug" [*dukduk*], a secret society [...] about whose aims and ceremonies I have to date been able to obtain as little precise information as any other white man'.[45] Possibly his comments in 'Cannibals in New Britain' were intended rhetorically rather than literally; nonetheless the entire text is riddled with inconsistencies. In the paragraph quoted above, the freedom, simplicity, ease and equality supposedly characterising Tolai life were presented as objects of envy, but in the immediately preceding paragraphs it was the sophistication of their society that attracted Finsch's praise:

> The naked inhabitants of New Britain are by no means as bad as their reputation, and [...] are far more advanced than has previously been assumed [...] a people which practises a regulated cultivation of the soil, produces its staple diet through its own industriousness, possesses a medium of exchange corresponding to our money, a rich language, [and] a great love of music [...] cannot be described by ethnologists as completely backward, even if it wears no clothing. Mere nakedness, therefore, is neither a criterion for the developmental stage of a human race, nor an indication of its original state.[46]

Finsch gave an equally flattering report of Tolai morals, asserting that their 'chastity and morality [...] can be termed exemplary'. Alcoholism, he declared, was 'completely unknown' in New Britain; marriage, although polygamous, was 'bound by strict laws', and household theft a rare occurrence, 'even though there are many wealthy people whose heaped-up treasures of shell money [...] could be just as great a temptation to crime as the Arnheims amongst our magnates'.[47] His arguments for the superiority of Tolai morals, especially as compared to those of societies he had encountered in Micronesia, tended to present the former within the noble savage paradigm:

> The strict morality [in New Britain] is very striking and pleasant in contrast to the peoples of Micronesia; it is hardly to be reconciled with the prevailing nakedness, but it seems the people here live as did the first pair in Paradise before the Fall: they are not aware of their nakedness and do not know shame as we understand it! One never observes obscene acts or gestures, and their sexual life is free from the bestial desires and vices of the Micronesians.[48]

Finsch explicitly 'refute[d] the claim, postulated in so many books', that 'chastity, modesty and honour as we understand them [...] only began to disappear little by little [from Micronesian societies]' following contact with whites, but remained unclear on whether Micronesians had ever enjoyed an existence as noble savages.[49] Furthermore, he was quick to discard the noble savage paradigm altogether, without any apparent cognitive dissonance, when he wished to emphasise an aspect of Tolai society it could not satisfactorily explain. In 'From the Pacific', he confirmed that theft was 'infinitely rarer' amongst the Tolai 'than amongst us [...] coconut palms and their fruits, as well as plantations, are absolutely inviolable'. However, he also stated baldly that '[a] kanaka without diwara [shell money] is a poor man, just as social status is

[ 54 ]

determined primarily by the possession of diwara', directly contradicting the social egalitarianism he then posited in 'Cannibals in New Britain'.[50] *Tapinowanne Torondoluan* again highlighted the use of shell money as evidence of sophistication: 'those small nassa shells, which substitute for our "money" in large areas of Melanesia [...] can even be lent out as such, namely in return for – interest! Truly, a remarkable indication of civilisation which one would least of all have expected [to find] amongst these "savages"'.[51]

What is evident, amongst all the inconsistencies and paradigm switching, is that Finsch's experiences in the field had substantially complicated his understandings of savagery and civilisation. Prior to his voyage, he seems to have assumed that 'savage' societies would display a consistent series of characteristics, as the following excerpt suggests:

> The inhabitants [of the area] along the Princess Marianne Strait in the south-west [of New Guinea] are without doubt the crudest. In them we behold those so-called savages who are becoming ever rarer on our planet. Completely naked, with the exception of a loin-covering [...] the Papuan of these regions roams the extensive territory of his home, and has no fixed abode. He makes his living by hunting; in addition, various wild-growing fruits serve him as food. It is also generally alleged that the Papuans are man-eaters, but reliable and unequivocal reports [of this practice] do not yet exist.[52]

Having experienced Tolai society, however, he discovered that apparently unequivocal markers of savagery from a European perspective, notably nakedness and cannibalism, could in fact co-exist with equally unequivocal markers of civilisation. Colleagues like Julius Lohmeyer remained content to sum up the level of development of Germany's various colonial subjects in a word or two: whereas German East Africa was inhabited by 'peoples of many kinds [...] from the marauding nomad to the semi-civilised coastal dweller, who can read and write Arabic, clothes himself decently and would be most reluctant to do without foreign import goods', the Bismarck Archipelago was merely 'populated by cannibals'.[53] Finsch, however, wished to differentiate. Like James Cook before him, he was particularly concerned to '[disassociate] people he liked from a practice that repelled him'. As Cook had done when discussing Maori practices, Finsch 'insisted that [Tolai cannibalism] was a fact, but was equally insistent that the people were good'; the Tolai, he declared, 'possess a good nature that in general is roundly denied such creatures, burdened as they are with the original sin of cannibalism'.[54] He was clearly aware of, and exploited to the full, Europeans' fascination with cannibalism – 'Cannibals in New Britain' included a full-page depiction of a cannibal feast he claimed to have witnessed on 7 March

1881 – but was careful to emphasise aspects of the 'dreadful spectacle' that did not conform to stereotypical expectations. 'No wild howl of victory was raised, as one expects from "savages"; on the contrary, everything proceeded as quietly as though something quite ordinary were taking place.'[55] Both 'Cannibals in New Britain' and 'From the Pacific' also stressed the limitations to cannibal practices:

> As far as I was informed by my friends, people are by no means fattened and slaughtered merely for enjoyment, as used to be the case in Fiji [...] instead, only those slain in battle are devoured [...] including women, but not children. The latter, as well as the women, are not permitted to participate in the enjoyment of human flesh. Moreover, in a feud between members of the same tribe or blood relatives, who are considered by these tribes too as sacred, the dead are not eaten, but are buried as usual [...] It is also worth mentioning that of the five white men slain during my stay in New Britain, not one was eaten.[56]

But what of Tapinowanne himself? Although Finsch devoted seventeen pages of text to a detailed description of their travels together, his various, sometimes conflicting motivations for writing make it difficult to attempt an objective analysis. A few basic facts can perhaps be taken at face value: Tapinowanne's approximate age – Finsch estimated that he was 'perhaps 13 to 14 years old' when they met, and 'around fifteen' by the time they reached Berlin – and the duration and geographical extent of their joint travels.[57] Finsch departed Matupit Island for Sydney on the brigantine *Southern Cross* in late March 1881; Tapinowanne, whom he had employed during his stay in New Britain to assist him with hunting and skinning bird specimens, 'would not be rebuffed, despite all the remonstrances and warnings from me and from his countrymen, and clambered aboard from his canoe at the very last moment, when the ship had already begun to move'.[58] The two men reached Sydney in late April 1881. Subsequent stops included Tasmania, New Zealand, Torres Strait, Cape York Peninsula, south-east New Guinea, Batavia (now Jakarta), Singapore, Ceylon (now Sri Lanka), Naples and finally, in October 1882, Germany. Here they remained, moving between Berlin, Bremen, and the Giant Mountains of Silesia, until October 1883. Finsch then arranged for Tapinowanne to return to New Britain 'by direct ship from Hamburg'.[59] His arrival in February 1884 was independently confirmed by the German trader Eduard Hernsheim, who reported:

> [T]he schooner *Hans* [...] had arrived. There was a Matupi boy on board, whom Dr Finsch had at one time taken with him to Germany. Typically, in spite of several years spent among Germans, this boy had learnt no German but only bad pidgin English, and made a very poor impression in his strange get-up.[60]

The 'strange get-up' presumably included a Royal Hawaiian Army cap and cockade, obtained by Finsch from a manufacturer in Bremen as an alternative to Tapinowanne's request for the German equivalent (available only to German citizens), and an 'eagerly longed-for' vasculum (cylindrical tin for carrying botanical specimens).[61] Hernsheim's sour tone contrasts markedly with Finsch's self-congratulatory depiction of his protégé's subsequent career as 'an itinerant preacher who helped to spread a great deal of light amongst his dark countrymen [...] an enthusiastic native promoter of Germany's reputation and significance'.[62] While neither account can be considered objective, together they hint at the very different interpretative possibilities opened by an alternative view of the same events.

Unfortunately, very little of *Tapinowanne Torondoluan* can be tested in this manner. We do have independent confirmation of Tapinowanne's introduction to the members of the Berlin Society for Anthropology, Ethnology and Prehistory on 11 November 1882; Adolf Bastian, chairing the monthly meeting, regretted the absence of the President, Rudolf Virchow, but spoke of 'the pleasure of seeing amongst us again [...] Dr Otto Finsch', who 'introduced the New Briton Papíno Wáne Toróndo Lúan [*sic*] from Matupi' and 'commented on the latter's intellectual characteristics, as well as on his homeland and the agriculture [practised] there'. Even this dry summary raises questions, given Finsch's later assertion that Tapinowanne had been 'introduced to the circle of the Anthropological Society by none other than its doyen, Virchow'.[63] Potential avenues for further investigation of alternative views include scanning German newspapers for the relevant period – although Finsch's painstaking compilation of published sources relating to his work leaves little hope of finding anything he missed – and engaging present-day Tolai communities in oral history research.[64]

In addition, there are useful insights to be gleaned from Finsch's descriptions of occasions on which Tapinowanne's engagement with specific events or circumstances did not correspond to expectations. Several incidents suggest that Tapinowanne, far from being a docile reflection of Finsch's colonial ambitions, asserted his own agency in ways Finsch occasionally found confronting. In south-east New Guinea, he ran away temporarily to join a group of locals living along the Goldie River after receiving 'a box on the ear' for having invited 'strange black guests to [share] our meagre supplies'. In Naples, Finsch was 'obliged soberly to forbid him from laughing loudly and pointing' at cripples on the streets. He had plenty to say about Italian sculpture, interpreting a statue of Siegfried and the dragon as depicting 'a "pukpuk" (crocodile)', and instructing Finsch to inform the sculptor that '[e]ven a white man was not strong enough to defeat the pukpuk in this way'. And despite his enthusiastic appreciation of a German military parade, he responded firmly to Finsch's threat 'to put him in amongst the soldiers' with a dark look and the words: 'I did not come to Berlin to become a soldier'. Why, then, did he choose to come? The question is as tantalising as the answer is opaque, though Finsch's explanation – that Tapinowanne wished 'to see the world, in particular Germany' – cannot be dismissed out of hand.[65] Finsch doubtless welcomed Tapinowanne's decision to board the *Southern Cross*; some months earlier, he had optimistically suggested to his mentor Virchow that he could 'bring with me, when I return home, several New Britons and New Irelanders' if Virchow could 'mobilise [the necessary] funds'.[66] However, I have found nothing to suggest that Tapinowanne was kidnapped or deceived into boarding, and he could well have had his own reasons for 'clamber[ing] aboard'. Drawing on individual biographies of Oceanian voyagers on Euroamerican vessels, David A. Chappell lists various possible motivations for their participation, 'from escaping from a bad situation to being "volunteered" by chiefs to personal adventure and material gain', adding: 'Given their seafaring heritage and growing interaction with foreign shipping, it would be surprising if Oceanians had *not* begun to voyage on the new vessels'.[67]

Finally, more recent anthropological work has the potential to complicate historical descriptions of encounters. A good example is Finsch's commendation of what he perceived as a straightforward gesture of generosity and friendship:

> My Tapino was always glad to share with other children [...] It was touching at his departure in Hamburg when he handed over to me at the last minute a beautiful Japanese parasol, which he loved with all his heart, with the words 'for Senta' – his most beloved little friend in Bremen.[68]

At one level, it is understandable that Finsch would wish to present Tapinowanne, as representative of Germany's newly acquired colonial subjects, in a positive light. At another, the enormous volume of recent work on Melanesian cultural alterities – especially in relation to sociality, gift exchange, 'multible' and 'partible' personhood, gender symbolism and gender relations – suggests that the deeper meaning of this gift to its giver, Tapinowanne, is something that neither its intermediary, Finsch, nor its recipient, Senta, nor we can ever fully understand.[69]

## Notes

1  This chapter draws on research conducted in association with the Australian Research Council Discovery Project 'European Naturalists and the Constitution of Human Difference in Oceania: Crosscultural Encounters and the Science of Race', based at the Australian National University under the direction of Bronwen Douglas

and Chris Ballard. Terms such as 'kanaka' reflect nineteenth-century usage. All translations are my own.

2   Elisabeth Haus (in operation 1908–81) was named after Elisabeth von Sachsen-Weimar-Eisenach, who founded the Women's League of the German Colonial Society. It now houses the Rectorate of Namibia University of Science and Technology. Anon., 'Neues Leben im "Storchennest"', *Allgemeine Zeitung* (17 April 2007), www.az.com.na/lokales/neues-leben-im-storchennest.19492.php, accessed 20 January 2016.

3   Anon., 'Eingänge für das Elisabeth-Haus in Windhuk', *Deutsche Kolonialzeitung* 24:51 (21 December 1907), 529; O. Finsch, *Tapinowanne Torondoluan, der erste Weltreisender Neupommerns (1882)* (Braunschweig: Julius Krampe, 1907).

4   B. Douglas, 'Encountering Agency: Islanders, European Voyagers, and the Production of Race in Oceania', in E. Hermann (ed.), *Changing Contexts, Shifting Meanings: Transformations of Cultural Traditions in Oceania* (Honolulu: University of Hawai'i Press, 2011), pp. 74–92.

5   O. Finsch, 'Tapinowanne Torondoluan. Eine Plauderei aus vorkolonialer Zeit Neupommerns', in J. Lohmeyer (ed.), *Unter dem Dreizack. Neues Marine- und Kolonialbuch für Jung und Alt* (Bielefeld and Leipzig: Velhagen & Klasing, 1902), pp. 419–35.

6   H. Abel, 'Otto Finsch. Ein deutscher Kolonialpionier', *Der Schlüssel* 3 (1938), 317–22; H. Abel, 'Finsch, Otto Friedrich Hermann', *Neue Deutsche Biographie* 5 (1961), 163–4, www.deutsche-biographie.de/pnd116524030.html, accessed 21 January 2016; I. Cazan-Simányi, 'Versuch einer biographischen Annäherung an Otto Finsch', in I. Cazan-Simányi and G. Weiss (eds), *Aus dem Pazifik. Ein Sammler aus Leidenschaft – F.H. Otto Finsch (1839–1917)* (Vienna: Museum für Völkerkunde, 2012), pp. 12–17; F. Cunze, 'Professor Dr. Otto Finsch†', *Braunschweigisches Magazin* 23:3 (March 1917), 21–5; O. Finsch, *Systematische Uebersicht der Ergebnisse seiner Reisen und schriftstellerischen Tätigkeit (1859–1899)* (Berlin: R. Friedländer & Sohn, 1899), pp. 11–29.

7   Finsch, *Systematische Uebersicht*, p. 14; O. Finsch, *Kaiser-Wilhelmsland. Eine friedliche Kolonialerwerbung. Separatabdruck aus Lohmeyer-Wislicenus 'Auf weiter Fahrt', Deutsche Marine- und Kolonialbibliothek Band IV* (Leipzig: Wilhelm Weicher, 1905), p. 2.

8   Berlin-Brandenburg Academy of Sciences (hereafter BBAW), Sig. II-XI, 74: Vorgang zur Unterstützung eines Forschungsvorhabens von O. Finsch durch die Humboldt-Stiftung für Naturforschung und Reisen aus den Jahren 1878–1882, letter from the Prussian Academy of Sciences to 'Eurer Excellenz' [A. Falk?], 18 December 1878.

9   BBAW, Sig. II-XI, 74: Vorgang zur Unterstützung eines Forschungsvorhabens … , excerpts from the minutes of meetings of the Physical-Mathematical Class of the Prussian Academy of Sciences, 3 May 1880 and 19 May 1881.

10  Finsch, *Systematische Uebersicht*, p. 15.

11  E. Achterberg, 'Hansemann, Adolph von', *Neue Deutsche Biographie* 7 (1966), pp. 625–6, www.deutsche-biographie.de/pnd118701428.html, accessed 22 January 2016; Finsch, *Kaiser-Wilhelmsland*, pp. 1–8; H. Gründer, 'Die historischen und politischen Voraussetzungen des deutschen Kolonialismus', in H. J. Hiery (ed.), *Die deutsche Südsee 1884–1914. Ein Handbuch* (Paderborn, Munich, Vienna and Zürich: Ferdinand Schöningh, 2001), pp. 44–5; K. Hildebrand, 'Kusserow, Heinrich von', *Neue Deutsche Biographie* 13 (1982), 343–4, www.deutsche-biographie.de/pnd116626933.html, accessed 22 January 2016; H. Mückler, *Kolonialismus in Ozeanien* (Vienna: facultas. wuv, 2012), pp. 171–2.

12  O. Finsch, *Samoafahrten. Reisen in Kaiser Wilhelms-Land und Englisch-Neu-Guinea in den Jahren 1884 u. 1885 an Bord des deutschen Dampfers 'Samoa'* (Leipzig: Ferdinand Hirt & Sohn, 1888), p. 7.

13  Anon., 'The German Annexation', *Maryborough Chronicle, Wide Bay and Burnett Advertiser* (31 December 1884), 3; cf. Finsch, *Systematische Uebersicht*, pp. 18–20, 130–2.

14  Anon., 'Germany in the Pacific. Statement by the *Standard*. Extensive Annexations Agreed to by England', *Argus* (23 December 1884), 5; cf. Anon, 'Cablegrams. Germany

and the Pacific. Comprehensive Annexation Scheme', *Evening News* (23 December 1884), 4; Anon., 'Special Telegrams', *Tasmanian* (27 December 1884), 15.

15  O. Finsch, 'Wie ich Kaiser-Wilhelmsland erwarb', *Deutsche Monatsschrift für das gesamte Leben der Gegenwart* 11 (1902), 742–3; Finsch, *Systematische Uebersicht*, p. 26 note 4; cf. Finsch, *Kaiser-Wilhelmsland*, pp. 22–3; P. Sack and D. Clark (ed. and trans.), *Eduard Hernsheim: South Sea Merchant* (Boroko: Institute of Papua New Guinea Island Studies, 1993), pp. 96–7.

16  Cazan-Simányi, 'Versuch einer biographischen Annäherung', p. 17.

17  BBAW, NL R. Virchow, No. 607, letter from O. Finsch to R. Virchow, 5 October 1899.

18  Berlin State Library (hereafter SBB), Manuscript Department, Sig. Darmstaedter, Asien (1876): Finsch, Otto, letter from O. Finsch to Minister [K. von] Studt, 24 September 1902; Federal Archive, Berlin, Deutsche Kolonialgesellschaft Sig. R 8023/823: Dr. Finsch, Leiden. Correspondenz betreffend Auswirkung eines Ehrensoldes für denselben, Sept. 1902 – Jan. 1904, letters from O. Finsch to J.A. Herzog zu Mecklenburg, 24 September 1902; from O. Finsch to Fürst [H.] zu Hohenlohe-Langenburg, 24 September 1902; and from J. Lohmeyer to 'Herr Direktor' [O. Stübel?], 4 April 1903; Finsch, 'Wie ich Kaiser-Wilhelmsland erwarb', *Deutsche Monatsschrift für das gesamte Leben der Gegenwart*, 9–12 (1902), 406–24, 570–84, 728–43, 875–89; Finsch, *Kaiser-Wilhelmsland*, pp. 1–23; E.M. Brockhoff, 'Lohmeyer, Julius', *Neue Deutsche Biographie*, 15 (1987), 133–4, www.deutsche-biographie.de/pnd117196614.html, accessed 26 January 2016.

19  Finsch, *Tapinowanne Torondoluan*, p. 4.

20  Finsch, *Tapinowanne Torondoluan*, p. 4.

21  Finsch, *Tapinowanne Torondoluan*, p. 4.

22  J. Samson, *Imperial Benevolence: Making British Authority in the Pacific Islands* (Honolulu: University of Hawai'i Press, 1998), pp. 25, 29.

23  O. Finsch, 'Aus dem Pacific. IX. Neu Britannien', *Hamburger Nachrichten* 153 (30 June 1881), 154 (1 July 1881), 155 (2 July 1881), 156 (4 July 1881), n.p.

24  O. Finsch, 'Menschenfresser in Neubritannien', *Illustrirte Zeitung* 81:2107 (17 November 1883), 445, 450.

25  H.B. Gardner, *Gathering for God: George Brown in Oceania* (Dunedin: Otago University Press, 2006), pp. 65–6, 84.

26  Finsch, 'Menschenfresser in Neubritannien', p. 445.

27  A.L. Epstein, *Matupit: Land, Politics, and Change among the Tolai of New Britain* (Canberra: Australian National University Press, 1969), pp. 13–14.

28  Epstein, *Matupit*, pp. 14–15; Jacob L. Simet, 'Tabu: Analysis of a Tolai Ritual Object' (PhD Dissertation, The Austraian National University, 1991), p. x.

29  Samson, *Imperial Benevolence*, pp. 40–1.

30  K. Neumann, *Not the Way It Really Was: Constructing the Tolai Past* (Honolulu: University of Hawai'i Press, 1992), pp. 6, 99.

31  BBAW, NL R. Virchow, Nr. 607, letter from O. Finsch to R. Virchow, 27 October 1880; Finsch, 'Aus dem Pacific', n.p.; Finsch, *Samoafahrten*, pp. 24–5.

32  H. Howes, 'Between Wealth and Poverty: Otto Finsch on Mabuyag, 1881', *Memoirs of the Queensland Museum – Culture* 8:1 (2015), 221–51.

33  Finsch, 'Aus dem Pacific', n.p.

34  O. Finsch, *Neu-Guinea und seine Bewohner* (Bremen: C. Ed. Müller, 1865), pp. 44–6.

35  O. Finsch, 'Skizzen von Neuguinea', *Illustrirte Zeitung* 46:1186 (24 March 1866), 204–2.

36  Finsch, 'Aus dem Pacific', n.p.

37  Finsch, *Tapinowanne Torondoluan*, p. 13.

38  Braunschweig Municipal Archives, Finsch H VIII A: 1130, letter from O. Finsch to unknown correspondent, 25 March 1892.

39  Finsch, *Tapinowanne Torondoluan*, pp. 4–6. On whaling-era contacts, see Alastair C. Gray, 'Trading Contacts in the Bismarck Archipelago during the Whaling Era, 1799–1884', *Journal of Pacific History* 34:1 (1999), 23–43.

40  Finsch, *Tapinowanne Torondoluan*, p. 5.

41   J. Specht, '"The German Professor": Richard Parkinson', in J. Dennison and J.P. White (ed. and trans.), *Thirty Years in the South Seas: Land and People, Customs and Traditions in the Bismarck Archipelago* ... (Sydney: Sydney University Press, 2010), pp. xv–xxxiii.
42   R. Parkinson, *Dreißig Jahre in der Südsee. Land und Leute, Sitten und Gebräuche im Bismarckarchipel* ... (Stuttgart: Strecker & Schröder, 1907), pp. 73–4.
43   Finsch, 'Menschenfresser in Neubritannien', 445.
44   H.S. Howes, *The Race Question in Oceania: A.B. Meyer and Otto Finsch between Metropolitan Theory and Field Experience, 1865–1914* (Frankfurt am Main: Peter Lang, 2013), p. 236.
45   Finsch, 'Aus dem Pacific', n.p.
46   Finsch, 'Menschenfresser in Neubritannien', 445.
47   Finsch, 'Menschenfresser in Neubritannien', 445. The phrase 'the Arnheims amongst our magnates' may refer to the von Arnim dynasty, prominent members of the landowning Prussian nobility; alternatively, Matt Fitzpatrick has suggested a connection to the 'inconceivable wealth' inherited by the protagonist of Edgar Allan Poe's short story *The Domain of Arnheim* (1842). See F. Hartung, 'Arnim-Suckow, Harry Kurt Eduard Carl von, Graf', *Neue Deutsche Biographie* 1 (1953), 373–5, http://www.deutsche-biographie.de/pnd118650297.html, accessed 28 January 2016; D.B. Sova, *Critical Companion to Edgar Allan Poe: A Literary Reference to His Life and Work* (New York: Facts On File, 2007), p. 57; F. Stern, *Gold and Iron: Bismarck, Bleichröder, and the Building of the German Empire* (London: Allen & Unwin, 1977), pp. 234–42.
48   Finsch, 'Aus dem Pacific', n.p.
49   O. Finsch, 'Ueber die Bewohner von Ponapé (östl. Carolinen). Nach eigenen Beobachtungen und Erkundigungen', *Zeitschrift für Ethnologie* 12 (1880), 319; Howes, *The Race Question in Oceania*, pp. 251–9.
50   Finsch, 'Aus dem Pacific', n.p. Although Finsch consistently applied the term *diwara* or *diwarra* to the shell currency used on Matupit Island, Albert B. Lewis later clarified that shell currency was 'called *diwara* on Duke of York Islands and New Ireland, *tambu* on New Britain'. See A.B. Lewis, *Melanesian Shell Money in Field Museum Collections* (Chicago: Field Museum of Natural History, 1929), p. 12 note 1.
51   Finsch, *Tapinowanne Torondoluan*, p. 5.
52   Finsch, 'Skizzen von Neuguinea', 205.
53   J. Lohmeyer, 'Die deutschen Kolonien am Beginn des 20. Jahrhunderts. Eine Übersicht mit fünf Karten', in Lohmeyer (ed.), *Unter dem Dreizack*, pp. 457–65.
54   Nicholas Thomas, *Discoveries: The Voyages of Captain Cook* (London: Penguin Books, 2004), p. 255; Finsch, *Tapinowanne Torondoluan*, p. 13.
55   Finsch, 'Menschenfresser in Neubritannien', 445, 450.
56   Finsch, 'Aus dem Pacific', n.p.
57   Finsch, *Tapinowanne Torondoluan*, pp. 3, 5; cf. BBAW, NL R. Virchow, No. 607, letter from O. Finsch to R. Virchow, 17 August 1881, in which Finsch describes Tapinowanne as 'a pretty New Briton of ca. 12 years'.
58   Finsch, *Tapinowanne Torondoluan*, p. 6.
59   O. Finsch, 'Zeichnungen und Malereien seines jungen Neubritanniers', *Verhandlungen der Berliner Gesellschaft für Anthropologie, Ethnologie und Urgeschichte* 15 (15 December 1883), 566.
60   Sack and Clark, *Eduard Hernsheim*, p. 80.
61   Finsch, *Tapinowanne Torondoluan*, pp. 14–15.
62   Finsch, *Tapinowanne Torondoluan*, p. 16.
63   A. Bastian, O. Finsch and R. Hartmann, 'Begrüssung von Finsch, lebender Neu-Britannier', *Verhandlungen der Berliner Gesellschaft für Anthropologie, Ethnologie und Urgeschichte* 14 (21 October 1882), 527; Finsch, *Tapinowanne Torondoluan*, p. 14.
64   Finsch, *Systematische Uebersicht*, pp. 93–7, 123–46.
65   Finsch, *Tapinowanne Torondoluan*, pp. 4, 10, 12, 14.

66  BBAW, NL R. Virchow, No. 607, letter from O. Finsch to R. Virchow, 15 August 1880.
67  David A. Chappell, *Double Ghosts: Oceanian Voyagers on Euroamerican Ships* (Armonk: M.E. Sharpe, 1997), pp. 17, 40.
68  Finsch, *Tapinowanne Torondoluan*, p. 13.
69  Key works include Marilyn Strathern, *The Gender of the Gift: Problems with Women and Problems with Society in Melanesia* (Berkeley: University of California Press, 1988); Robert Foster, *Social Reproduction and History in Melanesia: Mortuary Ritual, Gift-Exchange, and Custom in the Tanga Islands* (Cambridge: Cambridge University Press, 1995). Partial overviews of further contributions to what Foster terms the 'New Melanesian Ethnography' can be found in Mark Mosko, 'Partible Penitents: Dividual Personhood and Christian Practice in Melanesia and the West', *Journal of the Royal Anthropological Institute* 16:2 (2010), 215–40; Michael W. Scott, 'Neither "New Melanesian History" nor "New Melanesian Ethnography": Recovering Emplaced Matrilineages in Southeast Solomon Islands', *Oceania* 77:3 (2007), 337–54.

CHAPTER FOUR

# The goddess and the beast: African–German encounters

Eva Bischoff

On 26 August 1913, a young actress named Emma (Meg) Gehrts embarked on a journey to the German *Schutzgebiet* Togo. She accompanied the explorer and film-maker Hans Schomburgk to perform the female lead in the first movie filmed on site with African supernumeraries, revealingly called *The White Goddess of the Wangora*. As she was the first European woman to set foot into many villages of the hinterland, her pale skin sent little children screaming. Gehrts's description of her first encounter of this kind was published in her travel journal *A Camera Actress in the Wilds of Togoland* in 1915.

> Here [in Blita] I realised for the first time that my personal appearance might possibly inspire fear, or even disgust and aversion, for when I went into the market-place in the afternoon to have a look round as usual, the children fled screaming with terror, and even their mothers looked askance at me. [...] I felt really hurt at the attitude of their offspring, for I am very fond of children, and they of me, as a rule, and in Kamina we had been great chums together. But then in Kamina there were always white people about, whereas I was the first white woman, at all events, that these nude little ebony imps had ever set eyes on. Consequently, I suppose, they regarded me as a sort of pale-faced bogey, to be avoided promptly, and at all hazards.[1]

Gehrts's travel journal has been lauded by Gudrun Honke and János Riesz as one of the primary examples of German 'humanistic' colonial literature, characterised by a growing respect for African peoples and their cultures.[2]

In this chapter, however, I would like to suggest a more complex reading of her journal. On the one hand, Gehrts's text provides insight into the expedition's everyday life and the practicalities of film-making in the tropics. As such, it gives information about a specific subset of the African–German encounter at the beginning of the twentieth century. A careful, contrapuntal reading of the text allows for reconstructing part of the misunderstandings and bargaining processes that structured the African–German encounter during an expedition conducted in Germany's model colony just prior to the outbreak of the First World War.[3]

On the other hand, Gehrts's publication is a textbook example of German and British colonial popular cultures at the beginning of the twentieth century. Her account is riddled by racist preconceptions. This aspect becomes most apparent when focusing on questions of femininity and gender performativity,[4] namely Gehrts's continued self-stylisation in relation to European men as well as in relation to the Togolese population. According to her own words, Gehrts travelled to Togo as an actress 'posing as the white woman in Anglo-African cinematograph dramas'.[5] In these dramas she embodied a number of different figurations of white womanhood that were pervasive in both German and British colonial discourse: the young bride coming out, the settler's wife, the queen of a 'savage' tribe.[6] Her performance, I would like to argue, did not end with the sound of the shutter wrapping a day's shoot. In publishing her travel account, in a discursive act of self-making, Gehrts assumed another role or position: that of the female traveller who spoke authoritatively about Africa, thereby transforming her own experiences into an indirect, mediated version of the African–German encounter. As a result, Gehrts's journal enables us to reflect critically on these mediated forms of encounter which were the norm for the vast majority of German and British citizens who never travelled to the colonies. There were only small Afro-German communities in the larger cities such as Hamburg or Berlin.[7] Germans 'knew' Africa and its inhabitants from adventure novels, travel reports, colonial exhibitions or *Völkerschauen*, postcards, collectibles, photographs, films, to name but a few examples.[8] Gehrts's journal contributed to this multimedia complex of colonial popular culture.

This chapter combines both avenues of investigation by juxtaposing Gehrts's descriptions, often referring to racialised gender categories, with a contrapuntal reading of her account of how the Togolese population interacted with Schomburgk's expedition in general and her in particular.

In doing so, my analysis contributes to a growing body of literature: travelling women have caught the attention of feminist historiography since the 1980s and scholarly interest has not subsided since.[9] Histories of the involvement of women in the German colonial project are another continuously growing field of research, which initially concentrated on German South-West Africa, and which recently has begun to shift to other, non-settler colonies.[10] Still lacking, however, is a systematic investigation of their involvement in media and colonial popular culture, notwithstanding a few studies of Frieda von Bülow and Tobias Nagl's reconstruction of the white woman as an icon in colonial films.[11]

## A homemaker's duty and a mother's pity: Gehrts on trek

Emma Gehrts (1891–1966) arrived in Lomé, the capital of German colonial Togo, in autumn 1913. She accompanied Hans Hermann Schomburgk (1880–1967) on his journey to the colony after a considerable debate with her upper-middle-class parents who had strong objections to their barely twenty-two-year-old daughter joining his expedition. Schomburgk was an established 'great white hunter' by the time the expedition to Togo started. After joining the Natal Mounted Police in 1898 he had spent most of his life in southern Africa. Just prior to the journey to Togo, he had conducted expeditions for the British government and Carl Hagenbeck.[12] Realising the economic potential of colonial films, he started experimenting with the new technology and led an expedition to West Africa (today's Liberia) in 1912/13. Its filmographic results were meagre, due to technical difficulties.[13]

The location of Schomburgk's second film expedition, Togo, came under German rule in 1884.[14] Located at the Bight of Benin, its southern, coastal parts and the area dominated by the Ewe-speaking groups among Togo's population had been deeply affected by the transatlantic slave trade in multiple ways.[15] On a demographic level, the trade induced a dramatic overall population decline, with 15–20 per cent of the estimated 1.8 million slaves taken between 1640 and 1870 coming from the Bight of Benin. Since slave traders targeted men in particular, gender relations shifted. Women moved into more independent positions, especially economically. Mothers enjoyed a high level of respect, receiving tokens of their sons' affection in an elaborate economy of gift giving.[16]

The slave trade had also created a transatlantic cultural contact zone in which Europeans, Africans and Afro-Brazilians, who had moved to the Bight of Benin during the late eighteenth century and established themselves as social and political elite, interacted frequently.[17]

With the end of the slave trade, the production and trade of palm oil became the most important source of revenue in the region. Women became successful palm oil merchants and dominated the exchange between producers and European trading companies. European traders, among them a growing number of Germans, considered dealing with these female merchants an unsettling experience, since European gender norms restricted women to the domestic sphere.[18]

By the time Gehrts arrived in the colony, Togo was considered the *Kaiserreich*'s model colony. In contrast to other African colonies, German rule was not openly challenged by violent uprising or war after its annexation and initial 'pacification' in 1902.[19] It was also the site of several reform projects that breathed the spirit of Bernhard Dernburg's new colonial policies. From his appointment in 1907, the head of the Imperial Colonial Office called for regulating colonial populations, not subjugating them by force.[20] As a result, Schomburgk's endeavour operated under very favourable conditions. Moreover, the hunter and explorer was held in high regard in Berlin: Schomburgk was commissioned to film the visit of Wilhelm Solf's visit to the colony in his capacity as Secretary of the German Colonial Office.[21] Local officials endorsed his project as well: Adolf Friedrich Duke of Mecklenburg (1873–1969), governor of the colony from June 1912 to August 1914, gave the project his full support.[22] Whereas Schomburgk's earlier expeditions had aimed at acquiring specimens, the one to Togo, by contrast, was of filmographic interest. It intended to appropriate the ethnic particularities of the colony's indigenous population visually. 'Our object', Gehrts declared, 'was to film scenes and plays of native life amongst absolutely virgin and unspoiled surroundings.'[23]

Practically speaking, the expedition revisited places Schomburgk had been to during previous sojourns. It employed a combination of modern technology (railway, motorcar, telephone, submarine cable, short-wave radio transmitter), colonial infrastructure built by forced labour (roads, rest houses) and an extensive African support network of porters, local guides and intermediaries.[24] In addition, the project also relied on Schomburgk's expertise in leading African expeditions. This expertise included a clear concept of the social role of the expedition leader. Africans interpreted this role within established African norms and values as that of the 'provider'. Europeans assumed that the head of an expedition embodied European cultural and technological supremacy. This supremacy had to be established and constantly (re) affirmed by bodily practices such as hunting with firearms and eating meat, by dispensing European medicine and by imposing what Europeans considered 'proper' discipline. The instrument of choice was corporal punishment, ranging from slaps to severe beating with sticks or whips. The expedition thereby reiterated the openness of the black body (in the sense of availability and vulnerability), while reconfirming the hygienic, whole and untouchable white body.[25] According to his own descriptions, Schomburgk acted in full conformity with these norms, boasting that his African honorific 'Bwakukama' had been earned by his violent and strict disciplinary regime.[26]

In case of the expedition to Togo in 1913/14, the participation of Emma Gehrts added an additional element to this racial order. In addition to her commitments as the lead actress, Gehrts also performed 'housewifely' duties throughout their journey through the Togolese hinterland. Her responsibilities corresponded to established metropolitan bourgeois gender norms: she organised and co-ordinated the preparation and packing of their supplies, she supervised what in Europe would have been called household servants (cook, washerwoman/man, maids and valet) and she prepared the prestigious venison for the Europeans' consumption, as well as regular meals if the need arose.[27] In fulfilling these housewifely duties, Gehrts acted as a paragon of the competent homemaker, who was considered the embodiment of white womanhood in German colonial discourse.[28]

In this vein, Gehrts's log gave detailed information of the everyday 'caravan life and cookery from a white woman's point of view',[29] discussing the duties of (household) servants and their payment. She specified availability, prices, preparation, storage and transportation of European food items.[30] Gehrts put particular emphasis on the constant supervision of the servants to guarantee high standards of cleanliness and hygiene. If not properly monitored, the author warned, Africans would lick the plates clean instead of washing them, to get 'a taste of the white man's "chop"'. Clothes would be beaten to rags by the washerman, and all meals would be rendered 'inedible' by a cook who would season it using the fruits of the 'wild pepper plant' (i.e. chilies) 'with no sparing hand'.[31] Her warnings and recommendations mirrored those given in traditional advice manuals for women migrating to the colonies.[32]

Apart from that of a colonial homemaker, Gehrts's role also encompassed other, decidedly maternal qualities. In view of Schomburgk's strict disciplinary regime, she assumed the role of an intercessor on behalf of the African members of their expedition. On numerous occasions, she persuaded the expedition's leader to accept leniency or even mitigated the sentence pronounced by Schomburgk herself by performing small acts of mercy.[33] Servants and porters alike recognised her compassion and mitigating powers by calling her their 'little mother' or 'little white mother'.[34] Gehrts even recorded appeals such as: 'Little mother! Little mother! Have pity on your poor tired children!'[35]

The appeals bear a striking resemblance to supplications or prayers to the Virgin Mary, which was not coincidental. The Catholic Church had been represented in Togo since 1892. In 1913, a total of 47 priests, 15 monks and 25 nuns, supported by 228 lay catechists, laboured on 13 main and 197 auxiliary stations throughout the colony.[36] Only 363 Europeans lived in Togo in early 1913; among them 67 women. About 24 per cent of the colony's white population were Catholic missionary personnel, and 37 per cent of the white female population were nuns.[37] In 1907, the percentage had been even higher, with 40 per cent of the colony's white women having taken the vows.[38] Apart from teaching girls and young women, their main duties involved visiting indigenous households in proximity to their convents and nursing the sick and disabled.[39] Geographically speaking, the Catholic missionaries' activities concentrated on the coastal region (Lomé, Aného) and the territory of the Ewe-speaking population (Kpalimé, Atakpamé, Kpandu).[40] In 1913, Catholic schools taught 6,764 male and 1,699 female registered students.[41] Male graduates were often employed in intermediary positions because of their language skills. To them, obtaining Western education represented an opportunity to establish themselves socially and economically outside of existing local hierarchies. The overwhelming majority acquired English language skills, since English served as the *lingua franca* in trading with Europeans throughout the region.[42] Only a small minority learned German.[43]

Alfred, the chief interpreter on Gehrts's expedition, was one among them. He had acquired his language skills, according to his own words, at 'the Catholic Mission', referring indirectly to the school established by the Steyler Missionaries (also known as the Society of the Divine Word) in 1892.[44] Just like other Togolese from the southern part of the colony educated in Catholic schools, Alfred would have been familiar with Catholic gender imagery and ideals, most prominently those relating to the Virgin Mary, and with her relevance as a role model of white womanhood. If they had encountered a white woman personally before, it was likely a nun in a nursing and caring capacity.[45]

Coming from the southern region of the colony, Alfred would also be familiar with influential women, especially mother figures. He was not the only one. The 120 Africans hired for Schomburgk's expedition, ranging from cook to interpreter, manservants to porters, were all recruited in Atakpame and its outlying villages.[46] In supplicating to Gehrts as their 'little mother' and depicting themselves as her 'poor children', these Togolese members of Schomburgk's expedition creatively employed Catholic gender concepts to their advantage, they created a go-between who would mediate on their behalf.

Gehrts (as well as Schomburgk) missed this creative act of cultural translation entirely. Schomburgk collapsed her intercessory role with the one as the mother of the company (*Mutter der Kompanie*): 'Miss Gehrts also took charge of the commissariat, and I am sure that every member of the expedition will be only too pleased to certify that a better could not have been evolved than the one that was run so easily and beautifully by "our little mother," as the "boys" used to call her.'[47] Both Schomburgk and Gehrts grew up in Hamburg, a Protestant environment, and it can be safely assumed that they were unfamiliar with Catholic religious practices, let alone prayers (such as the 'Hail Mary'). Yet they both accepted the social roles resulting from the African appellation, as these expressions of their acceptance of a subordinate position in a racialised and gendered colonial hierarchy fitted into their racialised self-conceptualisations. To their minds, Africans were either savages or children.[48] The former had to be studied, subjugated and civilised, the latter had to be governed by the firm hand of a father and the loving care of a mother.

### Articulating white womanhood: bodily practices and mutual (mis)conceptions

The colonial expedition created a 'contact zone' in itself, a social space which intersected with its physical and social environment in multiple ways.[49] Within this zone, Gehrts was, as I have demonstrated above, constructed as homemaker and 'little white mother'. Yet Gehrts's travelogue also contains numerous descriptions of practices which articulated white womanhood on a corporeal level and which regulated physical as well as social boundaries. All these practices rested upon one central premise: the White Woman had to be handled with care.[50]

Protection from the alien environment, most of all sunshine but also mosquitoes, was of paramount concern in this context. Schomburgk's personal servant was detailed to tuck in the mosquito net covering her bed. For each insect that transgressed the boundary and stung her, his body was violated in turn. He received one slap to the face for each mosquito discovered. The punishment was executed in public, adding shame to injury.[51] If necessary, Gehrts's body was enveloped 'from head to foot in blankets and tablecloths' like that of 'an Egyptian mummy'.[52] German colonial officers gave up their personal quarters or houses to ensure that the White Woman was accommodated in an enclosed space that resembled European housing as closely as possible.[53]

Transportation was equally precarious: Due to her fragile constitution and the 'enervating, [...] moist, hot West African climate' she was carried long distances in a rudimentary palanquin, which could be covered for shade in hot weather and which she called a hammock, while the male European participants of the expedition walked, cycled or travelled on horseback.[54] Contrastingly, white men who were carried by hammock were ridiculed by other Europeans as weak and unfit for colonial duty.[55] The African personnel of the expedition emulated the white men's deference to Gehrts's special status. When she fell asleep in her hammock, the men carrying her did not dare to wake her upon arrival. They feared the wrath of the expedition leader for disturbing her.[56] Servants worried about her safety and begged her to stay behind during a particularly dangerous section of the expedition's journey.[57]

Arrivals were heavily ritualised, public affairs throughout her journey, and German officers and African dignitaries alike organised welcoming committees on multiple occasions. Gehrts recounted all of them with gusto. As a result, her travelogue also reads as a triumphal procession of the First White Woman through the colony. Station commandants such as Alexander von Hirschfeld at Sasane-Mangu set 'flags [...] flying from every point of vantage' and 'canter[ed] out [...] accompanied by a mounted bodyguard' to meet her, 'the first white woman in Mangu'.[58] African villagers gathered along 'the roads to see [her] pass, the women "ul-ul-ulling" a wild welcome, the men capering and singing'.[59] This came to a climax on their way to Tschopowa:

> The road used to be lined three and four deep by hundreds on hundreds of Konkombwa men, women, and children, all in gala attire, and I had to tell my boys to throw up the curtains of the hammock, so that I could sit up and smile my acknowledgments right and left, just as royalty does when it appears on a festive occasion in the streets of, say, London or Berlin. [...] At Tschopowa the whole affair culminated in a big dance, given in my honour.[60]

Such appearances were numerous. Schomburgk paraded a white woman across the territory as a symbol of German control and power, more than a decade after the violent 'pacification' of the colony, a process that has been likened to racketeering with the massacre as its primary form.[61] If it was safe for her to travel in Togo, the conquest was absolute.[62] In recounting her reception in the colony, Gehrts too transported the image of German colonial power to her readers in Europe. For a German reader, her description would also have connected to the ongoing debate about the 'civilising' role of white women in the *Kaiserreich*'s colonies. In this debate the role of European women as wives, homemakers and mothers was seen as crucial in preserving the 'racial purity' of the colonisers' offspring by curtailing the integration of the colonisers into African social networks through (informal) marriages with African women.[63]

Yet the further the expedition progressed into the colony's hinterland, the more frequently Gehrts received a very different kind of welcome, the one with which this chapter opened, of sending little children screaming.[64] Gehrts was deeply disturbed by these reactions and, with the help of the expedition's interpreter, tried to determine the reason for this behaviour. Upon arrival in Paratau, she cornered a little girl, who after initial refusal gave an answer which the interpreter translated very reluctantly and nervously into one word: 'shefearstolookupon-nyoubecauseyouaresougly'.[65] The actress, quite proud of her physical appearance,[66] was baffled and sought confirmation. A few days later, she asked a little boy whether she was really that ugly: '"Really and truly you are [...]" he replied, with childish frankness. "But," he added in extenuation, and as a balm perhaps for [her] wounded feelings, "you cannot help that. The good God made you so, did he not? We cannot all be black and beautiful." '[67] Gehrts interpreted these reactions in her own terms. She 'suppose[d] that they regarded [her] as a sort of pale-faced bogey' or 'ogre'.[68]

It is difficult to draw any specific conclusions from Gehrts's brief and rather self-centred descriptions about the concepts or notions that motivated the behaviour of the Togolese the actress encountered. It becomes apparent, though, that the Africans she met had clear notions about what to expect, and they were nothing positive. In Sumbu the 'old chief' was amazed by her laughter, stating that he had 'never seen a white woman before, but [had] always been told that they are unable to laugh'.[69] In many African societies a white body (often painted) was associated with death, witchcraft, and in turn with cannibalism. As mentioned above, Togo's shores were part of the West African Slave Coast. Among the population of its hinterland, rumours about white cannibals circulated, supported by the, from an African perspective often inexplicable practices, such as medical venepuncture and the anthropophagic rituals of the Catholic mass.[70] Prior to conversion to Christianity, the Ewe-speaking population of the southern parts of the colony adhered to religious practices which had inspired Vodou among the slaves of the Caribbean.[71] Today, practitioners of Vodou revere a powerful female lwa or gede, called Maman Brigitte (also Maman Brijit), who is associated with transitions of life and death and cemeteries. She is the wife of Baron Samedi, the head of the gede pantheon, and is also believed to rule over money and children. She also responds to petitions by those in need of help, especially the terminally ill.[72] As such, the fear spread amongst the Togolese population might have been the flipside of the reverence shown to Gehrts by the members of Schomburgk's expedition.[73]

### Of drudges and other healthy animals: the imperialist feminist speaks

In addition to her open and continued self-stylisation as the First White Woman, the actress and travelogue author also presented herself as an expert on African women and their role in African societies by including a chapter entitled 'A Woman Palaver', which explicitly dealt with 'womanly' questions.[74] The information given here, she proudly proclaimed, had been 'obtained at first hand' combining conventional anthropological observation with her privileged access as a woman during 'many long and confidential talks with the women of many diverse native tribes'.[75] The term 'confidential' suggests a shared bond, a form of sisterhood across ethnic boundaries and despite colonial power relations.

The topics covered included marriage and marriage ceremonies, polygamy, birth, child care and personal hygiene.[76] In presenting the customs and practices 'discovered,' she often compared European gender norms and gendered practices with what she believed to be their African counterparts. These descriptions combined racist stereotypes (indigenous woman as an animal, and/or as a passive object of exploitation by lazy indigenous men), with class prejudice, and white, middle-class feminism. In describing 'typical' African women's experiences of childbirth, for instance, Gehrts stated that for them 'none of those fears and misgivings that so frequently beset her civilised sister[s]' troubled them. On the contrary, as a 'perfectly healthy female animal' the 'savage woman looks forward to [...] childbirth' since her 'strong, supple body has never been compressed by corsets, or had its natural growth and development hindered by tight-fitting skirts, heavy "tailor-made" costumes, and other similar sartorial abominations'.[77] In clear contradiction to the image of the unfettered female African body conveyed here, however, Gehrts also mentioned a 'painful, and to our minds revolting operation of introcision, corresponding to the rite of [male] circumcision' (now known as female genital mutilation), to be performed on girls between ten and twelve years of age when they also received instruction in midwifery.[78]

In contrast to their healthy bodies, however, 'the great mass of the native women' were 'drudges' according to Gehrts's assessment.[79] African women's lives, she explained, 'might well serve the advanced suffragettes at home as a typical "terrible example" of what my sex has to put up with from the "tyrant man"'.[80] Unsurprisingly, she neglected to mention the successful female merchants who troubled the minds of German traders in Lomé and other coastal regions of the colony. Yet, contrasting the situation of the majority of women in Europe with the bleak picture of African women's lives drawn in her own descriptions, Gehrts concluded that African women 'are neither better nor worse off' than married women of the working classes. To her, women in Africa 'appear[ed] to be happy and contented; conjugal quarrels are comparatively rare; and poverty, as we understand the term in Europe, is practically unknown',[81] despite the fact that females were considered 'marketable commodities, just as are cattle, or goats, or fowls'.[82]

These comparisons seem to suggest that Gehrts questioned racist concepts of white superiority.[83] A closer look, however, demonstrates that Gehrts used these comparisons systematically either to criticise existing European practices and conditions (corsets, the situation of working-class mothers) or to brand male anti-feminism as uncivilised and primitive. The African Other was employed by her as a rhetorical device for interventions into intrinsically European debates. One of the most striking examples of this strategy is Gehrts's description of her reaction to her interpreter's rejection of the notion of formal female education as subverting gender hierarchies:

> I was inclined to laugh just at first at this example of negro philosophy, when it suddenly struck me that I had listened to very similar sentiments expressed by men in far more civilised communities. 'The girl I shall choose for my wife,' I once overheard an eminent lawyer remark, 'will not be one of your new-fangled sort, all fads and fancies, but one of the good old-fashioned kind, who will faithfully minister to the comfort of my home and willingly share my bed.' London lawyer and Togo interpreter – there was scarcely a pin to choose between them as regards their outlook on marital life and its duties and obligations. Both cherished at bottom precisely the same sentiments, and neither's ideal of femininity was one whit higher than the other's.[84]

Togolese gender norms and practices were thus utilised as a mirror to reveal the anti-feminist and misogynist sides of European societies, who supposedly should have 'evolved' beyond this level. We find this line of argument in many publications written by white middle- or upper-class women who actively and publicly supported the colonial cause in both Britain and Germany.[85] In these texts, African women and their lives became tools to promote the aims of white feminists in the metropole.

In addition to this form of rhetorical appropriation, elements of a decidedly colonial discourse on African women can be found, manifest in what Gayatri Spivak famously called the tendency towards 'saving brown women from brown men' in her analysis of the campaign for the prohibition of *sati* or widow-burning in British colonial India.[86] Building on Spivak, scholars have demonstrated how, in extending their motherly duties to the public sphere, British feminists appropriated imperial ideologies for their own, including the claim that 'brown women' or colonised women needed saving, namely by white women.[87] The topos of the 'white woman's burden', as Antoinette Burton refers to it, had multiple effects: it rendered Indian women helpless, installed British women as their caretakers and 'helped to neutralize powerful arguments about the monstrous, antisocial nature of the women's movement that opponents of women's suffrage were apt to mobilize in order to devastate the legitimacy of the Cause'.[88]

Gehrts explicitly referred to these efforts in two ways. First, she emphasised that a practice she perceived as the African equivalent of *sati*, namely burying a chief's wife along with him (alive but with broken limbs), had been successfully banished. '[N]ow the widow simply shaves her head,' she wrote, 'and wears a white bandage round her forehead, as signs of mourning.'[89] Secondly, she pointed out potential areas in which 'white women in Africa might do a lot of good on lines similar to those achieved by the Zenana missions in India'.[90] '[N]ative mothers', she stated, needed instructions on the 'importance of personal hygiene' after childbirth, and their husbands were made to understand the 'necessity of permitting women with new-born babies to be released for a time from their hard domestic duties'.[91] It is important to note that this form of feminist activism or concern on behalf of African women, however twisted and altered by colonial power relations, cannot be found in publications of German female colonial activists. In fact, as Martha Mamozai has shown, a distinct lack of concern for African women, even animosity, has been recorded. Most of their publications concentrated on the German settler colony South-West Africa, and in this context white women treated African women with contempt and cruelty.[92] In adopting imperial feminist views, Gehrts's publication aimed specifically at Anglophone readerships in Britain. Yet her articulation of white womanhood connected elements of German and British colonial discourse as is most apparent in her representations of the colonial female Other.

## A woman's touch: collecting films – representing the Other

The early 1900s saw a surge in colonial popular culture across Europe and the United States. Colonial topics, as well as racist and imperial imagery, permeated turn-of-the-century consumer culture and the new mass media such as pulp magazines or films.[93] This increase was accompanied by a continued interest in traditional colonial media such as the travel report.[94] Among the most prominent examples of this genre is Mary Henrietta Kingsley's *Travels in West Africa*, which described her journey to West Africa in 1893 (Sierra Leone to Angola) and in 1894–95 (Gabon). Her publication set standards in the book market: it described how she had famously set out to go where no white woman had gone before. Kingsley's report saw its third edition in 1897.[95] There are many indicators that Gehrts aimed at capitalising on the popularity of the colonial genre: firstly by connecting to Kingsley's success, and secondly by enmeshing her own book with the new medium of film, thereby creating a colonial multimedia experience.

Gehrts's travel account was published in 1915 in London and Philadelphia simultaneously. Her book was not rendered into German prior to 1999, when it appeared as *Weiße Göttin der Wangora: Eine Filmschauspielerin 1913 in Afrika* translated by Bettina Schiller. Gehrts was aided by the 'author and journalist' C.L. McCluer Stevens, who edited the manuscript, prepared it for presentation to the publishers and made suggestions about content and scope of the individual chapters.[96] Considering his contributions, he can be acknowledged as the co-author of the book: it contains numerous references to British culture which Gehrts could not have been familiar with at this point in time, suggesting that he contributed whole passages to make her account more palatable to an Anglophone audience.

In addition, Gehrts explicitly referred to well-established figurations of European and African femininity (the homemaker, the drudge, the animal). She endorsed key concepts of imperial feminism. Moreover, she described herself in terms of a 'new woman': smoking, flirting, travelling in a men's world.[97] The latter sets her travel journal strictly apart from that of her most prominent literary predecessor; Mary Kingsley emphatically dissociated herself from feminist movements and took great pains to appear as 'womanly' as possible in dress and appearance. Gehrts, by contrast, deliberately presented herself in breeches, participating in manly pursuits such as hunting.[98]

Gehrts's text was, however, more than a woman's travel book. It was what twenty-first-century readers would call a 'production blog'. The book took its readers not only along her journey as the First White Woman but also along that of a team of film-makers who produced a collection of movies ranging from documentaries to fiction. Following the typically circular structure of colonial narratives,[99] Gehrts's travelogue gave information just like a modern-day production blog would do. Readers were introduced to the technical side and practical difficulties of filming in Africa. High temperatures threatened to melt or even inflame the film material. It had therefore had to be kept in special vacuum cases, wrapped in 'green banana leaves'.[100] Cameras were also vulnerable: handles became too hot to be operated, mechanisms warped and wooden casings cracked. In the end, the expedition was left with only one out of originally two cinematic cameras.[101]

Gehrts also gave information on their interaction with African supernumeraries. Film-making, this becomes apparent very quickly in her journal, relied on the co-operation and participation of the African population just as much as organising and conducting an expedition. As there was (in contrast to the expedition) no established protocol for recruiting amateur actors, the film-makers had to improvise. Their strategies included negotiating with the local chief with the help of their interpreter, showing pictures taken during Schomburgk's previous visit, and paying the participants in tobacco, kola nuts, clothing and money.[102] Gehrts's descriptions indicate that potential supernumeraries held considerable bargaining power: 'The requisite number of natives

[ 75 ]

had to be laboriously collected from a score or more of villages scattered over a wide area of country.' Then, filming (and very likely also the subsequent payment) 'had to be explained to them over and over again through the medium of three or four different interpreters'. As a result, Gehrts concluded in exasperation, 'it was nothing but talk, talk, talk, palaver, palaver, palaver, from morning till night'.[103]

The actress also described many of the locations where pictures were shot and shared anecdotes about the filming process she considered entertaining. The first scenes of the *White Goddess of the Wangora*, Gehrts disclosed, were actually taken just before they left Togo after considerable problems to ensure the appearance of the central protagonist: a little girl of appropriate age, size and (most of all) light skin colour. 'It really looked at one time as if we should have to film the scene at some English seaside resort, with a squad of burnt-cork beach "niggers" as supers, an obviously most unsatisfactory alternative,' Gehrts reported.[104] Eventually, just about when the crew was about 'to despair, a coast girl turned up with a half-caste, khaki-coloured infant, of about the right age', who 'by the liberal use of a powder puff' was made 'to come out white on the film'.[105]

Readers of Gehrts's travel account also learned how each of the dramas shot in Togo was conceptualised. Two of them (*Odd Man Out* and the *White Goddess*) had been planned and scripted beforehand.[106] The two other cinematic dramas, *The Outlaw of the Sudu Mountains* and *The Heroes of Paratau*, were invented on the spot, inspired by the landscape or information gathered en route.[107] The documentaries, according to Gehrts's account, were shot in an even less premeditated manner. The team often decided spontaneously what they considered of interest to their potential audience. Topics included moving (and non-moving) pictures of dances, costumes, hunting techniques, industry and artisanship ranging from iron extraction, masonry and lime burning to the traditional cotton industry which was to be displaced by German colonial projects.[108] Their documentaries followed the visual strategies of the ethnographic archival *dispositif* of colonial film-making: capturing 'primitive' cultures, just as taxidermists prepared their specimen in order to preserve them for prosperity and scientific scrutiny.[109]

In describing their creations, Gehrts repeatedly highlighted her own contributions to the creative process. According to her report, several of those films, which were all well received by the London audience, were initiated by her. These often included representations of the mundane practices that Schomburgk, as an experienced traveller, took for granted, such as the distribution of salt among the expedition's porters as payment for their services, breaking down the expedition's camp and heading out for the day's march, or the 'daily life and work of a native woman'.[110] Many of the expedition's documentaries were shown at the Royal Geographical Society after Schomburgk's and Gehrts's arrival back in London in 1914. Gehrts proudly pointed out how sequences shot on her initiative were particularly appreciated by the audience.[111]

Schomburgk and his crew also used photography to capture what they considered to be 'typical' African practices. Again, Gehrts emphasised her contributions to the expedition's findings and displayed them to her readers by including stills and/or photographs in her book. This is another resemblance to twenty-first-century production blogs, which are often published previous to the release of the film in question. In a similar manner, Gehrts's travel account included a visual component, printing a total of 65 pictures, including stills from the films, accompanied by explanations and descriptions, many of them taken by Schomburgk and published with his explicit consent.[112]

All of these aspects indicate that in publishing *A Camera Actress in the Wilds of Togoland* Gehrts intended to capitalise not only on the public's interest in colonial adventure literature in general and on women's interest in particular but also on an audience which would see the moving pictures shot during the expedition. The timing of her publication supports this interpretation: Schomburgk's films were first shown in London in May and June 1914.[113] Gehrts finished her book on 1 July 1914.[114] Meanwhile, Moving Pictures Sales Agency, the British company Hans Schomburgk collaborated with to develop and distribute his films, worked on their American release. Schomburgk and Gehrts started a promotion tour to France and Germany but were stopped short in Paris after Germany and Britain declared war in August 1914.

## Conclusion: the goddess and the beast

When *A Camera Actress in the Wilds of Togoland* was finally published in 1915, the moment of prime publicity had passed. The war had disrupted all plans for international distribution. Most of Schomburgk's film material was lost and, as far as has been reconstructed so far, no copy of the adventure dramas shot in Togo survived.[115] For this reason, *The White Goddess of the Wangora*, the film whose production Gehrts described in her travel log most extensively, is inaccessible for historical research today. Its plot structure, however, can be reconstructed from Gehrts's descriptions and contemporary cinematic journals, as Tobias Nagl has shown.[116] It follows Henry Rider Haggard's colonial adventure novel *She* (first published in 1887) in telling the story of a white girl, orphaned by shipwreck, destined to be found by 'savages' and raised as their divine queen. Grown into a beautiful woman, she discovers her 'true' racial identity the moment her subjects bring forward a white hunter, imprisoned to be killed, saves him, and they escape the wrath of her former worshippers together as he takes her back into civilisation.[117]

Adopting the position of the female traveller, Gehrts's production or travel log articulated several aspects of white womanhood, namely the competent homemaker, the embodiment and symbol of German colonial power ('First White Woman') and the imperial feminist. Gehrts drew on elements of both British and German colonial discourses alike in her descriptions. In publishing her travel account in conjunction with the film releases, she created a multimedia experience that capitalised on a distinct public interest in white women in the colonies. Moreover, my analysis of Gehrts's journal indicates that colonial films emerged as part of an international multimedia complex which in turn, logistically speaking, rested on established international networks, trans-imperial careers and co-operation: Meg Gehrts's travel account emerged from one of the many instances in which German citizens collaborated with British institutions and employers.[118]

In addition, a contrapuntual reading of Gehrts's journal reveals glimpses at the ways and means in which Africans entered the moving pictures, so to speak. Encountering Gehrts's and Schomburgk's film expedition, they provided logistical support as porters or cooks and functioned as interpreters and intermediaries between Togolese leaders and the expedition. Exercising a considerable amount of bargaining power, they participated in Schomburgk's films on their own terms as supernumeraries and chief characters. They also negotiated the racial hierarchy of the expedition imposed by Schomburgk by employing Catholic imagery, creating an intercessor on their behalf (the 'little mother'). However, the reaction of the Togolese population was not a homogenous one. While some addressed Gehrts as their benevolent mother, others reacted with fear, identifying her white female body with that of beast or a bogey-(wo)man.

Systematic research on the history of (popular) visual culture of German colonialism has only just begun. So far, most authors examining colonial films concentrate on the (dis)continuities between Weimar and the *Kaiserreich*.[119] The results of the case study I have presented here demonstrate that the creation of these media experiences was structured by strong commercial interests, which explicitly counted on the marketability of white women's colonial experiences among Anglophone audiences. They also indicate that colonial films were the product of complex interactions between Europeans and Africans, beset by misconceptions and translational processes, in which Africans took an active interest and role. In this way my case study shows that investigating the production of colonial media can provide new insights into the entangled history of African–German encounters at the beginning of the twentieth century.

## Notes

1 M. Gehrts, *A Camera Actress in the Wilds of Togoland: The Adventures, Observations & Experiences of a Cinematograph Actress in West African Forests whilst Collecting Films Depicting Native Life and when Posing as the White Woman in Anglo-African Cinematograph Dramas* (London & Philadelphia: Seeley, 1915), p. 64. I would like to thank Matt Fitzpatrick for helpful and important comments on earlier versions of this paper.

2 G. Honke and J. Riesz, 'Nachwort. Meg Gehrts – Eine Filmschauspielerin auf Entdeckungsreise in der deutschen Kolonie Togo', in M. Gehrts, *Weiße Göttin der Wangora: Eine Filmschauspielerin 1913 in Afrika* (Wuppertal: Hammer, 1999), pp. 258–76, here p. 272. For a summary of this view on German colonial discourse, see: R.A. Berman, *Enlightenment or Empire: Colonial Discourse in German Culture* (Lincoln: University of Nebrasca Press, 1998), pp. 10–15.

3 The method of contrapuntal reading was first developed by Edward W. Said in his study *Culture and Imperialism* (New York: Knopf, 1994), p. 51.

4 Following Judith Butler's concept of gender performativity, I understand gender performances as dual acts, simultaneously representing and producing gender identities (J. Butler, *Gender Trouble: Feminism and the Subversion of Identity* (London: Routledge, 1990), pp. 134–41, 145; E. Haschemi Yekani, A. Klawitter and C. König, 'Aufführen', in Netzwerk Körper in den Kulturwissenschaften (ed.), *What Can a Body Do? Praktiken und Figurationen des Körpers in den Kulturwissenschaften* (Frankfurt am Main: Campus, 2012), pp. 30–46, here pp. 32–3). Gehrts's journal is an extraordinary example of this simultaneity as the author presents details on the practicalities of the theatrical aspect of white femininity and her contribution to perpetuating the racist gender concepts (e.g. bride, wife, queen, homemaker) by adopting another (female traveller).

5 As stated in her publication's subtitle.

6 Gehrts, *A Camera Actress*, p. 24 (*The Odd Man Out*), pp. 87–8 (*The Outlaw of the Sudu Mountains*), p. 35 (*The White Goddess of the Wangora*).

7 K. Oguntoye, *Eine afro-deutsche Geschichte: Zur Lebenssituation von Afrikanern und Afro-Deutschen in Deutschland von 1884–1950* (Berlin: Hoho, 1997); F. El-Tayeb, *Schwarze Deutsche: Der Diskurs um 'Rasse' und nationale Identität 1890–1933* (Frankfurt am Main: Campus, 2001); M. Bechhaus-Gerst and R. Klein-Arendt (eds), *AfrikanerInnen in Deutschland und schwarze Deutsche – Geschichte und Gegenwart* (Münster: Lit, 2004).

8 In addition to Langbehn (ed.), *German Colonialism*, see: A. Dreesbach, *Gezähmte Wilde: Die Zurschaustellung 'exotischer' Menschen in Deutschland 1870–1940* (Frankfurt am Main: Campus, 2005); J. Jäger, 'Bilder aus Afrika vor 1918. Zur visuellen Konstruktion Afrikas im europäischen Kolonialismus', in G. Paul (ed.), *Visual History: Ein Studienbuch* (Göttingen: Vandenhoeck & Ruprecht, 2006), pp. 134–48; D. Ciarlo, *Advertising Empire: Race and Visual Culture in Imperial Germany* (Cambridge, MA: Harvard University Press, 2011).

9 See, for instance: D. Birkett, *Spinsters Abroad: Victorian Lady Explorers* (Oxford: Blackwell, 1989); K.U. Schestokat, 'German Women in Cameroon: Travelogues from Colonial Times' (PhD Dissertation, University of Southern California, 1995); D. Jedamski, H. Jehle and U. Siebert (eds), *'Und tät das Reisen wählen!': Frauenreisen, Reisefrauen* (Zürich: EFeF, 1994); G. Habinger, *Ida Pfeiffer: Eine Forschungsreisende des Biedermeier* (Venna: Milena, 2004).

10 Key publications being: M. Mamozai, *Schwarze Frau, weiße Herrin: Frauenleben in den deutschen Kolonien* (Reinbek: Rowohlt, 1989); L. Wildenthal, *German Women for Empire, 1884–1945* (Durham, NC: Duke University Press, 2001);

A. Dietrich, *Weiße Weiblichkeiten: Konstruktionen von 'Rasse' und Geschlecht im deutschen Kolonialismus* (Bielefeld: transcript, 2007); M. Bechhaus-Gerst and M. Leutner (eds), *Frauen in den deutschen Kolonien* (Berlin: Links, 2009); L. Loosen, *Deutsche Frauen in den Südsee-Kolonien des Kaiserreichs: Alltag und Beziehungen zur indigenen Bevölkerung, 1884–1919* (Bielefeld: transcript, 2014).

11 J. Warmbold, 'Germania in Afrika: Frieda Freiin von Bülow, "Schöpferin des deutschen Kolonialromans"', *Jahrbuch des Instituts für Deutsche Geschichte* 15 (1986), 309–36; M. Czernin, *'Jenes herrliche Gefühl der Freiheit': Frieda von Bülow und die Sehnsucht nach Afrika* (Berlin: List, 2008); E. Bischoff, 'Tropenkoller: Male Self-Control and the Loss of Colonial Rule', in M. Reinkowski and G. Thum (eds), *Helpless Imperialists: Imperial Failure, Fear and Radicalization* (Göttingen: Vandenhoeck & Ruprecht, 2012), pp. 117–36; T. Nagl, *Die unheimliche Maschine: Rasse und Repräsentation im Weimarer Kino* (Munich: Edition Text + Kritik, 2009), pp. 279–308.

12 Nagl, *Die unheimliche Maschine*, pp. 230–1. On Hagenbeck and his influence on creating colonial spectacles: E. Ames, *Carl Hagenbeck's Empire of Entertainments* (Seattle: University of Washington Press, 2008).

13 Schomburgk was not the only film-maker who experienced these difficulties. See W. Fuhrmann, *Imperial Projections: Screening the German Colonies* (New York: Berghahn, 2015), pp. 165–74.

14 There is a rich literature on the history of German Togo starting with Peter Sebald's seminal study *Togo 1884–1914: Eine Geschichte der deutschen 'Musterkolonie' auf der Grundlage amtlicher Quellen* (Berlin: Akademie, 1988) which gives an exhaustive overview of the development of the colony. It has been reprinted in 2013 in an abridged version entitled *Die deutsche Kolonie Togo 1884–1914: Auswirkungen einer Fremdherrschaft* (Berlin: Links, 2013).

15 On the history of the Ewe, see J. Spieth and W.K. Amoaku, *The Ewe People: A Study of the Ewe People in German Togo* (Accra: Sub-Saharan Publishers, 2011).

16 A. Zimmerman, *Alabama in Africa: Booker T. Washington, the German Empire, and the Globalization of the New South* (Princeton: Princeton University Press, 2010), pp. 114–15.

17 Zimmerman, *Alabama in Africa*, p. 114.

18 R. Erbar, *Ein 'Platz an der Sonne'? Die Verwaltungs- und Wirtschaftsgeschichte der deutschen Kolonie Togo, 1884–1914* (Stuttgart: Franz Steiner, 1991), pp. 112–19; Zimmerman, *Alabama in Africa*, pp. 115–19. It is important to keep in mind, however, that the concept of the 'separate spheres' was an ideal and did not necessarily reflect social practices. L.K. Kerber, 'Separate Spheres, Female Worlds, Woman's Place: The Rhetoric of Women's History', *Journal of American History* 75:1 (1988), 9–39; K. Hausen, 'Öffentlichkeit und Privatheit. Gesellschaftspolitische Konstruktion und die Geschichte der Geschlechterbeziehungen', in Karin Hausen (ed.), *Frauengeschichte – Geschlechtergeschichte* (Frankfurt am Main: Campus, 1992), pp. 81–8.

19 T. von Trotha, *Koloniale Herrschaft: Zur soziologischen Theorie der Staatsentstehung am Beispiel des 'Schutzgebietes' Togo* (Tübingen: J.C.B. Mohr, 1994), pp. 33–44; Sebald, *Die deutsche Kolonie Togo*, pp. 48–60.

20 B. Dernburg, *Zielpunkte des Deutschen Kolonialwesens: Zwei Vorträge* (Berlin: Mittler & Sohn, 1907), p. 9. A. Zimmerman, *Alabama in Africa*, pp. 128–72; S. Beckert, 'From Tuskegee to Togo: The Problem of Freedom in the Empire of Cotton', *Journal of American History* 92:2 (2005), 498–526.

21 Fuhrmann, *Imperial Projections*, p. 188. As a result, the expedition followed Solf's itinerary up to Kamina; a fact not mentioned by Gehrts.

22 Gehrts, *Camera Actress*, p. 51.

23 Gehrts, *Camera Actress*, pp. 50–1. This aim connects back to the German discourse on the lethal threat that civilisation and colonisation posed for indigenous societies and cultures. Anthropology was thus often understood as a form of salvage operation, saving indigeneity from extinction (P. Grosse, *Kolonialismus, Eugenik*

*und bürgerliche Gesellschaft in Deutschland, 1850–1918* (Frankfurt am Main: Campus, 2000), pp. 124–44).

24  Gehrts, *Camera Actress*, pp. 69, 213, 117–18, 129–30, 236–7. The railway track to Atakpame had just been completed in 1913; the transmitter station was still under construction. See R. Klein-Arendt, *'Kamina ruft Nauen!': Die Funkstellen in den deutschen Kolonien 1904–1918* (Cologne: Herbst, 1996), pp. 199–207. Depending on such a network was a key characteristic of expeditions to African colonies in general. See M. Pesek, *Koloniale Herrschaft in Deutsch-Ostafrika: Expeditionen, Militär und Verwaltung seit 1880* (Frankfurt am Main: Campus, 2005), pp. 109–39.

25  Pesek, *Koloniale Herrschaft*, pp. 118–39; Gehrts, *Camera Actress*, pp. 216, 229–30. Gehrts rarely reported corporal punishments. Her mitigating influence on Schomburgk is discussed more often (see below).

26  H. Schomburgk, *Bwakukama: Fahrten und Forschungen mit Büchse und Film im unbekannten Afrika* (Berlin: Deutsch-Literarisches Institut, 1922), pp. 124–5.

27  Gehrts, *Camera Actress*, pp. 49, 55, 132, 172–3.

28  N.R. Reagin, 'The Imagined Hausfrau: National Identity, Domesticity, and Colonialism in Imperial Germany', *Journal of Modern History* 73:1 (2001), 54–86; *Sweeping the German Nation: Domesticity and National Identity in Germany, 1870–1945* (Cambridge: Cambridge University Press, 2007); K. O'Donnell, 'Home, Nation, Empire: Domestic Germanness and Colonial Citizenship', in K. O'Donnell, R. Bridenthal and N.R. Reagin (eds), *The Heimat Abroad: The Boundaries of Germanness* (Ann Arbor: University of Michigan Press, 2005), pp. 40–57; E. Bischoff, ' "Heimischwerden deutscher Art und Sitte": Power, Gender, and Diaspora in the Colonial Contest', *Itinerario* 37:1 (2013), 43–58.

29  Gehrts, *Camera Actress*, pp. 275–9, quotation p. 263.

30  Gehrts, *Camera Actress*, pp. 37, 49, 172, 276–9.

31  Gehrts, *Camera Actress*, pp. 53, 173, 275.

32  For instance F.A.W. Steel and G. Gardiner, *The Complete Indian Housekeeper and Cook*, edited by Ralph J. Crane and Anna Johnston (Oxford: Oxford University Press, 2010), pp. 78–9, 82. In a similar vein: Anon., *The Englishwoman in India: Containing Information for the Use of Ladies Proceeding to, or Residing in, the East Indies, on the Subject of their Outfits, Furniture, Housekeeping, the Rearing of Children, Duties and Wage of Servants, Management of the Stables and Arrangement for Travelling … , by a Lady Resident* (London: Smith, Elder, 1864), pp. 42–60. Medically inclined manuals explicitly warned against hot spices and recommended 'simplicity in diet'. See L. Hunt and A. Kelly, *Tropical Trials. A Handbook for Women in the Tropics* (London: W.H. Allen, 1883), p. 117.

33  Gehrts, *Camera Actress*, p. 245.

34  Gehrts, *Camera Actress*, pp. 179, 180, 229, 245, 278, 309. In appealing for extra money or an advance, African expedition members also used another nickname: 'puss' (ibid., p. 53).

35  Gehrts, *Camera Actress*, p. 245.

36  H. Gründer, *Geschichte der deutschen Kolonien* (Paderborn: Schöningh, 2004), p. 127. J. Schmidlin, 'Togo, Apostolisches Vikariat', in H. Schnee (ed.), *Deutsches Kolonial-Lexikon* (Leipzig: Quelle & Meyer, 1920), Vol. 3, pp. 526–7.

37  B. Zurstrassen, *'Ein Stück deutscher Erde schaffen': Koloniale Beamte in Togo 1884–1914* (Frankfurt am Main: Campus, 2008), pp. 48–59. Total numbers for 1913 taken from J. von Zech, 'Togo', in Schnee (ed.), *Deutsches Kolonial-Lexikon*, Vol. 3, pp. 497–526, here p. 507. The Catholic missionary organisation active in Togo was the Society of the Divine Word (Steyler Gesellschaft des Göttlichen Wortes or Societas Verbi Divini) and its female counterpart, the Servants of the Holy Spirit (Missionsgenossenschaft der Dienerinnen des Heiligen Geistes). On the formation of the latter and its relationship to the Society, see: K. Stornig, *Sisters Crossing Boundaries: German Missionary Nuns in Colonial Togo and New Guinea, 1897–1960* (Göttingen: Vandenhoek & Ruprecht, 2013), pp. 34–46.

38  Only 44 of 288 Europeans living in the colony were female and 18 of them nuns. Stornig, *Sisters Crossing Boundaries*, p. 14.

39  Stornig, *Sisters Crossing Boundaries*, pp. 232–4.
40  Stornig, *Sisters Crossing Boundaries*, pp. 13, 170. Missionary activities had been prohibited by the government to extend north of Atakpame until 1913 because of security concerns (Zimmermann, *Alabama in Africa*, p. 124).
41  Schmidlin, 'Togo, Apostolisches Vikariat', pp. 526–7.
42  Zimmermann, *Alabama in Africa*, pp. 123–8.
43  This trend continued despite the German colonial administration's efforts to encourage missionary societies to teach German, especially during Governor Graf Julius von Zech auf Neuhofen's administration (1905–10) (C. Sokolowsky, *Sprachenpolitik des deutschen Kolonialismus: Deutschunterricht als Mittel imperialer Herrschaftssicherung in Togo (1884–1914)* (Stuttgart: Ibidem, 2004), pp. 45–50). The so-called 'Sprachenfrage' was a matter of deep concern since English language skills provided access to newspapers published in the neighbouring British Gold Coast colony. They also raised doubts about the loyalty of Togolese colonial subjects. Much to the colonial administration's dismay, the missionaries would have preferred to instruct their pupils in a local language, preferably a standardised version of Ewe (Erbar, *Ein 'Platz an der Sonne'*, pp. 287–302; Sokolowsky, *Sprachenpolitik des deutschen Kolonialismus*, pp. 55–76).
44  Gehrts, *Camera Actress*, pp. 43 (information on education) and 53 (name given). Initially, the Catholic missionaries had conducted German classes only but had to abandon this practice after being faced with declining student numbers (Sokolowsky, *Sprachenpolitik des deutschen Kolonialismus*, p. 47).
45  Stornig, *Sisters Crossing Boundaries*, pp. 172–215, 351–2.
46  Gehrts, *Camera Actress*, p. 50.
47  Gehrts, *Camera Actress*, p. vii.
48  Gehrts employed the term 'savage' forty-seven and 'children' seventeen times in direct reference to Africans. She used the derogative 'boy' for African employee 131 times in *A Camera Actress*.
49  Pesek, *Koloniale Herrschaft*, pp. 109–39; M.L.Pratt, *Imperial Eyes: Travel Writing and Transculturation* (London: Routledge, 2000), p. 6.
50  A. L. Stoler, 'Making Empire Respectable: The Politics of Race and Sexual Morality in Twentieth-Century Colonial Cultures', in A. McClintock, A. Mufti and E. Shohat (eds), *Dangerous Liaisons: Gender, Nation, and Postcolonial Perspectives* (Minneapolis: University of Minnesota Press, 2004), pp. 344–73.
51  Gehrts, *Camera Actress*, pp. 229–30.
52  Gehrts, *Camera Actress*, p. 31.
53  Gehrts, *Camera Actress*, pp. xi, 28–9, 111, 128, 252–3, 300.
54  Gehrts, *Camera Actress*, pp. 61–6, 186, 220, 227, 233, 292, quotation on p. 64.
55  Von Trotha, *Koloniale Herrschaft*, p. 176–8. See also Gehrts, *Camera Actress*, p. 61 (Gehrts stressing her resilience in comparison to a male doctor travelling by hammock).
56  Gehrts, *Camera Actress*, p. 62.
57  Gehrts, *Camera Actress*, p. 179.
58  Gehrts, *Camera Actress*, pp. 126–7.
59  Gehrts, *Camera Actress*, p. 221.
60  Gehrts, *Camera Actress*, pp. 221–2.
61  Von Trotha, *Koloniale Herrschaft*, pp. 35–6, 42–4, 58–79.
62  This depiction omitted the presence of other European women in the colony especially that of the Servants of the Holy Spirit who during the course of their everyday missionary work also would have travelled 'where no white woman had ever been before' (Gehrts, *Camera Actress*, p. 17).
63  This colonial role for German women in Africa was weighed against concerns about female health issues and the drop in motivation among married colonial civil servants. Zurstrassen, *Ein Stück deutscher Erde*, pp. 78–93. This discourse has been reconstructed best with regard to the German settler colony German South-West Africa. See O'Donnell, 'Home, Nation, Empire', p. 44; Wildenthal, *German Women for Empire*, pp. 80–2.

64 Gehrts, *Camera Actress*, pp. 64, 75, 160.
65 Gehrts, *Camera Actress*, pp. 74–5, quotation on p. 75.
66 Gehrts, *Camera Actress*, p. 75.
67 Gehrts, *Camera Actress*, p. 75.
68 Gehrts, *Camera Actress*, pp. 64, 75.
69 Gehrts, *Camera Actress*, p. 177. This expectation might also reflect the solemnity with which nuns were expected to comport themselves.
70 H. Behrend, 'Witchcraft, Evidence and the Localisation of the Roman Catholic Church in Western Uganda', in R. Rottenburg, B. Schnepel and S. Shimada (eds), *The Making and Unmaking of Differences* (Bielefeld: transcript, 2006), pp. 43–60; R.C. King, 'The (Mis)uses of Cannibalism in Contemporary Cultural Critique', *Diacritics* 30:1 (2000), 106–23, pp. 110–12.
71 Zimmerman, *Alabama in Africa*, p. 114; H. Klose, 'Religiöse Anschauungen und Menschenopfer in Togo', *Globus* 81:12 (1902), 187–94.
72 M. Fernández Olmos and L. Paravisini-Gebert, *Creole Religions of the Caribbean: An Introduction from Vodou and Santería to Obeah and Espiritismo* (New York: New York University Press, 2011), pp. 116–54, here p. 128; J.E. Anderson, 'Gede', in J.E. Anderson (ed.), *The Voodoo Encyclopedia: Magic, Ritual, and Religion* (Santa Barbara: ABC-CLIO, 2015), pp. 107–14.
73 Considering that the actress gave very little information, if any, on the cultural and religious practices of the people she met, this preliminary interpretation can only be a first attempt to develop the outline for future research on the topic.
74 Gehrts, *Camera Actress*, pp. 263–79.
75 Gehrts, *Camera Actress*, p. 263.
76 Gehrts, *Camera Actress*, pp. 263–8.
77 Gehrts, *Camera Actress*, p. 268.
78 Gehrts, *Camera Actress*, pp. 272–4, quotation p. 272. This partial or total removal of the external female genitalia and connected medical practices often causes severe difficulties during childbirth. FGM was included in the United Nation's 'Declaration on the Elimination of Violence Against Women' (Resolution 48/104) in December 1993. Historical information on the topic is difficult to access and to evaluate; see B. Shell-Duncan and Y. Hernlund (eds), *Female 'Circumcision' in Africa: Culture, Controversy, and Change* (Boulder: Lynne Rienner, 2000). It is important to keep in mind, however, that FGM was also historically part of European medical treatments to 'cure' masturbation and hysteria. See M. Hulverscheidt, *Weibliche Genitalverstümmelung: Diskussion und Praxis in der Medizin während des 19. Jahrhunderts im deutschsprachigen Raum* (Frankfurt am Main: Mabuse, 2002).
79 Gehrts, *Camera Actress*, p. 274.
80 Gehrts, *Camera Actress*, p. 41.
81 Gehrts, *Camera Actress*, p. 274.
82 Gehrts, *Camera Actress*, p. 264.
83 As, for instance, Honke and Riesz assume in their commentary on the journal's German translation (Honke and Riesz, 'Nachwort', p. 275).
84 Gehrts, *Camera Actress*, p. 44.
85 A. Burton, *Burdens of History: British Feminists, Indian Women, and Imperial Culture, 1865–1915* (Chapel Hill: University of North Carolina Press, 2007), pp. 63–96; Dietrich, *Weiße Weiblichkeiten*, 272–80.
86 G. C. Spivak, 'Can the Subaltern Speak?', in C. Nelson and L. Grossberg (eds), *Marxism and the Interpretation of Culture* (Urbana: University of Illinois Press, 1988), pp. 271–313, here p. 296.
87 V. Ware, *Beyond the Pale: White Women, Racism and History* (London: Verso, 1993), pp. 1–46; Burton, *Burdens of History*, pp. 5–28; C. Midgley, *Feminism and Empire: Women Activists in Imperial Britain, 1790–1865* (London: Routledge, 2008), pp. 65–91.
88 Burton, *Burdens of History*, p. 18.
89 Gehrts, *Camera Actress*, 274–5, quotation p. 275.
90 Gehrts, *Camera Actress*, p. 269.

91 Gehrts, *Camera Actress*, p. 269.
92 Mamozai, *Schwarze Frau, weiße Herrin*, p. 156. As Lora Wildenthal points out, German white women were, however, anxious to curtail male (sexualised) violence against colonised women, worrying that life in the colonies might erode men's civilisatory standards in general (Wildenthal, *German Women for Empire*, pp. 73–8.
93 V. Langbehn, 'Introduction: Picturing Race: Visuality and German Colonialism', in Langbehn (ed.), *German Colonialism*, pp. 1–33.
94 A.P. Oloukpona-Yinnon (ed.), *Reiseliteratur und Wahrnehmung der Fremdheit am Beispiel Afrikas* (Lome: Presses de L'UL, 2011); particularly interesting in view of Togolese history: O.A. Assemboni, 'Achtung, Baby an Bord! Die Reise der kleinen Erika im Jahre 1912 aus dem Reisebericht "Sommerfrische in Togo" von Else Meyer' in ibid., pp. 119–37.
95 M.H. Kingsley, *Travels in West Africa: With an Introduction by Anthony Brandt* (Washington: National Geographic Society, 2002). This is the reprint of the third edition published in 1897.
96 Gehrts, *Camera Actress*, pp. xi–xii. Stevens would become a successful author in his own right in the 1920s. See, for instance C.L. McCluer Stevens, *Famous Crimes and Criminals* (London: Stanley Pauls, 1924). The book was reprinted between 1924 and 1929 in 14 editions.
97 Gehrts, *Camera Actress*, pp. 22 and 58.
98 For example: Schomburgk, 'Authoress and Dead "Hippo"', in Gehrts, *Camera Actress*, between pp. 188 and 189.
99 L. Veracini, 'Telling the End of the Settler Colonial Story', in F. Bateman and L. Pilkington (eds), *Studies in Settler Colonialism: Politics, Identity and Culture* (New York: Palgrave Macmillan, 2011), pp. 204–18, p. 205.
100 Gehrts, *Camera Actress*, pp. 46–7, quotation p. 47.
101 Gehrts, *Camera Actress*, pp. 36, 136. These were problems many early film expeditions encountered according to Fuhrmann, *Imperial Projections*, pp. 165–74.
102 Gehrts, *Camera Actress*, pp. 33, 219–20, 305.
103 Gehrts, *Camera Actress*, p. 33.
104 Gehrts, *Camera Actress*, pp. 304–5, quotation p. 305.
105 Gehrts, *Camera Actress*, p. 305.
106 Gehrts, *Camera Actress*, p. 90.
107 Gehrts, *Camera Actress*, pp. 86–90.
108 Gehrts, *Camera Actress*, pp. 92–4, 138. See also Beckert, 'From Tuskegee to Togo'; Zimmerman, *Alabama in Africa*, pp. 128–72.
109 Nagl, *Die unheimliche Maschine*, pp. 272–5.
110 Gehrts, *Camera Actress*, pp. 118–19, 191, quotation on p. 46.
111 Gehrts, *Camera Actress*, p. 201.
112 For example: Schomburgk, 'Playing an "Interior" Scene in a Native Drama', in Gehrts, *Camera Actress*, between pp. 36 and 37.
113 R. Low, *The History of British Film Vol. 2: The History of British Film, 1906–1914* (London: Routledge, 1997), p. 155.
114 According to the date on which she signed the preface. Gehrts, *Camera Actress*, p. xii.
115 Part of the film material was cannibalised to create other movies combining it with new studio takes or sequences filmed during his journeys prior to the one with Gehrts in 1913–14. The documentary 'Im deutschen Sudan' (1917) produced in this manner is the only one of Schomburgk's movies still in existence today. It was republished by the Institut für den Wissenschaftlichen Film in Göttingen in 2006 (Hans Schomburgk, *Im Deutschen Sudan* (Göttingen, 2006), 76 min., b/w, mono).
116 Nagl, *Die unheimliche Maschine*, pp. 285–6.
117 In Germany shown as *Die Weisse Göttin der Wangora* and *Die Fetischgöttin der Wangora* in 1916–17. According to Nagl, Schomburgk's movie inspired the genre of the 'Jungle Queen' serials of 1930s Hollywood (Nagel, *Die unheimliche Maschine*,

p. 286). As Nagl emphasises, the film depicted a highly sexualised notion of the White Woman (see ibid., p. 283).

118 For instance Eduard Schnitzer (Emin Pascha) or Dietrich Brandis to name only two examples. E. Bischoff, *Kannibale-Werden: Eine postkoloniale Geschichte deutscher Männlichkeit um 1900* (Bielefeld: transcript, 2011), pp. 84–6; R. Rajan, 'Imperial Environmentalism or Environmental Imperialism? Colonial Foresters and the Agendas of Forest Management in British India, 1800–1900', in R.H. Grove, V. Damodaran and S. Sangwan (eds), *Nature and the Orient: The Environmental History of South and Southeast Asia* (New Delhi: Oxford University Press, 1998), pp. 324–71. On the complex interplay between transimperial competition and co-operation see U. Lindner, *Koloniale Begegnungen: Deutschland und Großbritannien als Imperialmächte in Afrika, 1880–1914* (Frankfurt am Main: Campus, 2011). On the relationship between film and nationalism at the turn of the twentieth century, see R. Abel, G. Bertellini and R. King (eds), *Early Cinema and the 'National'* (Bloomington: Indiana University Press, 2016).

119 In addition to the aforementioned Nagl, *Die unheimliche Maschine* and Fuhrmann, *Imperial Projections* see W. Struck, *Die Eroberung der Phantasie: Kolonialismus, Literatur und Film zwischen deutschem Kaiserreich und Weimarer Republik* (Göttingen: Vandenhoeck & Ruprecht, 2010), and G. Waz, 'Heia Safari! Träume von einer verlorenen Welt: Expeditions-, Kolonial-, und ethnographische Filme', in K. Kreimeier and A. Ehmann (eds), *Geschichte des dokumentarischen Films in Deutschland: Band 2 Weimarer Republik (1918–1933)* (Stuttgart: Reclam, 2005), pp. 187–218.

## CHAPTER FIVE

# Wine into wineskins: the Neuendettelsau missionaries' encounter with language and myth in New Guinea

### Daniel Midena

'Yet another difficulty of mission work', wrote an anonymous author in the main organ of the Neuendettelsau mission society in 1888, is the 'art of translation'.[1] The short commentary explained that while Martin Luther's German-language Bible was undoubtedly an incredible achievement, Luther nevertheless had 'the advantage in that he was translating the Bible into the language of a cultured people [*gebildeten Volks*]'.[2] The neo-Lutheran missionaries from the small Bavarian town of Neuendettelsau who arrived in German New Guinea only two years earlier faced, in contrast, a far greater challenge than even Luther. They had to pour 'the wine of the gospels into the wineskins of barbaric languages [*barbarischer Sprachen*]' and 'uncivilised' [*uncivilisierter*] languages.[3]

The barbaric-versus-civilised discourse of this short text is of course both familiar and noteworthy. And it echoed the views of German contemporaries: In 1885, to give but one example, the former director of the Rhenish Mission Society, Friedrich Fabri (1824–91), wrote that German missionaries were ideally positioned to reshape the 'mentality, intelligence and moral and religious conceptions of uncivilized, still barbaric peoples'.[4] What I want to show in this chapter, however, is that this particular dichotomy does not in itself perform the main work in how the Neuendettelsau missionaries came to characterise New Guinean languages. Indeed, the rhetoric of barbaric and civilised peoples (and the stadial view of peoples it implied) is relatively rare in the everyday letters and diary entries held in the Neuendettelsau mission archive in Nuremberg.[5] Instead these documents express a more concrete concern. As the anonymous author in 1888 went on to explain, the distinguishing characteristic of a 'barbaric' and an 'uncivilised' language was 'the lack of any expressions for abstract things, that is, things not perceivable by the senses, a lack characterised by the absence of intellectual, transcendental views and concepts'.[6] This complaint – that there was a want for expressions for 'abstract things' and 'transcendental views' – resonated among Neuendettelsau missionaries from their arrival in German New Guinea in 1886 until at least the interwar period when Australia was the new colonial power.[7]

We should note however that there were in fact two interrelated complaints here. For the missionaries, abstract expressions not only designated specific things or concepts that were 'intellectual [and] transcendental' (*geistig* and *übersinnlich*) but also entailed a whole different regime of assumptions – a distinctive New Guinean 'semiotic ideology', to draw on Webb Keane's terminology – about 'what signs are and how they function in the world' that conflicted with the worldview of the Lutheran missionaries.[8] As such, the Neuendettelsau missionaries came to believe not only that New Guineans lacked certain abstract ideas but also, importantly, that New Guineans did not always treat signifiers as arbitrary and, as such, without any inherent relationship to or power over the things they signified.[9] This recognition, which formed the crux of how Neuendettelsau and other Protestant missionaries understood New Guinean linguistic ideology in this period, caused theological tensions for the missionaries for reasons we will see later. Once articulated, the missionaries' characterisation of how language functioned in New Guinea became key to portraying how New Guineans were different from Europeans as well as, in turn, one of the central bulwarks to be overcome in the conversion of New Guineans. Translating the Gospel was no longer a matter of merely introducing new words for missing abstract concepts, but required, the missionaries believed, a fundamental conversion of the New Guinean attitude towards language. This was, however, only half the story. In this chapter, the desire to radically change the New Guinean 'semiotic ideology' is placed in tension with another of their evangelical aims, namely, to radically indigenise Christianity. This latter goal had the opposite aim of leaving the 'form' of indigenous life (and language) untouched.

The Neuendettelsau views on language appear particularly frequently in the context of the missionaries' writings on New Guinean myths. Their thoughts about myths thus provides a useful means to illuminate the dynamic between the two goals in the short space of this chapter. On the one hand the Neuendettelsau missionaries believed that myths (German or New Guinean, it did not matter) reflected an indelible local way of thinking into which Christianity should be translated. And yet the missionaries also criticised the ritual function of myths in New

Guinea as evidence of a misguided view of the power of language – a view that was incompatible with the missionaries' theology of nature and had to be changed.[10]

The chapter is structured around these two evangelical aims. The first half explores the origins and implications of the belief that one's mother tongue fundamentally structures one's religious life and that one should, therefore, know the Christian God only within one's local linguistic and cultural context. The second half highlights the competing belief (held equally strongly) that the function of New Guinean languages needed to change to accommodate the 'abstract' themes of Christianity. The contention is that there existed a certain tension between these two points – between the localising and universalising demands of the evangelical project – that characterised Protestant missionary attitudes to evangelism at this time.

There are a variety of competing terms in German (and English) at play in this chapter: *Mythos*, *Mythe* (myth), *Märchen* (fairy tale), *Sage* (saga), *Erzählung* (story), *Geschichte* (story, history), *Gerücht* (rumour), *Fabel* (fable), *Schwank* (amusing anecdote) etc. Word choice of course matters and for this reason I have left these competing terms in the original German throughout the chapter. The missionaries themselves strongly preferred *Erzählung*, *Sage* and, more often than not, *Märchen* – for reasons that we will be in a better position to speculate on later. The Neuendettelsau missionaries rarely ever used the term 'myth' or German variants (*Mythos*, *Mythe*). They did not regard New Guinean myths in themselves as any more or less inherently valuable than their own German folk myths. For convenience, I will use the term 'myth' in this chapter as a loose catch-all for any and all types of stories.[11] My aim is not to provide a new theory of myths or to make an argument for any theory in favour of another.[12] In this chapter, the Neuendettelsau missionaries' documentation and discussion of myths serves rather as a lens to view the tensions in the missionaries' understanding of how the New Guinean 'semiotic ideology' stood in comparison to their own.

## Indigenising Christianity: myths as the key to the Papuan's soul

Documenting myths has long served a mundane practical purpose in the history of linguistic fieldwork. Myths were and remain an obvious place to start when first trying to come to terms with the structure and idioms of any unknown language.[13] The Neuendettelsau missionaries were no different in this – even though, in many respects, their education equipped them poorly for the task. From its inception in the 1840s, the

Gesellschaft für Innere und Äußere Mission im Sinne der Lutherischen Kirche – better known as the Neuendettelsau mission – aimed primarily to train young Protestant men from the surrounding rural areas in northern Bavaria to serve as pastors for overseas German-speaking congregations located in North America and Australia.[14] Students therefore studied only biblical languages (Hebrew, Latin and Greek) and English.[15] Over time, however, Neuendettelsau seminary graduates also began evangelising among 'heathens': first among Native Americans in North America in the 1850s, then a couple of decades later among Aboriginals in central Australia, and then finally in New Guinea from 1886 onwards. In spite of this growing focus, the majority of seminary students in Neuendettelsau were still training to work as pastors in German congregations abroad. The seminary curriculum education did not change to include knowledge of indigenous languages and cultures until 1923.[16] The first generations of graduates to New Guinea had little experience of life beyond the gentle hills of middle Franconia prior to travelling.

Perhaps the one major exception was the first Neuendettelsau missionary to New Guinea, Johann Flierl (1858–1947). He had been evangelising among Aboriginal peoples in central Australia since 1878 when, in 1884, German Chancellor Otto von Bismarck accepted a proposal to make the north-east of the New Guinean mainland and the surrounding islands a German protectorate under the administrative and financial responsibility of the German New Guinea Company (Deutsche Neuguinea-Compagnie).[17] Flierl immediately recognised Germany's South Pacific acquisitions as an opportunity for a fresh start. He later wrote that he had it 'in his unconscious' at the time to start a mission in an area of 'still untouched tribes'.[18] The mission director back in Neuendettelsau saw a mission within the new German colony as an opportunity to ride the wave of national support for colonialism in Germany. In September 1885 he replied enthusiastically to Flierl's proposal: 'a new [missionary] undertaking in the German protectorate [of New Guinea] would support the prevalent excitement for colonialism in Germany [...] *In God's name, onwards to New Guinea*'.[19] Flierl was the first Neuendettelsau missionary to begin evangelising on the mainland of German New Guinea. Such was his enthusiasm, he arrived at the main administrative port of Finschhafen in July 1886 less than a year after the arrival of the first German administrators. Following closely on his heels were the Lutheran Rhenish missionaries from Barmen, who arrived on the mainland in 1887, and the Catholic Society of the Divine Word in 1896. The harsh climate and intimidating mountainous terrain, especially along the Finschhafen coast, meant that contact with these other mission societies was minimal and German settlers were few. Flierl set up his first mission base at Simbang, some distance south from the colonial administrators at Finschhafen.[20] Over time, other Neuendettelsau missionaries gradually joined Flierl: by 1890, there were five Neuendettelsau missionaries (and their families); by 1900, nine; by 1908, twenty-one; and by the outbreak of the First World War, there were twenty-five evangelists as well as their families and a small number of manual workers.[21] Such were the missionaries' isolation and freedom, a visiting German District Officer described the cluster of independent Neuendettelsau mission stations as constituting a 'state within the state'.[22]

Very little was known about the land and the people before Flierl's arrival. From the beginning, Neuendettelsau missionaries treated collecting myths as a means to greater linguistic competence in Kâte and Jabêm, the two main language groups in the local area. This practice also enabled them to overcome some early challenges in their relationship with New Guinean informants. Missionaries noted early on that New Guineans were reluctant to reveal secret details about religious practices.[23] Moreover, New Guineans – whether out of sympathy, politeness or perhaps just exasperation – chose on occasion to adopt the missionaries' grammatical mistakes rather than correct them.[24] Finally, the New Guineans sometimes grew tired at having to explain every new word and thus self-limited their vocabulary. In a letter to the mission house in 1897, Flierl described how documenting stories proved a means to circumvent these challenges and simultaneously gain insight into the local language and religion:

> And thus it goes with the research of the Kai [i.e. Kâte] language – forwards, even if slowly. What the missionary employs in daily communication with the Papuans becomes familiar; but this is not enough. Since [the missionaries] now rarely discover a new word in their interactions with the people (because the people concentrate on only ever using those expressions that they know the missionaries understand), the missionaries therefore allow the people to tell small stories [*Geschichten*], which they write down in order to enter ever more deeply into the spirit of the language. That is absolutely necessary. For when it comes to translating the Word of God into their language, so hardship is heaped upon hardship. They have namely as good as no words into and with which to be able to express spiritual and religious concepts.[25]

Flierl's belief in 1897 that New Guinean languages lacked 'spiritual and religious concepts' did not at this time coalesce into a more general critique of New Guinean views about the function of language. He was concerned with collecting myths as a linguistic practice to overcome, in the first instance, difficulties of working with informants. More than that, however, Flierl believed that myths provided a useful window into 'the spirit of the language', that is, what he imagined to be the essential heart of New Guinean intellectual and religious life.

The question of whether thinking, religion and myths were essentially structured by one's native tongue motivated and divided many professional and amateur German linguists and anthropologists in the late nineteenth century. For some, such as Adolf Bastian (1826–1905), who was the central figure in German anthropology in the late nineteenth century, all peoples shared the same 'elementary thoughts' (*Elementargedanken*), even if these were disguised by local cultures:

> [I think it likely that] we will find the same tight core of ideas in all places and times. There are definite analogies in mythological thoughts and world views amid both the fetishism of the savage and the aesthetics of the civilized [...] in all these, after removing the cloak of local and temporal variations in language and idiom, we encounter the same small number of psychological kernels.[26]

Bastian and his supporters thought myths were best studied after removing 'the cloak of local and temporal variations in language', while his opponents regarded language as inseparable in theory and reality from such modes of thinking and religion. In his day, some of Bastian's main opponents on this point were Heymann Steinthal (1823–99) and Moritz Lazarus (1824–1903). Both were professors at the University of Berlin and, in 1860, founders of the *Zeitschrift für Völkerpsychologie und Sprachwissenschaft* (*The Journal for Folk Psychology and Linguistics*).[27] As members of Bastian's Berlin Anthropological Society, they found themselves in frequent battles over whether language was an appropriate object of anthropological study. In contrast to Bastian, Steinthal, for example, understood language in such a way that it provided the 'key to all aspects of humanity'.[28] Furthermore, he regarded knowledge of 'the spiritual content of the national consciousness [*Voksbewusstsein*], its views, how it feels and judges' as part and parcel of studying languages.[29]

An early and influential proponent of language-as-innate in German-speaking lands was the eighteenth-century philosopher and theologian Johann Gottfried Herder (1744–1804). For Herder, language was already right there at the origins of religion: 'in order to understand the language of the gods on Olympus the human being must already have reason and consequently must already have a language'.[30] Since reason and religion were both historical and linguistic, Herder concluded that religious expressions were unique to each language group.[31] Significantly, this thinking led him to see human beings as essentially divided according to the languages they spoke.[32] Herder's views inspired an interest in sagas, folk tales, folk songs and myths as expressions of a people-group's original and essential 'modes of thinking'.[33] A century before the arrival of the Neuendettelsau missionaries in New Guinea, Herder even considered New Guinean myths: 'In the end, however different its garb may be, religion can be found even among the poorest and rudest peoples on the edge of the earth. The natives of Greenland and Kamchatka, of Tierra del Fuego and Papua New Guinea, have religious expressions, illustrated by their sagas and customs.'[34] While Jacob and Wilhelm Grimm heeded Herder's call to collect folk songs and folk tales in Germany, the Neuendettelsau missionaries – inspired by a similar belief about language and the soul of peoples – led the effort to gather myths in New Guinea as a way to get to know their peculiar modes of thinking and religion.[35]

It should not surprise us that Herder's ideas about language were strongly reflected in Neuendettelsau. The influential founder of the Neuendettelsau mission seminary, Wilhelm Löhe (1808–72), reportedly read all of Herder's theologically relevant writings.[36] Löhe studied theology at the University of Erlangen in the 1830s, at a time when Herder's writings paved the way for the so-called Erlangen School within nineteenth-century German Protestantism. Herder's importance in Erlangen was such that the theologian Karl Barth later claimed that 'Without Herder there would have been no Erlangen group'.[37] We should nevertheless be cautious about placing too much weight on Herder's direct influence on the Neuendettelsau theology of language; Herder's name does not appear in either of the two main seminary textbooks used in Neuendettelsau in the late nineteenth and early twentieth centuries.[38] In her investigation of German mission linguistics in Africa, Sara Pugach recently pointed out that missionaries and German romantics like Herder were both 'inheritors of the seventeenth-century German pietist tradition that stressed a personal bond with Christ. ... The missionary belief in the deeply mystical, revelatory power of language stemmed as much from pietism as did that of individuals like Herder.'[39] The indigenising ambition of missionary linguistics reflected an underlying *pietistic* concern for a deep relation with Christ over Church doctrine.[40] In this way, a more important direct source of pietistic and romantic ideas about language for the Neuendettelsau missionaries in the decades around 1900 was the missiologist Gustav Warneck (1843–1910), the most prominent missionary educator in Germany in the late nineteenth century, who argued that 'each nation's soul comes to the Word in the vernacular [*Volkssprachen*]'.[41]

Translated into the context of German New Guinea, the Neuendettelsau missionaries defended the many New Guinean language groups as natural social units against the socially disruptive encroachment of 'Zivilisation' (civilisation).[42] With the strong support of the Neuendettelsau mission director, the mission's most gifted musician, Heinrich

Zahn (1880–1944), devoted himself from around 1915 onwards to finding unique indigenous melody structures which might carry Christian lyrics:

> Our European melodies are and remain foreign to the natives. Just as it is impossible for the European, who clings to European things and who measures the natives by a European scale, to become accepted by natives as a 'native', in the same way a native tribe cannot step into European circumstances, or spiritual world – here in the music – in such a way that it means to him what it means to us. That our chorale melodies were strange to the natives was evidenced from the beginning by the impure, unrhythmical, and downright mutilating singing of the hymns.[43]

The radical otherness of New Guinean life in Zahn's account ultimately fostered in the Neuendettelsau missionaries generally a relatively positive attitude towards local culture, even when it was different. Incomprehensibility was itself merely a sign of difference rather than necessarily an indication of cultural inferiority. To make this point, Zahn gave examples to demonstrate that one can appreciate New Guinean culture only from within. He wrote that a line from one of the local songs such as 'you are like a betelnut and like the stem of a fern' might mean nothing to an outsider. But it stimulated an image of 'splendour' for the New Guinean who knows that these items are used for dyeing bark cloth.[44] Such sentences in song and *Märchen*, wrote Zahn, are 'beautiful' and 'charming' within their own local context.[45]

The belief that God encountered human beings within their own language drove the desire to indigenise Christianity. Simultaneously, the elevation of myths as key to the soul of a people group provided the means to achieve this goal. Together these views explain why Neuendettelsau missionaries took such a close interest in myths. It accounts for why we find today so many collections of myths in their publications and, unpublished, in the mission archive.[46] Heinrich Zahn was one of the more prolific collectors and alone gathered over 450 pages of myths.[47] According to this particular Neuendettelsau evangelical aim, Christianity could become part of local life without changing traditional New Guinean ways of being.

## Abstracting Christianity: overthrowing Papuan mythological thinking

The missionaries' search within New Guinean myths for 'the spirit of the language', as Flierl put it earlier, inspired an optimistic rhetoric about the possibility of indigenising Christianity. But what then became of those beliefs and practices that were deemed incompatible with Christianity? These included the sex-themed dances and the *Balum* spirit-festival – to name two practices the Neuendettelsau missionaries particularly strongly opposed in the Finschhafen area.[48] Why were these not also regarded by the missionaries as somehow essential to a New Guinean way of life? Or perhaps, more to the point: how were these problematic elements detached discursively from less controversial practices and beliefs? The answer, I suggest, lies in an observation by Webb Keane. 'By the end of the nineteenth century,' Keane pointed out, 'the decision of what to salvage in colonial societies commonly hinged on whether the practice or idea in question could be defined as culture, and therefore more or less harmless, or as false religion.'[49] We find this reflected in the Neuendettelsau missionaries' rhetoric in New Guinea. In his argument for indigenising Christian liturgical music, for example, missionary Heinrich Zahn explicitly argued that New Guinean melody structures (which were inherently indifferent to the Christian message) were mere local 'form' – corresponding with Keane's sense of 'culture' – that might be filled with the universal 'content' of the Christian message.[50] In contrast, the missionaries characterised more theologically problematic aspects of New Guinean myths through the derogatory term 'animism' – and placed this in opposition to the 'abstract' ideas and concepts of a proper religion, such as Christianity. The final part of this chapter therefore looks at the ways in which missionaries tried to cleanse New Guinean languages of animism by introducing 'abstract concepts' and encouraging a view of signs as arbitrary.

*The function and definition of myths*

One of the first Neuendettelsau missionaries to speculate about which word to use to describe New Guineans' myths was Konrad Vetter, who worked among the Jabêm people prior to Heinrich Zahn and until his death from tropical illness in 1906. Writing in 1892, Vetter equivocated about how best to categorise the New Guinean stories which he had been collecting so as to provide a 'view into the way of thinking'.[51] For Vetter, the central question to determining the difference between *Sagen* and *Märchen* (the only two categories he considered) was whether the local Jabêm regarded the stories as in some sense true or not. He acknowledged, however, that his research proved inconclusive. On the one hand he noted that indigenous people themselves confessed to him that their stories made no claim to reality.[52] And, to this extent, he reflected on the way the locals told their stories around a fire at night time – that it was perhaps not unlike a German child listening to a good storyteller narrating *One Thousand and One Nights*.[53] On the other hand, he recognised that he could also identify instances when this was clearly not the case – when the Jabêm really seem to have believed their own stories to be literally true. The Jabêm possessed for example one particular story, wrote Vetter, in which dwarves come down from the forests and caves in the night to go fishing. Their long hair acting as bait, the dwarves stand in the water and throw their catch on to the beach. This was then how the Jabêm explained the presence of dead fish on the beach in the morning. Vetter concluded, on balance, that 'one can hardly call the *Sage* of the fishing dwarves a *Märchen* in the mind of New Guineans, since they themselves appear to believe in the existence of this creature of phantasy'.[54]

Where Vetter recognised the extent to which New Guinean myths were sometimes taken as literally true or historically accurate, other Neuendettelsau missionaries began observing the spell-like power of the myths themselves in local practices. In 1911, Christian Keyßer documented a number of myths in Neuhauss's *Deutsch Neu-Guinea* under the heading of the '*Sagen* of the Kai'. In his introduction he explained that 'It is perhaps not superficial to note that these are simply *Sagen*, not *Märchen*, not *Fabeln*. Additionally, that which we see as *Fabeln* are, for the Kai, *Sagen*.'[55] Georg Pilhofer, another missionary of the same generation as Keyßer, similarly wrote that *Sagen* were 'for the Papuans not simply *Geschichten* [because] these *Erzählungen* served a religious purpose'.[56] Pilhofer gave the example of a particular New Guinean *Sage* that could only be told at nighttime, lest one get grey hair.[57] In each instance, Keyßer and Pilhofer thought that the New Guineans held the myths to be historically true – and possibly also, more to the point, powerful.

Some of the missionaries' most sustained reflections on New Guinean myths emerged in retirement, when they had the time and space to synthesise several decades of experiences. They also received encouragement to share their views in Germany, where they proved popular speakers. Between 1921 and 1954, Christian Keyßer, the most well-known of the retired Neuendettelsau missionaries, gave a remarkable 4,829 sermons, lectures and talks, as far afield as France.[58] His presentations drew on his past experiences in German New Guinea and drummed up support for the mission's ongoing work. Moreover the lectures kept alive the memory of the German empire during the uncertain interwar years, when nostalgia for lost colonies further fuelled frustrations about Germany's weaker global position after the Versailles Peace Treaty.[59] It was in this political climate, in the midst of the Second World War, that Heinrich Zahn gave a series of three lectures on the topic of 'Jabêm Märchen und Sagen' (Jabêm Fairy Tales and Sagas, 1942) to an audience in the town of Bayreuth – an important Protestant base of support at the time for both the Neuendettelsau mission society and National Socialism. Zahn told the audience that the aim of his lectures was not to provide a new theory for *Märchen* and *Sagen*. Rather, he hoped to illustrate all manner of aspects of Jabêm life through the hundreds of stories he had collected (while evangelising among the Jabêm people on the north-east coast of New Guinea) as a rich source of data. Through the content of Jabêm myths, he wanted to be able to describe, in short, the whole Jabêm 'mental world and spiritual life'.[60] In his three lectures, Zahn then worked through, one at a time, a fairly standard list of ethnographic topics: the Jabêm conception of the soul, death, marriage, suicide, dancing, spirits, music and so on. Under each topic, Zahn gave evidence for the Jabêm approach or view based on the content of one or another myth that he had documented. One of the few moments during his 1942 lectures where he broke from this structure was when he briefly considered the significance and status of *Märchen* and *Sagen* in Jabêm society. Zahn told his audience that the concept of 'animism' explained everything. It was a worldview (*Naturanschauung*) that underlay New Guinean magical thinking in general, and enabled New Guineans to attribute spell-like power to the words of myths:

> That the magic spell is most often a completely innocent *Märchen*, a *Sage* or a piece from one them, always puzzled us [missionaries] from the beginning. In any case, the content of the spell always had a specific associated with that on which it was supposed to have an effect. A *tertium comparationis* can always be identified.[61]

Zahn observed that the Jabêm religious worldview assumed that the words of a *Märchen* held a certain power over things they named via a logic of resemblances or similarities, where the signifier resembles the signified through a *tertium comparationis*, a quality that brought them together

In their Jabêm dictionary, Heinrich Zahn and J.F. Streicher (a later Neuendettelsau missionary) identified the spell-like function of myths as a defining characteristic in New Guinea. They included this aspect in their Jabêm dictionary entry under *sẽboacõ*, the Jabêm term (they tell us) for 'fairy-tale, story, tale, legend' – noting that 'all fairy tales were charms'.[62] Zahn and Streicher made this even more explicit in their dictionary entry on the traditional Jabêm conclusion to a 'fairy tale' (*sẽboacõ*):

> sululuaèŋ siŋgôc boaŋgôc ... traditional conclusion of fairy tales (sẽboacõ), as a kind of magic blessing of the fruit growing in the newly planted gardens. sululuaèŋ siŋgôc boaŋgôc, gêŋ wê jaucjaucgeŋ, mokolo ŋajamata kapôêŋgeŋ, tê ŋaguŋ baliŋgen ma X ŋakwalim baliŋgen Ha! another fairy tale, crickets, tongue shells: May the crops grow plentifully (with many suckers), may the mokolo taroes grow big at the fireplace (jamata), may

the sugarcane grow long tap roots (grow as long as poles (guŋ), for punting canoes), may the bananas develop mighty bunches! (The longer the fairy tales the longer the vines, roots, etc. were believed to grow, the larger the crop would be! That was the logic of magic thinking and the conviction based on animistic tradition. The seed-plot of cargo cults – irrational and utterly unrealistic.)[63]

Parts of this must have been added later by Streicher. The term 'cargo cult', for instance, did not appear in literature until after Zahn's death.[64] But the main element of this colourful definition reiterates what Zahn identified in his 1942 Bayreuth lectures: New Guineans viewed the ritual telling of tales as a way to influence things through an analogical process of resemblance. In the example given in the dictionary, 'length' operated as a *tertium comparationis*, linking the duration of a fairy tale and the resulting size of a crop. In brief, the central reason this animistic approach to myth and language threatened the Neuendettelsau Christianity was that it blurred the duality of their world. For the missionaries, the animistic logic led to numerous theological errors, including misattributing spiritual or religious significance to things in nature. This was something the Neuendettelsau missionaries were familiar with from the reactions of New Guineans whenever there appeared in New Guinea an earthquake, comet or sickness.[65]

*Christian and abstract vocabularies*

We can now begin more fully to understand what the Neuendettelsau missionaries meant by 'abstract' expressions in their critique of New Guinean language systems. The missionaries' notion of abstraction was quite peculiar. This becomes more pronounced if we first consider it in light of competing contemporary scientific notions of abstraction. Take, for example, the work of the Austro-Hungarian psychologist Max Wertheimer (1880–1943). As a student in Berlin, Wertheimer studied under the ethnomusicologist Carl Stumpf and became interested in the 'thinking of primitive peoples'. In 1912, Wertheimer published a paper entitled 'Über das Denken der Naturvölker' (later translated as 'Numbers and Numerical Concepts in Primitive Peoples').[66] Not unlike the missionaries, he treated thinking as linguistically and locally constrained, even when analysing something as seemingly universal as numbers:

It is not enough to ask which numbers and operations of *our* mathematics are used by the peoples of some other (especially a so-called primitive) culture. Instead the question must be: What thought processes do they employ in this domain? What are their problems? How do they attack them? What are the results?[67]

[ 97 ]

Again, as with the Neuendettelsau missionaries, Wertheimer did not account for difference through locating *Naturvölker* ('natural peoples') on a scale – at 'a mere primitive stage' of a path towards civilisation, as he put it – but rather held (as the proper starting point for any 'genuine inquiry')[68] the possibility that non-European peoples might practise non-European ways of handling numbers. For Wertheimer, *Naturvölker* nevertheless lacked abstract concepts. He believed that the way *Naturvölker* handled numbers was somehow less abstract, less universal than in Germany. 'The ideal of universal transferability (i.e. abstractness) of thought structures is not necessarily the aim of all thinking in this sphere. There are structures [*Gebilde*] which, less abstract than our numbers, nevertheless serve analogous ends.'[69] He gives the example that if a member of a family were missing at a dinner table, it is clear to those present that someone is missing without necessarily needing to count those present.[70] Similarly, the thinking and language of *Naturvölker* therefore did not go beyond the 'natural context and natural relationships'.[71] In contrast, both Wertheimer and the missionaries treated their objects (Christianity, for the missionaries; numbers systems in Europe, for Wertheimer) as abstract because of their supposed universal transferability (*Übertragbarkeit*).[72]

However, Wertheimer's reasoning only mirrored the missionaries' ethnographic thinking this far. There was one particularly unique aspect to the Neuendettelsau missionaries' conception of abstraction. For Wertheimer – who was thinking about numbers – abstract ideas could be abstracted *from* material contexts or nature. The real world related to abstract ideas through a process of *induction*. The Neuendettelsau missionaries, on the other hand, did not believe the type of religious abstract terms they were concerned with could be induced or deduced through studying and meditating on the natural world. The type of abstraction knowledge that concerned the missionaries came through a process of *revelation*.

The peculiarly evangelical nature of Neuendettelsau missionaries' approach to abstraction is further demonstrated by looking at the concepts that they claimed the New Guineans lacked. Mission letters published in the main mission journal, *Kirchliche Mitteilungen*, occasionally listed and discussed the 'spiritual concepts' (*geistige und geistliche Begriffe*),[73] 'higher concepts'[74] and 'specific Christian concepts' for which the missionaries at one time or another could find no New Guinean equivalent. These included: *Vater Unser* (Our Father),[75] *Himmelreich* (the Kingdom of Heaven),[76] *Glauben* (belief),[77] *Geist Gottes* (the spirit of God),[78] *lieben* (to love),[79] *glücklich* (happy, lucky), *selig* (blessed), *anbeten* (to worship), *richten* (to direct), *beherbergen* (to accommodate),

*Wunder* (wonder, miracle), *Gleichnis* (parable), *Fest* (festival), *Braut* (bride), *Bräutigam* (bridegroom), *Hochzeit* (marriage), *müssen* (must), *sollen* (shall), *antworten* (to answer) etc.[80] Missionaries felt these terms were needed to give an account of Christian theology and establish Christian society.

In 1912 *Kirchliche Mitteilungen* provided its readers with an overview of the current state of missionary linguistic research in New Guinea. By this time, the Neuendettelsau missionaries' language proficiency was such that they could begin translating large passages of the Bible. The article explained that it took a lot of work to find 'biblical words and concepts' in foreign languages: 'This is possibly relatively easier among the cultured peoples [*Kulturvolk*], because they are also concerned with intellectual [*geistig*] things.'[81] The article proceeded to discuss a lecture on 'Missionsarbeit unter primitiven Völkern' (Mission work amongst primitive peoples) given in Berlin in 1910 by the Lutheran Rhenish missionary Albert Hoffmann. The content of his lecture gives us an indication that the theme of abstraction extended to other Protestant communities and was not limited to the Neuendettelsau society.[82] Hoffmann, who evangelised in an area adjacent to the Neuendettelsau missionaries, detailed the central challenge of translation in New Guinea in these terms:

> The first thing that was clear to us was that the Gospel is about spiritual and heavenly goods and not earthly [*irdisch*] – however, things one cannot see. How then to find the words for these unseeable things. The savages [*Wilde*] indeed had and used words for every little grass type and insect, but concepts were distant. With regards to thinking, he was also very focused on that which was perceptible with the senses [*das sinnlich Wahrnehmbare*]. ... How should we then explain to the people Biblical expressions such as belief, hope, eternal life, holiness etc.?[83]

Here Hoffmann conflated the scientific notion of an abstraction (i.e. a general rule that one might arrive at inductively by, say, a knowledge of numerous types of insects) with a sense of abstraction as all those terms which signify transcendental 'things'. Whatever the relation between the two, the fact remains that the Neuendettelsau missionaries did not believe that the second type (transcendental things) could under normal circumstances be arrived at through an inductive study of nature. Human beings could not, by their own efforts, come to a knowledge of God; and in any case, they had the Bible, which was the primary place where God revealed himself. This view is summarised in the Neuendettelsau seminary's main textbook for dogmatics, which seminary students had to copy out word-for-word throughout the late nineteenth and early twentieth centuries. It taught that revelation played a necessary evidentiary role in religious life – 'it is the objective side of religion, the subjective side is belief'.[84] Observing nature could only lead to God when God chose to reveal himself through 'natural revelation', which existed only 'so that the heathen could seek and find him'.[85] As Christian Keyßer wrote in 1929: 'people should not remain at this level after they come to know the clear Word of God [i.e. the Bible]'.[86] Once the New Guineans gained access to translations of the Bible, they were to look for God in nature no longer.

## Conclusion

Two competing attitudes towards myths existed within the Neuendettelsau mission. Myths were at once both a window into New Guinean worldviews and also, in their traditional spell-like function, incompatible with modern Protestant theology. The first generations of Neuendettelsau missionaries to New Guinea deployed the notions of abstract concepts and animism as a way of understanding the problematic side of myths and thereby classifying what they felt New Guineans lacked. Along with this belief in abstract expressions also came a belief that Webb Keane associated with global Protestantism in general at the time, that is, 'a sharp distinction between signs and the world they signified'.[87] The peculiarity of the missionaries' view of abstraction shows exactly why Keane's use of 'sharp' here is no mere rhetorical flourish. The views of modern Protestant missionaries overlapped significantly with those found within professional science circles of the day: nature was governed by natural laws; signs were arbitrary; and human beings could not, by their own efforts, influence the material world by merely speaking, whether by reciting spells, myths or, indeed, prayers. To this extent, the missionaries' view of God's place (or absence) in the world was not only compatible but in fact largely dependent upon these general natural scientific assumptions about independent natural laws. However, the missionaries also added a unique twist. Abstract religious concepts came through revelation, not through the scientific practice of abstraction – religious abstract concepts were in this sense even more detached from nature than scientific ones. A history of Christianity's relationship to abstraction and, indeed, a history of abstraction itself are still to be written. This chapter nevertheless offers an episode in these histories – one that shows that a discourse of 'abstraction' operated within both the history of Christianity and German colonialism to differentiate peoples according to their relationship to language. For the Neuendettelsau missionaries, New Guineans seemed trapped in their local context. Without intervention, New Guinean languages – as evinced by the magic-like function of myths – seemed incapable of accommodating words that claimed no power over the things they named. It was in these terms that the missionaries most frequently imagined what evangelism in New Guinea required – what was necessary, that is, to be able to pour 'the wine of the gospels' into New Guinean wineskins.

## Notes

1 'Auch eine Schwierigkeit bei der Missionsarbeit', *Kirchliche Mitteilungen aus und über Nordamerika, Australien und Neu-Guinea* (hereafter *Kirchliche Mitteilungen*) 10 (1888), 77. The anonymous author was most likely Johannes Deinzer (1842–97), the then director of the Neuendettelsau mission and editor of the *Kirchliche Mitteilungen*. Although commonly known as the Neuendettelsau mission, the official title of the mission society was the Gesellschaft für Innere und Äußere Mission im Sinne der Lutherischen Kirche (Society for Inner and Outer Mission of the Lutheran Church). Translations in this chapter are mine unless otherwise indicated.
2 'Auch eine Schwierigkeit bei der Missionsarbeit'.
3 This played on Matthew 9:17.
4 Quoted in Stewart Firth, *New Guinea under the Germans* (Melbourne: University of Melbourne, 1982), p. 136.
5 The Neuendettelsau mission records are today kept together as part of the Mission Eine Welt archival records housed at Das Landeskirchliche Archiv der Evangelisch-Lutherischen Kirche in Bayern (hereafter MEW LAELKB).
6 'Die größte Schwierigkeit, die sie zu bewältigen haben, liegt wohl in dem Mangel aller Ausdrücke für abstrakte, d.h. nicht mit den Sinnen wahrnehmbare Dinge, der sich natürlich aus dem Fehlen geistiger, übersinnlicher Anschauungen und Begriffe erklärt.' 'Auch eine Schwierigkeit bei der Missionsarbeit'.
7 Following present convention, in this chapter I will refer to the villagers in the German colonial sphere as New Guineans. It is important to note, however, that the Neuendettelsau missionaries and other Germans used multiple terms in their writing and were in fact strongly inclined to using the stylistically more elegant term *Papuan*. I have retained the missionaries' usage in my translations.
8 Webb Keane, 'Semiotics and the Social Analysis of Material Things', *Language & Communication* 23 (2003), 419.
9 My thinking on this point has been strongly shaped by Webb Keane, *Christian Moderns: Freedom and Fetish in the Mission Encounter* (Berkeley: University of California Press), 2007.
10 For a sense of the Neuendettelsau mission's theology of nature, see Friedrich Bauer, Johannes Deinzer and Martin Deinzer, *Christliche Ethik auf Lutherischer Grundlage* (Neuendettelsau: Selbstverlag der Missionsanstalt, 1904).
11 In this I am following Segal's usage. See R. Segal, *Myth: A Very Short Introduction* (Oxford: Oxford University Press, 2004), p. 4.
12 There is already well developed anthropological and philosophical literature on the topic. For a useful overview of this literature, see Segal, *Myth*.
13 *The Linguists Encyclopaedia* recommends, for example, that fieldworkers 'delay analysing conversations until a number of the more straightforward narrative texts have been transcribed and analysed'. Kirsten Malmkjær (ed.), *The Linguistics Encyclopedia* (London: Routledge, 1991), p. 126.
14 Christine Winter, *Looking after One's Own: The Rise of Nationalism and the Politics of the Neuendettelsauer Mission in Australia, New Guinea and Germany, 1921–1933* (Frankfurt am Main: Peter Lang, 2012), pp. 1–3.
15 For typical course outlines, see MEW LAELKB 2.42.

16 Harriet Völker, ' "Missionare als Ethnologen": Moritz Freiherr von Leonhardi, Australische Mission und Europäische Wissenschaft', in Reinhard Wendt (ed.), *Sammeln, Vernetzen, Auswerten: Missionare und ihr Beitrag zum Wandel Europäischer Weltsicht* (Tübingen: Gunter Narr, 2001), p. 179 n. 36.
17 Firth, *New Guinea under the Germans*, pp. 7–20.
18 Johann Flierl, *Als Pioniermissionar in das ferne Neu Guinea: Johann Flierls Lebenserinnerungen* (Wiesbaden: Harrassowitz Verlag, 2015), Vol. I, p. 352.
19 Quoted in Paul Steffen, *Missionsbeginn in Neuguinea: Die Anfänge der Rheinischen, Neuendettelsauer und Steyler Missionsarbeit in Neuguinea* (Nettetal: Steyler Verlag, 1995), p. 96. (Emphasis appears in Steffen's text.)
20 In the early 1890s the New Guinea Company moved its headquarters away from Finschhafen after a malarial outbreak killed over a third of the white population. Firth, *New Guinea under the Germans*, p. 31.
21 Hewig Wagner and Hermann Reiner (eds), *The Lutheran Church in Papua New Guinea: The First Hundred Years, 1886–1986* (Adelaide: Lutheran Publishing House, 1986).
22 Christian Keyßer, *Eine Papuagemeinde* (Neuendettelsau: Freimund-Verlag, 1950), p. 247.
23 See, for example, Georg Bamler's difficulty in learning about the Balum ceremony. Georg Bamler, 'Über Religion, Sitten und Geräuche der Eingebornen in und um Simbang', *Kirchliche Mitteilungen* 8 (1889), 63–4.
24 See Jürgen Stadler, *Die Missionspraxis Christian Keyßers in Neuguinea 1899–1920: Erste Schritte auf dem Weg zu einer einheimischen Kirche* (Nürnberg: VTR, 2006), p. 130.
25 Johann Flierl, 'Vom Sattelberg', *Kirchliche Mitteilungen* 11 (1897), 84.
26 Quoted in Klaus-Peter Koepping, *Adolf Bastian and the Psychic Unity of Mankind* (St Lucia: University of Queensland Press), p. 57.
27 Andrew Zimmerman, *Anthropology and Antihumanism in Imperial Germany* (Chicago: University of Chicago Press, 2001), p. 52.
28 Zimmerman, *Anthropology and Antihumanism*, p. 52.
29 Quoted in Zimmerman, *Anthropology and Antihumanism*, p. 53.
30 Johann Gottfried von Herder, *Philosophical Writings*, trans. Michael N. Forster (Cambridge: Cambridge University Press, 2002), p. 96.
31 Marcia Bunge, 'Introduction', in Herder, *Against Pure Reason: Writings on Religion, Language and History*, trans. Marcia Bunge (Eugene, OR: Wipf & Stock, 1993), p. 2.
32 Herder, *Against Pure Reason*, p. 78.
33 Herder wrote: 'Mythical expressions also provide us with a people's oldest symbolism and tactics of the heart and mind.' Herder, *Against Pure Reason*, p. 80.
34 Herder, *Against Pure Reason*, p. 86.
35 Richard M. Dorson, 'Folklore in the Modern World', in Richard M. Dorson (ed.), *Folklore in the Modern World* (The Hague: Mouton Publishers, 1978), p. 12.
36 David C. Ratke, *Confession and Mission, Word and Sacrament: The Ecclesial Theology of Wilhelm Löhe* (St Louis: Concordia, 1989), p. 31.
37 Quoted in Bunge, 'Introduction', p. 4.
38 The two main seminary textbooks were Friedrich Bauer, Johannes Deinzer and Martin Deinzer, *Christliche Ethik Auf Lutherischer Grundlage* (Neuendettelsau: Selbstverlag der Missionsanstalt, 1904); *Christliche Dogmatik auf lutherischer Grundlage* (Neuendettelsau: Missionsanstalt, 1921). Although these were eventually published in 1904 and 1921, the mission was using unpublished versions of these texts in the second half of the nineteenth century.
39 Sara Pugach, *Africa in Translation: A History of Colonial Linguistics in Germany and Beyond, 1814–1945* (Ann Arbor: University of Michigan Press, 2012), p. 25.
40 Pugach, *Africa in Translation*, p. 22.
41 Gustav Warneck, *Evangelische Missionslehre: Ein Missionstheoretischer Versuch*, 5 vols (Gotha: Frederich Andreas Perthes, 1887–1905), p. 17. For his influence in Neuendettelsau, see Stadler, *Die Missionspraxis Christian Keyßers*, p. 133.

42  For clear evidence of this distinction in German Protestantism at the time, see for example Walter Freytag, 'Volk, Zivilisation und Christenheit in Neuguinea', in Walter Freytag (ed.), *Die Junge Christenheit im Umbruch des Ostens: Vom Gehorsam des Glaubens unter den Völkern* (Berlin: Furche-Verlag, 1938).

43  Heinrich Zahn, trans. Philip W. Holzknecht, *Mission and Music: Jabêm Traditional Music and the Development of the Lutheran Hymnody* (Boroko: Institute of Papua New Guinea Studies, 1996), p. 143.

44  Heinrich Zahn, *Mission and Music*, p. 168. The New Guinean uses of metonym and simile in these cases were not taken by Zahn as examples of abstract thinking. The subject matter perhaps remained still too close to things 'perceivable by the senses'.

45  Zahn, *Mission and Music*, pp. 168, 245. For more on Zahn's ethnomusicology, see my chapter, 'The Ethnomusicology of Emotions in the Neuendettelsau Mission to the Papuans', in Claire McLisky, Daniel Midena and Karen Vallgårda (eds), *Emotions and Christian Missions: Historical Perspectives* (London: Palgrave Macmillan, 2015).

46  The main published collections can be found in Richard Neuhauss, *Deutsch Neu-Guinea*, 3 vols (Berlin: Dietrich Reimer, 1911); Stephan Lehner, 'Märchen und Sagen des Melanesierstammes der Bukawac', *Baessler-Archiv* Sonderabdruck aus Band XIV, 2 (1931), 35–72; Stephan Lehner, 'Sagan, Traumdeutungen, Trauergesänge', *Mitteilungen aus dem Museum für Völkerkunde in Hamburg* 14 (1930); Emil F. Hanemann, *Keys to the Papuan's Soul: Some Practices and Legends Current among the Natives of the Madang Mission Field, New Guinea* (Columbus, OH: Lutheran Book Concern, 1935).

47  'Jabem Märchen (Seboaco) gesammelt von Heinrich Zahn nach dem Diktat von Dawidi (David, Anam,) 1930/1', MEW LAELKB 6.109.

48  Stephen Lehner, 'The Balum Cult of the Bukaua of Huon Gulf, New Guinea', *Oceania* 5:3 (1935), 338–45; Zahn, *Mission and Music*, p. 256.

49  Keane, *Christian Moderns*, p. 85.

50  Zahn makes this form–content distinction explicit. See Zahn, *Mission and Music*, p. 160 n. 29.

51  'Märchen der Eingebornen in Neu-Guinea', *Kirchliche Mitteilungen* 6 (1892), 47.

52  'Märchen der Eingebornen in Neu-Guinea'.

53  'Märchen der Eingebornen in Neu-Guinea'. Vetter did not acknowledge here that *One Thousand and One Nights* did not originate in German-speaking lands.

54  'Märchen der Eingebornen in Neu-Guinea'.

55  Christian Keyßer, 'Aus dem Leben der Kai-Leute', in R. Neuhauss (ed.), *Deutsch-Neuguinea* (Berlin: Dietrich Reimer, 1911).

56  D. Georg Pilhofer, *Die Geschichte der Neuendettelsauer Mission in Neuguinea: Von den ersten Anfängen bis zum Kriegsausbruch 1914* (Neuendettelsau: Freimund, 1961), Vol. 1, p. 159.

57  Pilhofer, *Die Geschichte der Neuendettelsauer Mission*, Vol. 1, p. 159.

58  MEW LAELKB 5.329. See also 4.29.

59  For an overview of German interwar colonial nostalgia, see Volker Max Langbehn and Mohammad Salama (eds), *German Colonialism: Race, the Holocaust, and Postwar Germany* (New York: Columbia University Press, 2011).

60  Heinrich Zahn, 'Jabêm-Maerchen und Sagen' (1942), MEW LAELKB 6.34.

61  Heinrich Zahn, 'Jabêm-Maerchen und Sagen (2. Vortrag, s. 2)' (1942), MEW LAELKB 6.34.

62  'Sêboacô', *Jabêm–English Dictionary*, revised by J.F. Streicher; compiled by Heinrich Zahn in 1917 (Canberra: Australian National University, 1982), p. 527.

63  'sululuaèŋ siŋgôc boaŋgôc …', *Jabêm–English Dictionary*.

64  Lamont Lindstrom, 'Cargo Cult at the Third Millennium', in Holger Jebens (ed.), *Cargo, Cult & Culture Critique* (Honolulu: University of Hawai'i Press, 2004), p. 19.

65  On the New Guinean reaction to the appearance of Halley's Comet, see Zahn, 'Beurteilung der Eeemasang-Bewegung' (7 January 1933) MEW LAELKB 5.350.

66  Max Wertheimer, 'Numbers and Numerical Concepts in Primitive Peoples', in Willis D. Ellis (ed.), *A Source Book of Gestalt Psychology* (Abingdon: Routledge, 1938).
67  Wertheimer, 'Numbers and Numerical Concepts', p. 265.
68  Wertheimer, 'Numbers and Numerical Concepts', p. 265.
69  Wertheimer, 'Numbers and Numerical Concepts', p. 265.
70  Wertheimer, 'Numbers and Numerical Concepts', p. 266.
71  Max Wertheimer, 'Über das Denken der Naturvölker, Zahlen und Zahlgebilde', *Zeitschrift für Psychologie* 60 (1912), 323.
72  Wertheimer, 'Über das Denken der Naturvölker, Zahlen und Zahlgebilde', 323.
73  'Auszug aus einem Jahresbericht Flierl Erstattet an den Herrn Landeshauptmann E.V. Hagen', *Kirchliche Mitteilungen* 6 (1897), 44. This comes from Johann Decker's report.
74  'Die Urlaubsreise von Miss. Flierl und die gegenwärtige Lage in Neu-Guinea', *Kirchliche Mitteilungen* 5 (1898), 36.
75  'Auch eine Schwierigkeit bei der Missionsarbeit', 6.
76  'Aus einem Bericht von Miss. Vetter in Simbang (Schluß)', *Kirchliche Mitteilungen* 3 (1896), 18.
77  'Aus einem Brief von Miss. Bamler auf Tami', *Kirchliche Mitteilungen* 5 (1896), 38. Also 'Etwas aus dem Kapitel missionarischer Sprachforschung', *Kirchliche Mitteilungen* 11 (1912), 83–4.
78  Johann Flierl, 'Vom Sattelberg', *Kirchliche Mitteilungen* 13 (1897), 18.
79  'Die Urlaubsreise von Miss. Flierl und die gegenwärtige Lage in Neu-Guinea', *Kirchliche Mitteilungen* 5 (1898), 36.
80  See 'Aus einem Bericht von Miss. Vetter in Simbang (Schluß)', 19.
81  'Etwas aus dem Kapitel Missionarischer Sprachforschung', 83.
82  See also William B. McGregor, 'Missionary Linguistics in the Kimberley, Western Australia: A History of the First Seventy Years', *Historiographia Linguistica* 30:1 (2008), 132.
83  'Etwas aus dem Kapitel missionarischer Sprachforschung', 83.
84  Bauer et al, *Christliche Dogmatik*, p. 4.
85  Bauer et al, *Christliche Dogmatik*, p. 4.
86  Keyßer, *Eine Papuagemeinde*, p. 78.
87  Keane, *Christian Moderns*, p. 84.

## CHAPTER SIX

# Signs of the savage in the skull? German investigations of Australian Aboriginal skeletal remains, *c.* 1860

Antje Kühnast

In the Australian colonial context, Germans have largely been described as humanitarian forces in the relations between settlers and indigenous peoples.[1] Critical of harsh British colonisation practices, Germans ostensibly showed more sympathy towards the plight of Aborigines and appeared to have a better understanding of their rights as human beings.[2] German physical and cultural anthropologists of the mid- to late nineteenth century have similarly been described as following a more humane, less racialising approach to the investigation of colonised peoples in general.[3] This chapter explores this idea, to offer a sense of how Indigenous Australians figured in German anthropological investigations.

Australian Aborigines initially came to the attention of German naturalists with an interest in human diversity and its origins in the 1790s, when Germany's eminent 'father of physical anthropology', Johann Friedrich Blumenbach, acquired the skulls of two Australian Aboriginal men for his 'anthropological researches'.[4] He used these *Neuholländer* skulls and contemporary travel literature to construct his long-lasting monogenetic division of humanity into five varieties or races.[5] It was the beginning of the relentless appropriation, trading and racialising interpretation of Australian Aboriginal skeletal remains, not exclusively in Germany but in the entire northern hemisphere. In the decades following Australia's colonisation, mainly British anatomists and physical anthropologists rendered the skulls and bones of Australia's indigenous peoples into highly sought-after scientific 'specimens'.[6] In Germany, however, it took around another seventy years before a new generation of scientists picked up the threads of Blumenbach's work. Inspired by their famous anthropologist pioneer but also regarding his methodology as scientifically insufficient, they turned to the supposedly objective, empirical-inductive and comparative-statistical method for the investigation of human diversity. This approach fostered the large-scale acquisition of human remains for the purposes of 'comparative anthropometry or race-anatomy'[7] and (anti-)evolutionary theorising. In the 1860s, they set out to establish their area of research as a decidedly natural science discipline, physical anthropology.[8] At the same time, so-called 'anthropological material' from Australia began to arrive in Germany, appropriated through the individual and organisational scientific networks between Germany and Australia.

Among those who maintained ties with their homeland's scientific world was the artist, naturalist and explorer Ludwig Becker, who made himself a name in the scientific communities of both Melbourne and Germany in fields as diverse as geology, meteorology, ornithology and anthropology.[9] In 1859, Becker contributed to a government investigation into the state of the indigenous population of the colony of Victoria, providing information about their living conditions and their physical nature. To demonstrate the latter he presented the portraits of two young Aborigines and three Aboriginal skulls. Becker's testimony quickly found its way into the hands of some of the founding figures of the German discipline of *Anthropologie*. During the following years, Alexander Ecker and Gustav Lucae used their compatriot's statements to varying degrees as reference for their own investigations of Australian Aboriginal skulls and bones.

By then, Charles Darwin's theory of evolution was being debated in Germany's biological sciences, with the majority of physical anthropologists dismissing outright the *Affentheorie* for a number of methodological and ideological reasons. It has been argued that this rejection of Darwinian evolutionary principles shows that German physical anthropologists had a less racialising, or non-racist, attitude towards the investigation and evaluation of human diversity. Their claim of separating questions of physical diversity from the sphere of cultural, mental and moral investigation has similarly been interpreted as a sign of a less hierarchical view of human diversity.[10]

In this chapter I shall examine how Becker's well-intentioned cultural and physical anthropological statements, aimed at changing the devastating living conditions of Australia's indigenous peoples, were rendered by physical anthropologists in Germany into evidence for their racialising scientific discipline. Via the examples of Alexander Ecker and Gustav Lucae, this chapter demonstrates that the interpretation of Australian Aboriginal skeletal remains proved to be difficult and offered only ambiguous results. Through a variety of manoeuvres, such as recourse to the cultural anthropological sphere or a change in categories, these scientists attempted to interpret their ambiguous findings into clear evidence for the inferior state of Australian Aborigines.

## Ludwig Becker's 'well-formed' Aboriginal heads

In the 1850s, the colonial government of Victoria became worried about the welfare and population demise of Australia's original inhabitants.[11] Motivated by humanitarian concerns expressed in the British metropole, it established a Select Committee of the Legislative Council on the Aborigines in 1858 'with the view of endeavouring to ameliorate their present condition'.[12] The Select Committee interviewed government officials, missionaries and other colonists who 'they thought competent to reply' due to their various interests and interactions with Aboriginal people.[13] From these investigations it was concluded that '[t]he great and almost unprecedented reduction in the number of the Aborigines is to be attributed to the general occupation of the country by the white population; to vices acquired by contact with a civilized race, more particularly the indulgence in ardent spirits; and hunger, in consequence of the scarcity of game since the settlement of the Colony; and, also in some cases, to cruelty and ill-treatment'.[14] To alleviate their suffering it recommended the establishment of reserves under the guardianship of missionaries whose tasks included 'to induce the Aborigines to take an interest in the occupations of civilized life'.[15] The report resulted in the creation of the Victorian Board for the Protection of Aborigines.

As Leigh Boucher has noted, the Select Committee 'was as much directed by ethnographic enquiry as it was by humanitarian intervention'.[16] Accordingly, it handed out a questionnaire of eighty-nine questions of which the overwhelming majority related to matters of cultural, intellectual and physical characteristics. The first part, based on fourteen highly suggestive questions about their treatment by and responses to British settler society, related to the living conditions of Aborigines and suggestions as to their betterment. The second part was predominantly concerned with cultural anthropological issues such as Aboriginal linguistics, cultural, religious and political organisation. It also sought information about physical anthropological and anthropometric measurements, experiences with the impact of 'intermixture on physical and moral character' as well as 'intellectual character'.[17] The information supplied in response to this section featured to a minimal degree in the Select Committee's report. According to the Chairman Thomas McCombie, the resulting document should be regarded as an important historical document, 'prized by the learned societies of Europe'[18] who were 'most anxious' to prevent 'the irretrievable loss which science must sustain'[19] through the feared extinction of the Australian Aborigines.

Among those who contributed to the Select Committee's findings were three Germans – the Moravian missionaries Friedrich Wilhelm Spieseke and Friedrich August Hagenauer and the artist, naturalist and explorer Ludwig Becker.[20] One of the 'Forty-Eighters', Becker had arrived in Australia in 1851, making a living from portrait painting and newspaper illustrations. He is probably best remembered for his participation in and death during the ill-fated Burke and Wills Expedition of 1860/61 and his portraits of Aboriginal men and women: namely the 'sympathetic, if sad, representations' of Aboriginal Tasmanians in the deadly reserve of Oyster Cove in 1852, and his 'excellent likeness[es]' of two Aboriginal men from the Australian colony Victoria.[21] As Marjorie Tipping has stated, these miniature paintings reflected his 'compassion for the native people'. Accordingly, he 'portrayed them as flesh and blood human beings with a realism and dignity rarely, if ever, surpassed in colonial likenesses of Aborigines.'[22]

Following his Humboldt-inspired interest in natural history, Becker became an industrious member of Melbourne's scientific community, in particular its Philosophical Institute where he presented papers on a range of natural historical topics, such as zoology, meteorology and anthropology. In December 1856, he presented the nest and eggs of a lyrebird that he had acquired through a transaction with the local Aboriginal people of the Kulin nation.[23] Becker had directly negotiated the collecting of the nest and the gathering of Aboriginal knowledge about the bird with Simon, 'the son of the Yarra tribe chieftain, who, with other chiefs of the country [...] brought the curious land sale with Batman to conclusion'. Becker thought this man 'possess[ed] a higher degree of civilization and intelligence than the rest and [was] looked upon by his tribe as a sort of leader'.[24]

It seems highly probable that Becker here referred to the famous Wurundjeri leader Billibellary and his son (Simon) Wonga.[25] Roughly twenty years earlier, in 1835, the Aboriginal peoples of the Kulin nation, living in today's Melbourne area, encountered a group of British colonisers led by John Batman. Aspiring to secure pastoral land and a new settlement, Batman brought with him a treaty for the 'purchase' of land in exchange for material goods and a yearly rent. This was settled upon by Billibellary and seven other Aboriginal head men, resulting in the only (though contentious and speedily revoked by the colonial government) land treaty ever negotiated in Australia between the Europeans and Indigenous Australians.[26] His son Wonga was present at the time, together with his cousin Barak. Both would become respected indigenous leaders in the political struggle for Aboriginal land rights in the 1850s and 1860s, achieving the establishment of the Aboriginal reserve Corranderk in the wake of the 1858/59 Select Committee's recommendations.[27] By then, Simon Wonga had become head man of his people, following his father's death in 1846. He had witnessed the deterioration of his people's relationships with Europeans: from the infrequent 'well-meaning, confused and violent'[28] encounters of the early 1830s to the ensuing, initially quite amiable, relations between indigenous peoples and colonists around Melbourne, to the violent disruption of Aboriginal ways of life through colonial pastoralism which resulted in fatal frontier wars. As Leigh Boucher has described it, by the late 1850s, the surviving 'decimated communities had been completely terrorised and traumatised by violence and death' and they 'were struggling to find a social and economic space in amongst a settler community that was indifferent at best and hostile at worst'.[29] Europeans now dominated all areas of life in colonial Victoria, appropriating Aboriginal land and its resources while the indigenous population decreased significantly owing to violence, cultural disruption and disease.[30] However, despite their marginal position, Aborigines also negotiated and ascertained a resilient presence in colonial society by, for example, working for farmers and pastoralists.[31]

While it remains unknown when exactly, how often and under which circumstances Becker and Simon Wonga met, it has been documented that in November 1855 Becker stayed at the surveyor-general Andrew Clarke's farm on the Merri Creek.[32] There, people of the different Kulin tribes camped regularly to perform traditional and economic business,[33] such as performing corroborees and selling lyrebird tails to Melburnians.[34] It seems probable, however, that Becker and Simon Wonga met more than once, as Becker's part of the deal was to provide the head man with 'photographic portraits' of himself and 'one of his relations'.[35] Becoming increasingly interested in indigenous people, Becker maintained friendly relations with a number of local Aborigines. He 'was well received by them', being allowed to witness and even sketch some corroborees.[36]

The Philosophical Institute's proceedings from a meeting on 8 September 1858, however, also state that Becker 'exhibited and described some specimens of interest in natural history and the ethnography of Australia [...] illustrated by several aboriginal skulls, shell necklaces, tomahawks and other native weapons, belonging to the true Australian race, the aborigines of Tasmania, New Zealand, New Guinea, and the Feegee Islands'. He used these items to speculate on the genetic relations between the respective peoples, suggesting 'that our own aborigines, in Australia, are of a much higher class than as usually [sic] and wrongly stated in works treating of the same subject'.[37] Only a few weeks later, the Select Committee sent out its questionnaire, addressing Becker presumably on the basis of his portraits of Aborigines and his anthropological engagement at the Philosophical Institute.[38]

Becker answered the Select Committee's questionnaire and was apparently also interviewed in person.[39] He responded to eight of the eighty-nine questions, arguing that alcohol should not be supplied to Aborigines, that he supposed they stole 'impelled by necessity' and that they were 'not below the average intelligence of all other uneducated masses of nations, may they belong to the black, colored or white races of man'.[40] Of the second part, inquiring about the physical condition of Victoria's Aboriginal inhabitants, Becker answered the first five questions. These sought to determine their 'physical characters' such as body measurements, 'any prevailing disproportion between different parts of the body' and craniological information including their assumed phrenological implications, based on 'the corresponding development of moral and intellectual character'.[41] According to Becker, Australian Aborigines were strong, with limbs 'not actually disproportioned' but 'leaner than in the negro race'. Provided with 'sufficient food and shelter during the cold season they improve their external appearance very soon' and, as he admiringly added, their black hair 'when combed and oiled falls in beautiful ringlets down the cheeks and neck'. He had noticed, however, a 'peculiar odor' similar to that supposedly emitted by Africans but not as strong and 'not for want of cleanliness'.[42]

Questions 4 and 5 concerned the investigation of Australian Aboriginal heads and skulls, thoroughly elaborating on the significance of skulls for race determination and even giving instruction on how to obtain craniologically usable measurements and illustrations. The Select Committee was particularly interested in the skulls' long- or round-headedness and the facial profile, including the shapes of the frontal and rear parts of the head (or skull), the position of the head on the neck, 'the advance or recession of the chin' and 'the character of the lips and nose [...] in profile'.[43] All of these implicitly refer to contemporarily common race markers; for instance Peter Camper's 'facial angle' and Anders Retzius's 'cephalic index'. Camper construed the facial angle in the late eighteenth century with the aim of facilitating the drawing of human and animal head profiles. According to the Dutch anatomist and artist, it calculated the angle created by 'a line, drawn along the forehead and the upper lip' and the horizontal line, thereby illustrating the 'national physiognomy' of the different human races.[44] Camper's series started with Europe's contemporaneous epitome of beauty, the head of the classic statue of the ancient Greek god Apollo (100°), followed by those of a European (80°), a 'Kalmuck' (Asian) and an African (both 70°). Although Camper suggested there existed another human race on a fifth continent comprised of the inhabitants of the South Sea islands, New Holland and New Zealand, he did not include it in his series, considering too little was known about it in his times. Camper did not stop at arranging the facial angles of humans but also related the angle of his African skull to those of apes, namely an orang-utan (58°) and a tailed monkey (42°).[45]

The Swedish craniologist Retzius devised his index in the 1840s on the basis of the ratio between skull length and width, differentiating between long-headed (dolichocephalic) and short- or round-headed (brachycephalic) races. He divided each of these further into those with protruding and non-protruding jaws, calling them prognathous and orthognathous races respectively. According to Retzius, this craniometrical method enabled the 'correction' of race classification based on skin colour and/or geographical distribution.[46] For example, instead of grouping dark-skinned Africans with 'Papuans' of similar hue, Retzius classed the former with less dark-skinned 'New Hollanders' as long-headed races while 'Malayans' (usually described as of brown colour) and 'Papuans' belonged to the short-headed races. All of them, however, were unfortunate in having the 'countenance disfiguring feature'[47] of protruding jaws that identified them not only as prognathous but also as 'lower races'. With the form of the forehead seen as being linked to the intellectual capacities of the human brain, these measurements were viewed as testimony regarding the levels of intelligence in human races. As Stephen Jay Gould has aptly termed it, the dictum was 'front is better'; that is, it was supposed that 'higher mental functions were localized in anterior regions of the cortex, and that posterior areas busied themselves with the more mundane, though crucial, roles of involuntary movement, sensation, and emotion. Superior people should have more in the front, less behind'[48] – and the other way round.

Becker's most detailed contribution to the Select Committee's inquiry concerned these craniological questions when he presented portraits of the two young Australian Aboriginal men already mentioned and the illustrations and descriptions of three Aboriginal skulls (which might have been the same presented at the Philosophical Institute meeting three months earlier). The portraits depicted Billy and Tilki (or Jemmy), two young men Becker had met and painted in 1854 when visiting Kulkyne Station on the Murray River.[49] Nothing certain is known about these two young men whose English names were commonly used for Aboriginal people throughout Australia. On the basis of the scarce information Becker provided, Marjorie Tipping has suggested that both men were employed by the Melbourne acting coroner, Richard Youl, at the time. Youl was the licensee of Kulkyne Station, which was located approximately 500 kilometres north-west of Melbourne, within traditional Tati Tati country. Thus, the twenty-year-old Tilki was in all likelihood a Tati Tati man who, as he told Becker, lost part of his thumb in a violent encounter between his people and Thomas Mitchell's exploring expedition in 1836. Billy, who was a strong, tall and broad-chested man with a 'fine manly baritone', and 'a native from Port Fairy', was very likely a Gunditjmara man who, according to Becker, was two years younger than Tilki and had been a member of the native police before he was employed by Youl.[50]

On the basis of their likenesses, representing the 'neatly dressed and well-groomed'[51] individuals in profile, Becker answered the scientific questions about their head shapes. According to his observations, both men presented similar craniological features. Becker described 'jaws, very much projecting; mouth, large' and 'chin, small and receding' but also 'head, well-formed; forehead, rising nearly perpendicular from horizontal'. Whereas Tilki too presented a 'well-formed man's profile', Becker had more to say about his tribe's weapons, language and encounter history.

Turning to the three skulls, one of a young man and two of 'very old' individuals, they all measured the same in their widths and lengths. The juvenile skull of 'King John, a chief of the Adelaide tribe' (possibly Kaurna) was made of strong bones and its skullcap had a 'pyramidal shape, which [Becker] found to be the case with all the native skulls [he] had under examination'. Apart from this 'typical characteristic of the Australian race', Becker elaborated on the 'obliquity of the jaw' which, he thought, was caused by the configuration of the upper jaw ('slants so much forwards') and chin ('falls backwards') so 'that the facial angle is lowered to 85 degrees'. The second skull, belonging to 'a native from Port Phillip district' and thus also of the Kulin nation, exhibited the same facial angle, whereas the third skull of 'a native of the Warnambool tribe', possibly a Gunditjmara man, presented a shorter upper jaw, indicating a lesser degree of prognathism.[52]

A nineteenth-century polymath, Becker appears to have had some knowledge of the physical anthropological literature of the time; or he might just have attempted to meet the Select Committee's craniological requests. In any case, while his descriptions show that he adopted the scientific terminology of physical anthropological investigation, he betrayed his amateurish approach by his statement about the skulls' 'lowered' facial angle – an error instantly picked up by Alexander Ecker in Freiburg, to whom I shall return below. Even though nineteenth-century physical anthropologists often criticised Camper's angle composition and continuously changed its reference points, they generally stayed within his angular craniometrical delineations. That meant a facial angle of eighty-five degrees would by no means have been regarded as 'low'; quite to the contrary, King John's skull would have replaced Camper's European skull on the second-best position following Apollo's facial line.

In view of his evidence before the Select Committee, however, Becker's expertise on Australian Aborigines provides an interesting insight into the simultaneity of racialising and humanist attitudes towards Australia's indigenous peoples. Becker depicted Aboriginal people as individuals, showed respect for their culture and emphasised that they were wrongly treated as a low 'class' of the South Pacific's original inhabitants. As his remark about the level of intelligence among humanity's 'uneducated masses' indicates, he saw intelligence in strikingly modern terms, as a sociological category rather than a racial trait. His earlier comment about his lyrebird nest collector's 'higher degree of civilization and intelligence than the rest' of his tribe may also be interpreted in this vein. At the same time, utilising his portraits (conveniently showing Billy and Tilki in full side view) and skulls, Becker nonetheless engaged with physical anthropological race investigation – accepting its claim of scientific utility and validity for the purposes of the Select Committee's ameliorating intentions. In the case of Tilki, he combined these investigations with cultural observations, whereas he described the skulls as demonstrating 'the peculiar character of the Australian race'. Nevertheless, Becker drew no conclusions from these peculiarities regarding their racial status, mental capacities or state of civilisation.

## Alexander Ecker's surprising superior skeleton of the Australier

As the Select Committee's chairman had hoped, the report found its way into the hands of 'men of learning in Europe'.[53] Among them were the German physical anthropologists Alexander Ecker and Gustav Lucae, who used Becker's evidence in order to support their own physical anthropological investigations of Australian Aboriginal skulls and bones. In 1861, Alexander Ecker published a paper 'on the knowledge about the natives of South Australia',[54] comparing the skeleton of an Australian Aboriginal man with those of an African and a German (as representative of 'the European'). As one of the founding figures of physical anthropology in Germany, the anti-Darwinian Freiburg professor of anatomy considered this study made a significant contribution to the nascent discipline of 'the anatomy of the races'.[55] Based on the measurement of skeletal remains, physical anthropology was designed to collect as much data as possible about human physical diversity. Ecker had already begun to compile a 'special anthropological collection' of skulls and bones sent to him by 'friends and former students who lived in foreign countries'.[56] At the time of his death in 1887 he had amassed around five hundred human skulls.[57]

Two skeletons of a man and a woman from Australia were sent to him in the German summer of 1860, as a 'gift'[58] by Anton Vogt, a former student of Ecker, who worked as a doctor in a small town in South Australia.[59] In his free time, Vogt plundered Aboriginal burial sites near his residence to strengthen his connection with his former professor.[60] One skeleton belonged to a young man who probably died from a fractured skull after he 'had fallen off a cart', and whose remains Vogt 'dug up himself' a few kilometres out of town.[61] The second skeleton resulted from Vogt's neighbourly collaboration with a British colonist, who had informed him about the burial place of a woman behind a bush – as Vogt admiringly noted, her body was 'wrapped in a blanket of possum skins, which the natives' women know to sew beautifully together'. Vogt excavated the not-yet fully decomposed corpse and shipped it to Freiburg.[62] On the basis of his examination of her remaining teeth and her skeleton Ecker suggested that she had suffered from syphilis and died aged around forty years.[63]

Comparing the skeleton of the man with those of an African and a German, Ecker was in for a surprise, which, I suggest, made the Select Committee's report a useful tool for the interpretation of the Aboriginal skeletal remains. Ecker began by emphasising the individuality of each of the skeletons, asserting that 'when I talk here of the Negro or Australian, I do not claim that the circumstances are valid for all Negroes or all inhabitants of mainland Australia'. As Ecker added, the time for generalisations in the science of the 'anatomy of the races' had to be postponed to the future.[64] His introductory individualisation, thus, was not of the same kind as Becker's concern with Aboriginal individuals as living social beings. It resulted from the methodological shift from Blumenbach's description of single representative skulls to the (aspired) statistically based comparison of masses of skeletal remains. For the time being he had to be content, so to speak, with Blumenbachian single specimens for establishing a metric racial scale of Africans, Australians and Europeans.

Ecker examined the skeletons following the new methodological approach of assessing bones in absolute and relative measurements, arranging meticulous lists of numbers that calculated the lengths and thicknesses of the skulls, long bones, hands and feet, hips, spines and teeth; even estimating missing finger bones that Vogt had failed to unearth.[65] The Australian skeleton's arms and legs were not as long as those of the African but still longer than the European's. The arms were also relatively shorter than their own legs whereas the reverse condition applied to the 'Negerscelet'. According to Ecker all of this showed that 'the Negro approximated the ape type' whereas 'regarding the proportions of the extremities [...] the Australian stands closer to the European'. He conceded that this middle position 'as I willingly admit, was a very unexpected one, because the conformation of the skull, as shall be illuminated in the following, assigned the Australian a rather lower stage than the Negro and I would have hoped this character would be expressed in the remaining skeleton'.[66] In other words, Ecker's measurements did not merely describe the skeletons' physical nature but indicated stages in a racial hierarchy. Although he did not explicitly formulate the question from the outset, Ecker expected that the *Australier* stood 'below' allegedly apish Africans. As it turned out, he found that his Australian skeleton's measurements approximated the German's.

On first impression, Ecker's craniological investigation consisted of neutral anatomical statements, but from his comment it appears that he had a clear notion of a 'low' skull's characteristics. He offered no possible meanings of features that he rated as lower than Africans' and those that distanced the *Australier* from the lowest position on the race ladder. Nonetheless, Ecker declared that the Australian skull was the most inferior of the three by emphasising its smallness, lowness and narrowness in combination with its 'extension' between the frontal and rear parts and the facial angle. According to Ecker's measurements the Australian Aboriginal skull's facial angle was 'hardly 70 [degrees]'.[67] Matching Camper's Asian and African angles, this statement hardly needed explanation as Ecker could expect his readers to be knowledgeable about the Camperian facial angle scale. The African's angle of an impressive 80°, however, demanded an explanation. Matching Camper's measure for nearly ideally shaped Europeans, it surely could not have belonged to a 'real' *Neger*. Ecker therefore suggested this skull approached the less prognathous 'skull formation of the Bushmen'[68] (who had a lighter skin and were regarded among anthropologists as presenting more Asian facial features).

In a second step, Ecker linked the facial angle to the degree of prognathism and the shape of the skullcap, referring to the Australian Aboriginal skull's 'narrowness and lowliness, in general the small extension of the forehead'[69] and a flatness of the skull's back. He again did not have to translate these features into presumptions about lower

[ 115 ]

levels of intelligence and civilisation, which were also clearly implied in the Select Committee's questions about Aboriginal skulls and heads. Ecker could count on his colleagues' familiarity with, for example, the brain dissections undertaken in the preceding century by Blumenbach's student and friend Samuel Thomas von Soemmering, who presumed that Europeans' intelligence and culture resulted from the convoluted contents at the front of their skulls. Soemmering claimed they had larger brains that required straight, extensive foreheads with a rounded transition to the rear.[70] In contrast, 'in the Moor the transition from the back of the head to the spine is hollowed out flatter, less deep, than in us, just as if something is deduced from the brain-containing skull towards the rear; this is the case to a much stronger degree in the ape'.[71] Linking human brain and skull features to different levels of intelligence and civilisation, he went on to posit clearly unanatomical remarks on Africans' alleged low mental capacity that only reinforced the very biases he claimed to interrogate in his quest against African slavery in the Americas.[72]

While Ecker refrained from such explicit statements, I argue that his emphasis on particular skull features positioned the *Australier* on the lowest stage of humanity both physically and intellectually. The 'particularly noticeable limited development of the forehead'[73] of the *Australier* skull, for example, indicated a smaller size of the frontal lobe and, therefore, a lower level of intelligence and civilisation. At the same time, he understated a number of features that could have disputed the lower ranking, such as the lack of 'the significant thickness of the skull bones generally regarded as characteristic for the Australian race'. Ecker eschewed damaging the skull by sawing it apart, but he discovered that the Aboriginal man's skull injury allowed him to conveniently measure its 'not unusual' thickness.[74] The thinner bone however, according to Ecker's standards, would have placed the Australian skull closer to the European's.

If the interpretational tension created by the skeleton's 'superiority' and the skull's 'inferiority' appeared unresolvable by Ecker's metric investigation, the Victorian Select Committee's report offered a way to interpret his disparate findings. Finding the measurements provided by the report 'scanty',[75] Ecker nevertheless used it, albeit selectively, to add weight to the overall inferiority indicated by the Australian skull. This becomes clear in his partly summarising, partly translating references to the report. Especially with regard to Australian Aboriginal skulls, Ecker cited Becker but simply ignored the discrepancies between Becker's descriptions and his own investigation.

Citing his compatriot, Ecker turned Becker's description of Billy's and Tilki's heads as 'long and narrow, the forehead rising nearly perpendicular, jaw very protruding' into a general statement about Australian Aboriginal heads. He reiterated that their heads were 'well formed', although Billy's and Tilki's foreheads did not compare to the receding flattened foreheads Ecker described for his Australian skulls.[76] While Ecker made no comment about this discrepancy, he did detect Becker's seemingly incongruent facial angle measure. In his nearly verbatim translation of Becker's description of King John's skull, he highlighted the passage about the skullcap and the upper jaws, putting a conspicuous question mark behind Becker's facial angles: 'only 85° (?)'.[77] Again he did not comment further, but his questioning can be interpreted in two ways that do not necessarily contradict one another. He might have simply questioned either Becker's interpretation of the measure as a 'low' angle and/or the accuracy of a low-ranking *Australier* skull with a 'high' facial angle.

Whether Becker got it wrong, or Ecker could simply not imagine straight Australian faces, remains unclear. More importantly, although Becker pointed to the skulls' jaw and chin shapes as signs of a protruding facial profile he did not link it to the forehead conformation or its content. Ecker omitted Becker's statements about Aboriginal intelligence, but reported on a number of different opinions regarding 'the Australians' mental disposition', ranging from 'a very low stage on the intelligence scale' to equality with European intellectual capacities. On the basis of the Select Committee's conclusive remarks, he also differentiated between sufficiently developed perceptive skills (such as memory, mimicking, senses for language, hearing and location), 'little capacity for moral instruction and scientific education' and a number of statements about religion and other cultural practices that 'without a doubt assigns them a lower stage in relation to other natural peoples'.[78] In the conclusion of his investigation, Ecker perpetuated the committee's view that 'the influence of the Europeans on the black race can be regarded as destructive'.[79] He added, however, to the trope of the looming extinction of Australia's indigenous peoples, putting the blame on them for 'learning' only the European vices and losing their 'feeling for independence'. Furthermore, according to Ecker, it was the Australian Aborigines who 'regard[ed] the Whites as a higher, and themselves as a doomed lower race'. In conclusion he emphasised the rhetorical question 'some observers' asked as to 'whether it was desirable and worth the effort, to undertake steps to prolong the existence of such a race?'[80]

In contradistinction to Becker, it seems that for Ecker the supposed lowly racial status of Australian Aborigines justified calling into question their future existence, which was quite at odds with what the Select Committee had in mind with their recommendation for a reservation to preserve the remaining population. In whichever way Ecker would have answered that question, his usage of the committee's accumulation of statements, including Becker's, made it possible to align the irregularly 'higher' skeleton with the typical 'low' skull.

### Gustav Lucae's Australian glue brains

At the same time as Ecker, Johann Christian Gustav Lucae also undertook research on Australian Aboriginal skeletal remains. A prolific member of the local scientific society, the Frankfurt anatomist and craniologist is remembered mainly as the inventor of a geometric drawing device, the *Lucae'scher Orthograph*. This instrument was one of a variety of apparatuses developed with the aim of transforming 'ethnographic craniology'[81] into a standardised natural scientific discipline that would progress beyond Blumenbach's and Camper's merely descriptive insights. Projecting three-dimensional physical objects on to flat paper, Lucae anticipated that it depicted 'the truth and the reality'[82] of skull and brain characteristics, making them measurable and comparable.[83] Drawings of skull profiles created by such devices were then used to determine hierarchical facial angles that far superseded Camper's categorisations.[84]

In 1861, Lucae used six Australian Aboriginal skulls to intervene in the contemporary discussion about the best calculation of the facial angle, or the 'indeed well-founded differentiation of skulls in prognathous and orthognathous'.[85] He suggested its determination comprised the investigation of three regions of the skull; namely the facial profile, the size and shape of the forehead, and the brain as the latter's shaping agent. As representatives of the facial angle 'in the most extreme skull forms of the so-called lowest and highest human races', Lucae chose the Aboriginal skulls and ten European skulls for comparison. The latter were a collection of more or less famous and infamous Germans such as the Romantic 'genial poet' Johann Jacob Wilhelm Heinse, the poet and philosopher Friedrich Schiller, a man named Schumacher (who 'murdered the judge and injured several judicial clerks out of mean vindictiveness') and three unnamed men identified only by their collection numbers, plus one Hessian woman.[86] I shall not analyse Lucae's use of these German skulls in detail, but he probably mixed the skulls of convicted criminals with highly esteemed 'interesting personalities'[87] as signifiers for respectively 'lower' and 'higher' brain and face development. However, correlations of German social standing with skull and brain configurations did not show in Lucae's measurements, and, if he expected to find a correlation between 'low' German skulls and Australian Aboriginal skulls, he would have been disappointed. In fact, the acclaimed poet Heinse's skull, for example, according to this criterion presented quite unfavourable traits, whereas the murderer Schumacher turned out to have the best shape.[88]

The Australian Aboriginal skulls had been plundered from their burial sites and sent as scientific donations by Karl Ludwig Wilhelm Kirchner. The merchant, immigration agent and German consul in Sydney provided some information about the individuals they had belonged to. Dug up on one of his properties next to the Clarence River in the colony of New South Wales, they belonged to a woman who was 'Babys Mutter' and five men. According to Lucae, the woman's skull showed 'destruction by syphilis' and two of the men, 'Jomey' and 'Billey', had been 'killed in battle'.[89]

Lucae was uninterested in the skulls as indicators of their bearers' lives and deaths. He simply declared them as representative of the *Australneger* as they 'very much match[ed] the descriptions and illustrations of other authors' such as Blumenbach and 'Herr Ludwig Becker' who 'provided [the Select Committee] with a few very splendid pictures of the New Hollanders', namely Becker's skull illustrations. Citing almost Becker's entire notes on the skulls, Lucae was particularly interested in that of 'King John'. Representing, as Becker had stated, 'the peculiar character of the Australean [*sic*] race' it was a 'companion piece' to Lucae's skull no. XXII 10, or Jomey's skull.[90] Establishing the typicality of his Australian specimens, Lucae (like Ecker) additionally invoked the ape imagery. Without claiming it as his own, he cited some of his Anglophone colleagues, such as the American James Aitken Meigs,[91] who thought of one Australian Aboriginal skull as 'a truly animal head' whose upper jaw 'almost degenerates into a muzzle', and the English naturalist William Charles Linnaeus Martin who contended that Aboriginal eyebrows 'remind [...] us of some of the larger Apes'.[92]

The 'material' remains themselves, however, proved stubborn, presenting 'conspicuous individual differences'.[93] Lucae saw instantly that 'the prognathous form [was] by no means equally strong developed' in all of his Australian skulls, ranging from 'nearly orthognathous' to 'the highest degree of prognathism'.[94] Similarly, forward-jutting jaws were manifest in his European sample.[95] Proposing to include the curvature of the forehead in relation to a vertical line, against which to measure the facial angle, he hoped that 'maybe thereby measurements will emerge that approximate the truth and correspond with reality more'.[96] In other words, Lucae established the 'reality' of Australian prognathism by, first, insisting on their forward-jutting jaws despite his contrary findings, and then 'correcting' the measurement parameters so as to 'truly' represent this adjusted reality.

As a result, Lucae compiled a table 'that on the whole very truly follow[ed] nature's conditions'.[97] In fact, however, nature still showed that there were variations in both European and Australian skull shapes: a number of Australian foreheads 'approximat[ed] the most perfect of the Europeans' and some of the European jaws 'adjoin[ed] the least prognathous of the Australians'.[98] He subsumed these individual variations under the racial categories established from the outset of his study. Accordingly, 'the maximum forehead expansion occur[red] in our Europeans, but the maximum of the jaws in the Australians'.[99] Additionally, 'the pro- and orthognathism of a skull is not always based on the absolute size of the forehead or the jaw, but in a correlation between forehead and jaw; because we see skulls with a favourable forehead conformation become prognathous through a more protruding jaw, and less favourable forehead shapes gain an orthognathous conformation by a less protruding jaw'.[100] In effect, Lucae levelled out the individual variations through this change of parameter, re-evaluating heterogeneous human remains so that they remained within their racial 'type'.

Consequently, it becomes clear that, to preserve the paradigmatic assumptions underlying his investigation, Lucae's 'lower race' needed to be intricately linked with 'lower' skull features. According to these assumptions, the size and shape of the foreheads pointed directly to the quantity, and thus the mental quality, of the organ that formed them. Lucae and his colleagues thus appeared convinced that the sizes of European skull cavities were the direct result of their larger frontal lobes. Additionally, argued Lucae, the curvatures of the more and less favourable foreheads of Europeans and Australians were highly significant for the determination of the facial angle.

Interested in the 'interior skull surface of race heads', he investigated the skull-shaping forces of the brain by creating gluey models, mocking those who 'reject[ed] a simple means of gaining a rich lesson, in order to not damage the precious relic-like skull'.[101] Contrary to Ecker, he had no qualms about cutting through skulls in order to 'go directly' to 'the core', using the two skull halves as moulds to make 'a substitute for the missing brain'[102] for its capacity estimation. Made from dehydrated glue, these cerebral models could be weighed, measured and drawn, both in their entirety and in their different parts. They were thereby made comparable for the determination of their metric (and intellectual) volumes and, when drawn with his *Orthograph*, also supplied even more reliable data than the original natural brains that were lost to science. Or so Lucae claimed, who consistently referred to his models simply as 'brains'.[103]

Comparing his glue brain models, Lucae extended his link between forehead and jaw line to the interior of the skull, thereby anatomically correlating mental capacity (signified by the size and position of the frontal lobe) to the facial angle. Again, nature demonstrated the individuality of human anatomy as Lucae recorded 'plenty of differences' among the Australian brain models. He had to admit, however, 'not without some disconcertion' that there were brain shapes similar to those of the Australians in the European sample.[104] I suggest that, because the glue brains of Australians and Europeans were on the whole quite similar, Lucae had to clarify that 'for a well-developed forehead apart from the height the protruding of the middle and upper regions of the frontal lobe is of particular importance'. This specification allowed him to state 'that the entire profile of the frontal lobe lies in the Europeans more to the front, but in the Australians more to the rear'.[105] The latter's glue brains' rear region was larger than the former's, indicating the dominance of what Gould has termed the 'mundane' brain functions, and, consequently, less developed intellectual properties.[106] As a result, Lucae claimed, European brains sat above the eye sockets whereas Australian brains were stuck 'in the face', 'sunk between the eye cavities, even beneath the cheekbone'.[107]

## Conclusion

These case studies have examined the way German physical anthropologists of the mid-nineteenth century investigated the skeletal remains of Australian Aborigines. As their attempts to determine and interpret the 'facial angle' show, the notion of 'the low ranking Australian' was prevalent in their minds prior to the first Aboriginal skeletal remains even arriving in their dissecting rooms. In fact, these long-existent ideas of the 'savage' nature of Australia's original peoples were the reason for appropriating their remains in the first place.

In the event, these remains proved to be stubborn evidence for the dominant paradigm which taught the savagery of the Australian Aborigine. Confronted with the individuality of human anatomy, neither Alexander Ecker nor Gustav Lucae took up those parts of Becker's testimony that added complexity to the picture, as well as a sense of his experience of having lived alongside Indigenous Australians (and not just having inspected their remains), and instead developed strategies that allowed them to arrive at the outcome they seem to have anticipated from the outset of their investigations. To varying degrees, both prefaced their own investigations by invoking ape analogies that had long existed about Africans and were now extended to Australian Aborigines. Despite his initial claim to investigate individuals, Ecker could not accommodate their physical individuality without harmonising the perceived discrepancy between a 'higher' skeleton and its 'lower' skull. He turned to the Select Committee's colonial narrative to establish the lower state of his *Australier*, including Becker's evidence but ignoring his contradictory statements. In order to make sense of his inconclusive investigation, Ecker selectively consulted the report's information about Australian Aboriginal cultural and mental disposi- tions. To him it did not matter whether this source expressed more optimistic views, such as those of Becker, that regarded the behaviour and position of Australia's colonised peoples as a sociological rather than a natural aspect of their lives.

So too, Lucae would not accept that there were individual variations at work when his Aboriginal and German skulls presented more and less forward-projecting facial profiles and rounded foreheads. Far from raising doubts about the premises of his examination, he simply altered the parameters and referred to Becker's craniological contribution to the Select Committee's inquiry. Unlike Ecker, however, Lucae omitted Becker's statements about Aboriginal intelligence and their social condition altogether. His implicit assessment of Aboriginal intellectual capacity resulted from his manipulative investigation and interpretation of Aboriginal skulls and glue brains.

In view of this attitudinal discrepancy between the naturalist German 'on Australian ground' and those in the distant anthropologi- cal institutions of Germany, the humanist reputation of the German anthropological tradition needs to be qualified. Becker's Humboldtian humanist approach did indeed enable him to see Aboriginal people as individual humans in a specific historical and social setting. This might have led him to refrain from linking the 'typical' craniological characteristics he thought to have discovered to their intellectual capacity or potential. It, nevertheless, did not prevent him from acquiring and measuring Aboriginal skulls or from using his sympathetic portraits of Billy and Tilki as racial representations.

Whereas Becker seems to have engaged in these dehumanising inves- tigations in the belief this would contribute to the 'amelioration' of the living conditions of Australia's colonised peoples, Ecker and Lucae had no interest in the living individuals whose remains they investigated, other than as representatives of their 'race'. As first-generation physi- cal anthropologists in Germany, they claimed to be committed to a fact-gathering approach. Further, they sought to separate the physical from the cultural and mental spheres of investigation, even though their reading of the physical evidence before them was largely driven by cultural assumptions. Harbouring deeply ingrained views of Aboriginal 'savageness', they complied with none of the tenets of objectivity in their investigations of the first Aboriginal skeletal remains to arrive in Germany since the time of Blumenbach.

# Notes

1   I would like to thank the editors of this collection for their kind feedback on the early draft of this chapter. I am very grateful to the peer reviewers whose insightful suggestions significantly contributed to the improvement of this piece. All translations from German to English are my own.

2   M. Tipping, 'Ludwig Becker and Eugène von Guérard: German Artists and the Aboriginal Habitat', in J. Tampke and D. Walker (eds), *From Berlin to the Burdekin: The German Contribution to the Development of Australian Science, Exploration and the Arts* (Kensington: New South Wales University Press, 1991), pp. 81–107; D. Dodd, 'The Aboriginal Contribution to the Expedition, Observed through Germanic Eyes', in I.D. Clark and F. Cahir (eds), *The Aboriginal Story of Burke and Wills: Forgotten Narratives* (Collingwood, Vic: CSIRO Publishing, 2013), pp. 81–108.

3   H.G. Penny and M. Bunzl (eds), *Worldly Provincialism: German Anthropology in the Age of Empire* (Ann Arbor: University of Michigan Press, 2003); B. Massin, 'From Virchow to Fischer. Physical Anthropology and "Modern Race Theories" in Wilhelmine Germany', in G.W. Stocking Jr (ed.), *Volksgeist as Method and Ethic: Essays on Boasian Ethnography and the German Anthropological Tradition* (Madison: University of Wisconsin Press, 1996), pp. 79–158; A.D. Evans, 'A Liberal Paradigm? Race and Ideology in Late-Nineteenth-Century German Physical Anthropology', *Ab Imperio* 8:1 (2007), 113–38.

4   Johann Friedrich Blumenbach to Joseph Banks, 1 May 1795 (Letter 903) in F. Dougherty, *The Correspondence of Johann Friedrich Blumenbach*, Vol. 5: 1791–1795, Letters 645–965. Rev., aug., ed. by N. Klatt (Gottingen: Norbert Klatt Verlag, 2012), p. 395; see also J. Gascoigne, *Joseph Banks and the English Enlightenment: Useful Knowledge and Polite Culture* (Cambridge: Cambridge University Press, 1994), p. 154.

5   R. Bernasconi, 'Kant and Blumenbach's Polyps: A Neglected Chapter in the History of the Concept of Race', in S. Eigen and M. Larrimore (eds), *The German Invention of Race* (New York: State University of New York Press, 2006), pp. 73–90. See also my analysis of Blumenbach's investigation of the *Neuholländer* skulls, A. Kühnast, 'Racialising Bones and Humanity. The Scientific Abuse of Australian Aboriginal Human Remains in Nineteenth-Century German Physical Anthropology', in I. Wigger and S. Ritter (eds), *Racism and Modernity* (Berlin: LIT Verlag, 2011), pp. 162–78.

6   P. Turnbull, 'Ancestors Not Specimens: Reflections on the Controversy over the Remains of Aboriginal People in European Scientific Collections', *Electronic Journal of Australian and New Zealand History*, www.jcu.edu.au/aff//history/articles/turnbull.htm (Article publ. 4 July 1997, 18 pages); C. Fforde, 'English Collections of Human Remains, an Introduction', *World Archaeological Bulletin* 6 (1992), 1–4; C. Fforde, *Collecting the Dead: Archaeology and the Reburial Issue* (London: Duckworth, 2004).

7   A. Ecker, *Hundert Jahre einer Freiburger Professoren-Familie. Biographische Aufzeichnungen* (Freiburg im Breisgau, Akademische Verlagsbuchhandlung J.C.B. Mohr, 1886), p. 116.

8   As Andrew Zimmerman has convincingly argued, the discipline was also established as a decidedly antihumanist science. A. Zimmerman, *Anthropology and Antihumanism in Imperial Germany* (Chicago: University of Chicago Press, 2001).

9   T.A. Darragh, 'Ludwig Becker, a Scientific Dilettante: His Correspondence with J.J. Kaup and Others', *Historical Records of Australian Science* 11:4 (December 1997), 501–22, here 507–8.

10  See e.g. Evans, 'A Liberal Paradigm', and Massin, 'From Virchow to Fischer'.

11  L. Boucher, 'The 1869 Aborigines Protection Act: Vernacular Ethnography and the Governance of Aboriginal Subjects', in L. Boucher and L. Russell (eds), *Settler Colonial Governance in Nineteenth-Century Victoria* (Canberra: Australian National University Press, 2015), pp. 63–94, here pp. 69–72.

12  *Report of the Select Committee of the Legislative Council on the Aborigines* (Melbourne: John Ferres Government Printer, 1859), p. 25.

13 *Report of Select Committee*, p. v.
14 *Report of Select Committee*, p. iii.
15 *Report of Select Committee*, p. v.
16 Boucher, '1869 Aborigines Protection Act', p. 90.
17 *Report of Select Committee*, p. 48.
18 *Report of Select Committee*, p. v.
19 *Report of Select Committee*, p. 25.
20 The biographical information on Becker is based on Tipping, 'Becker and Guérard', and M. Tipping, *Ludwig Becker: Artist & Naturalist with the Burke & Wills Expedition* (Carlton: Melbourne University Press, 1979).
21 Tipping, 'Becker and Guérard', pp. 87, 90. See also G. Coslovich, 'Rare Portraits of Tasmanian Aborigines up for Sale', *The Age* (16 May 2011), www.theage.com.au/victoria/rare-portraits-of-tasmanian-aborigines-up-for-sale-20110515-1eoah.html; I.D. Clarke, 'The Members of the Victorian Exploring Expedition and Their Prior Experience of Aboriginal Peoples', in Clark and Cahir (eds) *The Aboriginal Story*, pp. 15–46, here p. 26.
22 M. Tipping, 'Becker's Portraits of Billy and Jemmy (Tilki)', *La Trobe Library Journal* 6:21 (April 1978), 1–7, here 1.
23 L. Becker, 'The Nest, Egg, and Young of the Lyrebird (Menura Superba)', *Transactions of the Philosophical Institute of Victoria*, 1 (1857), 153–4.
24 Becker, 'Nest of the Lyrebird', 153.
25 According to Presland, the Kulin 'confederacy' consisted of four tribes. The Wurundjeri are a clan of the Woiworung 'who claimed the area drained by the Yarra River and its tributaries'. G. Presland, *The Land of the Kulin: Discovering the Lost Landscape and the First People of Port Phillip* (Fitzroy: McPhee Gribble Publishers, 1985), pp. 25, 28.
26 R. Broome, *Aboriginal Victorians: A History since 1800* (Crows Nest: Allen & Unwin, 2005), pp. 10–11, 13; A.G.L. Shaw, *A History of the Port Phillip District Victoria before Separation* (Carlton: Melbourne University Press, 2006), pp. 46–8.
27 Broome, *Aboriginal Victorians*, p. 34; S. Furphy, '"They formed a little family as it were": The Board for the Protection of Aborigines (1875–1883)', in Boucher and Russell, *Settler Colonial Governance*, pp. 95–116, here pp. 97–8.
28 Broome, *Aboriginal Victorians*, p. 14.
29 Boucher, '1869 Aborigines Protection Act', p. 69.
30 Broome, *Aboriginal Victorians*, chapters 1–6.
31 Broome, *Aboriginal Victorians*, pp. 111–13.
32 Ludwig Becker to Johann Jakob Kaup, 14 November 1855, transl. and publ. by Darragh, 'Ludwig Becker', 517–18. As only four pages of this letter survived it remains unknown if Becker mentioned anything relating to Aborigines.
33 Broome, *Aboriginal Victorians*, pp. 104–6, 109.
34 Broome, *Aboriginal Victorians*, pp. 20, 104.
35 Becker, 'Nest of the Lyrebird', 153. See also J. Lydon, 'Photographing Kooris: Photography and Exchange in Victoria', in J. Lydon (ed.), *Calling the Shots: Aboriginal Photographies* (Canberra: Aboriginal Studies Press, 2014), pp. 103–30, here p. 111.
36 Tipping, *Ludwig Becker*, pp. 19–20.
37 'Proceedings of the Ordinary Meeting 18th December, 1856', *Transactions of the Philosophical Institute of Victoria* 3 (1859), xxi.
38 As Tipping has noted, Becker was 'one of the few qualified to make any scientific analysis' of the Aborigines' conditions. Tipping, 'Becker and Guérard', p. 92. Dodd has characterised Becker's contribution to the the meeting on 8 September 1858 as '[p]erhaps his most significant presentation at the Philosophical Institute's meetings'. Dodd, 'Germanic Eyes', p. 86.
39 Tipping, 'Becker and Guérard', p. 92.
40 *Report of Select Committee*, p. 82.
41 *Report of Select Committee*, p. 46.
42 *Report of Select Committee*, p. 82.
43 *Report of Select Committee*, p. 46.

44  P. Camper, trans. T. Cogan, *The Works of the Late Professor Petrus Camper on the Connexion between the Science of Anatomy and the Arts of Drawing, Painting, Statuary* (London: C. Dilly, 1794), p. 9. See also Fforde, *Collecting the Dead*, p. 11. On Camper's 'discovery of the facial angle' see M.C. Meijer, *Race and Aesthetics in the Anthropology of Petrus Camper (1722–1789)* (Amsterdam: Rodopi, 1999), pp. 105–9.
45  Meijer, *Race and Aesthetics*, pp. 106–8.
46  A. Retzius, 'Ueber die Schädelformen der Nordbewohner', *Archiv für Anatomie, Physiologie und wissenschaftliche Medicin* (1845), 48–129, here 87.
47  Retzius, 'Schädelformen der Nordbewohner', 86.
48  S.J. Gould, *The Mismeasure of Man* (New York: Norton, 1996), p. 129.
49  Tipping, *Ludwig Becker*, p. 90.
50  *Report of Select Committee*, p. 88. Tipping has questioned this on the basis of his young age when the native police was disbanded in 1852. Tipping, 'Becker's Portraits', p. 7 n. 4.
51  Tipping, 'Becker's Portraits', 1.
52  *Report of Select Committee*, 88.
53  *Report of Select Committee*, 25.
54  A. Ecker, 'Zur Kenntnis der Eingebornen Südaustraliens', *Berichte über die Verhandlungen der Naturforschenden Gesellschaft zu Freiburg im Breisgau* 22–4 (May–June 1861), 337–52, 353–68, 369–79.
55  Ecker, 'Kenntnis der Eingebornen Südaustraliens', 337.
56  Ecker, *Freiburger Professoren-Familie*, p. 116.
57  D. Möller, *Die Geschichte der Anthropologischen Sammlung Freiburg. Entstehung, Zusammenführung, Verlust* (Marburg: Tectum Verlag, 2015), p. 14.
58  A. Ecker, '3. Freiburg i. B. Catalog der Anthropologischen Sammlungen der Universität. Nach dem Stande vom 1. April 1878', in H. Schaaffhausen (ed.), *Die anthropologischen Sammlungen Deutschlands*, Vol. 3 (Braunschweig: Vieweg & Sohn, 1880), p. 6.
59  Ecker, 'Kenntnis der Eingebornen Südaustraliens', 337. See also D. Möller, 'Die Alexander-Ecker-Sammlung in Freiburg', in H. Stoecker, T. Schnalke and A. Winkelmann (eds), *Sammeln, Forschen, Zurückgeben? Menschliche Gebeine aus der Kolonialzeit in akademischen und musealen Sammlungen* (Berlin: Ch. Links, 2013), pp. 106–20, here pp. 116–17.
60  Ecker, 'Kenntnis der Eingebornen Südaustraliens', 337.
61  Ecker, 'Kenntnis der Eingebornen Südaustraliens', 339–40, 350, 360.
62  Ecker, 'Kenntnis der Eingebornen Südaustraliens', 359–60.
63  Ecker, 'Kenntnis der Eingebornen Südaustraliens', 354–7.
64  Ecker, 'Kenntnis der Eingebornen Südaustraliens', 338n.
65  Ecker, 'Kenntnis der Eingebornen Südaustraliens', 341.
66  Ecker, 'Kenntnis der Eingebornen Südaustraliens', 345.
67  Ecker, 'Kenntnis der Eingebornen Südaustraliens', 351.
68  Ecker, 'Kenntnis der Eingebornen Südaustraliens', 351n.
69  Ecker, 'Kenntnis der Eingebornen Südaustraliens', 348.
70  S.T. Soemmering, *Über die körperliche Verschiedenheit des Mohren vom Europäer* (Mainz, 1784), pp. 11–12.
71  Soemmering, *Körperliche Verschiedenheit des Mohren*, p. 8.
72  Soemmering, *Körperliche Verschiedenheit des Mohren*, p. 24. See also G. Lilienthal, 'Samuel Thomas Soemmering und seine Vorstellungen über Rassenunterschiede', in G. Mann and F. Dumont (eds), *Die Natur des Menschen. Probleme der Physischen Anthropologie und Rassenkunde (1750–1850)* (Stuttgart: Gustav Fischer Verlag, 1990), pp. 31–55, here p. 38.
73  Ecker, 'Kenntnis der Eingebornen Südaustraliens', 349.
74  Ecker, 'Kenntnis der Eingebornen Südaustraliens', 350.
75  Ecker, 'Kenntnis der Eingebornen Südaustraliens', 362.
76  Ecker, 'Kenntnis der Eingebornen Südaustraliens', 364.
77  Ecker, 'Kenntnis der Eingebornen Südaustraliens', 365.

78    Ecker, 'Kenntnis der Eingebornen Südaustraliens', 368.

79    Ecker, 'Kenntnis der Eingebornen Südaustraliens', 374.

80    Ecker, 'Kenntnis der Eingebornen Südaustraliens', 375.

81    G. Lucae, 'Zur Morphologie der Rassen-Schädel. Einleitende Bemerkungen und Beiträge. Ein Sendschreiben an ... den Akademiker Carl Ernst v. Baer in St. Petersburg', *Abhandlungen der Senckenbergischen Gesellschaft, Frankfurt am Main* 3 (1861), 483–535, here 499.

82    Lucae, 'Morphologie der Rassen-Schädel', 521.

83    Lucae, 'Morphologie der Rassen-Schädel', 485–98. See also C. Hanke, *Zwischen Auflösung und Fixierung. Zur Konstitution von 'Rasse' und 'Geschlecht' in der physischen Anthropologie um 1900* (Bielefeld: Transcript, 2007), pp. 191–2, and Zimmerman, *Anthropology and Antihumanism*, pp. 99–107.

84    Hanke, *Zwischen Auflösung und Fixierung*, p. 193.

85    Lucae, 'Morphologie der Rassen-Schädel', 520.

86    Lucae, 'Morphologie der Rassen-Schädel', 535–6. On the inclusion of Heinse's and Schiller's skulls into hagiographical celebrations of famous people, see M. Hagner, 'Skulls, Brains, and Memorial Culture: On Cerebral Biographies of Scientists in the Nineteenth Century', *Science in Context* 16:1–2 (June 2003), 195–218.

87    Lucae, 'Morphologie der Rassen-Schädel', 523.

88    Lucae, 'Morphologie der Rassen-Schädel', 514, 523.

89    Lucae, 'Morphologie der Rassen-Schädel', 535.

90    Lucae, 'Morphologie der Rassen-Schädel', 508–9.

91    On Meigs, see A. Fabian, *The Skull Collectors. Race, Science, and America's Unburied Dead* (Chicago: University of Chicago Press, 2010), pp. 128–30.

92    J. A. Meigs, *Catalogue of Human Crania in the Collection of the Academy of Natural Sciences of Philadelphia* (Philadelphia: J.B. Lippincott & Co, 1857), p. 96. and W.C. Linnaeus Martin, *A general introduction to the natural history of mammiferous animals, with a particular view of the physical history of Man, and the more closely allied genera of the order quadrumana, or monkeys* (London: Wright and Co. Printers, 1841), p. 312. Both cited by Lucae, 'Morphologie der Rassen-Schädel', 509.

93    Lucae, 'Morphologie der Rassen-Schädel', 511.

94    Lucae, 'Morphologie der Rassen-Schädel', 508.

95    Lucae, 'Morphologie der Rassen-Schädel', 524.

96    Lucae, 'Morphologie der Rassen-Schädel', 521.

97    Lucae, 'Morphologie der Rassen-Schädel', 523.

98    Lucae, 'Morphologie der Rassen-Schädel', 523–4.

99    Lucae, 'Morphologie der Rassen-Schädel', 523.

100   Lucae, 'Morphologie der Rassen-Schädel', 524.

101   Lucae, 'Morphologie der Rassen-Schädel', 500.

102   Lucae, 'Morphologie der Rassen-Schädel', 500, 502.

103   Lucae, 'Morphologie der Rassen-Schädel', 502–3.

104   Lucae, 'Morphologie der Rassen-Schädel', 513.

105   Lucae, 'Morphologie der Rassen-Schädel', 526.

106   Lucae, 'Morphologie der Rassen-Schädel', 514.

107   Lucae, 'Morphologie der Rassen-Schädel', 526.

# CHAPTER SEVEN

# 'Scientific tourism': colonialism in the photographs and letters of the young cosmopolitan Carl Heinrich Becker, 1900–2

Ulf Morgenstern

At the turn of the twentieth century the German orientalist scholar and later politician Carl Heinrich Becker (1876–1933) undertook a voyage to the north of Africa. The young man had already visited England, France, Italy and Spain as well as Switzerland and the Netherlands, the country of his birth. In 1900, the twenty-four-year-old Becker became heir to the fortune his father and grandfather had made from importing coffee from the Dutch East Indies to the Netherlands and, more importantly, selling coffee from there to the prosperous German Confederation.[1] Within a few decades around the middle of the nineteenth century they found themselves – despite being Germans – among the most important traders, speculators, bankers and bourgeois patrons of the Netherlands. Their assets allowed them to retire from business and to return to Germany in the 1880s. The townhouses in Amsterdam's exclusive Herengracht were sold and the family moved back to their home country in Hesse.

Besides a mansion in Frankfurt, a huge country residence built in 1863 in the nearby town of Gelnhausen as a summer resort became the centre of the family life.[2] It was in this villa that Becker, later known as the founder of modern Islamic studies (*Islamwissenschaften*) and as the liberal left-wing Prussian Minister of Culture and Education in the Weimar Republic, grew up. Rural Gelnhausen was also where his mother received his letters while he studied Theology and Oriental Languages in Lausanne, Heidelberg and Berlin,[3] as well as the place where he sent his correspondence while on his rambling overseas journeys.[4] These letters sent from his travels that took him to Morocco, Egypt, Sudan, Greece, Syria and Palestine between November 1900 and August 1902 are preserved in his (rarely used) personal papers in the Prussian

Privy State Archives.[5] Scholars from Arabic and Oriental studies have sporadically worked with them, mostly to illustrate the early scientific interests of the later professor.[6] None of these authors, however, has examined the nearly five hundred letters completely, and none of them has read them as what they are: impressive sources of the German *haute bourgeoisie* travelling through the colonies of other European powers. Moreover, they are fantastic sources for the study of the colonial *and* scientific interests of a young scholar from Germany's wealthy elite who at his own expense was – in German academic terms – on a two-year sabbatical between *Promotion* and *Habilitation*.

There are three reasons why the vast material has not been closely analysed. The first is its sheer volume, and the second is that later chapters of Becker's life seemed more interesting. His initial work in establishing Islamic studies, for example, meant nothing less than an early 'cultural turn' during the era of German colonialism around 1910. For other scholars, the study of the later Minister Becker has proved more appealing. As the famous head of German cultural politics and a sympathetic left-wing elder statesman, Becker was well acquainted with prominent figures of the 1920s and has often been seen fundamentally as a source for understanding the turbulent Weimar period.[7] Thirdly, the piles of private letters and photographs that are still in private ownership (some of which are studied here) have simply not been available to the public before. Just as Becker's biography, which has not yet been satisfactorily written,[8] could not begin without his gentrified and sophisticated family background, so too the life of Germany's first professor of 'History and Culture of the Middle East' cannot be written without due emphasis on these early and intensive practical experiences of Islamic Africa.

Generally speaking, the 'Africa expert' Becker appears occasionally in the literature on the Colonial Institute in Hamburg,[9] which was founded in 1908 and later became the nucleus of the University of Hamburg. In his five years there, Becker developed into an influential scholar within a burgeoning field of research. He was in close contact with international colleagues in his subject as well as with the traders of Hamburg who financed the institute. Besides these involvements in science and commerce, Becker was part of political networks, such as the leading figures of the Deutscher Kolonialverein, and maintained formal contact with foreign politicians in Berlin with their own interests in the academic exploration of the German colonies and their neighbouring territories. As Alexander Haridi has remarked, Becker 'devised the right concept at the right time and in the right place'.[10]

Haridi has also argued that Becker convinced the key circles in Hamburg and Berlin that 'colonial policy was, at its core, policy on

Islam'.[11] Haridi has further explained why there was such a great interest in a new scientific approach towards the Muslims in German colonies, with their respective cultures, history and languages. Becker's definition of Islam as a 'civilisation' rather than a religion or a bundle of languages intersected with pivotal questions plaguing the German colonial empire after 1900, and Haridi is absolutely right to point out that – alongside the pragmatic need to distinguish himself as an emerging scholar – there were pressing political and philosophical factors that shaped Becker's paradigm of *Islamwissenschaft*. Above all, there was a need to address the colonial problems of his time, and – from a world-historical, philosophical point of view – to develop the ability to underline and emphasise the supremacy of European societies.[12] Although this is well known, Becker's private experiences as a travelling millionaire in Islamic countries have not yet been investigated, despite the fact that they had clearly been the initial spark for his academic career and for the formation of his version of *Islamwissenschaft*.

## *Medieval and modern Islam: Becker's journey from Spain to Khartoum*

The term 'colonial' might appear misplaced for Becker's views on Spain, the first country he visited; however one cannot ignore a form of 'othering' both in the written and in the visual sources of his months there. He went there in September 1900 to study Arabic manuscripts in the library of the Escorial near Madrid.[13] He stayed in Fonda de Miranda for about four months, travelled around and took notes and dozens of photographs. In some ways, Becker's ethnographic eye was already on show here, with his shots often showing people who crossed his way in almost natural poses – unlike most photographs of the period. However, Becker also created stereotypically orientalist images,[14] using a reliable but heavy box-camera with glass negatives[15] and a then-new box-camera with roll-films. Becker's pictures therefore mark the transition from the aesthetics of static portraits (with the proportions of paintings of the nineteenth century)[16] to the blurred quick-shots of the era of the Kodak box-cameras of the early twentieth century.[17] He maintained this mixed way of photographing when he was approaching his actual destination, Egypt.[18]

Becker left Europe on a British steamer from Gibraltar to Alexandria. On the ship he enjoyed the company of a young couple he had got to know during a dinner at the German Embassy in Madrid. In letters to his mother Becker extensively described the von Bülows, Otto von Bülow being the designated German 'Juge aux tribunaux mixtes' in Egypt. In Madrid, Becker had also met diplomats, artists and other notable

[ 129 ]

figures from the most distinguished circles of the best society, including Ottmar von Mohl (1846–1922), of whom he wrote: 'Herr von Mohl, the German representative on the Caisse de la dette publique, has asked me to visit him; the people seem all very nice and, as far as I know, usually invite much company in Cairo.' Indeed, Mohl became a key figure for Becker, who instantly entered the diplomatic and scientific European elites of Cairo, with their invitations to tea and daytrips to Giza. These early encounters with the social elites of Germany set the tone for much of his time in North Africa. Soon after his arrival in Egypt he found that he had hardly enough time to study Arabic:

> The parlour is of course simple, but we have a huge working table, 2 couches, armchairs etc. The sleeping rooms are equipped with a comfort otherwise only found in England; there is one Arab as a servant exclusively for our storey [...] The management of the house is English. The very first day I visited the Bülows for tea and they immediately invited me on a trip to the Pyramids under the full moon; it is usual here to make the first visit by moonlight [...]. After our return we had tea at the Mohls'. Yesterday [...] Geheimrath von Mohl [...] took me to the club, introduced me there and especially to the German consul. We had breakfast with him, the Spanish consul, the German ambassador[19] and Sobernheim at the club. Afterwards Mr von Bülow visited me and invited me to dine with him. In the evening Sobernheim and I entertained Professor Strzygowski[20] as our guest, a charming Austrian scholar of renown. You can see how charming everybody here is and how well I fare here.[21]

In Becker's letters from Africa and in his later references to the journey the upper circles of the Europeans in Egypt seemed an international – or even supranational – colonial society. Diplomats, traders, military men and civilians (and women) met at evening parties, and, at least in Becker's depictions, shared high-class conversations in English and French, drank tea or port and left the native Egyptian, Sudanese or Ottoman elites well alone. Becker's letters are full of remarkable descriptions of these European gatherings in Africa;[22] however, he later also wrote with the same level of detail about the African people he encountered.

## Photographic and written images of colonialism

During his journey through British and French colonies Becker explored, measured and surveyed whatever he found philologically, historically, anthropologically or in other respects interesting. Whenever the Arabic lessons and the sketching and photographing of the Arabic backdrop of Cairo became tiring, Becker left the city for daytrips or longer journeys. Accompanied by other European scholars – professionals as well as laypeople – he roamed around Giza, travelled to Alexandria, journeyed to the Coptic monasteries near the Red Sea or headed up the Nile towards the second and the further cataracts in Sudan. On these journeys, which took on the character of expeditions, the closer he got to Omdurman and Khartoum, he filled notebook after notebook and wrote detailed letters to relatives and friends in which we clearly see the future *Privatdozent* who collects ideas and material for lectures to be held and articles to be written. However, besides these 'pure facts' collected by 'sober' observation, there were also always judgements of the country and its people which reflected common European stereotypes.[23]

> On the 2nd holiday – I took a donkey and a boy to carry my camera, to take some long-distance shots. A funny little lad, Abdel Kerim amused us greatly with his splendid eagerness; you can see him in some of the photographs. We went to a small village. For a long time Maghrebian bedouins have lived here around the Pyramids, who differ greatly from the population here both in their dress and their language. All the male and also the female villagers, who did not wear a veil, were only too willing to serve as accessories for a small baksheesh. In the end we graciously handed a whole mark over to the village in the person of the supreme mayor, which made our donkey drivers very mad due to this perceived squandering. We only intended to share the joy of the holiday with the people. Even though all Arabs are avaricious, one cannot cherish their constant good humour enough.[24]

Most of the letters were written in a clear and down-to-earth language. Reporting his experience with thoughtfulness and empathy in some passages seemed to be no barrier to presenting himself as an imperious contemporary of Churchill and Kitchener, Wilhelm II and Kipling elsewhere. In the context of his first visit to Luxor in February 1901, Becker informed his mother of an annoying accident:

> On our way a stupid fellah wench was run down, whose eyes and ears were covered with cloth like blinkers, and who consequently got hit repeatedly right in the middle of the street. We tried to evade, but she ran into my donkey, was sent stumbling against Dr Schmid's mount and finally fell to the ground, uninjured of course. The clothing of the harem is incompatible with modern traffic.[25]

Southwards on the Nile Becker extended his scientific sightseeing to Nubia, a common site on itineraries since Egypt had become a popular destination for Western archaeologists and even for some upper-class travellers eager to improve their education.[26] Once he arrived there, he planned to travel another 700 kilometres southwards to Khartoum. The Sudanese capital had quite recently become *terra incognita* again,

**Figure 7.1** 'That is the English cultural mission': Becker sees the Sudan in 1901

because in 1885 a defeat of the Ottoman-English troops had led to the rule of a Mahdist Islamic state lasting until 1898, when it fell to the British army following the battle of Omdurman.[27] Only two years after these battles Becker reached the capital of the Sudan as one of the first European scholars after the end of Mahdist theocracy.[28]

Becker's photographs, however, pictured a version of the colonial 'normality' he had become used to in Alexandria or Cairo. Despite there being far fewer white Europeans, the 'natives', as his imperial attitude led him to see them, were playing the same subordinate roles as they did in the more Europeanised and 'cultured' colonial metropolises such as Cairo or the rapidly growing Port Said on the Suez Canal.[29] This meant primarily that the Sudanese were portrayed as objects, servants and soldiers, or as native civilians in their 'natural surroundings'.[30] However, the Sudan was different from 'stable' Egypt. Rebellion and religious war had just been ended, and Becker repeatedly emphasised in photographs and in letters the necessity of being cautious.

> One cannot leave the city or use the desert railway without being filled with great admiration for Kitchener's historic deed. According to local judgement he was no soldier or general, but a most efficient manager, being

called 'The Sudan Machine' by Stevens (With Kitchener in Khartoum)[31] not without justification. A methodical Fabius Cunctator was the only possible saviour after all.[32]

The British Empire and its military strategist figured for Becker as symbols of European power challenged by African barbarians struggling for supremacy in the southern Mediterranean. His relief at Kitchener's reconquest was a colloquial deployment of the European discursive motif of the permanent 'safeguarding' of colonised territories,[33] which had become a steady 'white man's burden around 1900'.[34]

> The unrest is not far in the past, yet today we travel the country in luxurious trains – that is the English cultural mission. But I digress, let it simply be said that it is truly astonishing what British military instructors and officers have made of the Egyptian troops and especially the police forces. Also colonisation in Sudan, which – an example for Germany – is run completely by the military, is impressive: agrarian and commercial progress through military institutions.[35]

The colonial war disguised as a cultural mission seemed to Becker an appropriate means for 'civilising' countries.[36] While it is not clear how well informed he was about the particulars of the brutal British military campaign at Omdurman, what he had gleaned had earned his approval. 'The English had to destroy the *Qubbe* [tombs] for practical reasons', he argued, 'and they had to scatter the ashes of the Mahdi in the Nile, otherwise this place could have become a religious Islamic *Kyffhäuser*.'[37]

Freely mixing his newly acquired knowledge with what he had learned at home, Becker also shifted between political and anthropological observations:

> All the nationalities which fell prey to the Mahdi have been relocated to Omdurman and many feel right at home there today. All skin colours are to be found, from white Greeks to yellow Syrians and light brown Egyptian, to the red-brown Berber to the black-brown or pitch-black Negro type. They all live here most naturally and conduct their business in their own ways.[38] The city is densely populated, in the narrow aisles of the Bazaars there is much jostling and pushing; men and women usually go with their chests bare, men wear white or strong colours, while women tend to adopt more sober colours and usually carry some small thing, a bundle or picturesque clay pot elegantly on their head – a splendid oriental scenery. Europeans are scarcely seen, only the half-oriental Greeks are quite common here, they are commercially the cultural vanguard and have achieved astonishing results; with what little blood they still have from the antique Hellenes, they definitively have inherited their talent for trade and organisation.[39]

[ 133 ]

**Figure 7.2**   Destroyed Mausoleum of the Mahdi in Omdurman

Becker's letters and notes were frequently interspersed with such crude anthropological observations, yet rarely did his written opinions and the visual documentation correlate as directly as in the example of his description of the Bisharin,[40] 'a curious tribe, they have an aesthetic physique, black, curly hair, which they wear in long strands filled with butter or picturesquely fluffed up. They speak their own language and yet they are not of the Negroid type, I do not quite know where to place them.'[41]

As the Bisharin were settled in Aswan (between 1870 and 1875) they were the first tribe of the Beja-speaking nomads that European travellers could encounter on their way southwards to the Sudan. By chance they had become the first 'noble savages' that Western eyes and Western cameras got to see on the 'other side of the frontier'.[42] Their settlements were mentioned in the relevant travel reports of mostly British and French authors; from the 1860s there was German 'scientific' literature on the region as well.[43] It was only half a century after Becker that the Egyptian government prohibited foreigners from entering the camps, because the Bisharin felt molested and treated like animals in a zoo by tourists taking photographs.[44]

**Figure 7.3**  A random snapshot? Bisharin people seen through Becker's
Western lens

With its embrace of the taxonomic positivism of the day, and without
today's knowledge of the forty-year discussion of Edward Said's concept
of orientalism[45] or of the multidimensional interdependencies and mutual
reactions between occidental photographers and their oriental objects,
Becker's descriptions, and particularly his quest for 'authenticity', seem
naive and, for an emerging scholar, strangely undertheorised.[46] The idea
that he as a foreigner was an integral component of the colonial site he
was observing does not occur to him.[47] Rather, he believed in 'real', 'pure'
and 'unadulterated' experience and sought this among the 'savage people'
of Sudan. Yet, as was the case elsewhere, the documentary function
of Becker's oriental photography was overshadowed by the production
of staged realities.[48] Although Becker tried to look behind the scenes,
and although some of his photographs, like those of Sudanese women
and children, have a snapshot character, they remain reproductions of
stereotypes, as Becker's own description of them attests:[49]

> The soldiers' villages give an unadulterated picture of real African life.
> The black battalions have their harem in the garrison. They live together
> in small villages, the huts built only from straw mats, the children are
> naked and the women are not shy with their charms either.[50]

As a part of his attempt to capture authenticity, Becker took a keen interest in buying souvenirs, irrespective of whether they were antique artefacts or simply contemporary Islamic jewellery. Exemplifying the *Exotismus* typical of that era, Becker mixed personal and professional motivations in buying gifts for his relatives as well as objects for his scientific collection.[51]

> In that last place I did some considerable shopping; the natives in Nubia are surprisingly affluent and nearly all the women wear gold and silver jewellery which is very distinct and characteristic. In the middle of the forehead they wear a thin piece of gold, roughly the size of a *Thaler* with strange knobs, dangling from a short, broad chain made of glass pearls and pieces of wood or agate in their hair. Some wear two of these, over their ears and linked with leather straps to solid silver pendants. They also wear beautifully worked clasps around their arms and feet, chains, amulets, gold and silver earrings. I brought a whole such set with me, which I bought piece by piece. I took a very fine piece (of gold), which I intend to give to Frida, from the forehead of a comely Nubian woman. I think it can be made into an interesting unique brooch.[52]

The contrast between the European standards of culture and civilisation and the situation in what to him appeared as wilderness with the sporadic occidental presence are a recurring topic in Becker's letters. Although he journeyed in relatively comfortable conditions, his writings sometimes convey something like a longing for the impositions of tropical climate and the potential dangers of the 'wild' indigenous people.[53] In Abu Simbel he wrote:

> It is a smouldering heat, one has to drink enormous quantities, yet nearly no alcohol. The countless flies are annoying, they insolently cover especially our eyes in great numbers. The natives do not try to dispel them, their faces are often covered like flypaper, especially the children. Although it feels like sitting in a boiler room here, everybody puts on his dinner jacket in the evening – this will please many of them; Bär Crevenna wanted to bring his to the Matterhorn back in his day – it is definitely more appropriate here.[54]

## *Colonial images of Africa and Asia:*
## *an imperial meeting at home*

On his way back from Upper Egypt and Sudan Becker visited the Coptic monasteries, and in summer 1901 he returned via Greece and Istanbul to Germany, where his sister Frida married. One of his brothers-in-law, General Ernst von Blumenstein, represented another side of the contemporary German imperialism, having just returned from China, where he had been one of the leaders of the German expedition corps that defeated the so-called Boxer Rebellion. This coincidence was in a way unfortunate for Becker, because his Sudanese adventures were nothing compared to the real war experience of Blumenstein, who brought Chinese clothes as souvenirs. In their own ways, however, both were participants in the German Empire's entry into the politics of colonial rule after 1884–85.[55]

Before returning to Cairo in November 1901, Becker arranged to promote his *Habilitation* in Heidelberg with a lecture on 'The Mahdi in Islam'. His academic teacher Heinrich Bezold, who was Dean of the Faculty at that time, supported this unconventional choice, which they had discussed exhaustively in the months before.[56] Choosing this topic was a highly innovative move. It meant nothing less than putting contemporary history and current political issues on the academic agenda of oriental studies, which had traditionally been focused on questions of historical linguistics.[57] With the examination of a historical instead of a philological phenomenon, Becker was among the first who opened up a new cultural vista in university studies of the contemporary Orient as a neighbouring area of Christian Europe.[58] Although Becker was still looking for old Arabic manuscripts and ancient remains of former oriental societies, he developed a synchronic anthropological view, inseparably connected to colonial interests, leading him to a somewhat modern orientalist's enquiry into 'the political and social conditions of the present'.[59]

Becker spent the winter of 1901–2 in Cairo. His main aim was to improve his knowledge of the Arabic language. Further travels and colonial explorations where therefore reserved for his return journey. However, even within the city of Cairo Becker believed that he could gain knowledge about Egyptian culture and history. In fact Becker busied himself (re-)producing and collecting furnishings and items replete with the signature motifs of the colonised Orient. A letter to Bezold from 21. December 1901 shows how fuzzy the edges were 'between Orientalism as an academic discipline, a Western ideology, and a literary motif'[60] in the mind of a travelling scholar claiming to see his surroundings through scientific eyes. Back in the comfortable lodgings of his first stay in Cairo, Becker excitedly wrote, 'I decorated my room completely in the oriental fashion – everything is also for Keplerstraße 18; also a collection of Arabian pots, shards, bronzes adorn my room; how I will rejoice in showing you all of this one day.'[61]

While most of his oriental accoutrements were shipped from Alexandria to Germany in spring 1902, Becker's journey back home took him to Jerusalem, Damascus, Syria and Constantinople. For months he travelled on horseback and camelback, slept in tents and ended the trip with a stay in the Ottoman capital where he studied medieval manuscripts.

**Figure 7.4** Becker's sister Emma with her husband Ernst and their daughters in Chinese clothing, which he brought with him from the German Empire's campaign against the so-called Boxer Rebellion, 1901

When he was back in Heidelberg in May 1902, Becker held his public probationary first lecture as a *Privatdozent* on the topic 'The Woman in Islam' and was granted his *venia legendi* for Semitic Philology. In contrast to two years earlier he had now forged his own direction in the study of the Orient, recasting Islamic studies as a science that went beyond mere philological questions and integrated politically pressing concerns regarding contemporary religion and culture. This scientific perspective cannot be separated from the general political and societal interests of the German Empire. Indeed, this approach to the study of Islam increased in response to the growing contact with Islamic cultures, in south-east Europe and overseas, during Germany's imperialist and colonialist phase, moving beyond the oriental antiquarianism of the nineteenth century to explorations of the present.[62]

## Conclusion

Becker, the young son of a wealthy banker, was not merely a curious German or European who travelled the Middle East on his own in the era of *Weltpolitik*. Nor was he the only one to do so. While some studies have focused on the imperial linkages forged by political or scientific organisations,[63] investigations of the many informal, private actors who interacted with these organisations remain rare. Histories of diplomacy have taken the nexus between the formal and informal spheres into account only since political history has been opened to encompass cultural factors. Even so, private actors like Becker appear only marginally in the literature, greatly understating their impor-tance as creators and multipliers of the images of 'savages' in the 'civilised' West.

Becker's journeys through the Middle East can be seen to exemplify the traversal of colonial spaces by the wealthy upper middle class. The fact that he was a German travelling through the colonies of other European powers adds another, political as well as cultural layer to the descriptions in his letters. Becker presents colonialism without being a representative of the colonial power active on the region of his travels.[64]

Becker wrote and took photos long before he became known in scientific circles; indeed he became a professor only in 1908. The private and unofficial character of his letters, notes and pictures, and the lack of a clear mission, are most evident. Apart from the 'savage' people of Africa who were ostensibly the object of his study, other Europeans were described in great detail. Yet his letters nonetheless abide by the scientific standards of the time and eschew the trivia found in the travel writings of other affluent private travellers of his days.[65]

Unlike other travellers, Becker was also aware that his journey had – apart from the scholarly purpose – political dimensions. His exploration of colonies of other nations automatically meant political observations of the British and Ottoman colonial rivalry.[66] The Sudan experience after the end of the Mahdist state, when the British and Egyptian troops slaughtered eleven thousand enemies while losing just 48 men,[67] was a crucial experience in his intellectual development as an orientalist.

German orientalism, orientalist science and colonialism were inextricably linked at that time, and Becker built a university career on untangling the complicated web of relations between science and colonialism in an era when Germany was establishing dedicated colonial sciences.[68] The time of 'armchair scholarship' was over, and men like Becker, personally linked to Germany's political class, having read the works of Mungo Park and carried Kipling's novels in their travel libraries,[69] brought back vivid impressions from their expeditions. Besides the social networks they established, the most important impact of these travellers was to disseminate colonial images in the form of pictures they had taken and then used in lectures for the next generation of colonial experts as authentic and scientific impressions of Africa.[70]

Carl Heinrich Becker played a great part in the multifaceted depiction of the Orient and colonisation in Africa both in science and in the media.[71] Using 'frontier' imagery that suggested a pure and unspoiled wilderness and the proverbial empty spaces south of the Arabian language border in Sudan, he emphatically endorsed the European mission to spread 'civilisation'.[72] His early travel impressions greatly influenced Becker's later, highly complex works in Islamic studies.[73] Even though his cultural, religious and linguistic studies are best known, the academic scientist can never be separated from the colonial traveller. As a professor at the Institute for Colonial Studies in Hamburg, responsible for educating future civil servants for the colonies in Africa and Asia (as well as touristic and scholarly travellers),[74] he concisely expresses this relationship between culture and imperialism in a letter in 1910:

My dear Herzfeld,[75] we have to get rid of our damned German modesty. Our ghastly objectivity. We do not have to be as naive as the English, who mistake national egoism for the categorical imperative. We can consciously accept our national egoism but must not be distracted from realising it by a thousand considerations and worries. Cultural and economic influence are inseparable, and in the endless blabbering in the Reichstag about the exclusively economic nature of the German oriental policy there is a great amount of English hypocrisy.[76]

To be sure, Becker did not succumb to the same crass illusions of superiority and the same Eurocentrism as many of his contemporaries where cultural and religious studies were concerned,[77] yet, as his early letters and photographs from his travels between 1900 and 1902 illustrate, he remained in his perspective on 'the other' a colonial man of his time.[78] Apart from others before him (Georg August Schweinfurth) and after (Adolf Friedrich of Mecklenburg), Becker's European views and reflections on the oriental landscapes and surroundings that he 'explored' help to counter the common misperception that Germans were latecomers to colonialism. This is true only in a narrowly constitutional and political sense. More broadly, however, and following Edward Said, it is clear that Germans too embraced the practices of imperial orientalism that Said identified as characterising British and French endeavours in the Middle East.[79]

## Notes

1  Julia Laura Rischbieter, *Mikro-Ökonomie der Globalisierung. Kaffee, Kaufleute und Konsumenten im Kaiserreich 1870 – 1914* (Cologne: Böhlau Verlag, 2011); William Gervase Clarence-Smith and Steven Topik (eds), *The Global Coffee Economy in Africa, Asia, and Latin America, 1500–1989* (Cambridge: Cambridge University Press, 2003).
2  Kristina Michaelis, and Ulf Morgenstern (eds), *Kaufleute, Kosmopoliten, Kunstmäzene: Die Gelnhäuser Großbürgerfamilien Becker und Schöffer* (Hamburg: Am Goldenen Fuss, 2013).
3  Carl Heinrich Becker, 'Ibn Gauzi's Manaqib Omar Ibn' Abdelaziz' (Unpublished Dissertation, University of Heidelberg, 1899).
4  Gelnhausen is the place where in 2012 in the attic of the former servant's house of the Becker villa the author discovered the long-forgotten photographs of Becker's journey of 1900–2. I am especially indebted to Dr Kristina Michaelis, friend, co-author and owner of this attic full of family history.
5  Geheimes Staatsarchiv Preußischer Kulturbesitz, GStAPK, VI. HA, Nachlass C.H. Becker.
6  See for example Alexander Haridi, *Das Paradigma der islamischen Zivilisation – oder die Begründung der deutschen Islamwissenschaft durch Carl Heinrich Becker (1876–1933). Eine wissenschaftsgeschichtliche Untersuchung* (Würzburg: Ergon, 2005).
7  Guido Müller, *Weltpolitische Bildung und Reform. Carl Heinrich Beckers Wissenschafts- und Hochschulpolitik 1908–1930* (Cologne: Böhlau Verlag, 1991).
8  There are several articles and books focusing on Becker as a scientist or as a politician, however, Becker's family background and his early life are just mentioned as an aside, e.g. Hellmut Ritter, 'C.H. Becker als Orientalist', *Der Islam* 24 (1937), 175–85; Marc Batunsky, 'Carl Heinrich Becker: From Old to Modern Islamology', *International Journal of Middle East Studies* 13 (1981), 287–310. For the politician Becker see Béatrice Bonniot, *Homme de culture et républicain de raison. Carl Heinrich Becker, serviteur de l'Etatsous la République de Weimar (1918–1933)* (Frankfurt am Main: Lang, 2012). The only biography is rather outdated: Erich Wende, *C.H. Becker. Mensch und Politiker. Ein biographischer Beitrag zur Kulturgeschichte der Weimarer Republik* (Stuttgart: Deutsche Verlags-Anstalt, 1959). For further examples see Sabine Mangold, *'Eine weltbürgerliche Wissenschaft': die deutsche Orientalistik im 19. Jahrhundert* (Stuttgart: Franz Steiner, 2004), p. 251. Informative as historical sources but almost completely uncritical are the chapters of Hans Heinrich Schaeder, *C.H. Becker. Ein Gedenkbuch* (Göttingen: Vandenhoeck and Ruprecht, 1950).

9   Jens Ruppenthal, *Kolonialismus als Wissenschaft und Technik. Das Hamburgische Kolonialinstitut 1908 bis 1919* (Stuttgart: Steiner, 2007).

10  Haridi, *Das Paradigma der islamischen Zivilisation*, p. 199.

11  Haridi, *Das Paradigma der islamischen Zivilisation*, p. 11.

12  Haridi, *Das Paradigma der islamischen Zivilisation*, p. 17. Becker agreed to learn the languages of Islamic East Africa before his appointment as Professor in Hamburg, but he never did.

13  The famous orientalist Eduard Sachau in Berlin (Becker jokingly referred to him as the 'Deus Maximus omnipotens' in a postcard to Bezold, 15 July 1905, University library Heidelberg, Heid. Hs. 1501, 10) called the young man's attention to a manuscript in the Escorial library. Out of consideration for the funding of a journey to Spain Becker resolved to visit the Moorish sources there before leaving for a longer stay in North Africa.

14  For patterns of photographical representation of the Orient, see Ali Behdad (ed.), *Photography's Orientalism. New Essays on Colonial Representation* (Los Angeles: Getty Research Institute, 2013); Frank Berzieri, *Sûra. Écrivians, voyageurs et photographes en Egypte au XIXe siècle* (Paris: Phebus, 2012); Ken Jacobson, *Odalisques & Arabesques. Orientalist Photography* (London: Quaritch, 2007); Thomas Walther, *Focus Orient. Orientalist Photography from the Late 19th and Early 20th Centuries* (Cologne: König, 2010).

15  Becker to his mother, 1 December 1899 (Geheimes Staatsarchiv Preußischer Kulturbesitz, GStAPK, VI. HA, Nachlass C.H. Becker, 8604.

16  For the traditional views, see e.g. Sophie Gordon, *Cairo to Constantinople. Francis Bedford's Photographs of the Middle East* (London: Royal Collection Trust, 2013), documenting the four-month educational tour of the Prince of Wales in 1862. For the change of techniques and perspectives after 1900 see Charles-Henri Favrod, *Orient 1904–1930* (Heidelberg: Umschau, 1998).

17  Bernd Stiegler and Felix Thürlemann (eds), *Orientbilder: Fotografien 1850–1910* (Frankfurt: Weissbooks, 2015), 154, 168.

18  It is likely that, besides the popular literature on arts and history of Egypt that was common in the libraries of the sophisticated European bourgeoisie, Becker also possessed albums with classical subjects of the Orient and that he wanted not just simply to reproduce them but also to find new motifs and to develop an own view. A bestseller among the high-quality folios was Georg Ebers, *Aegypten in Wort und Bild. Dargestellt von unseren ersten Künstlern*, 2 vols (Stuttgart and Leipzig: Hallberger, 1879); cheaper but still sophisticated were scientific travel handbooks such as Georg Steindorff, *Die Blütezeit des Pharaonenreichs* (Bielefeld and Leipzig: Velhagen & Klasing, 1900), or Franz Pascha, *Kairo* (Leipzig: Seemann, 1903).

19  Felix von Müller 1857–1918, German consul general in Cairo 1897–1902.

20  Josef Strzygowski 1862–1941, Austrian art historian, 1892–1909 professor at the University of Graz.

21  Even without the telegraph the time and space-compression was impressive. It took only five days for letters and postcards from Cairo to reach Gelnhausen.

22  See for example, 'Wednesday the 13th I left Cairo at 8 pm, – the train had a restaurant car and a sleeper. By chance I met over dinner an Englishman who had been raised in Germany. He was the chief of police in Sudan, dealing with the slave trade, and was on his way back there. What he told me was very interesting. In 1900 this English-Egyptian agency still arrested 12 slavers and freed 1680 slaves.' Becker to his mother, 18 February 1901, GStAPK, VI. HA, Nachlass C.H. Becker, 8604. See also Ulrike Lindner, 'German Colonialism and the British Neighbour in Africa before 1914: Self-Definitions, Lines of Demarcation and Co-Operation', in Volker Langbehn and Mohamad Salamaa (eds), *German Colonialism: Race, the Holocaust and Postwar Germany* (New York: Columbia University Press, 2011), pp. 254–72, and Volker Barth and Roland Cvetkovski (eds), *Imperial Co-Operation and Transfer 1870–1930* (London: Bloomsbury, 2015).

23  Russell A. Berman, *Enlightenment or Empire. Colonial Discourse in German Culture* (Lincoln and London: University of Nebraska Press, 1998). See further Marianne

Bechhaus-Gerst and Richard Klein-Arendt (eds), *Die (koloniale) Begegnung. Afri-kanerInnen in Deutschland. Deutsche in Afrika 1880–1918* (Frankfurt am Main: Lang, 2003); Marianne Bechhaus-Gerst and Sunna Giesecke (eds), *Koloniale und postkoloniale Konstruktionen von Afrika und Menschen afrikanischer Herkunft in der deutschen Alltagskultur* (Frankfurt am Main: Lang, 2006).

24  Becker to his mother, 26 December 1900, GStAPK, VI. HA, Nachlass C.H. Becker, 8604. Unfortunately, the photographs referred to here are not preserved.

25  Becker to his mother, 20 February 1901, GStAPK, VI. HA, Nachlass C.H. Becker, 8604.

26  Angelika Lohwasser, '"Ueber Aegypten hinaus!" Die Archäologie Nubiens', in Verena M. Lepper (ed.), *Karl Richard Lepsius: der Begründer der deutschen Ägyptologie* (Berlin: Kadmos, 2012), pp. 149–70.

27  Michael Asher, *Khartoum. The Ultimate Imperial Adventure* (London: Penguin, 2006).

28  Douglas H. Johnson, 'Political Intelligence, Colonial Ethnography, and Analytical Anthropology in the Sudan', in Helen Tilley (ed.), *Ordering Africa. Anthropology, European Imperialism, and the Politics of Knowledge* (Manchester: Manchester University Press, 2007), pp. 309–35.

29  Valeska Huber, *Channelling Mobilities: Migration and Globalisation in the Suez Canal Region and Beyond* (Cambridge: Cambridge University Press, 2013); or Liat Kozma, Cyrus Schayegh and Avner Wishnitzer (eds), *A Global Middle East: Mobility, Materiality and Culture in the Modern Age, 1880–1940* (London and New York: IB Tauris, 2015).

30  Invaluable on the issue of European views in colonial photography is Ali Behdad and Luke Gartlan (eds), *Photography's Orientalism. New Essays on Colonial Representation* (Los Angeles: Getty Research Institute, 2013).

31  George W. Steevens, *With Kitchener to Khartum* (London: Dodd, 1898).

32  Becker to his mother, 1 March 1901, GStAPK, VI. HA, Nachlass C.H. Becker, 8604. Quintus Fabius Maximus Verrucosus, named Cunctator (one who hesitates), Roman general and dictator, who, using very careful and circumspect tactics, managed to defeat the Carthagian general Hannibal in the Second Punic War and was initially maligned for his 'hesitant' approach to warfare. Familiar with imperial literature of his time, Becker was citing Steevens, *With Kitchener to Khartum*.

33  Manuel Köppen, 'Im Krieg mit dem Fremden: Barbarentum und Kulturkampf', in Alexander Honold and Oliver Simons (eds), *Kolonialismus als Kultur: Literatur, Medien, Wissenschaft in der deutschen Gründerzeit des Fremden* (Tübingen: Francke, 2002), pp. 263–87.

34  Becker read novels by Kipling in the nights in tents in the Sudanese desert. Becker to his mother, 1 February 1901, GStAPK, VI. HA, Nachlass C.H. Becker, 8604. On this process of 'reading empire', see Jeff Bowersox, *Raising Germans in the Age of Empire: Youth and Colonial Culture, 1871–1914* (Oxford: Oxford University Press, 2013), pp. 119–64.

35  Becker to his mother, 6 March 1901, GStAPK, VI. HA, Nachlass C.H. Becker, 8604.

36  See the comprehensive work of Dierk Walter, *Organisierte Gewalt in der europäischen Expansion. Gestalt und Logik des Imperialkrieges* (Hamburg: Hamburger Edition, 2014).

37  Becker to his mother, 7 March 1901, GStAPK, VI. HA, Nachlass C.H. Becker, 8604. The Kyffhäuser is a low mountain range in Thuringia. The medieval emperor Barbarossa, who died 1190 during a crusade, was said to be sleeping in the mountain until he returned and renewed the empire.

38  See Marianne Bechhaus-Gerst, 'Nubier, Beja, Griechen, Kopten und Araber in Dongola. Der Nordsudan als kosmopolitischer Raum im mittelalterlichen Jahrtausend', in Michael Borgolte and Matthias M. Tischler (eds), *Transkulturelle Verflechtungen im mittelalterlichen Jahrtausend: Europa, Ostasien, Afrika* (Darmstadt: Wissenschaftliche Buchgesellschaft, 2012), pp. 21–33.

39  Becker to his mother, 7 March 1901, GStAPK, VI. HA, Nachlass C.H. Becker, 8604.

40  Becker spelled them Bisárin; they are one of the major ethnic groups belonging to the nomadic population of southern Egypt and the Sudan.

41  Becker to his mother, 23 February 1901, GStAPK, VI. HA, Nachlass C.H. Becker, 8604.

42  Steven E. Sidebotham, Martin Hense and Hendrikje M. Nouwens, *The Red Land. The Illustrated Archaeology of Egypt's Eastern Desert* (Cairo: American University in Cairo Press, 2008).

43  Becker owned the most famous books among them, in which the Bisharin are mentioned as well: Georg Schweinfurth, *Au Cœur de l'Afrique, 1868–1871* (Paris: Hachette, 1875), Vol. II, pp. 28–9.

44  Jane Starkey, 'Perceptions of the Ababda and Bisharin in the Atbai', *Sudan Studies* 26 (2001), 25–43.

45  Edward Said, *Orientalism* (New York: Routledge & Kegan Paul, 1978). Part of the controversy on Said's slightly Marxist argument is documented in Daniel M. Varisco, *Reading Orientalism: Said and the Unsaid* (Seattle: University of Washington Press, 2007).

46  In contrast to the people shown in exhibitions around Europe as 'primitive natives' (Anne Dreesbach, *Gezähmte Wilde. Die Zurschaustellung 'exotischer' Menschen in Deutschland 1870–1940* (Frankfurt am Main: Campus, 2005)), Becker assumed an unadulterated authenticity when studying the people in their native 'habitat'. See Thomas Theye, 'Optische Trophäen. Vom Holzschnitt zum Foto-Album: Eine Bildgeschichte der Wilden', in Thomas Theye (ed.), *Wir und die Wilden: Einblicke in eine kannibalische Beziehung* (Reinbek: Rowohlt, 1985,pp. 18–39; and Michael Wiener, *Ikonographie des Wilden. Menschen-Bilder in Ethnographie und Photographie zwischen 1850 und 1918* (Munich: Trickster, 1990).

47  Johannes Fabian had an enormous impact for understanding the 'othering' in colonial interactions: *Time and the Other. How Anthropology Makes Its Object* (New York: Columbia University Press, 1983); see also Matti Bunzl, 'Johannes Fabians "Time and the Other": Synthesen einer kritischen Anthropologie', *Historische Anthropologie* 6:3 (1998), 466–78.

48  See for this tendency Thomas Walther, *Focus Orient*. See also Ann Maxwell, *Colonial Photography and Exhibitions: Representations of the 'Native' People and the Making of European Identities* (London: Leicester University Press, 1999); T. Jack Thompson, *Light on Darkness? Missionary Photography of Africa in the Nineteenth and Early Twentieth Century* (Grand Rapids: WB Eerdmans, 2012). See too Gerhard Paul (ed.), *Visual History. Ein Studienbuch* (Göttingen: Vandenhoeck & Ruprecht, 2006); Helmut Lethen, *Der Schatten des Fotografen. Bilder und ihre Wirklichkeit* (Reinbek: Rowohlt, 2014); Franz X. Eder, Oliver Kühschelm and Christina Linsboth (eds), *Bilder in historischen Diskursen* (Wiesbaden: Springer, 2014).

49  For a brief summary of this, see Alexander Will, 'Das nahe Fremde. Islambilder in Deutschland 1871–1918', in Veit Veltzke (ed.), *Playing Lawrence on the Other Side. Die Expedition Klein und das Deutsch-osmanische Bündnis im Ersten Weltkrieg* (Berlin: Nicholai, 2014), pp. 29–39; Peter Burke, *Augenzeugenschaft. Bilder als historische Quellen* (Berlin: Wagenbach, 2003).

50  Becker to his mother, 7 March 1901, GStAPK, VI. HA, Nachlass C.H. Becker, 8604.

51  Stefanie Wolter, *Die Vermarktung des Fremden. Exotismus und die Anfänge des Massenkonsums* (Frankfurt am Man and New York: Campus, 2005).

52  Becker to his mother, 12 March 1901, GStAPK, VI. HA, Nachlass C.H. Becker, 8604

53  These desires for adventures were common among the European white travellers; see e.g. Urs Bitterli, *Die 'Wilden' und die 'Zivilisierten'. Grundzüge einer Geistes- und Kulturgeschichte der europäischen überseeischen Begegnungen* (Munich: CH Beck, 1991).

54  Becker to his mother, 27 February 1901, GStAPK, VI. HA, Nachlass C.H. Becker, 8604. Crevenna was a friend with whom Becker made mountain hikes during his university time in Switzerland in 1895. These bizarre attempts to maintain European social conventions under completely different conditions in Africa have become an interesting field of research: see Johannes Fabian, *Out of Our Minds: Reason and*

*Madness in the Exploration of Central Africa* (Berkeley: University of California Press, 2000); Hubertus Büschel, '"Starke Angst in den Tropen" – Männlichkeit und Krise in ethnologischen Texten 1900–1960', in Martin Sabrow (ed.), *ZeitRäume. Potsdamer Almanach* (Berlin: Transit, 2008); Eva Bischoff, 'Tropenkoller: Male Self-Control and the Loss of Colonial Rule', in Maurus Reinkowski and Gregor Thum (eds), *Helpless Imperialists. Imperial Failure, Fear and Radicalization* (Göttingen: Vandenhoeck & Ruprecht, 2013), pp. 117–36.

55  See therefore Hans Fenske, 'Ungeduldige Zuschauer. Die Deutschen und die europäische Expansion 1815–1880', in Wolfgang Reinhard (eds), *Imperialistische Kontinuität und nationale Ungeduld im 19. Jahrhundert* (Frankfurt am Main: Fischer, 1991), pp. 87–123.

56  See their letters in Bezold's papers in the University library, Heidelberg, Heid.Hs. 1501, 10, and in Becker's legacy, Geheimes Staatsarchiv Preußischer Kulturbesitz, GStAPK, VI. HA, Nachlass C.H. Becker, 6431. On 3 March 1901 Bezold wrote to Becker, saying that they could meet in Tunis: 'Next Saturday we want to travel directly to Tunis from here (via Marseille) and stay there for ca. 10 days. (do join us for a while!!) I will be glad to shake the dust of Europe from my shoes for once.'

57  Süleyman Kiziltoprak, 'The Egyptian Question and the Multilateral policy of Germany (1876 – 1904)', in Claus Schönig (ed.), *Türkisch-deutsche Beziehungen: Perspektiven aus Vergangenheit und Gegenwart* (Berlin: Klaus Schwarz Verlag, 2012), pp. 34–55.

58  For this shift of the academic interest, see e.g. Ahcène Abdelfettah, Alain Messaoudi and Daniel Nordman (eds), *Savoirs d'Allemagne en Afrique du Nord (XVIIIe–XXe siècle)* (Saint-Denis: Bouchène, 2012); Sabine Mangold-Will, *Eine 'weltbürgerliche Wissenschaft'. Die deutsche Orientalistik im 19. Jahrhundert* (Stuttgart: Franz Steiner, 2004); or Suzanne Marchand, *German Orientalism in the Age of Empire. Religion, Race and Scholarship* (New York: Cambridge University Press, 2009), pp. 33ff.

59  Suzanne Marchand, 'Popularizing the Orient', in *Intellectual History Review* 17:2 (2007), 176. See for a broader context Stefan Hauser, 'German Research on the Ancient near East and Its Relation to Political and Economical Interests from Kaiserreich to World War II', in Wolfgang Schwanitz (ed.), *Germany and the Middle East 1871–1945* (Princeton: Wiener, 2004), pp. 155–79.

60  Todd Kontje, 'Germany's Local Orientalisms', in James Hodkinson and John Walker 9eds), *Deploying Orientalism in Culture and History* (Rochester, NY, and Woodbridge: Camden House, 2013), pp. 55–77. See also Haridi, *Das Paradigma der islamischen Zivilisation*.

61  Becker to Bezold, 21 December 1901, University library Heidelberg, Heid. Hs. 1501,10.

62  For the current state of research, see Rebekka Habermas, 'Debates on Islam in Imperial Germany', in David Motadel (ed.), *Islam and the European Empires* (Oxford: Oxford University Press, 2014), pp. 231–53, and Dieter Heimböckel, 'Der Orient-Diskurs in der Kultur- und Zivilisationskritik um 1900', in Axel Dunker and Michael Hofmann (eds), *Morgenland und Moderne. Orient-Diskurse in der deutschsprachigen Literatur von 1980 bis zur Gegenwart* (Frankfurt am Main: Lang, 2014), pp. 13–33.

63  Susanne Voss, *Die Geschichte der Abteilung Kairo des DAI im Spannungsfeld deutscher politischer Interessen 1881–1929* (Rhaden/Westfalen: Verlag Marie Leidorf, 2013).

64  Birthe Kundrus, 'Von der Peripherie ins Zentrum. Zur Bedeutung des Kolonialismus für das deutsche Kaiserreich', in Sven O. Müller and Cornelius Torp (eds), *Das deutsche Kaiserreich in der Kontroverse* (Göttingen: Vandenhoeck & Ruprecht, 2009), pp. 359–73.

65  Isolde Lehnert, 'Vier Mann in einem Boot. Tagebuchfahrt einer Nubienfahrt', *Mitteilungen des Deutschen Archäologischen Instituts Kairo* 65 (2009), 253–70; see for further travels Anke Fischer-Kattner, *Spuren der Begegnung. Europäische Reiseberichte über Afrika 1760–1860* (Göttingen: Vandenhoeck & Ruprecht, 2015).

66  Martin Kröger, 'Spielfeld der Mächtigeren. Das osmanische Reich und der europäische Kolonialismus', in Charlotte Trümpler (ed.), *Das Große Spiel. Archäologie und Politik zur Zeit des Kolonialismus (1860–1940)* (Essen: DuMont, 2008), pp. 28–33. An intriguing example for expeditions of the transnational community of colonial

scientific explorers is Bernhard C. Schaer, *Tropenliebe. Schweizer Naturforscher und niederländischer Imperialismus in Südostasien um 1900* (Frankfurt am Main: Campus, 2015).

67 Myles Osborne and Susan Kingsley Kent, *Africans and Britons in the Age of Empire, 1660–1980* (London and New York: Routledge, 2015), pp. 105–14.

68 Todd Kontje, *German Orientalism* (Ann Arbor: University of Michigan Press, 2004); Ursula Wokoeck, *German Orientalism. The Study of the Middle East and Islam from 1800 to 1945* (London: Routledge, 2009); Marianne Klemun (ed.), 'Wissenschaft und Kolonialismus', *Wiener Zeitschrift zur Geschichte der Neuzeit* 9:2 (2009); Helen Tilley, 'Introduction: Africa, Imperialism, and Anthropology'. in Tilley (ed.), *Ordering Africa*, pp. 309–35.

69 Although he might have bought it later in life, it is a tempting speculation that Becker's copy of the famous book, Mungo Park, *Travels in the Interior District of Africa* (London: TS Arden, 1847), was already part of his library in 1900; see the catalogue made after his death in 1933 in GStAPK, VI. HA, Nachlass C.H. Becker, 6632.

70 Elisabeth Edwards, 'Photography and the Material Performance of the Past', *History and Theory* 48:4 (2009), 130–50.

71 Nina Berman, *Orientalismus, Kolonialismus und Moderne. Zum Bild des Orients in der deutschsprachigen Kultur um 1900* (Stuttgart: M&P, 1997).

72 Benedikt Stuchtey, '"Westward the course of empire takes its way". Imperialism and the Frontier in British and German Historical Writing around 1900', in Benedikt Stuchtey and Peter Wende (eds), *British and German Historiography 1750–1950* (Oxford: Oxford University Press, 2000), pp. 289–334.

73 Carl Heinrich Becker, *Islamstudien. Vom Werden und Wesen der islamischen Welt*, 2 vols (Leipzig: Hildesheim, 1924/1932).

74 See for instance, Carl Heinrich Becker, 'Der Islam', in *Baedecker: Ägypten* (Leipzig: Hildesheim, 1911), pp. LXXXI–XCVIII.

75 Ernst Herzfeld, 1879–1948, German archeologist and orientalist.

76 Becker to Ernst Herzfeld, 9 December 1910, GStAPK, VI. HA, Nachlass C.H. Becker, 4023.

77 Sabine Mangold, 'Carl Heinrich Becker und seine These vom orientalisch-abendländischen Kulturkreis. Ein Orientalist und die Grenzen Europas', in Sabine Penth, Martina Pitz, Christine van Hoof and Ralf Krautkrämer (eds), *Europas Grenzen* (St Ingbert: Röhrig, 2006), p. 165.

78 As the letters of Becker's longest expedition, which led him to Japan, China, the Dutch East Indies, India and Persia in 1931–32 demonstrate, Becker persisted in adhering to a basically hierarchical racial taxonomy (civilised Japanese in contrast to degenerated, almost savage Malays) (Susanne Kuss (ed.), *Carl Heinrich Becker in China. Reisebriefe des ehemaligen preußischen Kultusministers 1931/32* (Münster: Lit, 2004).

79 Contra the most prominent post-Saidian author on that topic, Marchand, *German Orientalism*.

CHAPTER EIGHT

# Through a German lens: the Australian Aborigines and the question of difference

Judith Wilson

*Civilisation and wilderness – a German* Sonderweg

In 1855, one of Germany's best-selling nineteenth-century authors, Friedrich Gerstäcker (1816–1872), published an article entitled 'Civilisation und Wildniß' (Civilisation and Wilderness) in the popular German magazine *Die Gartenlaube*. In the article he compared both realms, calling on the reader to decide whether savages or heathens would improve on entering a state of civilisation. Having returned only three years previously from a voyage around the world (1849–52) which had taken him through the wilds of South America to the Californian gold fields, from there to Tahiti and the wilderness of Australia, then back to Europe via Java, Gerstäcker was well qualified to judge, and his biting sarcasm leaves no doubt as to what conclusion the reader is meant to draw:

> If forced to adopt foreign customs and traditions, foreign civilisation and religion – he [the savage] lies down and dies, but that doesn't matter – the overpopulated countries occupy and cultivate his land and maintain that they have done civilisation a service. Strangely, they overlook the fact that the only ones to benefit are themselves and that what they were really after was trade and a place to anchor – if the people perish in the process, so be it.[1]

In his critique of colonial rapaciousness and European pretensions to cultural superiority, and in his knowledge of and sympathy for those scorned as savages,[2] Gerstäcker aligned himself with a discourse tradition that Russell Berman in *Enlightenment or Empire* (1998) identified as distinctively German and different from, more ambivalent and more nuanced than that of the major colonial powers, more open to the transformative impact of the encounter with Europe's others.[3] The position adopted by Berman was, in part, a response to the tendency of postcolonial accounts to equate Enlightenment with empire, to universalise British experience and make little or no allowance for other colonial circumstances and experiences.[4] His study is just one example of an increasing number of studies to challenge the convergent tendency of postcolonial narratives and attempt to provide a more differentiated account of Germany's development and colonial involvement.[5]

In the historiography of anthropology, nineteenth-century anthropology was traditionally seen as a colonial science, one that, in the German case, was inevitably linked to German imperial ambitions and the racist science used to legitimate them.[6] Like Berman's studies, H. Glenn Penny and Matti Bunzl's edited collection *Worldly Provincialism. German Anthropology in the Age of Empire* (2003) aimed to provide a corrective to the teleological trajectories of many of these accounts and shed new light on the development of German anthropology. In their introduction, Penny and Bunzl, like Berman, claimed that Germany was different, but they went a step further, declaring that German anthropology[7] in the nineteenth century was, unlike its British and French counterparts, characterised not by 'colonial concerns' at all but rather by a commitment to the acquisition of knowledge and a humanist interest in difference.[8]

Penny and Bunzl point to the work of Johann Gottfried Herder (1744–1803) as an early example of a uniquely German Counter-Enlightenment tradition that opposed the tendency of French philosophers to order human groups in an evolutionary hierarchy based on their degree of civilisation. While based on a fundamental belief in the unity of humankind, Herder's work, in foregrounding difference rather than sameness, gave rise, they claim, to a tradition in anthropology and ethnology that valorised 'the particularity of each national and ethnic entity', a tradition that was fostered by Germany's own particularity and provincialism. German scholars thus viewed the question of difference 'through a specifically German lens', coloured not by their colonial ambitions but rather by an interest in culture, the culture of others as well as their own. This in turn shaped Germans' encounters with non-Europeans.[9]

Because of its focus on anthropology as opposed to literature and its concern with the factors that caused German anthropologists to abandon their cosmopolitan tradition at the end of the nineteenth century, none of the contributors to *Worldly Provincialism* revisited the Enlightenment heritage of German anthropology, and only one of the contributions in the volume is devoted to travel accounts.[10] Yet, in the late eighteenth and early nineteenth centuries, travel accounts were the main medium of German engagement with other cultures.[11] The ethnographic information they contained provided the foundation for German Enlightenment theories on the nature and origin of humankind that led to the formation of anthropology as a new field of inquiry. Anthropological theories and the discussions to which they gave rise fed back into travel literature, influencing the way in which travellers responded to the cultures they encountered and the way they represented them. As Joan Pau Rubiés observed, travellers increasingly left Europe with an awareness of the debates to which they could contribute.[12]

In this chapter I want to make a contribution to the discussions initiated by Penny and Bunzl by exploring an area which played an important role in German deliberations on cultural diversity and in which the worldly and the provincial, travel literature and anthropology intersect: the representation of the Australian Aborigines. In the first section of the chapter I examine the representation of the Aborigines in works by central contributors to the German discourse of diversity in the Enlightenment, Georg Forster (1754–94), Johann Blumenbach (1752–1840) and Herder himself, all of whom are commonly regarded as representatives of the German liberal humanist tradition to which Penny and Bunzl refer. In the second section I turn to Gerstäcker and the representation of the Aborigines in Volume IV of his travel narrative *Reisen* (*Travels*) (1852–54)[13] and conclude with a further article by Gerstäcker on the Aborigines, 'Australien und die australische Race' (Australia and the Australian Race) that appeared in *Die Gartenlaube* in 1860.[14]

It may seem strange to include Gerstäcker in this study as he was clearly not an ethnographer, but the representation of other cultures did form an important component of his travel writing.[15] He not only had access to more information about the Aborigines than his Enlightened compatriots but also had first-hand experience of the Aborigines and their situation, and two chapters of his Australian travel narrative are devoted to a detailed ethnographic description of their lifestyle and customs. Gerstäcker was moreover a traveller who was aware of the ongoing debates in Germany on the issue of cultural difference and made his own contribution to them in the popular media.[16]

My enquiry will be guided by some of the questions raised by Penny and Bunzl's thesis. To what extent were the Germans' representations of the Aborigines determined by a worldly interest in their difference, to what extent by their own 'provincial' agendas? Were their views entirely devoid of colonial interest or necessarily implicated in the colonial enterprise? Did the view of the Aborigines change with increased cultural contact and is this reflected in Gerstäcker's account? And is there a discernible strand in the German engagement with the problem of Aboriginal difference that links these texts and can be identified as distinctively German and different?

## The Enlightenment dilemma: unity versus diversity

Gerstäcker was clearly familiar with Enlightenment debates on human diversity, or with popularised versions of them. In 'Zur Naturgeschichte des Menschen' ('On the Natural History of Humankind'), published in 1860 in the widely read magazine the *Hausblätter*,[17] he launched another attack on European attempts to define cultural difference, this time producing an entertaining parody of a typical natural history of humanity. In it he compared the ubiquity of humankind with that of the housefly, showed that the few things that distinguish humans from other mammals demonstrated the formers' deficiency rather than the opposite, and declared provocatively that there was no need to invoke divine providence to explain their dominance, that it was due solely to their intellect. He continued with a tongue-in-cheek exploration of the characteristics normally used to distinguish humans from animals and an equally facetious attempt to explain the difference between the terms genus, species and variety. This was followed by a discussion of the characteristics normally used to distinguish different human species such as skin colour.[18] Those who based any pretensions they might have on the lightness of their skin could change their minds, he suggested, if they knew that the Australian Aborigines used the same word 'grinkari' for the dead whose skin they have removed and the whites who resemble them.[19] The comment recalls Herder's warning in his *Briefe zu Beförderung der Humanität* (Letters for the Advancement of Humanity) (1793–97) that those who have been mistreated will one day turn the tables on their oppressors: 'The negro paints the devil white'.[20] But in Gerstäcker's text the 'civilised' European risks ridicule rather than revenge.

Gerstäcker's use of an Australian example was in part a piece of showmanship designed to display his familiarity with the wider world and Aboriginal custom, but it does draw attention to the place of the Aborigines in Enlightenment attempts to grapple with the challenges posed by cultural difference. In her introduction to *Foreign Bodies. Oceania and the Science of Race 1750–1940*, Bronwen Douglas has highlighted the significant role that experience of and examples from the Oceanic region, particularly Aboriginal Australia, played in the development of the science of race from the late eighteenth century.[21] In her own contributions to this volume, Douglas discusses in some detail the part that Blumenbach played in 'the biological turn' of the discourse of race,[22] and the contribution of the Forsters, father and son, to the classification of peoples in the South Seas and its impact.[23] However her investigation is focused mostly on debates in France and Britain and does not include Herder. As Douglas correctly observes, lack of information about the Oceanic region meant that discussions of its peoples were long dependent on the writings of William Dampier (1651–1715).[24] Dampier was the first to provide a first-hand description of the native inhabitants of New Holland, and his view of them as the 'miserablest people' was to prove remarkably resilient.[25] Despite the correctives provided in John Hawkesworth's account of Cook's first voyage of discovery (1768–71), the first German edition of which had appeared already in 1774,[26] Forster, Blumenbach and Herder all, directly or indirectly, based their assessment of the state, or status, of the Aborigines on Dampier. In my view this was due not only to the relative unavailability of alternative views but also to the discursive function of Australia's Aborigines in their texts.

This is best illustrated by Georg Forster's essay 'Neuholland und die brittische Colonie in Botany-Bay' ('New Holland and the British Colony in Botany Bay') which was completed for Spener's *Historisch-genealogischen Calender* (Historical and Genealogical Yearbook) in 1786.[27] As a result of their participation in Cook's second voyage of discovery (1772–75), Forster and his father, Johann Reinhold Forster (1729–98), enjoyed unprecedented authority as the main German mediators of knowledge on the South Seas in the late eighteenth and early nineteenth centuries.[28] Although they did not actually visit Australia, Georg Forster nonetheless felt well qualified to provide an account of the founding of the new colony and its prospects. He used the essay to celebrate civilisation, the European civilising mission and Cook's achievement, and to draw attention to the colonial potential of New Holland, its temperate climate, the vast expanse of territory still unknown and unexplored, the mountains of quartz that shimmered with the promise of future riches, the grasslands that could so easily be transformed into meadows and pastures.[29] This was in fact an essay dominated by colonial concerns and a perfect example of the type of precolonial 'colonial fantasy' which Susanne Zantop made the object of her study in *Colonial Fantasies*.[30]

The information Forster provided was largely based on his own reworking of Hawkesworth's account, but, when it comes to the native inhabitants, it was Dampier's view that dominated. The Aborigines were represented as 'the most miserable race'. No fields, no clothes, no houses, they lacked both the structures of civilised society and its basic rudiments. Given their numbers and nomadic lifestyle, he predicted that they would pose no threat to the colony, but move on and find somewhere else to live, and that they might even derive some benefit from European example.[31] This prediction was consonant not only with his faith in the civilising mission but also with his view of progress, which he saw as driven by a constant process of destruction and displacement.[32] Whereas in his own account of Cook's journey, *Voyage around the World* (1777), Forster was often critical of European expansionism and its impact, deploring not only the loss of inncocent lives but also the corruption of native morality,[33] here he turned a blind eye to the potential cost of colonisation in order to promote its benefits. In this context the Aborigines served largely as a negative foil to demonstrate the desirability of the state of civilisation and the advantages attendant on the establishment of the new colony.[34] Forster had a personal and provincial interest in European undertakings in the Pacific as a participant and a writer, and he was clearly set here on securing the 'cultural capital' that went with his expertise.[35]

The Forsters, father and son, made a major contribution both to the 'empirical material' from the South Seas that fuelled Enlightenment debates on human diversity and to its interpretation.[36] The new information they provided on the peoples inhabiting the Pacific Islands led Blumenbach, already a noted authority in the emerging field of anthropology, to reassess his major work *De generis humani varietate nativa* (On the Natural Variety of Mankind), which was first published in 1775, and expand his human taxonomy to include a fifth human variety, the Malay. In this group he located the two South Sea groups identified by Johann Forster as Polynesians and Melanesians. Unsure about exactly where the New Hollanders belonged, he located them between the Malay and the Ethiopian, leaving it open as to whether they might ultimately be classified rather as Ethiopian.[37] In keeping with the tentative nature of his classification and his views on the impact of climate, habitat and mode of life on human development, he noted that the features of the New Hollanders that had been observed by Dampier and Cook might be not endemic but attributable to the climate or the Aborigines' cultural practices.[38]

Blumenbach remained insistent that his distinctions were arbitrary and that the variations he described were much more fluid than the categories used to contain them;[39] nevertheless he continued to refine his system, developing a more rigid classificatory hierarchy in which Caucasians took pride of place as the primeval progenitors of humankind while Ethiopians and Mongolians were consigned to a position at the furthest extremes of their 'Ausartung'. Blumenbach's term 'Ausartung' is generally assumed to mean something more akin to deviation,[40] and this is certainly what he understood by it,[41] but the Biblical resonance of his ideal *Urstamm* (primeval type) inevitably links it with the Fall. In Johann Forster's *Observations Made during a Voyage round the World* (1778), and in the work of his theoretical guide Buffon, the term degeneracy was moreover clearly associated with decline. Forster described the inhabitants of the Western Isles in the South Seas as inferior in every respect to their eastern counterparts, attributing their 'degeneracy and debasement' to the harsher climate and their lack of education.[42] Not surprisingly 'degeneracy' became a catchword in descriptions of the Aborigines, as settlers and administrators were confronted with what seemed to be their insurmountable difference and hostility. Both Douglas and Gascoigne give the example of Barron Field (1786–1846), the judge of the Supreme Court of New South Wales, who in 1822 in an address to the Philosophical Society of Australasia, used Blumenbach's work to consign all of the Australian Aborigines to the one 'degenerate Ethiopian' group and to infer that they would therefore never be civilised.[43]

Most scholars agree that Blumenbach's primary concern was to create a more differentiated scientific scheme that would account for human difference without undermining Biblical authority and a commitment to the unity of humankind.[44] In a way the Ethiopians and the Mongolians were the necessary corollary of the *Urstamm* required to resolve the fundamental tension between these potentially contradictory positions. But to give his model a more scientific foundation, Blumenbach grounded it in human morphology, thereby contributing to a notion of race based not on tentative and fluid transitions but on fixed characteristics. And by adding colour and beauty to his mix of racial markers, he lent his authority to their use as racial discriminators. He also amassed a vast collection of skulls, amongst them two from New Holland, acquired courtesy of Joseph Banks in 1793 and 1799.[45] Although he did not share Forster's enthusiasm for the European civilising mission, his own provincial work was in this respect just as intimately connected to the British imperial endeavour. And it was to have a long-term and far-reaching impact – his fivefold division of races became the canonical taxonomy used by ethnographers in the nineteenth century.[46] In locating the Aborigines in close proximity to the Ethiopians, Blumenbach's work moreover provided an empirical foundation for Dampier's earlier assessment of them as the most primitive of races and scientific sanction for the trade in their skulls and skeletons that has remained a source of anger and sorrow for those whose ancestors were its victims.

Of Forster, Blumenbach and Herder, Herder was possibly the most critical of colonial conquest and Enlightenment notions of progress and European superiority. In the tenth letter of his *Briefe zu Beförderung der Humanität* he railed against European presumption:

> Name the land to which Europeans have come without abusing defenceless, trusting humanity [...] through encroachment, unjust wars, greed, deceit, oppression, through diseases and harmful gifts! Our part of the world should not be called wise, but arrogant, intrusive, cheating; it has not cultivated, but destroyed the germs of peoples' own cultures wherever and however it could.[47]

Herder's view of culture was developed, at least in part, in opposition to the notion of civilisation that was embodied by the French and embraced by many of his Enlightenment contemporaries.[48] The pioneering role attributed to him as the forefather of an anti-Enlightenment cultural relativist tradition is therefore not without foundation. This view has, however, been contested by Enlightenment scholars, amongst them David Denby. In 'Herder: Culture, Anthropology and the Enlightenment' Denby demonstrated that Herder's work, although critical of central aspects of Enlightenment thought – stadial theory, abstract universalism, colonialism – was still firmly anchored in the Enlightenment idea of progress.[49] Denby drew attention to the fundamental tension in Herder's work between two narratives of culture, one that affirmed cultural diversity using a 'language of fixity', another that outlined the development of culture in terms of transformation and progress. In the latter, he maintained, Herder's view of culture came much closer to the Enlightenment view of civilisation.[50]

This tension, which is evident throughout Herder's major work *Ideen zur Philosophie der Geschichte der Menschheit* (1784–91) (Reflections on the Philosophy of the History of Mankind), is also apparent in his representation of the natives of New Holland.[51] In sections of the text in which Herder was concerned to maintain an argument for the common humanity of all humankind, he assured the reader that, contrary to common perception, all primitive peoples, including the *Neuholländer*, did have some form of belief.[52] He rejected the stadial view of history, arguing that each group had developed the capacities required by its environment. Although the needs of the New Hollanders were constrained by the harsh climate, they adjusted their desires accordingly and therefore enjoyed their own type of felicity.[53] In the section of the *Ideen* devoted to his characterisation of different peoples, Herder, however, turned to Dampier and the remarks made by Johann Reinhold Forster in his *Observations*. This is surprising given that, as I have noted, Hawkesworth's account of Cook's first voyage was available in translation and had already been reprinted a number of times. Like Forster, Herder included the Aborigines among an older 'negro' stock which had inhabited a number of the Asian islands before being displaced by more recent arrivals.[54] The New Hollanders that Dampier described seem, he commented, to belong to the lowest class of this group and inhabit one of the most desolate tracts on this earth.[55] In this part of the *Ideen* the Aborigines were embedded in his narrative of historical transformation, and his representation of them was dictated by that narrative. Here the 'negro' (and by implication those of negro stock) was represented as the developmental antithesis of the European, fixed by climate and disposition at a more primitive stage of human development.[56] While Herder was insistent that each culture should be valued as a manifestation of the divine in nature, the development of humankind, its transformation, was driven by education, by commerce and ultimately by displacement and destruction. In his description of the natural world Herder expressed a view of development that was very similar to that of Georg Forster: Always and everywhere, he argued, nature needed to destroy in order to rebuild; it had to divide in order to reunite.[57]

Herder resolved the contradiction between his vehement opposition to colonial conquest and his promotion of commerce as a motor of progress by splitting commerce into good and bad and appealing to people's divinely ordained humanity. On this, he based the utopian hope that, with time and the advancement of reason, 'voyages of conquest will become voyages of trade, founded upon mutual justice and protection'.[58] To maintain a view of Herder as the pioneer of a Counter-Enlightenment tradition untainted by colonial concerns and Enlightenment hierarchies of development, it is necessary to ignore or downplay this clear strand of his narrative.

While the information available to Forster, Blumenbach and Herder was limited, it is evident here that the representation of the Aborigines, or the role they played, in the works examined was determined to a considerable degree by the function they had in other narratives, the narrative of discovery and progress (Forster), the scientific counterpart of the Biblical creation myth (Blumenbach), and the story of human transformation (Herder). Although it may not have been their intention, the fact that they relied on Dampier as their main source contributed to the persistence of his view of the Aborigines in the German discourse of human diversity, giving it new authority. Similarly, their attempts to explain development in terms of degeneration or destruction and displacement fed easily into the nineteenth-century discourses of cultural inferiority and extinction. Despite their criticisms of European society, in all of their works Europeans ultimately retained their pre-eminence as the pinnacle of human development.

### Gerstäcker and the Aborigines: Australia as a place of German colonial interest

By the mid-nineteenth century a different mood prevailed in the German states. Herder's scepticism about stadial models of progress had proved to be well founded. A combination of industrialisation, agrarian reform, population growth and crop failures had produced not progress but unemployment, poverty and famine. The resulting social problems led many German states to actively promote migration as a means of ensuring social stability. Political oppression and social dislocation led in 1848 to political upheaval and, for a brief period, to a new political order. Representatives of the new order saw migration not only as a means of alleviating Germany's social problems but also as a way of establishing German enclaves abroad that might serve as beachheads for German trade,[59] and secure Germany's standing as a nation and international power.[60] By virtue of its compatible climate, valuable mineral resources and strategic location, Australia was one of the countries considered suitable for the establishment of German settler colonies.[61]

A supporter of the new order, Gerstäcker was able to persuade the newly formed Frankfurt parliament and the Cotta publishing company to finance his voyage around the world to report on the success of overseas German settlements and explore new destinations for German migrants. Although the parliament was dissolved before Gerstäcker arrived in Australia, depriving him of his main source of funds, he spent in all some six months there. In that time he undertook an adventurous overland trek from Sydney to Adelaide, travelling first by mail coach to Albury, then by hand-built canoe along an uncharted stretch of the Murray, and finally, when his boat sank, on foot to South Australia where he visited German communities on the outskirts of Adelaide and in the Barossa Valley. His journey provided him with material for one volume of his five-volume travel narrative, as well as for a number of articles, short stories and novels.[62]

By 1851 Australia had realised some of the colonial potential that Forster had foreseen in 1786, but the Aborigines had failed to move on and find somewhere else to live. For many, Dampier's view of them as 'the miserablest people' was confirmed by the colonial encounter. Their perceived lack of culture, particularly their seeming failure to cultivate the land,[63] served to support the legitimacy of their displacement in the eyes of their colonisers, an application of Enlightenment theory that was enacted in the colonies with devastating effect.[64] The expropriation of Aboriginal lands and the destruction of their food sources led to violent clashes between settlers and Aborigines. On the path Gerstäcker was to follow to South Australia, the escalation of violence had led in 1841 to a bloody and much publicised massacre on the Rufus river.[65] Despite the Enlightenment belief in the common humanity of humankind and the human potential for improvement, the Aborigines seemed stubbornly resistant to the ostensible blessings of civilisation and Christianity. Far from benefiting from European example, they had, it was argued, succumbed to European vice and disease. As their numbers decreased, the conviction increased that they were a doomed race.[66]

Nevertheless, as a result of the work of Aboriginal protectors, colonial administrators and missionaries, a great deal more was known about Australia's indigenous peoples and their way of life by the time Gerstäcker arrived in Australia. Amongst this group were humanitarians who spoke up on their behalf, challenged popular prejudice and criticised the mistreatment of the Aborigines at European hands. The main sources of ethnographic information about the Aborigines in South Australia, the destination of Gerstäcker's overland journey, were the journals and reports of Matthew Moorhouse (1813–76), South Australian Protector of Aborigines from 1839 to 1856, the ethnographic accounts of the Dresden missionaries Christian Teichelmann (1807–93), Clamor Schürmann (1815–93) and Heinrich Meyer (1813–62) and the travel account of Edward Eyre (1815–1901), Resident Magistrate and Protector of the Aborigines on the Murray river from 1841 to 1844.[67] By his own acknowledgement, Gerstäcker did not spend long enough in Australia to give an informed account of the Aborigines and was therefore reliant on the additional information he could obtain from other sources.[68] These were the sources to which he turned.[69]

His appropriation of his English sources could in fact be seen as an act of textual colonisation. In the German version of his *Reisen*, Gerstäcker attributed the greater part of his information to Moorhouse, who had generously placed his journals at his disposal and allowed him to take notes.[70] In the English version of his *Travels* published only one year later, he claims to have had insufficient time to take advantage of Moorhouse's offer, directing English readers instead to the accounts of the two Dresden missionaries, Schürmann and Teichelmann. He made no mention of Eyre although the wording of some parts of his text indicates that he must also have used Eyre's account.[71] For his information on Aboriginal myths and legends Gerstäcker turned to Meyer. The Aboriginal section of Gerstäcker's German narrative was first published separately in serial form in Cotta's daily *Das Ausland* in 1852 where its author was given as Dr Gerstäcker.[72] Gerstäcker, like Forster, was clearly aware of the provincial capital, cultural and financial, that accrued to him as a traveller with first-hand experience of other cultures, and both here and in his *Reisen* he employed various strategies to blur the border between his sources and his own input, stamping his authority on the texts he translated, in some instances simply deleting unnecessary detail, in others removing references that clearly identify the author or the main target audience, and on occasion adding commentary of his own. But he had chosen his sources judiciously and they served him well.

Gerstäcker's account of the South Australian Aborigines was not the first account published in German, but it was possibly the first to reach a wider German reading public.[73] In his role as cultural mediator he not only provided his readers with new information about the Aboriginal culture of a particular region but also continued the critical Counter-Enlightenment tradition with which Herder's work is associated. His sources furnished him with most of the material contained in the two chapters of his *Reisen* dedicated to the Aborigines, and with the credentials of a well-informed ethnographer with an insider's knowledge of the tribes that inhabited the districts he visited. In this section of his text he provided valuable insights into the culture that the Aborigines were alleged not to have, giving a detailed and differentiated account of their lifestyle, dietary laws, weapons and implements, their ceremonies, burial rites and superstitions, and examples of their myths and legends. Although conceding that they might appear to be 'God's most neglected people', he attempted to explain some of their purported deficiencies in terms of their own culture and the land they inhabited,[74] drawing attention to their skill as hunters, trackers and mimics.[75]

He also corrected a number of other misconceptions about Aborigines that had persisted since the Enlightenment. He followed Blumenbach in declaring them to be an intermediate race, a mix of Negro and South Sea Islander or Malay, but challenged the view, reiterated by Forster in his 'Neuholland' essay, that they were the same throughout the land,[76] pointing to differences in their features, skin colour and hair.[77] Where it had long been assumed that they had no concept of property, Gerstäcker explained that greater understanding of their language revealed that they did in fact have territorial rights, that they possessed tracts of land that were passed on from father to son just as property was in Europe and other parts of the 'civilised' world.[78] While he did not explore the implications of this discovery in the travel narrative, he did in one of the novels based on it. In the novel *Die beiden Sträflinge* (The Two Convicts) (1856) the blame for Aboriginal hostility was put squarely on European failure to acknowledge their prior ownership of the land.[79] The failure of the civilising mission, in which Forster expressed such faith, was for Gerstäcker a cause not for disappointment or frustration but rather for amusement. He clearly took some pleasure in the fact that attempts to settle the natives and convert them had proved so fruitless. At the first call of their comrades from the bush, the Aborigines abandoned all vestiges of Europeanisation and returned to the wilds. As a result, the missionaries had been forced to abandon their schools and their mission, consigning the souls of their charges to eternal damnation. The Devil could not have wished for better agents, Gerstäcker concluded with a typical touch of sarcasm.[80]

Without question, the authors of Gerstäcker's sources were driven by colonial concerns. Moorhouse sought to provide the government and the settlers with the information needed to ensure stability in the colony, the missionaries were motivated by the need to be able to communicate with their potential converts, while Eyre looked to improve understanding of the Aborigines so as to alleviate their situation.[81] Gerstäcker's account, in comparison, does seem to represent a genuine attempt to provide his German readers with a more nuanced, less immediately utilitarian view of Aboriginal culture. But Gerstäcker was not only a myth breaker, he was also a myth maker. In 'Das Lager der Schwarzen' (The Blacks' Camp) published in the *Hausblätter* in 1856 he said: 'My expectations of a voyage are modest – I only require a beautiful foreign land and foreign people, or some danger to spice the boring journey.'[82] His journey through the monotony of the Australian wilderness needed spice, savages to provide interest and suspense, an adversary to underline his own role as adventurer and hero. This role fell to the Aborigines who, in this strand of the narrative, were represented accordingly as hostile, treacherous, malicious and murderous.[83] Having heard of the Aborigines' practice of extracting the kidney fat from their still living victims, he, and with him the reader, lived in constant fear that any encounter with the 'Blacks' would result in the loss of his 'Butter'.[84] Whereas Gerstäcker, the 'ethnographer', made an important, albeit textually mediated contribution to his readers' understanding of German culture, Gerstäcker the author of adventure perpetuated the stereotypical view of Aborigines as ignoble savages who had prevailed since Dampier, thereby undermining the critical impetus of his ethnographic contribution and its more empathic understanding of the Aborigines' situation.

*Gerstäcker's 'Australien und die australische Race':*
*diversity versus unity*

In 1860, Gerstäcker made a further contribution to debates concerning human variety and the origin of humankind with the title 'Australien und die australische Race'. In this article he, in characteristic fashion, asserted his authority as someone with first-hand experience of Australia to put paid to reports of a large inland stream in the interior of the country and the fantasies it had fuelled. But he also took the opportunity to make a much more radical intervention, proposing in the second part of the article, unexpectedly, a revision of Blumenbach's division of humankind. The Malays could be considered a separate race, he declared, whereas the Australian Aborigines most certainly were and should therefore take the place of the Malays as the fifth human variety in Blumenbach's taxonomy.[85] To support this revision, he used arguments that at first sight seemed to hark back to Herder's *Ideen*, emphasising the need to see the Bible as the product of a particular culture, as well as the connection between each species and the land that it inhabits. Gerstäcker, however, severed the ties that grounded these arguments in the scriptural account of a single common origin. Those who unnecessarily devoted their time and energy to trying to demonstrate that the peoples of the earth all evolved from one original couple were not even supported by the Bible itself, he declared.[86] Current knowledge indicated that plants and animals had already existed before the advent of human beings, and that they must have been equally distributed over different parts of the world, or at least have occupied different centres from which they had spread out in an area with a suitable climate. He then gave examples to demonstrate the improbability of migration theories – how would a tiger have managed to get from paradise to South America? Certainly not by sea, and by land it would have had to cross the polar region and swim across the Bering Strait. If there were not multiple centres of creation, one would moreover have to assume that other parts of the world had remained empty until fortuitously discovered and populated by one or the other traveller.[87] He went on to demonstrate that the Aborigines could not have originated from the Malays or the Ethiopians. To the Ethiopians they bore no resemblance, and it was inconceivable that such a non-migratory people would have travelled so far afield, while neighbouring island dwellers from the north kept their distance, repelled by the ferocity of the Australian natives, the barren land and lack of things to trade. With a typical Gerstäcker quip, he added that a people who inhabited such a salty, arid wasteland must have been created for it, or they would never ever have been able to endure it.[88]

In 1850 Louis Agassiz (1807–73), one of the most influential advocates of polygenism, had published an article entitled 'Geographical Distribution of Animals' in which he challenged the authority of 'the Mosaic record' and made a case for the existence of distinct zoological provinces in which animals and plants had been created for the particular habitat in which they were to be found.[89] It provided him with the natural historical foundation for his theory of human diversity which he outlined in 'The Diversity of Origin of the Human Races',[90] published in the same year. Here he made a similar case for multiple, distinct centres of creation, one of which was New Holland. Gerstäcker must have been familiar with Agassiz's work. In 'Australien and die australische Race' he reproduced Agassiz's central thesis as well as some of the points made to justify it.

Why the turn to polygenism? Some of the appeal of polygenist theory for Gerstäcker lay no doubt quite simply in the opportunity it afforded him to take on Germany's major anthropological authority and assert his own as someone with greater personal experience of the wider world. Polygenism, however, was already present as a potential in the work of Forster, Blumenbach and Herder. Its explanatory power was recognised by Forster, who in his debate with Kant on the issue of race entertained the possibility of different origins, but chose to leave the question open.[91] It was also inherent in Blumenbach's taxonomy and Herder's reflections on cultural particularity, but both Blumenbach and Herder demonstratively maintained their stance on the unity of humankind, recognising the threat posed by the polygenist position to Biblical authority, and to the very notion of humanity as the distinguishing feature of human beings and their moral compass.[92] The monogenist view prevailed in the early nineteenth century, but by the middle of the nineteenth century polygenism had gained ground, given support by the increased inflow of information on different cultures, the shift in attempts to explain human difference from climate and habitat to morphology and heredity, discoveries in geology and palaeontology that challenged Biblical chronology, and the sobering experience of increased cultural contact.[93] In Germany it remained a hotly contested issue and a source of acrimonious disputes to which Gerstäcker might well have intended to contribute.[94]

As biblical authority waned and colonial views hardened, poly-genism also gained increasing currency in Australia. In providing a clear demarcation of difference and an explanation for the resistance of some peoples to attempts to remedy their perceived deficiencies, polygenist theory provided a psychological salve for personal prejudice and colonial conscience. As Aboriginal numbers declined in Australia and attempts to civilise the natives were abandoned, their fate was increasingly attributed to their innate difference. [95] It is not clear whether Gerstäcker shared this view, but he would no doubt have been exposed to it during his Australian sojourn, and he did accept the inevitability of progress and the inevitability of its outcome for indigenous populations:

> and steamers will puff and locomotives wheeze where the proud palm, in silent majesty, still waves its crown [...] All of this will happen with an unmistakable necessity in order to provide the growing human race with space for its preservation – space for its restless activity – and he who has the space to spare – the native – will be the victim.[96]

## Conclusion

Enlightenment *or* empire, cosmopolitanism *or* colonialism, liberal humanism *or* racism? These oppositions and the 'or' that divides them are to some extent at least the creations of the broad brushstroke narratives of which they are a part, narratives that necessarily subordinate complexity and contradiction to coherence. The texts examined in this chapter demonstrate that the Germans' representations of the Aborigines were in part determined by the sources on which they drew, in part by the internal debates in which they were engaged, by a worldly interest in cultural difference on the one hand, and a desire to contain it on the other. While German anthropology can lay some claim to the moral high ground of a liberal humanism that was critical of colonial abuse and European self-aggrandissement, it was not divorced from empire, or from the Enlightenment notions of civilisation and progress that underpinned European views of cultural development, and this inevitably impacted on the Germans' view of the Aborigines. Ironically, it was Gerstäcker, the traveller with an explicit colonial brief, who, by virtue of the sources on which he drew, rather than his own encounter with the Aborigines, went furthest in challenging traditional preconceptions of the Aborigines and providing his German readers with a more informed and differentiated picture of Aboriginal culture.

Given the Germans' dependence on other sources, most of them English, it is difficult to make a case for a perspective on the Aborigines that was distinctly German and different. What links their texts is rather a tradition of cultural inquiry that grew out of the interchange between travel literature and anthropology and to which they contributed as Germans. It enabled them not only to engage seriously with the question of unity and the challenges posed by cultural difference but also to step outside their own culture and view it through a more critical lens.

Gerstäcker concluded 'Civilisation und Wildniß' with a sobering indictment of those who considered themselves to be more civilised – when they are gone, we will express some regret that we did not treat the inhabitants of the wilderness more kindly, he declared, but

[ 162 ]

their story will soon be forgotten; we have too much to do to reflect on their fate – 'and the world is civilised'.[97]

## Notes

1  Friedrich Gerstäcker, 'Civilsation und Wildniß', *Die Gartenlaube* 17 (1855), 224–5, at p. 225.
2  In *Liberal Imperialism in Germany* (2008) Matthew Fitzpatrick drew attention to this article in order to demonstrate that the 'racializing tendencies' of German popular literature were not always monolithic. He noted that Gerstäcker did not criticise colonialism as such but rather the moralising that accompanied it. See Matthew P. Fitzpatrick, *Liberal Imperialism in Germany. Expansionism and Nationalism 1848–1884* (New York and Oxford: Berghahn Books, 2008), p. 183.
3  Russell A. Berman, *Enlightenment or Empire. Colonial Discourse in German Culture* (Lincoln and London: University of Nebraska Press, 1998), pp. 10, 14–15.
4  Berman, *Enlightenment or Empire*, p. 16
5  A move away from totalising master narratives has seen scholars from different areas make similar calls for a greater focus on the complexity of particular local and historical contexts. Notable examples are Sara Eigen and Mark Larrimore, 'The German Invention of Race', in Sara Eigen and Mark Larrimore (eds), *The German Invention of Race* (Albany: State University of New York Press, 2006), pp. 1–10; Bronwen Douglas, 'Foreign Bodies in Oceania', in Bronwen Douglas and Chris Ballard (eds.), *Foreign Bodies. Oceania and the Science of Race 1750–1940* (Canberra: ANU E Press, 2008), pp. 3–30; George Steinmetz, *The Devil's Handwriting. Precoloniality and the German Colonial State in Qingdao, Samoa, and Southwest Africa* (Chicago and London: University of Chicago Press, 2007).
6  For a succinct survey of the history of anthropology and some of its main concerns, see Henrika Kuklick, 'History of Anthropology', in Rofer Backhouse and Phillipa Fontaine (eds), *A Historiography of the Modern Social Sciences* (Cambridge: Cambridge University Press, 2014), pp. 62–99.
7  Penny and Bunzl used anthropology as an umbrella term that included ethnology. I have expanded it here to include ethnography and ethnographic accounts. While this ignores the historical distinctions between the different fields of enquiry, it underlines the porosity of the boundaries which divide them. For a comprehensive discussion of the three areas and their origins, see Hans F. Vermeulen, *Before Boas: The Genesis of Ethnography and Ethnology in the German Enlightenment* (Lincoln and London: University of Nebraska Press, 2015), pp. 1–37.
8  Matti Bunzl and H. Glenn Penny, 'Introduction: Rethinking German Anthropology, Colonialism and Race', in H. Glenn Penny and Matti Bunzl (eds), *Worldly Provincialism. German Anthropology in the Age of Empire* (Ann Arbor: University of Michigan Press, 2003), pp. 1–30, at pp. 1–2. While acknowledging the importance of colonialism as a context for the development of German anthropology, the majority of contributors to the volume supported Penny and Bunzl's thesis, as others in the field have done. Andre Gingrich emphasised the non-colonial empirical spirit that guided early German studies of other cultures, Hans Vermeulen their scholarly agenda. See Andre Gingrich, 'The German-Speaking Countries', in Fredrick Barth, Andre Gingrich, Robert Parkin and Sydel Silverman. *One Discipline, Four Ways: British, German, French, and American Anthropolgy* (Chicago and London: University of Chicago Press, 2005), pp. 61–153, at p. 68; Vermeulen, *Before Boas*, p. 442. A notable exception was Andrew Zimmerman who, in *Worldly Provincialism* and the book on which his contribution was based, used the example of the 'skin trade' to establish a direct connection between colonial subjection and anthropological objectification and demonstrate that physical anthropology was, in theory and practice, not liberal at all but, on the contrary, both anti-humanist and anti-human. See Andrew Zimmerman, 'Adventures in the Skin Trade: German Anthropology and Colonial

Corporeality'. in Penny and Bunzl (eds), *Wordly Provincialism*, pp. 156–79; Andrew Zimmerman, *Anthropology and Antihumanism in Imperial Germany* (Chicago and London: University of Chicago Press, 2001).

9  Bunzl and Penny, *Worldly Provincialism*, pp. 11, 12, 14.
10  The exception is Liebersohn's comparison of Chamisso's and Krämer's Pacific travel narratives. See Harry Liebersohn, 'Coming of Age in the Pacific: German Ethnography from Chamisso to Krämer', in Penny and Bunzl (eds), *Worldly Provincialism*, pp. 31–46.
11  In *Colonial Fantasies* Susanne Zantop noted that, at the end of the eighteenth century, the Germans were the main consumers of travel accounts in Europe. Andre Gingrich devoted a separate section of his account of anthropology in the German-speaking countries to the 'travel-report side' of Enlightenment anthropology. Penny and Bunzl too commented on the increased German demand for travel reports in the nineteenth century, which they saw as a marker of German 'worldliness'. By the middle of the nineteenth century, it had, they noted, become a new market, with middle-class newspapers and magazines devoting whole sections to travel and ethnographic accounts. See Susanne Zantop, *Colonial Fantasies. Conquest, Family, and Nation in Precolonial Germany, 1770–1870* (Durham, NC, and London: Duke University Press, 1997), p. 32; Gingrich, 'The German-Speaking Countries', pp. 66–8; Penny and Bunzl, *Wordly Provincialism*, p. 5.
12  Joan Pau Rubiés, 'Travel Writing and Ethnography', in Peter Hulme and Tim Youngs (eds), *The Cambridge Companion to Travel Writing* (Cambridge: Cambridge University Press, 2002), pp. 242–60, at p. 257.
13  Friedrich Gerstäcker, *Reisen*, Vol. IV (Stuttgart and Tübingen: Cotta, 1854).
14  Friedrich Gerstäcker, 'Australien und die australische Race', *Die Gartenlaube* 30(1860) 473–5.
15  In *Ideology, Mimesis, Fantasy: Charles Sealsfield, Friedrich Gerstäcker, Karl May, and Other German Novelists of America* (1998), Jeffrey Sammons underlined the 'mimetic' dimension of Gerstäcker's work which he claimed was based on Gerstäcker's desire to provide the German reading public with realistic images of the other worlds he visited. See Jeffrey L. Sammons, *Ideology, Mimesis, Fantasy: Charles Sealsfield, Friedrich Gerstäcker, Karl May, and Other German Novelists of America* (Chapel Hill: University of North Carolina Press, 1998), pp. xi, 200. For this reason Gerstäcker is regarded as a representative of a new ethnographic realism in travel writing.
16  Gerstäcker's representation of the Aborigines has received some attention in German-Australian literary and intercultural studies, but, because his reputation is based primarily on his status as a popular author, the focus of these studies has thus far been literary, rather than ethnographic. For an overview of Gerstäcker's Australian writings, see Alan Corkhill, *Antipodean Encounters: Australia and the German Literary Imagination 1754–1918* (Bern, Frankfurt am Main, New York and Paris: Peter Lang, 1990), pp. 73–102. For a more recent literary study, see Alan, Corkhill, 'Space, Place and Identity in the Australian Fiction of Friedrich Gerstäcker', *Limbus Australisches Jahrbuch für germanistische Literatur- und Kulturwissenschaft* 6 (2013), 141–55. For intercultural literary studies of Gerstäcker's work, see Matthias Morgenroth, *Nachrichten aus dem Land der Gegenfüßler: Untersuchungen zur deutschen Australienliteratur* (Tübingen: Stauffenberg, 2001); Christiane Weller, 'Das fremde Ich. Begegnungen im pazifischen Raum' (PhD Dissertation, Monash University, 1998); Christiane Weller, 'Male Pursuits. Travelling Adventurers in Australia and the Pacific', in Alison Lewis, Lara Anderson and Heather Merle Benbow (eds), *Other Encounters: European Writers and Gender in Transnational* Context (St Ingbert: Röhrig Universitätsverlag, 2014), pp. 117–43; Judith Wilson, 'Enlightenment and/or Empire: Two German Perspectives on the Australian Aborigines', in Henriette von Holleuffer and Adi Wimmer (eds), *Australien: Realität – Klischee – Vision* (Trier: Wissenschaftlicher Verlag Trier, 2012), pp. 153–66. For a recent translation of Gerstäcker's travel account, see Peter Monteath (ed.), *Australia. Friedrich Gerstäcker. A German Traveller in the Age of Gold* (Mile End: Wakefield Press, 2016).

17 Friedrich Gerstäcker, 'Zur Naturgeschichte des Menschen', in Friedrich Hackländer and Edmund Hoefer, *Die Hausblätter*, Vol. I (Stuttgart: Adolph Krabbe, 1860), 68–80.
18 Gerstäcker, 'Zur Naturgeschichte des Menschen', 72–3.
19 Gerstäcker, 'Zur Naturgeschichte des Menschen', 73–4.
20 Johann Gottfried Herder, *J.G. von Herder's ausgewählte Werke in einem Band* (Stuttgandart Tübingen: J. G. Cotta'scher Verlag, 1844), p. 1195.
21 Douglas, 'Foreign Bodies in Oceania', in Douglas and Ballard (eds), *Foreign Bodies*, p. 13.
22 Douglas, 'Climate to Crania: Science and the Racialization of Human Difference', in Douglas and Ballard (eds), *Foreign Bodies*, pp. 33–96, at pp. 37–41.
23 Douglas, ' "Novus Orbis Australis": Oceania in the Science of Race, 1750–1850', in Douglas and Ballard (eds), *Foreign Bodies*, pp. 99–155. On Blumenbach pp. 106–10; on the Forsters pp. 102–6.
24 Douglas, ' "Nobus Orbis Australis" ', p. 101.
25 William Dampier, *A New Voyage Around the World* (New York: Dover Publications, 1968), p. 313. First published 1697. On Dampier, see Bernard Smith, *European Vision and the South Pacific* (Sydney: Harper and Row, 1985), pp. 169–71. First published 1960.
26 John Hawkesworth, *An account of a voyage round the world with a full account of the voyage of the Endeavour: in the year MDCCLXX along the east coast of Australia by Lieutenant James Cook, Commander of His Majesty's Bark Endeavour*, compiled by D. Warrrington Evans (Brisbane: W.R. Smith and Paterson, 1969). First published in 1773. For details of the German editions, see Leslie Bodi, Stephen Jeffries and Susan Radvansky, *Image of a Continent. A Bibliography of German Australiana from the Beginnings to 1975 – Bild eines Kontinents. Eine Bibliographie deutscher Australiana von den Anfängen bis 1975* (Wiesbaden: O. Harrasowitz, 1990), p. 199.
27 Georg Forster, 'Neuholland und die brittische Colonie in Botany Bay', in Deutsche Akademie der Wissenschaften zu Berlin (ed.), *Georg Forsters Werke: Sämtliche Schriften, Tagebücher, Briefe*, Vol. 5 (Berlin: Akademie-Verlag, 1985), pp. 161–80. First published 1787. The *Historisch-Genealogischer Calender* was a yearbook focused on new events and discoveries.
28 Cf. John Gascoigne, 'The German Enlightenment and the Pacific', in Larry Wolff and Marc Cipolloni (eds), *The Anthropology of the Enlightenment* (Stanford: Stanford University Press, 2007), pp. 141–71, at p. 145.
29 Forster, 'Neuholland', pp. 165–8.
30 Zantop, *Colonial Fantasies*.
31 Forster, 'Neuholland', pp. 174–8.
32 Forster's view of the forces driving development is outlined in a subsequent essay, 'Cook der Entdecker' (Cook the Discoverer) also published in 1787. See Georg Forster, 'Cook der Entdecker', in Deutsche Akademie der Wissenschaften zu Berlin (ed.), *Georg Forsters Werke: Sämtliche Schriften, Tagebücher, Briefe*, Vol. 5 (Berlin: Akademie-Verlag, 1985), pp. 191–302, at pp. 194–5.
33 Georg Forster, *A Voyage round the World*, in Deutsche Akademie der Wissenschaften zu Berlin (ed.), *Georg Forsters Werke*, Vol. 1, p. 133.
34 For a more detailed analysis of Forster's essay, see Judith Wilson, 'Abjection, Subjection, Redemption: Georg Forster's and Therese Huber's Perspectives on the Penal Colony', *Georg-Forster-Studien* 14 (2009), 133–87.
35 George Steinmetz uses the term cultural or ethnographic capital to describe the object of those competing for recognition of their ethnographic authority in the German colonies. See George Steinmetz, *The Devil's Handwriting. Precoloniality and the German Colonial State in Qingdao, Samoa, and Southwest Africa* (Chicago and London: University of Chicago Press, 2007), p. xiv.
36 Douglas, ' "Nobus Orbis Australis" ', p. 100.
37 Johann Friedrich Blumenbach, *Über die natürlichen Verschiedenehiten im Menschengeschlechte* (Berlin: Humboldt Universität zu Berlin, 2011), p. 124. Reprint of the original first published in 1798.

38  Blumenbach, *Über die natürlichen Verschiedenheiten im Menschengeschlechte*, pp. 139, 154.
39  Blumenbach, *Über die natürlichen Verschiedenehiten im Menschengeschlechte*, pp. 203–4.
40  cf. Douglas, 'Climate to Crania', p. 38.
41  Timothy Lenoir, 'The Göttingen School and the Development of Transcendental Naturphilosophie in the Romantic Era', *Studies in the History of Biology* 5 (1981), 111–205, at p. 140.
42  Johann Reinhold Forster, *Observations Made during a Voyage round the World* (Honolulu: University of Hawai'i Press, 1996), p. 342 (edited by Nicholas Thomas, Harriet Guest and Michael Dettelbach). First published 1778.
43  Douglas, '"Nobus Orbis Australis"', p. 135; John Gascoigne, *The Enlightenment and the Origins of European Australia* (Cambridge: Cambridge University Press, 2002), p. 165.
44  George W. Stocking, Jr, *Race, Culture and Evolution. Essays in the History of Anthropology* (New York: The Free Press, 1968), p. 40; John Zammito, 'Policing Polygenesis in German', in Sara Eigen and Mark Larrimore (eds), *The German Invention of Race* (Albany: State University of New York Press, 2006), pp. 35–54, at p. 45.
45  John Gascoigne, *Joseph Banks and the English Enlightenment. Useful Knowledge and Polite Culture* (Cambridge: Cambridge University Press, 1991), p. 151.
46  B. Ricardo Brown, *Until Darwin: Science, Human Variety and the Origins of Race* (London: Pickering and Chatto, 2010), p. 46.
47  Herder, *J.G. von Herder's ausgewählte Werke in einem Band*, p. 1195.
48  Wulf Koepke, 'Herder's Views on the Germans and Their Future Literature', in Hans Adler and Wulf Koepke (eds), *A Companion to the Works of Johann Gottfried Herder* (Rochester and New York: Camden House, 2009), pp. 215–32, at p. 223.
49  David Denby, 'Herder: Culture, Anthropology and the Enlightenment', *History of the Human Sciences* 18:1 (2005), 55–76, at pp. 59ff.
50  Denby, 'Herder: Culture, Anthropology and the Enlightenment', pp. 66–7.
51  Johann Gottfried Herder, *Ideen zur Philosophie der Geschichte der Menschheit* (Berlin: Holzinger, 2013). First published 1782–8.
52  Herder, *Ideen*, p. 278.
53  Herder, *Ideen*, p. 224.
54  Herder, *Ideen*, p. 173.
55  Herder, *Ideen*, p. 172.
56  For a critical assessment of Herder's views on Negroes see Zantop, *Colonial Fantasies*, pp. 66–81.
57  Herder, *Ideen*, p. 40.
58  The two different views of commerce in Herder's *Ideen* are outlined in John K. Noyes, 'Commerce, Colonialism, and the Globalization of Action in Late Enlightenment Germany', *Postcolonial Studies* 9:1 (2006), 81–98, at p. 93.
59  Renate Vollmer, *Auswanderungspolitik und soziale Frage im 19. Jahrhundert. Staatlich geförderte Auswanderung aus der Berghauptmannschaft Clausthal nach Südaustralien, Nord- und Südamerika 1848–1854* (Frankfurt am Main, Berlin, Bern, New York, Paris and Vienna: Peter Lang, 1994), p. 65.
60  In *Liberal Imperialism in Germany* (2008), Matthew Fitzpatrick argues that expansionism was central not only to German liberals' solution to the so-called *Sozialfrage* (social question) but also to their notion of the nation-state, providing them with the unifying concept needed to overcome German particularism and combat rival narratives of the nation-state. The liberals, he claims, engaged in 'an imperialism from below', considering very different types of colonial ventures, amongst them settler colonies and migration, as complementary means to achieving their expansionist goal. See Matthew P. Fitzpatrick, *Liberal Imperialism in Germany. Expansionism and Nationalism 1848–1884*. (New York and Oxford: Berghahn Books, 2008), pp. 1–24.
61  For an account of developments in this period, see David Blackbourn, *The Long Nineteenth Century* (Hammersmith: Fontana, 1997).

62  For more detail on Gerstäcker and his undertaking, see Monteath (ed.), *Australia*, pp. 261–75.
63  This view has been challenged by Bill Gammage who, in *The Biggest Estate on Earth*, described the forms of systematic land management employed by the Aborigines to ensure an abundant supply of plants and animals in the areas over which they ranged. See Bill Gammage, *The Biggest Estate on Earth. How Aborigines Made Australia* (Crows Nest: Allen & Unwin, 2011).
64  Douglas, '"Nobus Orbis Australis"', p. 134.
65  On frontier conflict, see Henry Reynolds, *Frontier. Aborigines, Settlers and Land* (St Leonards: Allen and Unwin, 1996). First published 1987. On the Rufus river massacre, see Robert Foster, Rick Hosking and Amanda Nettelbeck, *Fatal Collisions* (Adelaide: Wakefield Press, 2001), pp. 29–34.
66  Robert Foster, 'An Imaginary Dominion. The Representation and Treatment of Aborigines in South Australia 1834–1911' (PhD Dissertation, University of Adelaide, 1993), p. 175.
67  Foster, 'An Imaginary Dominion', pp. 148–55.
68  Gerstäcker, *Reisen*, p. 337.
69  Gerstäcker's primary sources were Moorhouse's journal, no longer extant, and his reports, some of which were published in local newspapers and the British Parliamentary Papers, (two have been republished by Robert Foster in *Journal of the Anthropological Society of South Australia* 28 (1990), 38–64); Edward John Eyre (1854), *Journals of Expeditions of Discovery into Central Australia and Overland from Adelaide to King George's Sound in the Years 1840–1*, Vol. II (London: T. & W. Boone; Heinrich Meyer); *Manners and Customs of the Aborigines of the Encounter Bay tribe* (Adelaide: Public Library of South Australia, 1962). First published 1846.
70  Gerstäcker, *Reisen*, p. 292.
71  For examples, see Judith Wilson, 'Enlightenment and/or Empire: Two German Perspectives on the Australian Aborigines', in Holleuffer and Wimmer (eds), *Australien: Realität – Klischee – Vision*, pp. 153–66, at p. 159.
72  Friedrich Gerstäcker, 'Die Indianer Australiens', *Das Ausland: Wochenschrift für Erd- und Völkerkunde* 25:62–8 (1852), 247–71.
73  Other information on the South Australian Aborigines that was available in German, but presumably not to a broader reading public, included the missionary reports published in the *Dresdner Missionsnachrichten* and the following accounts which appeared in the monthly reports of the proceedings of the Berlin Geographical Society: Hermann Koeler's 'Notizen über die Eingeborenen an der Ostküste des St. Vincent-Golfs in Süd-Australien. 1837 und 1838', *Monatsberichte über die Verhandlungen der Gesellschaft für Erdkunde zu Berlin* 1:3 (1842), 42–57; 1:5 (1844), 34–75; Schayer, 'Abhandlung über die Verhältnisse der Eingeborenen von Australien und die Ursachen der Abnahme dieser Bevölkerung', *Monatsberichte über die Verhandlungen der Gesellschaft für Erdkunde zu Berlin.* 4 (1847) – 8 (1847), 225–32; Dr Herm. Behr, 'Über die Urbewohner von Süd-Australien', *Monatsberichte über die Verhandlungen der Gesellschaft für Erdkunde zu Berlin* (1848), 89–93.
74  Gerstäcker, *Reisen*, pp. 333–4.
75  Gerstäcker, *Reisen*, pp. 282, 284, 333.
76  Forster, 'Neuholland', p. 174.
77  Gerstäcker, *Reisen*, p. 334.
78  Gerstäcker, *Reisen*, p. 347.
79  Friedrich Gerstäcker, *Die beiden Sträflinge* (Jena: Costenoble, 1856), p. 106.
80  Gerstäcker, *Reisen*, pp. 287–90.
81  Foster, 'An Imaginary Dominion', pp. 152–5.
82  Friedrich Gerstäcker, 'Das Lager der Schwarzen', *Die Hausblätter* 3 (1856), 116–125, at 116.
83  Gerstäcker, *Reisen*, pp. 13, 86.
84  Gerstäcker, *Reisen*, p. 203. For a more detailed discussion of this aspect of Gerstäcker's *Reisen* see, Wilson, 'Enlightenment and/or Empire', pp. 162–3.

85  Gerstäcker, 'Australien und die australische Race', 473.
86  Gerstäcker, 'Australien und die australische Race', 473.
87  Gerstäcker, 'Australien und die australische Race', 474.
88  Gerstäcker, 'Australien und die australische Race', 475.
89  Louis Agassiz, 'Geographical Distribution of Animals', *Christian Examiner and Religious Miscellany* 48 (1850), 181–204.
90  Louis Agassiz, 'The Diversity of Origin of the Human Races'. *Christian Examiner* (1850), 1–36.
91  Douglas, 'Climate to Crania', pp. 49–50.
92  Cf. Stocking, *Race, Culture and Evolution*, p. 40.
93  Stocking, *Race, Culture and Evolution*, pp. 37ff.
94  One such dispute, the clash between the physiologist Rudolph Wagner, a monogenist and conservative monarchist, and Carl Vogt, a polygenist and radical democrat, received a public airing in the *Augsburger Allgemeine Zeitung* of which Gerstäcker was a reader. Interestingly, from 1839 to1844, Vogt had been an assistant of Agassiz who at that stage had a position as a professor of natural history in Neuchatel. For an account of the Wagner–Vogt dispute, see Frederik Beiser, *The Genesis of Neo-Kantianism, 1796–1880* (Oxford: Oxford University Press, 2014), pp. 182ff.
95  In ' "The Miserablest People in the World": Race, Humanism and the Australian Aborigine', *The Australian Journal of Anthropology* 18:1 (2007), 18–39, Kay Anderson and Colin Perrin describe the hardening of attitudes that occurred as colonists were confronted with Aboriginal intractability. In fact, they make a direct causal connection between the rise of polygenism and perceived Aboriginal irremediability. The rise of polygenism was more complex than this, but some of its attraction no doubt lay in the explanation it provided for the failure of the civilising mission and the justification it gave for abandoning it.
96  Gerstäcker, 'Civilisation und Wildniß', p. 225.
97  Gerstäcker, 'Civilisation und Wildniß', p. 225.

# CHAPTER NINE

# The savagery of America?
# Nineteenth-century German literature
# and indigenous representations

Nicole Perry

During the long nineteenth century, one of the issues occupying the minds of German intellectuals was the phenomenon of mass emigration to America. Significant traces of this preoccupation can be found in the fiction of the time, reflecting the tensions and concerns of a deeply stratified and conflicted society. In the first half of the nineteenth century, travel between Europe and America was uncommon and sporadic at best; it was not until the latter half of the century and the advent of improvements in communications, methods of travel and eventually consistent emigration between the continents that a true 'transatlantic network' was formed and discourse began to reflect actual rather than imagined developments in the 'New World'.

As both Wynfrid Kriegleder and Oliver Simons have argued, the idea of America in the German consciousness was first realised through literary sources that transformed frontier experiences into a conceptual language that spoke to metropolitan concerns.[1] Despite their frontier topos, these writings were inherently internalist; focusing on German histories, politics and intellectual questions, with little regard for the affairs of indigenous peoples in North America save for where they intersected with the colonialist tactics of the young American republic. Although the works discussed in this chapter are both set in the United States and deal explicitly with the 'Indian Question',[2] the authors framed their discussions within a burgeoning German nationalist discourse, which located the beginnings of a German nation at the crossroads of global history. The works predate the colonies of imperial Germany, and although aware of the imperialist tendencies of other nations, both authors focus on America and its dealings with indigenous peoples so as to apply, via the medium of fiction, lessons learned there to their specific German concerns.

Further complicating the status of North American Indians in German works is the historiographical split that has emerged in recent scholarship on the extent to which Germans were more sympathetic than other settlers to Native Americans. Whereas H. Glenn Penny's *Kindred by Choice: Germans and American Indians since 1800* suggests that 'a striking sense of affinity for American Indians [...] has permeated German cultures for two centuries', Jens-Uwe Guettel's *German Expansionism, Imperial Liberalism, and the United States, 1776–1945* argues forthrightly that 'Germans, like Americans, had held pro-expansionist and at times exterminatory attitudes vis-à-vis Native Americans ever since the late eighteenth century'.[3]

Certainly, as Penny argues, there was a keen interest in things Native American; however there was also a clear lack of consistent and accurate information regarding North America and in particular its indigenous populations in the early nineteenth century. These circumstances allowed German authors to use the young American republic as a literary backdrop in novels where indigenous characters served the narrative function of driving the stories of white protagonists. In addition, many in enlightened circles in Germany viewed the United States and the new country's dealings with the indigenous populations with piqued interest in regard to their own colonial concerns and interests.[4] The construct and terminology of the 'noble savage' was an essential part of this discourse and the authors focused on either the 'noble' or the 'savage' dimension of the term to reflect their own, metropolitan desires or intentions within the text.

Demonstrating this are the two novels from the first half of the nineteenth century considered here, namely Sophie von La Roche's 1798 *Erscheinungen am See Oneida* (Appearances on Lake Oneida) and Charles Sealsfield's *Der Legitime und die Republikaner* (The Legitimate and the Republicans) from 1833. Both authors used indigenous characters to further their narratives and underlying messages, but in markedly different ways. While La Roche embraced the philosophical enthusiasm for the 'noble savage' of the late eighteenth and early nineteenth centuries when discussing indigenous populations in North America, Sealsfield deliberately depicted the state of the Oconee as primitive and archaic, so as to advocate for an American-style republic in the German-speaking principalities and Habsburg Empire of Europe. While both works can be read as anti-Indian narratives, upon deeper inspection it becomes clear that the indigenous characters are much more complicated than a simple 'red devil/noble savage' dichotomy might suggest. Throughout their stories both authors reveal the tensions, the contradictory images and the historical debates on both sides of the Atlantic surrounding America's first peoples. With different underlying purposes shaping their narratives, each author evokes images of savagery and primitiveness that exemplify and argue for the necessity of colonialisation of North America's indigenous peoples, while creating indigenous characters sufficiently complex to cause the reader to contemplate the question of who really is the savage.

## Sophie von La Roche and Erscheinungen am See Oneida (1798)

The oeuvre of the late Enlightenment female author Sophie von La Roche (1730–1807) has remained largely on the periphery of the German literary canon. A contemporary of the eighteenth-century giants of German literature, Christoph Martin Wieland and Johann Wolfgang von Goethe, La Roche's marginalisation and lack of recognition were primarily the result of her gender. Widely considered the first German-speaking female author able to live from her writing, she established herself as 'the best known and most prolific woman author in Germany',[5] largely on the popularity of her first novel Geschichte des Fräuleins von Sternheim (1771) and her monthly journal aimed at the education of young women, Pomona für Teuschlands Töchter, and yet she was unable to break into the mainstream market. La Roche was also widely regarded for her literary salon in Koblenz, which attracted the intelligentsia of the region and, like the salons of the day, became a place of philosophical debate. The novel Erscheinungen am See Oneida (1798) is most representative of her later writing and keenly reflects the interest and debate among the intellectual circles in Germany regarding the young, burgeoning American republic. At the centre of this debate was the question of America's indigenous peoples and their future in a rapidly changing societal framework. And while La Roche's astute observations reflect the overarching tensions in this debate, the actual intention behind her work, far removed from America, was to advocate for the necessity of education for Germany's young women through a veiled comparison of the Oneida women as 'daughters of Nature':[6] uneducated and primitive when juxtaposed with the enlightened aristocratic Frenchwoman Emilie Des Wattines. La Roche's views on gender and female education in the German context in the eighteenth century were truly revolutionary, but, without dismissing these underlying questions of gender and education,[7] her cliché-ridden descriptions of indigenous people require interrogation, highlighting as they do her interest in both America and its native population.

At the beginning of the text, the narrator takes the time to describe the indigenous population, and later, while Emilie is giving birth to her child, the narrator concentrates on the discussion between her husband Carl Des Wattines and an Onedia youth describing Nesquehiounah, the near-legendary Iroquois character who straddles the line between nobility and savagery. The conversation reveals the youth as the son of Nesquehiounah, who rose to the rank of colonel in the American army during the American Revolution, and whose own story had already traversed the Atlantic,[8] yet he rejects a European lifestyle to return to his indigenous roots. The ambivalence and ambiguity of the depiction of Nesquehiounah reveals La Roche's and indeed Germany's ambivalent attitude towards not only the newly minted American Republic but also the future of indigenous peoples in the United States in the early nineteenth century.[9] At the time of the story Nesquehiounah had died, yet his name and the mythology surrounding his military feats lived on a generation later. The nostalgia La Roche evokes for the famous warrior suggests both the admiration of a past age and primitive people, who were in the Rousseauian sense closer to Nature, while at the same time it reinforces what was seen as the perceived inevitable yet tragic fate of 'savages' in America, considered unable or unwilling to adapt to modern life. La Roche's work thus vacillates between the arguments set forth by Guettel and Penny. On the one hand La Roche's work sporadically expresses admiration for the noble savage of a generation earlier yet it is clear to her that their lifestyle cannot co-exist with the increasingly dominant Euro-American way of life. Accordingly, she argues for the expansion of America through a pedagogical framework, which, while not advocating the outright extinction of North American indigenous peoples, nonetheless argues for their assimilation and displacement.

La Roche's America novel vividly recounted the fascination, expectations and disappointments of a young European man travelling through the north-eastern United States as described in his letters home. Bored with cities such as Philadelphia or New York that reminded him of Europe, the narrator longed to experience his idea of America – wild and uninhabited. The narrator arrived at Lake Oneida in upstate New York, some four hundred English miles from Philadelphia, where he met among others the young French couple the Des Wattines, with whom he became fascinated. In his description of the settlers and his experiences, he was less taken with the children of European parentage than he was by the local Indigenous population he had seen trading and bartering. The Dutch and German children were not as strong or as beautiful as the local Indigenous tribe, he argues,[10] and the narrator evokes a litany of clichés conjuring the contradictory European idea of the noble savage as primitive, noble and divine:

> But the Dutch and German youth did not seem as strong or as beautiful to me as the tribes of Natives, some of whom I saw while trading beaver and bear skins, and whose beauty and power reminded me of the appearance in the painting by the great British painter, who was born in America, West, who in Rome at the first sight of the Apollo in the Vatican exclaimed: Oh what a similarity with the young Mohawk warrior, whose bow is drawn, his eye on the enemy, and quickly follows him! – only those, like me, who have seen these noble figures, would think that West could judge the art of the imitation, not as an American, but as an expert of the great, noble beauty of Nature and truth.[11]

Referring to the painter Benjamin West (1738–1820), the narrator used his overly sentimental fervour to augment his own experience in America: he created his own version of the noble savage myth. He compared the indigenous populations he saw with paintings of which his readers in Europe would at least have been aware, raising these young indigenous traders to godlike European forms as he compares the Mohawk warrior to the first breath-taking view of the Apollo *Gestalt* in Rome. West's painting *The Death of Wolfe* (1770) had been a sensation when it was exhibited in London in the spring of 1771, and, although the story the painting tells is almost entirely fictitious, it became one of the most reproduced paintings of the time, reflecting and increasing the popularity and interest in Europe of North America and its indigenous peoples. It depicts the death of the British Major-General Wolfe on the Plains of Abraham surrounded by his officers and a crouching and seemingly stoic Mohawk warrior. Of course, as Daniel Francis notes, Wolfe had actually died away from the action, in the company of only one of his men because he was so disliked by his officers.[12] Wolfe also despised the local indigenous peoples, the majority of whom would have been fighting on the side of the French. West's painting was known to La Roche, as a member of the educated elite in Germany, and she purposively reminded her readers of the noble savage ideal it encapsulated, providing them with a familiar cultural point of reference – replete with European ideals – which could later be evoked when the readers encounter the Oneida and more importantly the legendary Nesquehiounah.

*Erscheinungen am See Oneida* also utilised different narrative focalisations, which gave different perspectives of the lived experiences in upstate New York. The Des Wattines all tell the narrator separately about their isolated island life in the middle of Lake Oneida and their encounters with the Oneida tribe by virtue of Emile's pregnancy. Their encyclopaedias were the foundation of their education and the possessions that they value most, as they believed that *Bildung* (education) separated them from the savages. Yet Emile realised that she needed help from the daughters of Nature, and their practical experience, in birthing her child. Emilie's pregnancy provided the segue to the inevitable confrontation and clash of cultures between the European and indigenous worlds, as represented by the Des Wattines and the Oneida tribe. This encounter was primarily centred on the birthing process and Oneida domestic sphere as experienced by Emile; however La Roche also uses it to introduce Nesquehiounah, a character who, at times, owing to his ability to speak both European and North American indigenous languages, his military prowess and his geographical knowledge of the north-eastern seaboard, appears to be a true 'Renaissance Man'. Emilie and Carl swim from their island paradise to the shores of Lake Oneida and enter the Oneida village, uninvited and as outsiders. After the necessity of their arrival is made clear, Emilie was whisked away by the women to a wigwam as Carl collapsed, reduced to tears. The young chief of the tribe looked at him and told him quite literally to be a man – '[K]omm, sey Mann!'[13] The youth spoke fluent English and this surprised Carl until he learned that his father was Nesquehiounah, the legendary Iroquois colonel of the American army, and whose reputation also extended as far as Europe. Nesquehiounah's knowledge of not only *his* homeland, and other peoples and territories, but also of European languages and cultures was so extensive that he was, in his own terms, as cultivated as the Des Wattines, if not more so, without the physical hindrance of the encyclopaedias that Des Wattines had transported to his island paradise from France. At the same time, he remained an enigma, an unstable image. The story of Nesquehiounah was told to Des Wattines by the young, unnamed youth and was later recounted to the narrator by Des Wattines. Nesquehiounah the legend, although a more decorated soldier than many of his fellow white brothers in arms, had no desire to maintain and lead a Euro-American style of life.

In this *Rahmenerzählung*, he appeared in the city, most likely Philadelphia, wearing the traditional dress of an Iroquois warrior while waiting for his friend and fellow (white) soldier in the city, whom he had come to visit for the last time before leaving the densely populated metropolises of the Northeastern Seaboard for the 'wilds of America' described by the narrator. He was not 'going Native' but returning to his 'savage' roots. While in the city, Europeans who have recently arrived on the continent stared at him and remarked on his 'Indianness', his savagery, aghast at his appearance because they are confronted by the contradictions of frontier America; the cosmopolitan is juxtaposed with the ostensibly uncultured, savage indigene. Nesquehiounah responded to their comments and Eurocentric views in fluent French, as retold to Des Wattines and thereafter the readers, of course, in German:

> A savage! ... Me a savage! Oh I have lived long enough with the whites to be convinced that it is not the people in the forests who should be called savages. Do we have prisons and trials? Are we not free like birds and you slaves like dogs? Do we have as much emotion, vice, diseases and grief as you? No, we honour the Elder and you despise him. Your firewater often makes us mad, but me and my people say: the land where the day begins is an evil land, the sun only passes, it is not as good as ours, where the sun sets. Listen to me! A Jesuit told me in my youth that our life is too empty. I now know, that the life of the European is too full, that an evil spirit is inside of you and does not leave you in peace, until you have died.[14]

In this extensive and compelling critique of European life, Nesquehiounah exposes the hypocrisy of the luxuries and excesses that have become a part of everyday European enjoyment. His social critique was a poignant commentary on the debauchery of European life. He challenged the European notion of freedom, something La Roche herself would argue comes from education, as represented by the encyclopaedias, and he delivered a scathing attack on the European vices of vanity and alcohol. Nesquehiounah (who was from Canada),[15] invoked a Jesuit who claimed that indigenous life was too empty, to argue that the constant need to busy oneself was the root cause of the systemic problems of European society.

Nesquehiounah does not appear again in the story, but his legend of noble savagery hovers in the background throughout the rest of the novel. He is the man against whom all other indigenous characters are measured by Des Wattines and the narrator. His appearance occurs relatively early in the story, and the final mention of any indigenous content comes at the end of Book Two, when the narrator and the settlers discuss the amount of time needed for the successful cultural development of the North American indigenous population. The settlers determine that the indigenous peoples cannot survive, because, if the British needed nine hundred years to develop after Caesar came, the Oneida still need 937 years to reach a civilized standard.[16] The contrast between their pessimistic account of the 'civilising' process and Nesquehiounah's easy facility with but ultimate rejection of the norms of European life could not be clearer. The power and force with which Nesquehiounah's image is introduced into the narrative profoundly strikes both Des Wattines and the narrator, but it is just as abruptly erased as the settlers contemplate the fate of the current Oneida people. This erasure is the source of the novel's ambivalence towards indigeneity. Nesquehiounah represented the contradictions and ambiguity of the La

Roche's attitude towards the indigenous population. He appears in the novel as an exception, an individual who assimilated with but rejects the culture of the coloniser, depicted as both noble and savage, and, crucially, as a Native American successfully negotiating the difficulties of the frontier. His final rejection of European cultural forms places emphasis on his *savageness*. But the *noble* in Nesquehiounah is perhaps best reflected in his statement that it is not the people in the forests who should be called savages.[17] As a character, Nesquehiounah allows for La Roche to imagine the forms of agency open to indigenous peoples faced with colonisation. Yet at the same time, it situates him firmly as both an atavism and an exception, ultimately allowing for the colonial priorities of the settlers to prevail.

## *Charles Sealsfield and his early American novels*

Thirty-five years after La Roche's American novel, the Austrian-American Charles Sealsfield condemned the archaic lifestyle of the Oconee tribe, located in the southern state of Georgia. In contrast to La Roche's abstract and more removed consideration of the 'Indian Question', Sealsfield's work largely corroborates Guettel's findings, in its strident advocacy of either the assimilation or, if necessary, the annihilation of North American indigenous peoples, whose traditional lifestyle and resistance to the increasingly dominant settler way of life he viewed as hindering the inevitable and necessary expansion West. It was a sentiment that would find expression over a decade later with the concept of Manifest Destiny. His novels, *Tokeah and the White Rose* and *Der Legitime und die Republikaner* (The Legitimate and the Republicans), published in 1829 and 1833 respectively, compared the Oconee and other indigenous nations to the monarchies of Europe. The thinly veiled comparison allows for him to argue that these two forms of government, which he portrayed as sharing similar hierarchical and structural features, were obsolete atavisms when compared with the fledgling American democracy, a system grounded on the principles of equality and economic freedom. Sealsfield's championing of the ideals of American democracy became highly influential and can arguably be seen reflected in the French liberal thinker Alexis de Tocqueville's seminal *Democracy in America*, published in 1835. While Sealsfield's novels both exalted the ideals of American democracy, it was in his use of indigenous characters and the tensions present in his evolving depictions of 'savagery' that are best examined when comparing the two novels, as they reflect the development and refinement of Sealsfield's own political leanings. *Tokeah and the White Rose*, considered the first novel written about the American Southwest in any language,[18] was written in the style of a captivity narrative, similar to James Fenimore Cooper's *The Last of the Mohicans* (1826), and was, interestingly, printed by the same publishing house in Philadelphia: Carey, Lea and Carey. Sealsfield's German version, however, bordered on being a political treatise, underscoring his blind and enduring support for President Andrew Jackson's controversial Indian Removal Act of 1830 and Jackson's stand on slavery, along with his unabashed promotion of the adoption of an American-style democracy in Europe. His American experience was located in the Antebellum South, the birthplace of the populist President Jackson, and this is also reflected in his version of America. In his enthusiastic support of Jackson and the American Republic, Sealsfield viewed both the 'Indian Problem' and slavery as necessary evils, which could and should be overlooked, as the success of the (white) American Republic was of tantamount importance to his dream of a Europe devoid of monarchies.

A pseudonym for Karl Postl, Charles Sealsfield was a disillusioned Austrian priest who mysteriously fled the Metternich regime for the United States. His true identity was not discovered until his death and the reading of his will in Solothurn, Switzerland, in 1864, and he remains one of the most underrated and puzzling nineteenth-century authors on both sides of the Atlantic. He was called the 'Greatest American Author',[19] albeit by a German, and he remains unique primarily for two reasons. Firstly, he wrote in both German and English (his first novel was in English), and secondly he held unorthodox political views; for a German-speaking European, he was uncommonly pro-American. His unclear genealogy and bilingualism have contributed to his obscurity as well as his tenuous place in the German or American literary canons. But the reality is that Sealsfield was a hybrid author of sorts, a writer who should be considered part of both literary traditions. This claim is supported not only by his two early novels of the American Frontier discussed here but also by his alignment with the American political machine and his written work on America in general, which again contrasts starkly with that of his German contemporaries.

The most prominent nineteenth-century German writers of America (both in fiction and non-fiction or travel writing) belong to the generation after Sealsfield and included Friedrich Gerstäcker (1816–72), Ferdinand Kürnberger (1821–79), Balduin von Möllhausen (1825–1905) and, of course, two generations later, Karl May (1842–1912). Unlike other German authors who viewed America exclusively through a German lens, Sealsfield wrote from an obviously pro-American standpoint. He differed from his counterparts in that he viewed the American republic as the natural political progression of aristocratic Europe, he believed in an evolution from the outdated monarchies that in his opinion plagued

Europe to an American style of 'by the people for the people' democratic republic. He aligned himself unconditionally with Andrew Jackson and his politics, in part because Jackson was such a staunch believer in American democracy (best represented by Jackson's desire when President to sever America's ties with Britain, its influences and traditions).[20] Sealsfield's German version *Der Legitime und die Republikaner*, written specifically for a German readership, was overshadowed by the recently translated *Last of the Mohicans*, which was considered a blockbuster and quickly became the standard by which novels pertaining to America were measured. Unlike other German authors of the time, Sealsfield advocated from an overtly American standpoint, and consequently *Der Legitime und die Republikaner* was an arduous read for a German audience, lacking the romantic elements of Cooper's tale and relying heavily on detailed, local American knowledge. As a consequence, its pro-democratic message was often lost on the German readers inside the reactionary regimes he hoped would be overthrown.

The second half of *Der Legitime* deviated considerably from the English-language, Cooperesque version,[21] not least in its treatment of the indigenous characters, also contributing to the book's failure to gain popularity in Germany. Contrary to Penny's sense that Germans were more attuned and sympathetic to the plight of North America's indigenous peoples, Sealsfield effectively championed Jackson's Indian Removal Act of 1830 by arguing that the archaic political system of the Oconee, which he based on the Metternich regime, along with their unwillingness to accept the western expansion of the United States, would lead to the tribe's eventual demise. His comparison of two inflexible, archaic political systems, those of the European monarchies and of the Oconee, created a connection between the two. Both, he argued, were standing in the way of the American Republic and, more broadly, democracy as a whole, and thus both were to be read as savage atavisms.

The narrative changes in the German version of the novel offer a much more confrontational political treatise than the original English text. By focusing on the differences in the portrayal of the chief of the Oconee, Tokeah, and the figure of General Jackson in the two stories, the rise of Sealsfield's growing support of Jackson's controversial Indian Removal Policy[22] and Jacksonianism in general can be traced. By concentrating on the image of Tokeah, the chief of the Oconee, significant changes in the plot of the German novel are revealed. In the English version, Tokeah was a tragic character representing a past age, unable to come to terms with the fate of his people, whereas in the German version Sealsfield transformed Tokeah into a devious, manipulative character – a savage – interested only in profit, thus personifying Andrew Jackson's understanding of the 'Indian Problem' – and his solution to it.[23]

Within limits, the English version, *Tokeah and the White Rose*, was also politically didactic. It opened with the White Rose being taken by Tokeah and the Oconee as a baby during a midnight raid and fourteen years later Arthur Graham, the British aristocrat falling in love with her when the White Rose saved him from an alligator. Numerous adventures ensued as befits its episodic nature, but the entire time Arthur is told by different settlers about the benefits of American democracy. Tokeah, along with the youthful leader of the Comanche, El Sol, meets with General Andrew Jackson, who was in New Orleans preparing to fight the British in the War of 1812. In the conversation, Tokeah is chastised for not leading his people to the Texas Territory and giving up his traditional lands,[24] like El Sol, who had already committed his tribe to relocating to non-American land. While Tokeah tragically dies trying to rescue the bones of his father, the White Rose and Arthur marry. The final surprise is revealed on a plantation in Jamaica when White Rose's father arrives from Spain and establishes her noble birth.

Unlike the German version, *Tokeah and the White Rose* was essentially a love story and captivity narrative meant for an English readership which hinted at the tensions regarding the indigenous population in the southern United States.[25] Published in the first year of President Jackson's second term, however, *Der Legitime und Republikaner* underwent crucial early changes which subtly refocused the structure of its English predecessor. Arthur Graham was no longer a British aristocrat but was rechristened James Hodges, a British midshipman who was captured by a pirate and as a result much more suitable to be Americanised. In this context the story was 'no longer [about] class consciousness that needs to be overcome, but national traits',[26] including the perceived superiority of the British. The love story that had featured so prominently in the English version is negligible, as Hodges ignores Rosa's romantic overtures and marries one of Squire Copeland's daughters. The plantation owner Gentillon, a Creole from whom Arthur gently learned about the advantages of the American way of life in the English story, is replaced with a wealthy colonel and his wife, who teach Hodges about his democratic rights and principles. In the German version General Jackson is introduced earlier in the novel and he is much more revered, both by the narrator and by other characters. His talk with El Sol and Tokeah is greatly expanded upon, and he more overtly displays his displeasure with Tokeah.[27] In patiently explaining to Tokeah that the 'großer Geist' has made the land for both indigenous and American peoples, and that the Americans have paid the indigenous peoples for the lands, the General eventually calls Tokeah a bloodsucker, like the tyrants of the old world,[28] as the Americans are settling the land for all to use, including Tokeah's people:

> The fate of the red man [...] is cruel in many ways, but it is not inevitable; barbarism in its fight with the Enlightenment must always be softened, as the night softens the day; but you have the means at hand to affiliate yourselves with this Enlightenment and to join our civil way of life. If you, however, do not want this, and choose instead of respected citizens to be wild Legitimates, then you do not have to accept fate, which throws you aside like pretend tools after your nocturnal train has passed through.[29]

Echoing Sealsfield's formulation of the 'Indian Question' (and supporting Guettel's argument that Germans often lacked any sense of affinity with indigenous North American peoples), Jackson warns the old and haggard Chief in no uncertain terms that, if Tokeah and the Oconnee do not decide to assimilate to the dominant American society, their 'savage' lifestyle would simply be extinguished as being unconducive to the Enlightenment ideals of the burgeoning American republic.

The novel focuses more explicitly on the fight for American democracy than its predecessor. The War of 1812 is presented as necessary in the American struggle for independence from Britain, as is the role it plays in Jackson's ascension to the presidency. The second President of the United States, John Adams, who in *Tokeah* was mentioned as among the great men of America, is now viewed critically along with his son, John Quincy Adams, who won the American presidency over General Jackson with the 'Corrupt Bargain' in the 1824 election. Both are portrayed as enemies of the young American republic, mainly because of their strong connections to England and Europe. In regard to the 'Indian Question', in *Der Legitime und die Republikaner* it is asserted that even the proudest of braves must admit that the white race is superior:[30]

> See my son, how clever the white man is. The red men would never colour the tomahawk with their blood; they are irrepressible and proud, like the buffalo, but when the call of war is raised, they become gentle and do not follow one leader, like the red men, rather become many, who are all under one.[31]

Tokeah is speaking to El Sol regarding the military power of the white man and their ability to follow orders on the battlefield as an example of the organisational superiority of the Americans and their military prowess.

The most obvious political transition, however, is found in the title of the German version: *The Legitimate and the Republicans*.

Perfectly expressed by Jeffrey Sammons, Tokeah, as a representative of the original and legitimate possessors of the land is in conflict with the Republicans – the Americans – who wanted to settle the land for the American expansion West.[32] This leitmotif of differing claims of legitimacy is also conceived as a reflection of the aristocratic rulers of Europe, who claimed to rule by divine right, thereby foregrounding the inherent ideological conflict with American democracy. It is through his character Tokeah that Sealsfield reveals the noble savage to be both indigenous and European: 'Eloquence, the stoic style, and the solemnity of hierarchical style are noble *and* savage, dignified *and* obsolete, like the European aristocracy.'[33]

*Tokeah and the White Rose* relies upon the romanticised image of the noble savage, a physically strong, regal-looking man, lamenting the demise of his people, a member of a past age, reminiscent of La Roche's Nesquehiounah and later Karl May's Winnetou. This figure was and would remain a cliché which, as Penny has argued, was and still is very popular in German-speaking countries. In *Der Legitime und die Republikaner*, on the other hand, the nobility of the Native American was stripped away, while images of savagery were amplified. Tokeah himself is described here as physically small and weak, blinded by paranoia and stubbornness. In its depiction of how a young democracy might overcome savagery, Sealsfield's work became much more politicised, echoing the sentiment in Jackson's 'Second Annual Message' in December 1830 and his 'Message on Indian Affairs' in February 1831. American progress cannot tolerate nomadic peoples and their relationship to land; the indigenous peoples are strongly encouraged to settle as civilised farmers, but, if they do not, they will be forcibly removed from their lands or even eradicated. Sealsfield transformed his frontier romance into an anti-Indian novel which emphasised the savageness of the indigenous population, echoing a particular American sentiment of the time and vindicating Guettel's sense that a literary genre which included elements of the noble savage ideal could also easily accommodate assimilationist and eliminationist sentiments.

## Conclusion

In the thirty-five year-span between Sophie von La Roche's *Erscheinungen am See Oneida* and Charles Sealsfield's *Der Legitime und Republikaner*, it is possible to trace a transition in the representation of 'savagery' in German accounts of America and its Indigenous peoples. La Roche's America novel, set on the continent of North America but addressing European debates regarding women's emancipation, was guided by Johann Gottfried von Herder's idea of colonial alterity.[34] La Roche created a largely compassionate view of savagery informed by philosophical currents sympathetic to the colonised and romantic paintings of a new continent and its first peoples who, predominantly through a lack of knowledge, were viewed as wild, uncivilised, and undomesticated. Considered the first German author to critically engage with indigenous characters,[35] La Roche located the indigenous characters as 'savage' remnants of the past. Her ambivalence towards colonised Native Americans is apparent in her contrasting depictions of the culturally adept Nesquehiounah on the one hand, and the settlers' discussion of the time required to civilise the 'Oneida', on the other. In the end, La Roche's colonial ambivalence would be settled on the side of Europeanisation, colonialism portrayed not as a conflict between equals but as the necessary encroachment of European, white, and civilised sensibilities into a New World, with Indigenous Americans viewed as incomprehensible, atavistic and ultimately savage.

By the time of Sealsfield's novels in the 1830s, the discourse surrounding indigenous America had shifted, and the improvement to networks of travel and communication, along with the development of the American political landscape, especially in regard to the native population, had vaulted writings of lived experience and knowledge to the forefront of German interests in Indigenous Americans. In this context, Sealsfield's *Der Legitime und die Republikaner* emerged as a political treatise advocating an American-style democracy in Europe. In this narrative, the ostensibly archaic lifestyles of the Oconee and other tribes were doubly condemned, both in their own terms as indigenous atavisms incapable of adjusting to the realities of the colonised world and as a metaphor for Europe's own atavistic monarchs.

## Notes

1   Wynfrid Kriegleder, *Vorwarts in der Vergangenheit. Das Bild der USA im deutschsprachigen Roman von 1776–1855* (Tübingen: Stauffenburg, 1999), pp. 11, 35. Oliver Simons, ' "Amerika gibt es nicht": On the Semiotics of Literary America in the Twentieth Century', *The German Quarterly* 82:2 (2009), 196–7.
2   It should be noted that the 'Indian Question' was not addressed in the United States until the latter half of the nineteenth century.
3   H. Glenn Penny, *Kindred by Choice: Germans and American Indians since 1800* (Chapel Hill: University of North Carolina Press, 2013), p. xi; Jens-Uwe Guettel, *German Expansionism, Imperial Liberalism, and the United States, 1776–1945* (Cambridge: Cambridge University Press, 2013), p. 85.
4   Guettel, *German Expansionism*, p. 4.
5   Kevin Hilliard, 'Sophie von La Roche', in Hillary Brown (ed.), *Landmarks in German Women's Writing* (Bern: Peter Lang, 2007), p. 43.
6   Sophie von La Roche, *Erscheinungen am See Oneida*, ed. Heike Menges, 3 vols (Eschborn: Klotz, 1995), Vol. 2, p. 95.

7   See Linda Dietrick, ' "Schwimme mit mir hinüber zu den Hütten unserer Nachbarn":
     Colonial Islands in Sophie von La Roche's *Erscheinung am See Oneida* (1798) and
     Jacques-Henri Bernadin de Saint Pierre's *Paul et Virginie (1788)*', in Rob McFarland
     and Michelle Stott James (eds), *Sophie Discovers Amerika: German Speaking Women
     Write the New World* (Rochester, NY: Camden House, 2014), pp. 16–29; Elisabeth
     Krimmer, 'A Garden of Her Own: Noble Savages and Superior Europeans in Sophie
     von La Roche's "*Erscheinungen am See Oneida*" ', in Laura Martin (e.d), *Harmony
     in Discord: German Women Writers in the Eighteenth and Nineteenth Centuries*
     (Frankfurt am Main: Peter Lang, 2001), pp. 21–43; Nicole Perry, 'Education and
     *Erziehung* in the Wilderness of America: Sophie von La Roche's *Erscheinungen am
     See Oneida*.', in Wynfried Kriegleder and Gustav-Adolf Pogatschnigg (eds), *Literarische
     Narrationen der Migration Europa – Nordamerika im 19. Jahrhundert* (Vienna:
     Praesens Verlag, 2012), pp. 9–20.
8   La Roche, *Erscheinungen am See Oneida*, Vol. 2, p. 96.
9   Guettel, *German Expansionism*, pp. 83, 85.
10  La Roche, *Erscheinungen am See Oneida*, Vol. 1, p. 27.
11  'Doch dünkten mich die jungen Leute der Holländer und Teutschen nicht so stark
     und schön, als die Stämme der Eingebohrnen, von welchen ich einige bey einem
     Handel von Biber- und Bärenfellen sah, und mich bey ihrer Schönheit und Stärke an
     den Auftritt des großen englischen, in Amerika gebohrnen Mahlers: West, erinnerte,
     welcher in Rom bey dem ersten Blick auf den Apoll des Vaticans ausrief: O was
     für eine Aehnlichkeit mit einem jungen Krieger der Mohawks, welcher den Bogen
     gespannt, das Aug' auf den Feind gehestet, ihn mit schnellen Schritten verfolgt! – nur
     diejenigen, welche wie ich, diese edlen Gestalten sahen, werden finden, daß West
     nicht als Amerikaner, sondern als Kenner großer edler Schönheit der Natur und
     Wahrheit, die Kunst in der Nachahmung zu beurtheilen wußte.' Unless otherwise
     noted, all translations are my own.
12  Daniel Francis, *The Imaginary Indian: The Image of the Indian in Canadian Culture*
     (Vancouver: Arsenal Pulp Press, 1992), p. 13.
13  La Roche, *Erscheinungen am See Oneida*, vVol. 2, p. 94.
14  'Ein Wilder! ... Ich ein Wilder! O, ich habe lange genug bey den Weißen gelebt, um
     überzeugt zu seyn, daß sie, nicht die Menschen im Walde, Wilde genannt werden
     sollten. Haben wir Gefängnisse und Prozesse? Sind wir nicht frei wie die Vögel, und
     sie Sclaven wie Hunde? haben wir so viel Leidenschaften, Laster, Krankheiten und
     Kummer als sie? Nein, wir ehren das Alter und sie verachten es. Ihre brennenden
     Wasser machen uns oft toll, aber ich und die Meinigen sagen: das Land, wo der
     Tag anfängt, ist ein böses Land, die Sonne geht nur vorbey, es ist nicht so gut wie
     das Unsere, wo sie zur Ruhe geht. Hört ihr! ein Jesuit sagte mir in meiner Jugend,
     daß unser Leben zu leer sey. Ich weiß jetzo, daß der Europäer ihres zu voll ist; daß
     ein böser Geist sie treibt und ihnen keine Ruhe läßt, bis sie sterben.' La Roche,
     *Erscheinungen am See Oneida*, Vol. 2, pp. 100–1.
15  La Roche, *Erscheinungen am See Oneida*, Vol. 2, p. 98. It can be inferred here that
     by 'Canada' the region that is now Quebec, or Upper Canada is most likely meant.
     Jesuits had been acting as missionaries in the area.
16  La Roche, *Erscheinungen am See Oneida*, Vol. 2, pp. 159–60.
17  La Roche, *Erscheinungen am See Oneida*, Vol. 2, p. 100.
18  John T. Krumpelmann, 'Tokeah, the First English-Language Novel in Our Southwest',
     *The South Central Bulletin* 28:4 (1968), 142.
19  Theodor Mundt, *Geschichte der Literatur der Gegenwart* (Berlin: M. Simion, 1842),
     pp. 425–6.
20  Cf. Walter Grünzweig, *Das demokratische Kanaan: Charles Sealsfields Amerika
     im Kontext amerikanischer Literatur und Ideologie* (Munich: Fink, 1987), pp. 77,
     79.
21  Bernd Fischer, 'Baumwolle und Indianer Zu Charles Sealsfields *Der Legitime und
     die Republikaner*', *Journal of German-American Studies* 19 (1984), 85–96.
22  Cf. Gary Clayton Anderson, *Ethnic Cleansing and the Indian: The Crime that
     Should Haunt America* (Norman: University of Oklahoma Press, 2014); Stephen J.

Rockwell, *Indian Affairs and the Administrative State in the Nineteenth Century* (Cambridge: Cambridge University Press, 2010); Ron Soodalter, 'On Removing Seminioles: Andrew Jackson's Policy of "Indian Removal" Ran in to Trouble in Florida – His Name Was Osceola', *Military History* 29.2 (2012), 62–9; Sean Michael O'Brien, *In Bitterness and in Tears: Andrew Jackson's Destruction of the Creeks and Seminoles* (Westport: Praeger, 2003); Guettel, *German Expansionism*, p. 62; Robert V. Hine and John Mack Faragher, *The American West: A New Interpretive History* (New Haven: Yale University Press, 2000).

23  Jeffrey L. Sammons, *Ideology, Mimesis, Fantasy: Charles Sealsfield, Friedrich Gerstäcker, Karl May and Other German Novelists of America* (Chapel Hill: University of North Carolina Press, 1998), p. 32.

24  Texas did not become an American state until 1845.

25  Sammons, *Ideology, Mimesis, Fantasy*, p. 27.

26  Sammons, *Ideology, Mimesis, Fantasy*, p. 28.

27  Charles Sealsfield, 'Der Legitime und die Republikaner', in Karl J.R. Arndt (ed.), *Sämtliche Werke*, Vols 6–7 (Hildesheim: Olms Presse, 1972), Vol. 7, book 3, pp. 278–82.

28  Sealsfield, *Der Legitime und die Republikaner*, Vol. 7, book 3, pp. 279–80.

29  'Das Schicksal der rothen Männer [...] ist hart in vieler Hinsicht, aber es ist nicht unvermeidlich; die Barbarei muß im Kampfe mit der Aufklärung immer weichen, so wie die Nacht dem Tage weicht; aber Ihr habt die Mittel in der Hand, an diese Aufklärung Euch anzuschließen und unser bürgerliches Leben einzutreten. Wollt Ihr dieses jedoch nicht, und zieht Ihr vor, statt geachter Bürger wilde Legitime zu seyn, so müßt Ihr mit dem Schicksale nicht hadern, das Euch wie Spielwerkzeuge wegwirft, nachdem Ihr Eure nächtliche Bahn durchlaufen send.' Sealsfield, *Der Legitime und die Republikaner*, Vol. 7, book 3, p. 281.

30  Sealsfield, *Der Legitime und die Republikaner*, Vol. 7, book 3, p. 30 and pp. 38–9.

31  'Sieht mein Sohn, wie die Weißen schlau sind. Die rothen Männer werden nimmer den Tomahawk in ihrem Blute färben; sie sind unbändig und stolz, wie der Büffeltier, aber wenn sie das Kriegsgeschrei erheben, so werden sie zahm und folgen nicht Einem Führer, wie die rothen Männer, sondern vielen, die alle unter Einem sind.' Sealsfield, *Der Legitime und die Republikaner*, Vol. 7, book 3, p. 38.

32  Sammons, *Ideology, Mimesis, Fantasy*, pp. 31–4.

33  Sammons, *Ideology, Mimesis, Fantasy*, p. 3.

34  I agree with Linda Dietrick's argument that La Roche modelled her main characters' attitudes towards the Oneida on Herder's Enlightenment philosophies. Dietrick, "Schwimme mit mir hinüber zu den Hütten unserer Nachbarn": Colonial Islands', p. 17.

35  Wynfrid Kriegleder, 'The American Indian in German Novels up to the 1850s', *German Life and Letters* 53:4 (2000), 489.

# CHAPTER TEN

## Incompetent masters, indolent natives, savage origins: the Philippines and its inhabitants in the travel accounts of Carl Semper (1869) and Fedor Jagor (1873)

### Hidde van der Wall

Around 1870, two travel accounts of the Philippines were published in Germany. Both authors, Carl Semper[1] and Fedor Jagor,[2] had visited the Spanish colony for scientific purposes, combining geographical, biological and anthropological inquiry. They presented the archipelago to a general audience and provided data for the German scholarly discussions of the Philippines which emerged in the last quarter of the nineteenth century.[3] Their accounts emerged in the context of continued European imperialism marked by the decline of the Spanish empire, and the rise of German colonial fantasies and ambitions. This chapter analyses how these two texts described and categorised the various inhabitants of the Philippines, and how they evaluated the impact and conditions of colonialism. It asks how the observations of Semper and Jagor both reflected and impacted on the archipelago.

After completing his doctorate in zoology, Carl Semper (1832–93) left Germany in 1858 for the Philippines in order to observe nature in the tropics.[4] He stayed seven years, interrupted by a nine-month expedition to Palau.[5] He undertook numerous excursions from his base in Manila, and travelled for longer periods through northern Luzon, Mindanao and Bohol, doing zoological research which formed the basis for his life work,[6] but also ethnographic and anthropological studies.[7] His 1869 book consists of six lectures and was intended as the prelude to a more extensive popular travelogue which was never published.

Before coming to the Philippines, Fedor Jagor (1816–1900) visited the Dutch and British colonies in south-east Asia, experiences he used in his assessment of the Spanish colony. He travelled in central and southern Luzon as well as the Visayas, collecting anthropological, ethnographical and zoological material. After returning to Europe, he did research in the colonial archives in Madrid, embedding his 1873 book in a broader edifice of colonial knowledge.[8] In 1871 Rudolf Virchow reported research on human skulls from Luzon brought to Germany by Jagor,[9] although his travelogue does not mention such 'skin trade' explicitly.[10]

Syed Alatas accuses Jagor of having promulgated the 'myth of the lazy native', the discourse which, he argues, justified 'colonial capitalism'.[11] Jagor, like Semper, did indeed cast Philippine natives as lazy and lacking in morality and discipline; few commentators of the period avoided such racialised language.[12] But, as the following analysis shows, Jagor made important alterations to the myth by blaming indolence to a large extent on the impact of Spanish colonialism.

As travel writing, these texts deployed literary conventions and narrative strategies that presented the author-traveller as an impartial expert. Although the author was in control of the country constructed in his text, and stood in an uneven power relationship to the locals while physically in the colony, he presented his presence as self-explanatory and harmless, in what Marie Louise Pratt calls the 'narrative of the anti-conquest'.[13] This narrative is evident in both travelogues: the authors rely on the Spanish colonial infrastructure to provide them with servants drawn from forced labour, which they mention but never problematise (with one exception in Jagor, which I discuss below). If travel narratives functioned as ' "rituals of conquest" by which Europeans established legitimate claims to extra-European territories',[14] writing about colonies held by other European states had the potential to establish claims that competed with those of existing, established colonial powers.

While Spain had already lost its American empire, by the end of the nineteenth century the Spanish regime in the Philippines had been in existence for over three hundred years. It relied heavily on religion to cement its rule, and gave great influence to Catholic friars opposed to modernisation. To manage the demographic composition of the colony, the Spanish upheld a hierarchy of racial categories. Spaniards of so-called pure blood (generally those born in Spain: *Peninsulares*) formed the top of the pyramid, followed by Spanish creoles (*Insulares* or *Filipinos*) whose blood was deemed tainted by their birth in the colony. Thereafter came two groups of *Mestizos* (Spanish and Chinese),[15] and finally *Indios*. The last category encompassed a variety of peoples, who were supposedly the Christianised subjects of their Spanish Catholic masters, while non-Christians – Muslim *Moros* in the unsubjected south and pagan mountain dwellers – were disregarded and not considered legitimate parts of Philippine society. European birth, religion and biological kinship determined one's position in the racial stratification.[16] For his part, Semper employed the term *Eingeborene* (natives),[17] while Jagor mainly uses the term *Indier* to refer to the natives of the

Philippines, a direct translation of *Indios*, the generic Spanish term for all natives in the empire, which designated them as imperial subjects and disregarded the linguistic and cultural diversity of the scattered archipelago. The Spanish word *Filipino* – and with that the access to a Filipino identity – was reserved for creoles.[18]

Spanish dominance was challenged by socio-economic developments from the mid-nineteenth century onwards. After Spain opened the colony to international trade in 1834, increasing wealth created a middle class consisting of *Indios*, *Mestizos* and *Insulares* alike,[19] who articulated a 'desire for change'.[20] German businessmen were among those who profited from the new investment opportunities, among them the parents of the woman whom Semper married in Manila. Economic immigrants formed a powerful non-Spanish Western presence – an alternative expression of European imperialism which, while operating under the aegis of the Spanish empire, also rivalled its dominance. With the emerging middle class came a concomitant push for modernisation.[21] From 1869 to 1872 – following the short-lived liberal revolution in Spain – Governor-General Carlos de la Torre seemed to cater to such demands, but a violent reaction led to the return of the clerical traditionalist order.[22] Semper's book appeared right before the reformist spell, Jagor's just afterwards.

Both books were also written while the process of German unification was ongoing and acquiring colonies 'became a public issue'.[23] As it never materialised as political acquisition, Germany's interest in the Philippines has unfairly received little attention in the historiography of German colonialism.[24] But the Philippines, with its declining Spanish rule, became an area of focus for German ambitions. The 1873 Sulu incident indicates Spain's fear of German interference with its colony at a time when Germany had officially no colonial ambitions.[25] Spanish anxiety peaked in the 1880s as Germany acquired colonies in nearby New Guinea and contested Spain's claim over the Marianas. Meanwhile, Philippine intellectuals drew on mainly German knowledge to construct their nation.[26]

From the 1870s onwards German scholars took great interest in the Philippines,[27] and Semper and Jagor gave impulse to work by scholars such as Virchow,[28] Adolf Bastian[29] and the Bohemian Ferdinand Blumentritt.[30] In the final decades of the century, anthropologists such as Adolf Bernhard Meyer visited the archipelago, while the immigrant pharmacist Alexander Schadenberg used his spare time for anthropological fieldwork there.[31] As Resil Mojares notes, 'Germans were the most prominent among the non-Spanish Western scientists visiting the Philippines in the nineteenth century'.[32] Similar to economic activities, their work contributed to the existing structures of the colony (on which it depended), while it also formed an alternative to Spanish colonial knowledge. Given the 'logical alliance between Western science and political power' at work,[33] colonial competition also came to take place in the field of sciences. While operating in the colonial context, German anthropology provided Philippine nationalists with the building blocks of prehistory and race to construct a unified people predating Spanish-Catholic dominance.[34] For nationalists searching for racial and cultural origins, German anthropology became the prime alternative to Spanish knowledge.[35]

By 1870, a secular, scholarly discourse on the Philippines had not yet really developed. Megan Thomas argues that the cutting-edge colonial science of ethnology was only half-heartedly embraced by the scientific community of the colony, which was dominated by friars.[36] As Mojares writes, their scholarship was driven by 'the urge to organize, classify, and thus render the unfamiliar familiar', and imposed 'a European conception of order on a primitive "anarchy" of facts'.[37] The inhabitants of the islands became objects of a narrow line of scholarly inquiry which served explicitly colonial purposes. Although driven by similar urges, German anthropology was also characterised by liberal ideas of progress,[38] and German scholars asserted their approach as inherently superior to the Spanish Catholic tradition. This chapter investigates how Semper and Jagor's travel accounts, which would inform later German discussions on the Philippines, evaluated the colonial system, and how their accounts both described and affected its peoples.

Semper's depiction of non-Christian 'tribes' in the mountains both opened up the possibility of constructing a picture of precolonial society, and objectified natives as objects of study. Considering the lack of archaeological findings, he turned to these communities for evidence of the earliest inhabitants:

> In the Philippines, [...] the first appearance of Man is shrouded in almost impenetrable darkness. Whereas the remainders of stilt houses [...] support our imagination when reconstructing a pre-Celtic society in Europe, the first inhabitants of the Philippines have not left us any monuments; but the mores and manners of a number of living tribes give us a fairly faithful image of past centuries.[39]

Semper treated living people as archaeological artefacts, as atavistic remnants of a prehistoric society. He devoted one chapter to such peoples, most prominently those nowadays referred to as Aeta, whose distinctly darker and shorter appearance led to them being given the collective name *Negritos*, commonly used by Western observers, including Semper and Jagor.

Credited by Virchow for being one of the first authors to describe the physical characteristics of *Negritos*,[40] Semper speculated on their descent and kinship with the Papuans of New Guinea and the inhabitants of Micronesian islands like Fiji – questions which would be discussed in the early 1870s by Virchow, Jagor and others in what came to be known as the *Negritofrage*.[41] Presenting *Negritos* as free spirits, 'undemanding children of nature' and a naturally brave and friendly people, Semper calls them the original inhabitants of the Philippines.[42] This conclusion was shared by Virchow, who related *Negritos* to Aboriginal Australians and Papuans.[43] In his work, Semper was careful to correct the work of previous authors on the spread of *Negritos*, and thereby established his superiority over the existing scholarship.[44]

Semper's discussion of other tribal peoples followed a similar pattern of objectification and search for racial origins. He focused on the various groups in the mountains of northern Luzon and the Manobo people in the jungle of eastern Mindanao – in the far north and south-east of the archipelago. As these areas were the furthest from the supposed sites of first contacts with Muslim and Christian cultures, Semper presumed that they preserved the archipelago's original culture in its purest form. As with the *Negritos*, by calling them the living remains of ancient culture, he effectively reduced them to archaeological evidence by consistently highlighting their backwardness.[45] He characterised the supposedly non-Malay Igorots in northern Luzon as reliable and friendly, but the Malay Irayas as unwelcoming. Turning his attention to Mindanao, he depicted the Malay Manobos as violent and polygamous. Their religious fanaticism, replete with 'human sacrifice and cannibalism', served as an ostensible marker of their barbarity.[46] It is indicative of the speculative character of Semper's argument that he claimed that the original culture of the archipelago was somewhere on the spectrum between the friendliness of the Igorots and the violence of the Manobos, a claim which, despite its tendency towards racialisation, allowed nationalists scope for the construction of a Filipino people predating Spanish Catholic conquest. It also became a vehicle for racial prejudice towards the Malay native majority, with Semper's depiction of precolonial culture as violent effectively reinforcing the idea that colonisation brought civilisation.

Jagor described his encounters with *Negritos* and his visits to people living on the flanks of the volcanoes of the Bicol region in southern Luzon in similar terms. His first encounter with a *Negrito* family depicted them (as Semper did) as friendly and peaceful. Highlighting their primitive state, he observed that they traded their forest produce with the lowland population in exchange for food. They were not viewed as producers or even capable of basic forms of agency. When, for example,

Jagor joined them on a hunt, his account stated that they accompanied him, suggesting his sense of superiority: 'The male accompanied me on the hunt, armed with bow and two arrows which had points of two inches long, shaped like lances, of which one was coated in poison.'[47] While the *Negrito* man was cast as an accessory to Jagor's hunt, his equipment, supposed to be suggestive of his savageness, also proves that this was in fact his hunt, while Jagor was merely a guest.

Jagor's account includes images of *Negritos*, drawn from photographs taken in a different area. He also made direct drawings of *Negritos* during an unplanned stay at Mariveles, where his ship was forced to take shelter from stormy weather which lasted two weeks: 'Sadly I only learned in the final days that there was a settlement of Negritos in the mountains, and only shortly before my departure was I able to see and draw a man and a woman.'[48] *Negritos* remained of great interest to Jagor, as his disappointment at this missed chance for deeper investigation signals. He included his drawing of the male *Negrito*, showing his physical features as well as his clothes and equipment, as a contribution to the debate regarding the *Negritofrage*, in which he participated while writing his book. In essence, however, they interested him as a category, not as individuals.

The *Negritofrage* also framed his discussion of mountain dwellers on two volcanoes in Bicol: Mount Yriga and Mount Isarog. Asserting himself over existing scholarship, Jagor corrected supposed misconceptions about the racial constitution of these people. He described their physical features and cultural habits to determine their 'race', concluding that the people living on Mount Yriga were not, as previously assumed, *Negritos*.[49] He calls them instead 'mixed breeds of Indios and Negritos':

> Their skin is dark brown, not black [...]. Some, but certainly not all, have crinkly hair. Whereas [...] Negritos [...] do not engage in agriculture, live almost unsheltered outdoors, feed themselves with the products of nature, the half-savages [*Halbwilde*] of Mount Yriga live in comfortable cabins and cultivate several tubers and some sugar cane. [...] The few ranchos are very accessible, and have most friendly communication with the Indios [...]. In spite of these neighbourly connections they preserved much of their original nature. The men were naked except for a G-string, the women likewise or wore a skirt reaching from the hip to the knee. In the largest rancho the women were dressed very decently.[50]

Determining their racial constitution through physical and cultural features appears to have been his primary objective in visiting and describing these people. Jagor connected race and culture, labelling them partly *Negrito* and partly savage, and claiming they were more civilised and decent because their ranchos were larger and more sophisticated. Nakedness served as a marker of civilisation, and Jagor focused on what people did not wear. Contrary to his earlier mentioning of a *Negrito* settlement near Mariveles, he now asserted that *Negritos* were savages living outdoors. The settlements in Bicol indicated to him that people there were ahead of *Negritos* in terms of racial and cultural development. He included a drawing which showed villagers in what the text reveals to be a posed scene, following Jagor's instructions.

The notion that the cultural features of such communities preserved an assumed original Philippine character, corresponded to Semper's attempts to highlight their backwardness and objectify them as relics from the past. The same pattern applies to Jagor's depiction of the people of Mount Isarog, another Bicol volcano, who, he argued, 'preserved their independence and the mores of an earlier age'.[51] Time had seemingly stood still in these communities, which he concluded were remainders of a formerly widespread tribe that had withstood colonialism, and could therefore be investigated to construct an image of Philippine life before the Spanish conquest. Jagor furthermore claimed that the customary classification of the people living on Mount Isarog, as belonging to the Igorots, the name of mountain peoples in northern Luzon, is incorrect, once more asserting his scholarship.[52]

Both authors describe *Negritos* as a *Naturvolk* resisting civilising efforts, whereas they called other tribal people 'half-savages' who were capable of some form of development, but nonetheless remained at lower stages of civilisation than the Christianised lowlanders. Their analyses foreshadowed a theory of migration waves in which *Negritos* were seen as the indigenous inhabitants, who in prehistory were driven into the hills and woods by waves of increasingly superior immigrants. This theory, put forward by Blumentritt in the 1880s and embraced by Filipino nationalists like Jose Rizal,[53] still causes racial prejudice against mountain tribes today, even though its scientific grounding is questionable at best.[54] Both Jagor's and Semper's searches for the racial origins of the inhabitants of the Philippines predated Blumentritt's inquiry by a decade and appear to have been sources of data for the Bohemian ethnologist, who never visited the country he studied.

On one occasion, Jagor's presentation of tribal peoples clashes with his own observations. When discussing the multiple failed attempts of Europeans to extract copper from the hills around Paracale in Bicol, he gave expression to his astonishment that the 'savage Igorots' (whom he previously determined as 'half-savage') were successful where the Europeans had failed. They had mined, he noted, a high amount of copper through a necessarily sophisticated system (which Jagor does not describe) and made it into intricate kettles. Apparently, these supposed (half-)savages possessed technical skills unknown to Europeans! Jagor commented that as the art of gaining and reworking copper must have been known here before the arrival of the Spanish, they had probably learned it from the Chinese or Japanese.[55] To Jagor it seemed unthinkable that 'backward' natives could have developed such technology independently. Accordingly, he suggested that it was technology imported from ostensibly more civilised areas of Asia.

Racial stereotypes were also at the basis of the two travel accounts' depictions of the majority Christian native population as indolent, unreliable and dissolute ('*liederlich*'). According to Alatas, Jagor 'echoed very much the earlier views on the Filipinos' as lazy, and 'found them addicted to idleness and dissipation'.[56] But Jagor at times intimated that laziness was caused by exogenous factors, particularly Spanish colonialism. This exposed an interesting tension between his attempts to understand Philippine natives and to pin their supposed indolence on Spain, on the one hand, and the racial discourses within which he worked, on the other.

The accounts mentioned the theme of indolence in passing throughout their narratives; it appears as a self-evident truth generated by the colonial ideology in which these texts function. For instance, when Semper discussed the difficulties of seafaring in the archipelago, he listed a number of causal factors, including a lack of accurate maps, the threat of pirates, the frequency of heavy storms, and 'the innate carelessness of the crews'.[57] For Semper, such recklessness was intrinsic to the natives' nature. Similarly, Jagor's accounts of his sea journeys were customarily accompanied by examples of unreliable native seamen.[58]

Cockfighting, which regularly appeared in many nineteenth-century accounts of the Philippines as an expression of the supposed native indolence and moral deficit, was also discussed by Jagor,[59] who expressed his bewilderment at the custom. His mockery of this 'national vice' revealed his bias towards men, the part of the population usually involved in this activity: 'Almost all Indios have fighting cocks. Many never go out without their darling; [...] and overload him with the most tender caresses.'[60] His ostentatiously civilised revulsion at the fighting itself arises not from the cruelty towards animals but from the behaviour and appearance of the spectators: 'For Europeans, the sight is very repulsive: The ring-shaped auditorium is loaded with natives, who are sweating from all pores, their faces ecstatic with hideous zeal.'[61] His examples of the cruel treatment of the roosters draw attention to the barbarism of the natives, who are shown to be irresponsible, impulsive and dissolute:

> Each rooster is armed with a sharp, sickle-shaped, 3-inch-long knife that cuts deep wounds, always causing the death of one or both roosters through gruesome injuries. If a rooster cowardly runs away, it is plucked alive. Compared to the means of the players, incredibly high sums are being

waged. It is evident that these cockfights work extremely corruptively on a people so inclined to idleness and dissoluteness.[62]

Those who lose all while gambling reportedly resorted to robbery.[63] Jagor thus takes a moralistic stance on cockfighting, which, he argued, aggravated the natives' innate laziness and immorality.

He also highlighted the behaviour of native priests as a particularly poignant example of indolence. Upon entering the village of Batu in Bicol, the dirt and bad state of the roads confirmed for him that the parish priest was a native, who, it turned out, complained about the lack of revenue he received from his parish.[64] Jagor went on to deplore the state of the native clergy:

> Native priests generally bestow little honour upon their order. Incredibly ignorant, very dissolute, only educated in the formalities of their service, they spend a big part of their time playing, drinking and doing other sinful things. They do not even care to preserve decorum, except during mass, which they read in a comically dignified manner, without understanding a word of it. Often there are girls and small children in the Convento [...]. Of his own accord, the local priest [of Batu] introduced two beautiful girls to me as his poor sisters, whom he supported in spite of his reduced situation; their daughters, though, were blatantly called daughters of the Cura by the servants.[65]

The stereotypes Jagor attributed to these priests were the same he applied to natives in general: uneducated, dissolute, more interested in show than substance. Jagor explicitly stated that he did not observe such behaviour in Spanish clergymen. His comments appeared at a time when Spanish friars and administrators were increasingly hostile towards native priests (whom they suspected of corruption, incompetence and disloyalty), as they competed for the most lucrative positions.[66] In his 1842 policy report, the administrator Sinibaldo de Mas had pointed out the untrustworthiness of native priests (including *Mestizos* and creoles), who would still 'belong to a conquered people' and have a 'natural affection toward their own countrymen'.[67] In 1872, three creole priests were even publicly executed on charges of inciting a rebellion.

A similarly recurring theme was that of Jagor's abandonment by local helpers on his expeditions, which he consistently reported in an ironic, ridiculing tone. Even his account of his first excursion, through the province of Laguna, contained three such occasions, the first on his journey from Manila to Laguna by river boat:

> After the crew had tried to discontinue the journey under all sorts of pretences, they left the boat at the village of Pasig to get sails, but did not return. Only with the help of the night watch could they be taken from the houses of their friends, where they were hiding.[68]

[ 193 ]

Apparently too lazy to do their job, the crew needed to be disciplined by the colonial authorities. Jagor furthermore reported having to abandon his hike from the town of Los Baños to a nearby village because his guide pretended to be exhausted after half an hour's walk.[69] Another guide had run off on the way to Mauban, taking his advance payment with him, as Jagor does not fail to mention.[70]

The chapters on his travels through Bicol and the Visayas contain many further examples. He blames his failure to reach the summit of Mount Mayon on 'the unreliability of the Indios'; two men carrying supplies disappeared right at the start of the hike, whereas the man who was supposed to guard the base camp returned to the nearest town before noon. Jagor's ironic account culminates at nightfall:

> My servant, who carried a woollen blanket and an umbrella for me, disappeared suddenly in the darkness, as it started to rain, and only found me the next morning [...]. We spent the rainy night on the barren stones, freezing, [...] our teeth chattering.[71]

After staying for a while in a nearby town, his servants reportedly resorted to theft to prevent him from travelling onwards and avoid leaving the comforts and pleasures of lazy Philippine village life:

> My servants and their many friends liked the idle life in Daraga so much, that they wanted to enjoy it as long as possible. They often chose ingenious means to this end. Twice, as everything was ready for departure on the following morning, my shoes were stolen at night. Another time my horse was stolen.[72]

Numerous such examples could be cited here. On some occasions Jagor included Spaniards in his picture of indolence. He called the Philippines a 'paradise' (*Schlaraffenland*), where natives and (as he added in an offhand manner) Spaniards lived under the 'most comfortable circumstances', indulging in the abundance offered by the country's natural conditions.[73] But he then continued to focus on the indolence of colonials, describing a boat ride on the Pasig near Manila. The 'Tiendas' by the riverside lured passing boatmen with 'food, [...] leisurely company of both sexes, Hazard games, tuba [palm wine], betel nuts and tobacco'.[74] Apart from games and substances, loose sexual conduct – including homosexual acts – marked the natives' indolence and dissoluteness. He again invoked sexuality when he pointed out the ostensibly dissolute native traditions that characterised indigenous housing:

> Houses that have only one single room, in which *all* activities take place, are the cause of great dissoluteness and dirty routines: the whole family sleeps in it together and every traveller is a welcome guest.[75]

With no further explanation, it is assumed commonplace that sleeping together in one room caused dissoluteness. In two ways, though, Jagor nuances this picture of the lazy native, as becomes apparent in his account of another troubled hike, namely his climb to the summit of Mount Isarog:

> The Indios taken from Goa [the nearest town] were so lazy and cranky during the expedition, that almost all work, cutting a path through the forest, fell on the Igorots; the lazy Indio coolies even threw away the drinking water, the Igorots had to get fresh water from quite a distance [...] During all troublesome marches I always got along better with tribesmen than with Indios. I found the former compliant, reliable, decisive, knowledgeable, while the latter usually displayed defiant characteristics. But it would be unjust to draw conclusions from this regarding their respective natures; for the savages are at home in the forest [...] But the Indios are forced labourers who do the right thing, from their standpoint, when they do as little as possible.[76]

Here he depicted the uphill tribes as more reliable than the lowlanders, a contrast which fits in with his idealisation of tribal communities as natural peoples in a more original state. Similar descriptions can also be found in the Austrian geologist Richard von Drasche's reports of his travels through the mountains of northern Luzon in the 1870s.[77] Beyond this, Jagor explained native indolence by stating that his unwilling assistants were in fact resisting forced labour imposed upon them by the colonial regime. He does not attribute the unreliability of his servants to an inborn indolence, but rather to a form of passive resistance.

The remark which Alatas specifically criticised as a postulation of the natives' laziness is more complex when read in its context, namely a lengthy discussion of Spain's influence on the colony. Seemingly out of the blue, Jagor joked about the bamboo oars common for small boats: 'all the better if it breaks along the way, until it's fixed, the tiring work has to be paused'.[78] Jagor used this anecdote to illustrate a supposed lack of moral grounding and dignity. Stereotypical as this view was, Jagor concluded that this moral deficit was the consequence of a subjection to Catholicism, which resulted in the loss of the original native culture.[79] With the loss of original values, the pre-existing, indigenous moral grounding had been lost and forgotten. Ultimately, Jagor blamed the natives' laziness on their subjection to a foreign culture.

Jagor also maintained that the destruction of native traditions was made possible by the Philippines' cultural backwardness at the time of conquest, an argument which echoed eighteenth-century Spanish

views on Philippine natives as mere imitators,[80] and which indicated
his Eurocentric stance:

> The culturally undeveloped Filipinos [*Philippiner*] quickly adopted the
> appearances of the foreign religion and the appearances of the character
> of their new masters; they learned to despise their own customs as pagan
> and savage. Now they sing Andalusian songs and dance Spanish dances,
> but how! They copy everything, without understanding the spirit from
> which it proceeded. Therefore, they and their artworks are mostly boring
> and characterless.[81]

The inability of natives to understand the imposed culture seemed to
result not only from its foreignness but also from their underdevelop-
ment. Nevertheless, Jagor concluded that Philippine indolence was not
determined by 'race', but was a result of colonisation. He made reference
to the natives of British Malaya, who were supposedly akin to Filipinos,
and called them 'earnest, taciturn, dignified, fearfully solicitous about
their honour, and submissive to superiors'.[82] These adjectives reveal his
imperialist perspective: seriousness, silence and submissiveness could
be exploited for economic profit. Spain's allegedly mild regime had
failed to instil natives with an industrious spirit, as it did not require
hard labour and allowed the peasants to live off the riches of the land.[83]
Stereotypes of the Spanish informed his evaluation of their regime: both
Spaniards and Filipinos preferred an easy life over the industriousness
of colonial capitalism. Jagor's argument differed fundamentally from
Alatas's interpretation of it: indolence resulted from Spanish colonial
rule, instead of being a racial feature of the native. While he still held
that Philippine natives were capable of improvement, the guidance
of a colonial master remained necessary in his view. This raised the
question of whether the Philippines might not be better off under
another, more efficient colonial power.

Jagor's discussion of regions outside central Luzon implied a more
positive evaluation of colonialism's impact. He reported that the people
of Bicol had a distinct language and many characteristics setting them
apart from the Tagalogs to their north and the Visayans to their south.
He called Bicol the connection between Tagalogs and Visayans in terms
of language, ability and mores – physically and mentally inferior to the
Tagalogs, but superior to the Visayans. The superiority of the Tagalogs
was supposedly noticeable in the beautiful women in the part of Bicol
bordering on the Tagalog provinces, women with a fairer complexion.[84]
He thus constructed a hierarchy based on a connection between physical and mental capabilities on the one hand and development on the
other: the closer to the centre of colonial power, the more developed
the people. Here his argument again included racial elements. The

chapter on the Visayan islands of Samar and Leyte reaffirmed this hierarchy:

> The inhabitants of Samar and Leyte are more sluggish, not as clean as those of Luzon, and seem to be lagging behind the Bicol as much as the latter behind the Tagalogs. Near Tacloban, which has lively trade with Manila, these traits are less pronounced; the women there are pleasant and bathe a lot. Furthermore, the inhabitants of both islands are friendly, good-natured, obedient and peaceful.[85]

Civilisation, he argued, emanated from the colonial centre Manila, as shown by the hierarchy between Tagalogs, Bicol and Visayans, and by the notion that negative traits were less pronounced in the port connecting the islands with the centre. Women's cleanliness and attractiveness was a measure of development. The positive traits attributed to the locals in the final sentence once more indicate Jagor's colonial gaze, which stood in dynamic tension with his criticism of Spain as a colonial master.

Semper correspondingly saw that the Spanish failed to accommodate the development of a 'dignified civic spirit'.[86] In contrast to Jagor's argument which accused Spain of destroying precolonial culture, Semper presents Spanish influence on the natives as too superficial to instil dignity and diligence in the colonial subjects. Indolence thus appears as more natural to Philippine natives here than in Jagor's view.

Both authors emphasised a lack of economic development,[87] implying that there were possibilities for foreign investors. Discussing a plantation newly established in Bicol by a young Frenchman who praised the diligence of his employees, Jagor claimed that foreigners got along with native workers better than Spaniards did, because the latter often came from the lower classes and made unreasonable demands.[88] Indeed, the ineptitude of Spanish officials and managers did cause dissatisfaction among their employees, who saw themselves as far more able to run the country than the supposedly superior colonisers.[89] Jagor instead expected much from non-Spanish Western involvement, as he concluded that there were few colonies which offered better opportunities for plantation investment.[90] He presented the Philippines as a badly exploited, fertile land with a potentially hardworking population, offering economic opportunities to non-Spanish foreigners, Germans (the primary audience of his book) among them. A greater foreign presence, or a transition of power, he reasoned, could consequently drive forward development and free the people from their perceived indolence.

Although both authors mainly reported problems, the mid-nineteenth century actually witnessed considerable economic growth and social transformation. In contrast to other European observers (whose racial theories rendered this phenomenon unthinkable),[91] Jagor noted the emergence of a home-grown middle class. But he framed this class exclusively as *Mestizo*, disregarding the number of those categorised as *Indios* who had actually achieved middle-class economic positions and did not fit his image of the indolent native. The idea that racially mixed people were less indolent reveals that, despite Jagor's sophistication, he still upheld elements of the prevailing racial discourse. Neither author mentioned *Indio* entrepreneurs or businessmen and *Indios* appeared only as small peasants, fishermen or both. Semper, for instance, claimed that beyond the vicinity of the large cities, where there was some division of labour, every native was a peasant and fisherman at the same time, being interested only in satisfying his and his relatives' immediate needs.[92] They were not, for him, part of the modern economy. Business was in the hands of Westerners and *Mestizos*; small retail was almost exclusively run by Chinese who, Jagor noted, sold clothes and fake jewellery.[93] Chinese *Mestizos* appeared as hardworking, wealthy and entrepreneurial, but also as ruthless, cunning and exploitative:

> Mestizos, especially those of Chinese and Tagalogs, form the richest, most entrepreneurial part of the local population; they know all the good and bad qualities of the natives and relentlessly exploit these for their aims.[94]

Both authors envisaged *Mestizos* as the force of future development.[95] Semper called them intellectually and physically superior to the 'purely Malay indolent natives', who did not share their 'desire to amass riches'. Indolence here appears as an obvious feature of the Malays, Semper's racial definition of the majority native population. He furthermore presented *Mestizos* as possessing a 'sense of higher self-respect than the one shown by the Tagalogs or Visayans'. Their consciousness of belonging to a distinct 'tribe' had brought about an apparent 'desire to greater political independence and self-government'.[96] The hope for change Semper projected on to *Mestizos* derived from a racialised, stereotypical view not only of this group but also – a more negative one – of the *Indios*:

> To a Spaniard, whose wish is mainly to preserve the colony as a milk cow, the Mestizos may seem a dangerous enemy. Still, the hope of the country rests on them. An immigration of many Europeans, who would change the country – like the English did in New Zealand and Australia – into a European one, is unthinkable [...] The pure Malay today lives almost exactly like before, lacking consciousness of higher personal dignity, lacking interest in the common fate of the country.[97]

For Semper, only Europeans and Mestizos possessed the political and economic skills needed for development. His view on 'pure' natives as lacking an indispensable sense of dignity and common good produced a justification of colonialism. Many of these supposedly lazy natives actually did profit from and contribute to the economic growth that the Philippines underwent, as well as to its political development during the late nineteenth century. Indeed, a large part of the nationalist movement of the 1890s consisted of (usually *Indio*) office staff in companies and the expanding bureaucracies.[98] Even though he criticised the exploitative character of Spanish rule, Semper warned that the loss of colonial power would mean a return to the precolonial tyranny of clans:

> Should, by unfortunate circumstance, the country achieve political freedom and the only power be destroyed that, throughout the centuries, was able to force the inhabitants to adopt a higher culture, then an immediate collapse into the old clan system, which exists up to this day, would occur. This can only be prevented by the strong hand of a new lord.[99]

Semper employed the colonial argument of the civilising mission, which ostensibly brought higher culture and political justice for the natives' own good. He did not, however, specify which new foreign power he expected to take over to prevent a return to uncivilised precolonial society, though his stance could easily be interpreted to call upon an emerging Germany to take its responsibility in the region.

Jagor, who also feared a return to precolonial society, went into more detail regarding the future. He argued that the end of Spanish rule was imminent, as Spain – once a positive influence on the colony – resisted both the modernisation necessary for the new world economy and the liberalisation needed to satisfy a prosperous, enlightened and self-conscious *Mestizo* population.[100] He viewed Spain as unable to develop an efficient colonial bureaucracy like the Dutch or the English.[101] Crucially, he blamed the problems of the Philippines not on colonialism *per se* but on the backward nature of Spanish rule. To his mind, the colony would have fared better under a modern colonising power. Like Semper, Jagor claimed that Spanish rule failed to prepare the Philippines for independence and international competition. He deemed the guidance of a colonising power indispensable for the country's own good and correctly predicted that the United States of America would take on this role.[102]

The conclusions of Semper and Jagor regarding the state and future of the Philippines and its people under Spanish colonialism foreshadowed the Philippine Revolution of the 1890s and the subsequent transition to American colonial rule. Parallel to the two travellers, Philippine nationalists, such as Rizal in his 1887 novel *Noli Me Tangere*, lamented the backwardness of Spanish rule, with its powerful clergy, and its failure to modernise the colony. The rise of this Philippine nationalism seems to have been predicted in the remarks of Semper and Jagor that identified *Mestizos* as the force of change in the country. With reference to Jagor, Mojares has noted that political and economic expansion fostered 'new needs and new ways of looking at the world', resulting in the rise of an intelligentsia and the formation of a public sphere.[103] But this intelligentsia – which was to transform the country by pushing for modernisation and reforms, and increasingly also for independence – was not limited to *Mestizos*, as the observations of the two travelogues implied. Like education, economic participation also extended to so-called *Indios*. Consequently after 1872 – when both authors were back in Germany – a national movement transcending racial boundaries emerged in the Philippines.[104]

Both of these travel accounts' discussions of tribal groups show a paradox of romantic idealisation and denigrating objectification. Presenting these people as relics from a precolonial, savage past also ascribed to them a purity lost to the Christianised *Indios*, the supposedly more civilised lowlanders who were seen as corrupted by the imposed foreign culture. The search for cultural and racial origins served colonial knowledge, but also informed the discourse of an emergent nationalism. Moreover, in applying cutting-edge anthropology to Spain's colonial subjects, the authors challenged the dominance of Spanish colonial knowledge production.

The connections between German scholarship and the Philippine nationalist movement have been well documented.[105] Of the travellers in this chapter, Jagor seems to have interacted most intensively with Philippine nationalist intellectuals. As Mojares claims, the nationalist scholar Pedro Paterno drew much on Jagor for his observations about Philippine life.[106] And while he studied in Paris, Trinidad Pardo de Tavera hosted a dinner for Jagor.[107] Jagor's expectation of an American takeover, which would take place in 1898, caught the attention of Rizal,[108] who planned to translate his book but never finished the project.[109] Rizal also seems to have drawn on Jagor in writing his 1890 essay 'The Indolence of the Filipino', in which he defended his countrymen against the accusations of indolence in Western observations (which also shows how Semper and Jagor were part of a wider milieu discussing this topic). While admitting the existence of laziness, Rizal denied that it was in the natives' character; instead he joined Jagor in attributing it to outside factors: colonial mismanagement, corruption and exploitation, wrong examples set by Spaniards and the church, and also the hot climate.[110]

Philippine nationalism, and Spain's failure to respond to its calls for modernisation and political rights, culminated in the revolution of 1896. In December of that year, Rizal was executed in a vain attempt to put the genie back in the bottle.[111] The insurrection coincided with the Spanish–American War to bring about the end of Spanish rule in the archipelago, but it did not see the end of colonialism there. After defeating Spain, the Americans incorporated the Philippines into their own empire – as Jagor had expected and Semper had wished. Their argument, that guidance by a foreign power was indispensable for the well-being of the Philippines, resounded in American justifications of their hegemony as a 'tutelage' in democracy and civilisation.[112] In 1900, after the official end of hostilities between US and Filipino troops, William Beveridge justified US imperialism by claiming that good government was not in the blood of the Filipinos.[113] This example of the political afterlife of anthropological assumptions indicates that these liberal German scholars, while challenging specifics of Spanish colonial practice, ultimately reinforced the racial categories and stereotypes that upheld the unequal power relationships of imperialism well after the Spanish had retired from the scene.

## Notes

1 Carl Semper, *Die Philippinen und ihre Bewohner: Sechs Skizzen nach einem im Frankfurter geographischen Verein 1868 gehaltenen Cyclus von Vorträgen* (Würzburg: Stuber, 1869).

2 Fedor Jagor, *Reisen in den Philippinen* (Berlin: Weidmannsche Buchhandlung, 1873).

3 Megan C. Thomas, *Orientalists, Propagandists and Ilustrados: Filipino Scholarship and the End of Spanish Colonialism* (Minneapolis: University of Minnesota Press, 2012), p. 62.

4 See the short biography accompanying the volumes containing the evaluations of his zoological findings: August Schuberg, 'Carl Semper', in Carl Semper, *Reisen im Archipel der Philippinen: Wissenschaftliche Resultate, Zweiter Theil: Ergänzungsheft* (Wiesbaden: Kreidel, 1895), pp. vii–xviii.

5 Carl Semper, *Die Palau-Inseln im Stillen Ozean: Reiseerlebnisse* (Leipzig: Brockhaus, 1873).

6 After returning to Germany, Semper became professor of zoology at the University of Würzburg, where he and his students spent years evaluating the data he collected in the Philippines, resulting in the seven-volume *Reisen im Archipel der Philippinen: wissenschaftliche Resultate*. See for his groundbreaking findings regarding environmental effects on the evolution of animals Karl Semper, *Animal Life as Affected by the Natural Conditions of Existence* (New York: Appleton, 1881).

7 E.g. Carl Semper, 'Reisen durch die nördlichen Provinzen der Insel Luzon', *Zeitschrift für allgemeine Erdkunde* 13 (1862), 81–96; translated as 'Trip through the Northern Provinces of the Island of Luzon', in William Henry Scott (ed.), *German Travellers on the Cordillera* (Manila: Filipiniana Book Guild, 1975), pp. 17–34.

8 A prime source of Western knowledge on the Philippines, it was republished there during the American colonial period. Fedor Jagor, 'Travels in the Philippines', in Austin Craig (ed.), *The Former Philippines through Foreign Eyes* (Manila: Philippine Education Co., 1916), pp. 1–356.

9 Rudolf Virchow, 'Über den Schädelbau der Bewohner der Philippinen, insbesondere der Negritos', *Zeitschrift für Ethnologie* 3 (1871), 33–42 (p. 33).

10 Andrew Zimmermann, 'Adventures in the Skin Trade: German Anthropology and Colonial Corporeality', in H. Glenn Perry and Matti Bunzl (eds), *Worldly Provincialism: German Anthropology in the Age of Empire* (Ann Arbour: University of Michigan Press, 2003), pp. 156–78 (p. 171).

11  Syed Alatas, *The Myth of the Lazy Native: A Study of the Image of the Malays, Filipinos and Javanese from the 16th to the 20th Century and Its Function in the Ideology of Colonial Capitalism* (London: Crass, 1977), p. 55.

12  Otto van den Muijzenberg, *The Philippines through European Lenses: Late 19th Century Photographs from the Meerkamp van Embden Collection* (Quezon City: Ateneo de Manila University Press, 2008), p. 14.

13  Marie Louise Pratt, *Imperial Eyes: Travel Writing and Transculturation* (New York: Routledge, 1992), p. 7.

14  Harry Liebersohn, 'Coming of Age in the Pacific: German Ethnography from Chamisso to Krämer', in Perry and Bunzl, *Worldly Provincialism*, pp. 31–46 (p. 31).

15  People from present-day China migrated throughout south-east Asia well before European colonisers arrived and categorised the variety of them as a single Chinese entity. In the nineteenth century, more Chinese arrived as labourers. Benedict Anderson, *Spectre of Comparisons: Nationalism, Southeast Asia, and the World* (Quezon City: Ateneo de Manila University Press, 2004), pp. 13–14.

16  Paul A. Kramer, *The Blood of Government: Race, Empire, the United States, and the Philippines* (Quezon City: Ateneo de Manila University Press, 2006), p. 39.

17  Semper, *Die Philippinen*, p. 81.

18  Ambeth R. Ocampo, '1896 Philippines: Racial Context of the Revolution', in *Bones of Contention: The Andres Bonifacio Lectures* (Mandaluyong: Anvil, 2014), pp. 97–115 (p. 100).

19  Benito J. Legarda, *After the Galleons: Foreign Trade, Economic Change and Entrepreneurship in the Nineteenth-Century Philippines* (Quezon City: Ateneo de Manila University Press, 1999); Patricio N. Abinales and Donna J. Amoroso, *State and Society in the Philippines* (Pasig: Anvil, 2005), p. 80.

20  Ocampo, '1896', p. 109.

21  John Schumacher, 'Economic Factors in the Revolution', in *The Making of a Nation: Essays on Nineteenth-Century Filipino Nationalism* (Quezon City: Ateneo de Manila University Press, 1996), pp. 126–33 (p. 127).

22  Anderson, *Spectre*, pp. 228–9.

23  Woodruff Smith, *The German Colonial Empire* (Chapel Hill: University of North Carolina Press, 1978), p. 6.

24  Imperialism is not only expressed in conquests or hegemonic positions, but it contains multifarious processes of mutual influence between centre and periphery. See Dirk van Laak, *Über Alles in der Welt: Deutscher Imperialismus im 19. Und 20. Jahrhundert* (Munich: Beck, 2005), p. 10.

25  Peripheral Sulu was never subjected to Spanish dominance (retaining Islam under a sultanate). It was traditionally allied with Spain's competitors: the nearby Dutch empire and, more recently, Britain. When a German merchant ship broke through the Spanish blockade around Sulu, a diplomatic crisis ensued. Volker Schult, 'Sultans and Adventurers: German Blockade-Runners in the Sulu Archipelago', *Philippine Studies* 50:3 (2002), 395–415.

26  For instance, Jagor's account made a lasting impression on the works of Jose Rizal, who read it while he was a student. Floro C. Quibuyen, *A Nation Aborted: Rizal, American Hegemony, and Philippine Nationalism* (Quezon City: Ateneo de Manila University Press, 2008), pp. 114–16. T.H. Pardo de Tavera, for his part, was heavily influenced by Jagor, Virchow and Ferdinand Blumentritt. See Mojares, *Brains of the Nation*, p. 205.

27  Thomas, *Orientalists*, p. 206.

28  Rudolf Virchow, 'The Peopling of the Philippines', in Craig, *The Former Philippines through Foreign Eyes*, pp. 536–50.

29  Bastian briefly visited Manila and its surroundings in the 1860s. Adolf Bastian, *Die Völker des östlichen Asien: Studien und Reisen, fünfter Band: Reisen im indischen Archipel: Singapore, Batavia, Manilla und Japan* (Jena: Hermann Costenoble, 1869), pp. 256–99.

30 Blumentritt became an intellectual ally and adviser of Philippine nationalists. Benedict Anderson, *Under Three Flags: Anarchism and the Anti-Colonial Imagination* (Pasig: Anvil, 2006), pp. 102–3, 124–5.

31 Alexander Schadenberg, 'The Banao People and the Guinaangs, Gran Cordillera Central', in Scott, *German Travellers on the Cordillera (1860–1890)*, pp. 129–39; 'Tribes Living in the Interior of Northern Luzon', in ibid., pp. 140–60.

32 Resil B. Mojares, *Brains of the Nation: Pedro Paterno, T.H. Pardo de Tavera, Isabelo de los Reyes and the Production of Modern Knowledge* (Quezon City: Ateneo de Manila University Press, 2006), p. 387.

33 Edward W. Said, *Culture and Imperialism* (New York: Vintage, 1994), p. 153.

34 Thomas, *Orientalists*, pp. 201, 206.

35 See Filomeno V. Aguilar, 'Tracing Origins: Ilustrado Nationalism and the Racial Science of Migration Waves', *The Journal of Asian Studies* 64 (2005), 605–37.

36 Thomas, *Orientalists*, p. 63.

37 Mojares, *Brains of the Nation*, pp. 384, 387.

38 See Matti Bunzl and H. Glenn Penny, 'Introduction: Rethinking German Anthropology, Colonialism, and Race', in *Worldly Provincialism*, pp. 1–30 (p. 5); Woodruff D. Smith, 'Anthropology and German Colonialism', in Arthur J. Knoll and Lewis H. Gann (eds), *Germans in the Tropics: Essays in German Colonial History* (New York: Greenwood Press, 1987), pp. 39–58 (p. 44).

39 Semper, *Die Philippinen*, p. 48.

40 Virchow, 'The Peopling of the Philippines', p. 537.

41 Virchow, 'Über den Schädelbau der Bewohner der Philippinen, insbesondere der Negritos'; 'Ueber Negrito- und Igorroten-Schädel von den Philippinen', *Zeitschrift für Ethnologie, Verhandlungen der Berliner Gesellschaft für Anthropologie, Ethnologie und Urgeschichte* 4 (1872), 204; Fedor Jagor, 'Über die Negritos', *Zeitschrift für Ethnologie: Verhandlungen der Berliner Gesellschaft für Anthropologie, Ethnologie und Urgeschichte* 3 (1871), 43; Adolf Bastian, 'Die Negrito-Frage', *Zeitschrift für Ethnologie: Verhandlungen der Berliner Gesellschaft für Anthopologie, Ethnologie und Urgeschichte* 3 (1871), 44; C.E. Meinicke, 'Bemerkungen zu Wallace's Ansichten über die Bevölkerung der indischen Inseln', *Zeitschrift für Ethnologie* 3 (1871), 84–93.

42 Semper, *Die Philippinen*, pp. 50–1.

43 Virchow, 'The Peopling of the Philippines', p. 537.

44 Semper, *Die Philippinen*, p. 49.

45 Semper, *Die Philippinen*, p. 53.

46 Semper, *Die Philippinen*, p. 63.

47 Jagor, *Reisen*, p. 51.

48 Jagor, *Reisen*, p. 63.

49 During an 1871 discussion within the Berliner Gesellschaft für Anthropologie, Ethnologie und Urgeschichte, he used the same example (and almost exactly the same words) to counter reports that the Bicol volcanoes were home to *Negritos*. See Jagor, 'Über die Negritos', p. 43.

50 Jagor, *Reisen*, pp. 105–7.

51 Jagor, *Reisen*, p. 161.

52 Jagor, *Reisen*, pp. 161–2.

53 Aguilar, 'Tracing Origins', pp. 606–7.

54 Van den Muijzenberg, *The Philippines through European Lenses*, pp. 12.

55 Jagor, *Reisen*, p. 147.

56 Alatas, *The Myth of the Lazy Native*, p. 55.

57 Semper, *Die Philippinen*, p. 33.

58 For example he described a ship's captain who was forgetful, undisciplined and always on the lookout to steal food or livestock, in explicit contrast to Spanish skippers who sought to make the journey as quick as possible. Jagor, *Reisen*, pp. 66–7.

59 The French immigrant Paul de la Gironière noted the 'ferocious joy' of the 'Indians' at cockfighting. Like Jagor, he was mainly concerned with the appearance of the

natives involved. Paul de la Gironière, *Twenty Years in the Philippines* (Manila: Filipiniana Book Guild, 1962 (First published: Paris 1854)), p. 61.

60  Jagor, *Reisen*, p. 21.
61  Jagor, *Reisen*, p. 21.
62  Jagor, *Reisen*, pp. 21–2.
63  The Dutch colonial administrator in Java, J.A.B. Wiselius, who visited the Philippines in 1875, made a similar connection between the exaggerated passion for cockfighting and the virulence of armed robberies; supposedly the bands of robbers consisted of those who got indebted while betting. J.A.B. Wiselius, *A Visit to Manila and its Environs* (Quezon City: Ateneo de Manila University Press, 2016), p. 21.
64  Jagor, *Reisen*, p. 103.
65  Jagor, *Reisen*, pp. 103–5.
66  Kramer, *The Blood of Government*, p. 41.
67  Quoted in Quibuyen, *A Nation Aborted*, p. 128.
68  Jagor, *Reisen*, pp. 52–3.
69  Jagor, *Reisen*, p. 54.
70  Jagor, *Reisen*, p. 60.
71  Jagor, *Reisen*, p. 71.
72  Jagor, *Reisen*, p. 85.
73  Jagor, *Reisen*, pp. 31–2.
74  Jagor, *Reisen*, p. 33.
75  Jagor, *Reisen*, p. 126. Emphasis in the original.
76  Jagor, *Reisen*, pp. 173–4.
77  Richard von Drasche, 'The Military Districts of Benguet, Lepanto and Bontoc', in Scott, *German Travellers on the Cordillera*, pp. 35–45 (translation of 'Einige Worte über die Militär-Districte Benguet, Lepanto, und Bontoc auf der Insel Luzon und ihre Bewohner', *Mittheilungen der kaiserlich-königlichen geographischen Gesellschaft in Wien* 9 (1876), 509–15 and 638–43).
78  Jagor, *Reisen*, p. 30.
79  Jagor, *Reisen*, p. 31.
80  See Mojares, *Brains of the Nation*, p. 425.
81  Jagor, *Reisen*, pp. 29–30.
82  Jagor, *Reisen*, p. 38.
83  Jagor, *Reisen*, p. 33.
84  Jagor, *Reisen*, pp. 119–20.
85  Jagor, *Reisen*.
86  Semper, *Die Philippinen*, p. 76.
87  E.g. when Jagor asserts that the colony lags behind due to failures to develop a better road network. Jagor, *Reisen*, p. 159.
88  Jagor, *Reisen*, p. 157.
89  Michael Cullinane, *Arenas of Conspiracy and Rebellion in the Late Nineteenth-Century Philippines: The Case of the April 1898 Uprising in Cebu* (Quezon City: Ateneo de Manila University Press, 2014), p. 40.
90  Jagor, *Reisen*, p. 157.
91  As Otto van den Muijzenberg notes, the Dutch merchant Meerkamp van Embden, who resided in Manila, did not document the native and the *Mestizo* middle class, the existence of which contradicted racial theories. See Van den Muijzenberg, *The Philippines through European Lenses*, p. 13.
92  Semper, *Die Philippinen*, p. 31.
93  Jagor, *Reisen*, p. 125.
94  Jagor, *Reisen*, p. 26.
95  Bastian was less positive, ridiculing *Mestizo* ignorance and pedantery. Bastian, *Die Völker des östlichen Asien*, p. 265.
96  Semper, *Die Philippinen*, pp. 89–90.
97  Semper, *Die Philippinen*, pp. 90–1.
98  Cullinane, *Arenas*, p. 39.
99  Semper, *Die Philippinen*, p. 91.

100 He credited Spain with the achievement of civilising a people found at a 'lower cultural level, stricken by small wars and subjected to despotism'. Semper, *Die Philippinen*, p. 287.
101 Semper, *Die Philippinen*, pp. 101–2.
102 Jagor, *Reisen*, p. 289.
103 Mojares, *Brains of the Nation*, p. 419.
104 Mojares, *Brains of the Nation*, p. 443.
105 See Aguilar, 'Tracing Origins'; Anderson, *Spectre*; Anderson, *Under Three Flags*; Mojares, *Brains of the Nation*; Thomas, *Orientalists*.
106 Mojares, *Brains of the Nation*, p. 45.
107 Mojares, *Brains of the Nation*, p. 212.
108 Quibuyen, *A Nation Aborted*, pp. 166, 218.
109 John Nery, *Revolutionary Spirit: Jose Rizal in Southeast Asia* (Quezon City: Ateneo de Manila University Press, 2011), p. 47.
110 Jose Rizal, 'The Indolence of the Filipino' (1890), Project Gutenberg, http://archive.org/stream/theindolenceofth06885gut/8indf10.txt (acccessed 30 November 2016).
111 See Anderson, *Under Three Flags*, pp. 163–4.
112 See Quibuyen, *A Nation Aborted*, pp. 279–80.
113 Kramer, *Blood of Government*, p. 3.

# CHAPTER ELEVEN

# Social Democrats and Germany's war in South-West Africa, 1904–7: the view of the socialist press

Andrew G. Bonnell

Jens-Uwe Guettel recently published an article criticising what he called the 'myth of the pro-colonialist SPD', dealing with German social democracy and imperialism before the First World War.[1] For a reader closely familiar with the subject matter, it is initially counter-intuitive that the case would have to be made that the German Social Democratic Party before 1914 was critical of German colonialism. The Social Democratic press constantly attacked the fiscal policy of the Reich, which relied on indirect consumption taxes falling heavily on the working class to finance a rapidly growing navy, increased army spending and other expenditure related to colonialism and Germany's imperial ambitions. Social Democratic politicians were also vocal in exposing human rights abuses in Germany's colonies, such as those by the notorious Carl Peters in German East Africa.[2] Why, then, did Guettel feel the need to prove the anti-colonial credentials of the German Social Democrats? Partly it is because, since the work by the Australian historian Roger Fletcher on the pro-colonialist right-wing revisionists associated with Joseph Bloch's magazine the *Sozialistische Monatshefte*, a disproportionate amount of attention has been paid to this group of Social Democratic authors in discussions of Social Democracy and imperialism.[3] In contrast to this emphasis, John Philip Short, in a recent essay on the working class in the 1907 elections, makes a distinction between what he calls the 'local' anti-colonialism of workers (or the rank and file membership of the party) and the 'acquiescent leadership', although this still tends to give too much weight to the revisionist element in the leadership at this time – the leadership included highly divergent views, and the revisionists were still advancing a minority opinion when it came to colonialism.[4] A second factor in the tendency observed by Guettel to understate the anti-colonialism of German Social Democrats is the sometimes totalising critique of writers from a self-consciously postcolonialist perspective, who view all of German society in the *Kaiserreich* as complicit in imperialism, either as beneficiaries of the (in reality exiguous) fruits of the exploitation of the colonies or, more commonly, as caught in webs of colonialist and racialised discourse.[5]

One useful source for gaining access to the attitudes of the German Social Democratic Party's rank-and-file membership is the illustrated humorous-satirical paper *Der wahre Jakob* (published by the Social Democratic publisher J.H.W. Dietz in Stuttgart). *Der wahre Jakob* (The True Jakob) was visually appealing and accessible to a broad readership. Its graphic style was comparable with its more celebrated contemporary bourgeois rivals, such as *Simplicissimus*. Like *Simplicissimus*, *Der wahre Jakob* caricatured and pilloried such targets as intolerant priests, reactionary Junkers and the Prussian officer corps, and did so with an added political radicalism, which reached a new intensity in its coverage of the 1905 Russian Revolution, a period that also coincided with a large-scale strike of miners in Germany's Ruhr region. Unlike the more theoretically elevated 'scientific' journal of the party, *Die Neue Zeit*, *Der wahre Jakob* reached a genuine mass readership: 193,000 subscribers in 1905, increasing to 228,000 in 1907 (and eventually reaching 380,000 in 1912).[6] That each issue, on average, would have reached multiple readers can be safely assumed by what we know about how the paper was read. Subscription copies were delivered to large working-class households, which sometimes included lodgers, and copies in party or union workers' libraries also reached multiple readers.

Copies of the Social Democratic press were typically available for reading in pubs frequented by party members, and political police reports, such as the large collection of surveillance reports of workers' conversations in Hamburg pubs, indicate that not only did workers spend their time reading when they were not otherwise occupied in drinking, conversation or playing dice, but they would sometimes read articles aloud to each other and discuss them. *Der wahre Jakob* is occasionally mentioned in this connection (along with the Hamburg party paper the *Hamburger Echo*).[7] As Richard Evans argued in his analysis of these surveillance reports,[8] the opinion of workers was overwhelmingly critical of colonialism in general and the war in South-West Africa in particular, on the grounds of expense, reports of corruption and mismanagement, sympathy for the German troops who had been sent to such an inhospitable place, and the absence of a sufficient justification for Germany to be engaged in a war against the native population.[9] Accounts of party meetings in Berlin, recorded by the political police there, reinforce the picture of a strongly anti-colonial attitude among rank-and-file Social Democrats. In party meetings held in Berlin's left-leaning Social Democratic *Wahlvereine* (effectively, the party branches in the Reichstag electoral districts), there were rank-and-file calls for revisionists such as Max Schippel or Richard Calwer to be kicked out of the party for their conciliatory attitude towards imperialism.[10] The division between the anti-colonial majority of the party and the revisionist minority resulted in a set-piece debate between the radical Georg Ledebour and the more pro-colonial Max Schippel in a special general meeting of the party organisation for Berlin's Sixth Electoral District, held over two nights in December 1907 and February 1908, with over a thousand party members in attendance on each night. The debate ended in a humiliation for Schippel, who was heckled by the audience when he tried to argue for the necessity of colonies, and many audience members walked out of his closing speech.[11] Following the discussion of colonial policy at the 1907 Socialist International Congress in Stuttgart, and anticipating a major debate at the German party congress in Essen in September, the party's leading theoretician, Karl Kautsky, restated the party's fundamentally anti-colonial stance in a tract on socialism and colonial policy that was published in October of that year. Kautsky stressed the interests of the ruling classes in pursuing imperialism, and emphasised that these interests ran counter to those of the working class.[12]

Even if one avoids assuming a straightforward, unmediated reception by the readership, it is clear from the circulation figures over the thirty years from 1884 to 1914 that *Der wahre Jakob* was successful in reaching a very high proportion of party members, and also reached workers who were not members but who sympathised with the party and voted for it, and that, as it continued to enjoy a high degree of popularity, it will have succeeded in striking a chord with this readership. (Party members were also not shy in coming forward in meetings and party congresses if they were unhappy with the output of the party's press, as shown by the so-called 'Naturalism Debate' at the 1896 Hamburg Party Congress, and by records of many party meetings besides.)

How then, did *Der wahre Jakob* depict the South-West African war of 1904–7, and, in particular, how did it depict the Herero and other African peoples of the region who were at war with the German army? The war in South-West Africa (today, Namibia) was perhaps the most politically charged episode in Wilhelmine Germany's colonial rule, becoming the focus of the national elections for the Reichstag in 1907.[13] On the cover of the first issue of *Der wahre Jakob* for 1907, preceding the so-called 'Hottentot Elections', in which Chancellor Bernhard von

Bülow's government sought to capitalise on the opposition parties' lack of patriotic support for Germany's colonial efforts, the paper displayed a remarkable cover picture (see Figure 11.1). An allegorical female figure, representing Social Democracy (identifiable by her red Phrygian cap, the emblem of revolution), stood guard over a group of African women and men, while caricatures of Chancellor Bernhard von Bülow (incongruously depicted as a yellow Buddha) and Colonial Secretary Bernhard von Dernburg rode into the attack on a storm cloud pulled by a rather scrawny Prussian eagle. The portrayal of the Africans avoided stereotypical caricature; they are shown sympathetically, women cowering, one defending her small child, while the men stand in a defensive posture with shields and a spear, albeit sheltering behind the much larger white female figure, who wields her own sword and shield. The caption, alongside the title 'On the Reichstag election', is 'Peoples of Africa, defend your most sacred possessions', a clear allusion to the notorious allegory of the 'Yellow Peril' by Hermann Knackfuss, designed by Kaiser Wilhelm II personally, which this cover picture obviously parodied (hence Bülow as Buddha).[14] The illustration made a dramatic claim for solidarity between German Social Democracy and the African peoples in South-West Africa, and it stressed that the Herero had been fighting a legitimate war to defend their own lands against German imperialism.

Although this claim for solidarity between German socialists and the oppressed Africans in Germany's colonies was not (indeed could not have been) realised in practice, there are numerous examples in *Der wahre Jakob* of the paper vindicating the legitimacy of the resistance of the Herero and the Nama, or attacking the conduct of the German army in South-West Africa. The attacks are of a piece with the constant campaigns of the paper (and of the Social Democratic press more widely) against militarism, and against the way in which the Prussian officer corps embodied and upheld the class rule of the Junker aristocracy.[15] The paper also held the government's rhetoric of German cultural superiority up to ridicule, contrasting it with the reality of notorious abuses of colonised populations. *Der wahre Jakob* did not shy away from accusing the German army of atrocities. In its actual depictions of Africans, however, the paper ran the gamut from sympathetic portrayals that resisted stereotypical exaggerations of supposedly African features to more crass caricatures. Arguably, the latter should be viewed in their specific contexts, including against the background of the paper's frequent resort to extreme caricature of familiar *German* social types.

At the very outset of the rebellion against German rule in South-West Africa, *Der wahre Jakob*'s regular brief satirical verse rubric, *Hobelspäne*

Figure 11.1 'Peoples of Africa, Protect Your Most Sacred Possessions!',
*Der wahre Jacob*, No. 534, 8 January 1907, p. 5293

(chips from the workbench) commented on the peculiarities of the tribe of the Bondelzwarts:

This is the tribe of the Bondelzwarts,
A most peculiar breed apart.
They do not want to pay their tax,
Or to bow their knees and backs.

They want to live their lives on earth,
Just as they would choose from birth!
How can one give such a rabble
An understanding of our culture?[16]

Despite the frivolous register typical of this page of the paper, *Der wahre Jakob*'s doggerel mocked German pretentions of cultural superiority and showed sympathy for the Africans' natural desire for freedom to live their own lives.

This theme was developed in a longer piece of verse, called 'Insolence!', the following May. The 'little people of the Herero' (*Völkchen der Herero*) were clearly, in the eyes of all 'model patriots', a 'depraved rabble', displaying an incomprehensible attachment to their own land and cattle. The Herero were unwilling to do hard labour for whites for miserable pay, and were completely unimpressed by such German cultural achievements as 'our splendid lieutenants, the envy of the world'. Worst of all, the Herero had the impertinence to shoot back when they were shot at. German patriots thus called for the Herero to be 'hanged and shot', but, *Der wahre Jakob* pointed out, the Germans would have to catch the Herero first.[17] *Der wahre Jakob* again sympathised with the Hereros' right to resist, and introduced another trope: the wily natives outwitting the flat-footed German military. Similar sympathies for the cause of the Herero were evident in another poem printed in June 1904, this one by the anarchist writer Erich Mühsam, 'Der friedliche Michel' (the peaceful [German] Michel).[18] In November 1904, in one of the short jokes the paper mixed in amongst its satirical verses, short prose pieces and cartoons, *Der wahre Jakob* presented a teacher quizzing a schoolboy:

Now, Charlie, what did they call in olden days a man who fought bravely?
– Think about it – A h-e-r ...

Charlie (quick on the uptake): A Herero![19]

In December 1904, *Der wahre Jakob* went so far as to compare Hendrik Witbooi, the Nama chief who conducted a protracted resistance campaign against German rule, with the German national hero Arminius, or Hermann, of the Cherusci, the victor over the Roman legions in the Teutoburg Forest in AD 9. In a possibly calculated affront to the nationalist right, the anonymous Social Democratic poet branded Witbooi the 'new Arminius', taunting enraged 'German patriots' with the parallel that, if Witbooi had been an ally of the German occupiers before turning against them, he was doing much the same as the historical Arminius had once done in his dealings with the Romans.[20] This comparison actually echoed remarks by August Bebel at the very start of the war in January 1904, when in a speech to the Reichstag he compared the rebellion of the Herero to the resistance of the Germanic tribes to the Roman empire, which Germans now regarded as the greatest possible heroism.[21]

*Der wahre Jakob* also justified resistance by African subjects of the Kaiser by depicting them as victims of injustice under German colonial rule. The short prose piece 'Of the Negro who set out in search of justice' describes an African who seeks redress after a white man stole his cow: he is turned away by the police and the colonial authorities, goes to Europe to ask for justice, but is sent to prison, and once back home finally goes to fetch his Mauser rifle, to get justice.[22] A 1906 cartoon pilloried conditions in German Cameroon, showing natives fleeing a German bailiff armed with a whip, while in another frame a black sat in prison as a result of having the temerity to lodge a complaint against unfair treatment. (On the same page of the paper, a poem posed the question: 'who does Herero-Land belong to?', suggesting that the desert battleground would soon belong to the vultures.)[23] Another cartoon in 1906 showed an African reading a German judgement posted on a wall, and asking himself: 'If I defend myself with a gun, I get hard labour, if I defend myself by making a complaint I get hard labour. So I might as well stay with the gun!'[24]

At the same time as depicting the Herero as leading a justified defence of their own freedom, *Der wahre Jakob* applied its customary satirical treatment of militarism in general, and of the Prussian officer corps in particular, to the German colonial forces trying to suppress the rebellion. In May 1904, a stereotypical young Prussian lieutenant 'von Blowitz' was depicted holding his sword high but with his legs in athletic full retreat before an agitated swarm of African warriors in the background (Figure 11.2), while exclaiming in Berlin dialect that he had 'imagined this Africa entirely differently' (*'Det hab' ick mir anners vorjestellt, dieset Afrika – aber janz anners!'*).[25] In October 1904, in a full-page colour cartoon (Figure 11.3), the paper mocked General Lothar von Trotha's claim to have won a decisive victory at the Battle of Waterberg. Von Trotha is depicted on a hillock, surrounded by staff officers with binoculars scanning the horizon for a sign of the enemy, and saying: 'I have won the battle of Waterberg, but the gods only know where the Herero I defeated are hiding.' Meanwhile, an African in a German army

## Bei den Hereros.

Leutnant v. Blowitz: Det hab' ick mir anners vorjestellt, diefet Afrika, — aber janz anners!

Figure 11.2  A[lbert] Staehle, 'Among the Hereros', *Der wahre Jacob*, No. 464, 3 May 1904, p. 4344. Lieutenant von Blowitz: 'I imagined this Africa quite differently!'

uniform is discreetly stealing the champagne from the General's well-stocked picnic basket, almost under the officers' noses.[26] The motif of a wily native hiding in the general's picnic basket and eluding his pursuers was repeated in a cartoon strip during the month of the January 1907 elections.[27] In the same vein, *Der wahre Jakob* printed a joke in

Figure 11.3  H.G.J., 'After the "Victory"', *Der wahre Jacob*, No. 476, 18 October 1904, p. 4492. General von Trotha: 'I have won the battle of Waterberg, but the gods only know where the Herero I defeated are hiding.'

September 1905 in response to a report that General von Trotha had offered 5,000 Marks for the head of rebel leader Samuel Maherero. Maherero's alleged reply: 'I wouldn't give you five Marks for the head of a Prussian general.'[28]

Mockery of the officer corps did not mean that *Der wahre Jakob*'s writers and artists were indifferent to the fate of the ordinary enlisted man in what was, after all, a conscript army. In June 1904, the new troop transports to South-West Africa were shown being swallowed up by a cannon morphing into a ravenous monster: they are, literally, 'cannon-fodder'.[29] There were expressions of sympathy for parents of war dead (coupled with attacks on officialdom for alleged callousness towards the bereaved), and sympathy for disabled veterans, who would carry away from the campaign a medal and a wooden leg.[30] In a grim full-page drawing entitled 'The Blessings of Colonial Policy', vultures settled on a battlefield beside the bodies of dead German soldiers and Africans alike. The drawing carried the grimly ironic commentary: 'No meat shortage in South-West Africa'.[31] In a similar vein, another full-page cartoon entitled 'From our Colonies' showed an African desert littered with skeletons (including remains of German uniforms) under a large German flag. A pair of visiting dignitaries, one obviously a Junker aristocrat, the other a top-hatted capitalist, sum up the benefits of colonial expansion: 'Even if it hasn't brought anything in and there's not much to be got here as far as higher goods are concerned, it would be worth setting up a bone mill here.'[32]

The campaign in South-West Africa became the focus of fresh media and political attention in late 1906, when a wave of procurement scandals broke out, partly thanks to the parliamentary work of Centre party deputy Matthias Erzberger, involving the firm of Tippelskirch, a supplier of goods to the army, and Adolf Woermann's shipping company, which had both managed to secure excessively lucrative monopoly deals to supply the German forces there.[33] The Social Democratic press frequently pilloried the expenses incurred by the Reich's colonial commitments, which were seen (in most cases quite correctly) as disproportionate to the economic benefit the German people derived from the colonies.[34] A cartoon in *Der wahre Jakob* from November 1904 depicted Chancellor Bülow attempting to crush the Herero by dropping on them a boulder representing 200,000,000 million Marks in gold.[35] In the second half of 1906, *Der wahre Jakob* now also attacked the 'stink' coming out of the colonial office in the light of the latest corruption allegations, adding that all of Europe was already aware of the stench from Germany's colonies themselves. Colonial corruption proved to be a rich vein for satirical comment, which *Der wahre Jakob* worked assiduously for months.[36] In September 1906, *Der wahre Jakob* ran a full-page drawing of the allegorical figure Germania in a cart sinking deep into a corpse-ridden and skeleton-ridden 'colonial swamp'. The cart is drawn by a donkey representing the ever-hapless German 'Michel', while the nonplussed coachman, Chancellor Bülow, stands on the bank of the swamp, calling on 'St Matthias' for assistance, exclaiming that the 'cart has never been so deep in the mud before'.[37] In the same issue, a German parliamentary delegation to South-West Africa is shown surveying a desolate scene, with bodies hanging from gallows, while at the foot of the gallows are piles of empty champagne bottles and empty tins of caviar: the gentlemen of the Colonial Office had obviously been hard at work.[38] Meanwhile, on another page, a group of Herero consider the state of the war. A chief suggests that, if they can get a 25 per cent cut of Tippelskirch's war profits, they would keep fighting, otherwise they would make peace.[39] A subsequent cartoon shows the German governor preparing for a parliamentary delegation by painting the Schutztruppe soldiers black, because he could 'no longer rely on real Negroes', and the soldiers are instructed to tell the members of parliament that the local railway is twice as long as it actually is.[40] The German civilising mission had clearly reached its nadir, mired in corruption, and with German soldiers in blackface the closest the governor can find to a loyal native subject.

The debates over corrupt conduct in military and colonial procurement gave fresh impetus to publicity of abuses in the colonies. In the issue of *Der wahre Jakob* that preceded the January 1907 'Hottentot elections', along with the cover illustration depicting Africans defending their sacred possessions mentioned above, a cartoon strip in a graphic style very reminiscent of a Wilhelm Busch graphic story presented a narrative sequence on 'German Culture in Africa'. The story began: 'In the black continent there was a people who lived in a completely primitive and barbaric state and who stood on a low level of culture.' The words are somewhat undercut by the depiction of a happy and well-nourished African family. 'The good Germans then took pity on them and set forth to impart the blessings of civilisation to them': the caption to a picture of a missionary straight from the conventions of anti-clerical caricature, marching alongside a brandy-merchant's wagon. The 'ungrateful' 'savages' are then shown chasing the missionary and alcohol-seller away. The Germans were thus prompted to 'demonstrate their truly humane sentiments to the black people': the heavily armed military mow down the Africans. The Germans further demonstrate their humanity in a scene of flogging and hangings. The last panel showed the blessings of German culture: the now hungry Africans are robbed of their cattle, banished from their lands, and German signs reading *Verboten* sprout in the otherwise impoverished landscape.[41]

The ironic treatment of the blessings of German culture in the colonial setting was a staple of *Der wahre Jakob*'s treatment of the war. As early as May 1904, a 'Battle Song for South-West Africa' summed them up: militarism, missionaries, and schnapps:

> We bring salvation in parade-march step,
> We bring civilisation;
> Best of all we bring with us
> Christendom's religion!
> We bring you cannons, we bring you schnapps,
> And flags with black, white, red.
> And if you give us your fields and women and cows,
> Then – we won't even strike you dead![42]

Another short item in *Der wahre Jakob* measured the progress of the Christian religion in the colonies, with the natives learning to accept corporal punishment.[43]

A common motif in *Der wahre Jakob* was satire on bourgeois matrimonial customs, typically viewed as characterised by materialism, hypocrisy and double standards. The war in South-West Africa offered a fresh twist on the theme of the bourgeois marriage. In June 1904, a stout capitalist is shown asking his prospective son-in-law, in military uniform with an officer's sabre, why he is leaving for Africa when he had only just got engaged to the businessman's (stereotypically unattractive) daughter. The reply: 'I would be afraid otherwise in the three years of military service I might forget my trade as a butcher.'[44]

Not all representations of German army atrocities in Africa were as indirect as this; some, like the cartoon by Emil Erk (one of the paper's most prolific artists) 'No quarter given' from January 1905, was drastically direct, showing an African prisoner being held by one German officer while another soldier bayonets him. A missionary stands in the background piously forgiving their sins (Figure 11.4).[45] Two indolent young lieutenants feature in a cartoon from October 1905 in which the more experienced Africa hand explains the 'Trotha system' to the newcomer: 'The only good Herero is a dead Herero.'[46] Also confronting was the drawing in September 1906 of a German soldier in colonial uniform deliberately shooting down one African after another with the brutal caption: 'German tinned meat' (also an allusion to the contemporary controversy over meat prices and import restrictions on American tinned meat).[47] In a less drastic vein, *Der wahre Jakob* also took aim at reports of Trotha's suppression of critical press reporting.[48]

The depiction of German army abuses in Africa in *Der wahre Jakob* reflected the concerns raised by the party leadership in the Reichstag. From a very early stage of the war, in March 1904, the veteran party

**Figure 11.4** [Emil] Erk, 'No Quarter Given', *Der wahre Jacob*, No. 483, 24 January 1905, p. 4591. Missionary: '... and forgive us our sins, as we forgive our masters and protectors.'

leader August Bebel expressed concerns about the conduct of the war, citing reports of the killing of Herero prisoners, querying why no Herero prisoners were being taken alive and raising the acute question of what might *not* be being put in writing as far as orders in the field were concerned.[49]

As far as visual representations of the Herero and Nama go (and of Africans in general during this period – German representations tended not to differentiate too much between different African peoples), *Der wahre Jakob* contained a varied spectrum, depending partly on the register of the artwork: broadly comic or more serious and appealing to pathos and empathy. David Ciarlo has traced the development of visual images of Africans in German advertising in his impressive 2011 study *Advertising Empire*. He has identified a trend to more racist, infantilising representations of Africans in German print media after the war in South-West Africa. He suggests that *Der wahre Jakob* and its Munich-based Social Democratic counterpart *Der Süddeutsche*

*Postillon* joined in the trend, defining Africans by 'their black skin, bulging lips, and frizzy hair'.[50] The nature of visual representations of Africans in *Der wahre Jakob* did reflect the emerging conventions and visual shorthand in representations of Africans in German popular culture, but these representations also varied depending on the artist's intentions in each case.

In June 1904, in one of its full-colour, full-page cartoons, *Der wahre Jakob* broached the taboo subject of sexual relations with African women in the colonies. The point of the cartoon, the 'Shadow-side' (Figure 11.5), however, was not outrage at 'miscegenation' but the more familiar target of the sexual mores (double standard, exploitation of lower-class women) of the German upper classes. The blasé young officer is turning away from an African woman holding out her hand demanding support for the healthy and smiling brown baby she is carrying on her back. The lieutenant's response: 'That's the problem with disseminating culture, – now even the black women are asking chaps like us for child support.' The African woman is not the subject of caricature. She could perhaps be viewed as somewhat eroticised: her costume leaves one breast bare (providing the artist with an opportunity for a characteristic *art nouveau* curved line in keeping with the graphic style of the day), but the emphasis is less on her erotic qualities than on her forthright assertion of her rights as a mother: it is her outstretched hand that occupies the centre of the picture.[51]

A cartoon image early in the war shows recourse to the unflattering 'Hottentot' racial stereotype (a pot-bellied African with a prominent backside is shown in profile, accentuating the caricatured features). The point of the drawing was to mock the attempt to transplant German customs to Africa by depicting the new pot-bellied 'compatriot', decked out with incongruous items of European clothing like a top-hat and stiff collar but with no shirt, with German medals pinned to the rear of his loincloth.[52] A 1907 joke about colonial trade also played on a similar theme of African ignorance of European clothing and customs, even if its main point was how little benefit the German economy derived from trade with its African possessions.[53]

This stereotypical image of Germans' new 'compatriots' from March 1904 described above was counterbalanced a month later by a short story also titled 'Our "Compatriot"', which was a sympathetic pen portrait of an African labourer performing the heaviest labour in a German harbour city to get by on the minimum for survival, far from the sun and open spaces of his home: *'Armer Schwarzer!'* (poor black man), the writer, A.R., concluded.[54]

Perhaps the most stereotypical caricature of an African in the paper in this period is one of the German 'Duke of Gerolstein' meeting the

**Figure 11.5** H.G.J., 'The Shadow Side', *Der wahre Jacob*, No. 468, 28 June 1904, p. 4394. 'That's the problem with disseminating culture, – now even the black women are asking chaps like us for child support.'

King of 'Omeiahiland', from January 1907. The latter is a crude cartoon Negro, grinning with enormous lips and teeth, and a nose-ring, incongruously dressed in a German cavalry uniform. But the depiction of the chinless and dumpy German duke is if anything more grotesque, in keeping with the socialist media's often savage attacks on the aristocracy.[55] While there are certainly instances of this kind of caricature of Africans in *Der wahre Jakob*, there is a spectrum of different comic registers and different degrees of caricatural exaggeration. Alongside such 'Sambo'-style caricatures, there are some more serious depictions which avoid caricature and invite empathy.

Notwithstanding these instances of racial caricature, in *Der wahre Jakob*'s textual content there is also evidence of a programmatic rejection of any concept of racial superiority. A short satirical prose piece in *Der wahre Jakob* depicted Africans as innately no less intelligent than Germans: allegedly the *Deutsch-Ostafrikanische Zeitung* had reported that German colonists were complaining that the 'Negro children' were learning 'much too much'. The solution to this problem that German colonial experts allegedly came up with: transferring the African children to schools in the Prussian East-Elbian countryside, which could safely be expected to retard their intellectual progress.[56] Elsewhere, more generally, the paper rejected the racial ideology of antisemites and mocked the *völkisch* belief in the innate superiority of the Germanic peoples.

The attitude of Social Democrats towards the colonised people of Africa was partly conditioned by a progressive philosophy of history through successive higher stages of development, in which perspective the Herero and Nama represented a backward stage of development. At the same time, however, Social Democrat leaders and writers defended the human rights of Africans, and their elementary right to self-defence. On the one hand August Bebel himself, influenced by Social Democracy's version of the Marxist progressive view of historical stages of development, had referred to the Herero as a 'savage people' (*ein wildes Volk*) occupying a low stage of cultural development. However, he also spoke out against the 'dreadful contempt for this race', expressed both within and outside the Reichstag, which could have the effect of facilitating worse atrocities against the rebellious Africans.[57] He contrasted the 'low cultural level' of the Herero with reports of their merciful treatment of white women captives, suggesting that Herero women would have fared worse at the hands of white captors.[58] As the war continued, however, Bebel was able to empathise with the Herero, who were masters of their own land in their eyes and were exercising a natural and honourable right to self-defence in resisting foreign intrusion and seizure of their property.[59]

*Der wahre Jakob*'s strongly critical, anti-imperialist stance on the war in South-West Africa was shared across the Social Democratic party press. For example, the Munich-based counterpart of *Der Wahre Jakob*, the *Süddeutscher Postillon*, carried a drawing on the German campaign in South-West Africa entitled 'In the sign of the cross', in which a proud-looking German colonial officer plants his boot and the German flag emblazoned with the Iron Cross on the bodies of a slain Herero family (depicted without any caricatured features).[60] The party's 'central organ', *Vorwärts*, was outspoken in condemning the abuse of the Herero and Nama, and questioned the continuing prosecution of the war after the Herero had offered a negotiated peace, resulting in senseless bloodshed on both sides.[61] By the end of 1904, the party's leading newspaper was condemning what it now referred to as 'the annihilation of the Herero' by General von Trotha.[62] Important regional Social Democratic newspapers like the left-radical *Leipziger Volkszeitung* were militantly anti-imperialist and energetic in their criticisms of the conduct of the war.[63] In the party's theoretical journal, *Die Neue Zeit*, the Austrian Marxist Otto Bauer developed a critical economic analysis of colonialism, which opened with a reference to the fact that the German Empire was 'sacrificing the blood of its sons and the sweat of its workers in a cruel war for an African sandy desert'.[64] Even the revisionist journal *Sozialistische Monatshefte* (not actually a party publication but a private enterprise run by Joseph Bloch), which generally sought to pull party opinion to the right on 'national' issues, was critical of the conduct of the war in its short glosses on current events. While the journal was prepared to concede the need to protect the lives of Germans in the colonies, it went on to state:

> when one reads that a manner of warfare is being waged against the rebels in which any considerations of humanity are abandoned, then one has to be doubly and thrice-over critical of the maladministration that must have driven an uncivilised people to despair. Germany has suffered enough damage from its colonies, must shame be added to that account as well?[65]

The attitude of Social Democrats to the war in South-West Africa was most authoritatively articulated by the party leader August Bebel in his Reichstag speeches to the subject. The party initially (in January 1904) abstained from voting for or against the credits for the war, despite maintaining its in-principle opposition to colonialism (in the face of strident government insistence that the appropriations were necessary to defend the lives of white colonists, including civilians, women and children). Bebel justified this by arguing that it was too early to be sure of all the facts behind the outbreak of the rebellion, but the tenor of his speech was anti-colonialist, maintaining that the Hereros' defence of their freedom and property was understandable and legitimate, and pleading for the war to be conducted with humanity rather than vengefully.[66] A year later, debating the government's budget, Bebel declared himself in a position to make better founded judgements on the events in South-West Africa than he had been twelve months earlier. He gave a lengthy speech outlining the responsibility of German colonial policies for the uprising, exposed examples of mistreatment of the Herero by the Germans, and defended the right of an oppressed people to revolt against mistreatment. Moreover he attacked the 'barbaric methods of war' of the German forces under General von Trotha.[67] Bebel renewed his forthright attacks on von Trotha in the December 1906 budget debate that preceded the 'Hottentot elections', quoting von Trotha's notorious 2 October 1904 proclamation threatening the Herero with annihilation, and his practice of driving Herero women and children into the desert to starve. Bebel recalled the notorious 'Huns speech' of the Kaiser to the China expeditionary force in 1900, raising again the question of whether von Trotha acted on his own authority or on the basis of an unwritten order, which this time would not be made public in the way the Kaiser's 'Huns' speech had been.[68]

To what extent was the Social Democratic Party able to extend any solidarity to Germany's oppressed colonial subjects in practice, as the January 1907 cover picture of *Der Wahre Jakob* seemed to promise? In one of his speeches criticising the war, August Bebel pointed out that (as a National Liberal deputy had already stated):

> The Hereros don't read the newspaper, they don't get any newspaper, and even the Germans who are now fighting there, won't get any newspaper for the time being. Besides, all of these discussions of the causes of the uprising will have no influence on the course of events on either side.[69]

However, Bebel's criticisms of abuses by the German forces in South-West Africa very quickly came to the attention of the German officers there. Two weeks after this Reichstag speech, the son of the German Governor Theodor Leutwein was writing home to boast to a friend that he had written a parody of a proclamation by Bebel mocking Bebel's call for humanitarian conduct towards the Africans and posted it in the officers' mess in Windhoek to the loud approval of his brother officers.[70]

Practical solidarity was limited by factors such as communication, distance and the nature of the wartime conditions. As Robert Michels joked at the 1904 Bremen party congress, the party had no *Vertrauensmänner*, or local delegates, in South-West Africa.[71] Nor, for that matter, did any Social Democratic Reichstag deputy ever visit one of Germany's colonies before 1914.[72] There was also relatively little opportunity for interaction with Africans from the Kaiser's colonies within Germany around this time. As Robbie Aitken and Eve Rosenhaft have recently outlined, there were some Cameroonians who came into contact with Social Democrats in the late 1880s and early 1890s when they visited and worked in Germany, but after 1893 travel to Germany by Africans from Germany's colonies became more restricted.[73] This lack of direct contact between German Social Democrats and Germany's colonial subjects is perhaps a disappointing finding, but there may be some merit in noting the constraints that hampered even committed anti-imperialists in the metropolis from experiencing such contacts in person.

If the solidarity with the Herero and Nama remained theoretical and vicarious, the German Social Democrats, after the initial abstention from voting for or against credits for the war in January 1904, were remarkably consistent in their opposition to colonialism in general and to the South-West African war in particular (even if a minority on the party's right wing increasingly sought to undermine the party's anti-imperialist principles after 1907). The party press advanced a variety of reasons for this opposition, including fiscal grounds, and opposition to militarism, but the party's newspapers and its spokespeople also consistently gave out a message in support of human rights, and the right of peoples to self-determination. In their attitudes to African peoples, Social Democrats were not free from prevailing assumptions of backwardness *vis-à-vis* Europe's higher level of economic development (and therefore, it was assumed, cultural development), but the party's writers and leaders still recognised the essential human rights of the Herero and Nama and their fundamental right to revolt against German rule. In the actual depictions of Herero and Nama, and other Africans, in the illustrated Social Democratic press, there was, as outlined above, a spectrum of representations, from more stereotypical caricatures in some cartoons to the less clichéd images of dark-skinned, suffering, fellow human beings (depending on the comic or serious register of the specific image). One factor determining the depiction of Africans is that cartoonists and artists for *Der wahre Jakob* were typically less interested in accurate depictions of the Africans than in using them as a foil for the usual targets of left-wing satire: strutting Prussian lieutenants, creeping priests etc. The ruling class of Wilhelmine Germany was the main target of *Der wahre Jakob*'s barbed satire, and the natives of South-West Africa figured as either the victims or the adversaries of that class's representatives.

A reading of the Social Democratic press from 1904 to 1907, especially the most popular socialist paper, *Der wahre Jakob*, supports the notion of a strong anti-colonialist consensus in the party in this period. It is true that following the loss of Reichstag seats by Social Democrats in 1907 (despite a modest increase in votes in absolute terms), the revisionists and less theoretically inclined pragmatic reformists gained ground in the Social Democratic Party. However, the party's platform for the 1912 elections continued to give considerable prominence to its fundamental opposition to colonialism, condemning colonialism both for increasing the risk of war and for its subjugation and exploitation of foreign peoples.[74] As Jens-Uwe Guettel argues, despite their assumptions that historical progress was reflected in societies' differing stages of economic and cultural development – Social Democrats were not cultural relativists – in Reichstag debates over colonial policy (including over so-called 'miscegenation' laws in 1912), Social Democrats continued to emphasise the humanity of Germany's colonial subjects. Alfred Henke, for example, even drew parallels between the discrimination of 'mixed-race' people in South-West Africa and the treatment of Social Democrats within Germany, and affirmed his party's belief in 'the equality of all human beings, regardless of their skin colour'.[75] At the programmatic and theoretical level, the Social Democratic Party, especially after the 1890s, took a principled anti-racist stance, partly on 'scientific' grounds, partly on grounds of a commitment to human rights and partly because the party increasingly viewed racism as a political instrument of their adversaries in Germany's nationalist-*völkisch* right.[76]

## Notes

1 Jens-Uwe Guettel, 'The Myth of the Pro-Colonialist SPD: German Social Democracy and Imperialism before World War I', *Central European History* 45 (2012), 452–84.
2 See Arne Perras, *Carl Peters and German Imperialism, 1856–1918. A Political Biography* (Oxford: Oxford University Press, 2004), pp. 208, 216–22.
3 Roger Fletcher, *Revisionism and Empire. Socialist Imperialism in Germany, 1897–1914* (London: Allen & Unwin, 1984). See also Markku Hyrkkänen, *Sozialistische Kolonialpolitik. Eduard Bernsteins Stellung zur Kolonialpolitik und zum Imperialismus 1882–1914* (Helsinki: SHS, 1986); and, preceding Fletcher's work, Hans-Christoph Schröder, *Gustav Noske und die Kolonialpolitik des Deutschen Kaiserreichs* (Berlin and Bonn: J.H.W. Dietz Nachf., 1979). For broader treatments, see Hans-Christoph Schröder, *Sozialismus und Imperialismus* (Hanover: Verlag für Literatur und Zeitgeschehen, 1968); Franco Andreucci, *Socialdemocrazia e imperialismo. I marxisti tedeschi e la politica mondiale 1884–1914* (Rome: Editori Riuniti, 1988).
4 John Phillip Short, 'Colonialism, War, and the German Working Class', in Bradley Naranch and Geoff Eley (eds), *German Colonialism in a Global Age* (Durham, NC. and London: Duke University Press, 2014), pp. 210–27. See also Short, *Magic Lantern Empire. Colonialism and Society in Germany* (Ithaca and London: Cornell University Press, 2012), especially chapter 6, focusing on the 1907 'Hottentot elections' and the working class in Leipzig.
5 Guettel, 'The Myth of the Pro-Colonialist SPD', pp. 453–5; see, for example, Helmut Walser Smith, 'The Talk of Genocide, the Rhetoric of Miscegenation: Notes on Debates in the German Reichstag Concerning Southwest Africa, 1904–1914', in Sara

Friedrichsmeyer, Sara Lennox and Susanne Zantop (eds), *The Imperialist Imagination. German Colonialism and Its Legacy* (Ann Arbor: University of Michigan Press, 1998), pp. 107–23.

6 Dieter Fricke, *Handbuch zur Geschichte der deutschen Arbeiterbewegung 1869 bis 1917* (Berlin: Dietz, 1987), Vol. 1, p. 588. Fricke laments a decline in the journal's radicalism after 1907, however, ibid., p. 587.

7 E.g. Staatsarchiv Hamburg (StAHH), 331–3 Politische Polizei, 5320 Vigilanzberichte Schutzmann Mebus, report dated 8 December 1908 (unfoliated).

8 Richard J. Evans, *Kneipengespräche im Kaiserreich* (Reinbek bei Hamburg: Rowohlt, 1989). Evans's selection shows strong anti-imperialist sentiment among Hamburg workers, pp. 341–60; for a report on opposition specifically to the South-West African war, pp. 353–4.

9 In addition to the reports cited by Evans, *Kneipengespräche im Kaiserreich*, see StAHH, 331–3, 5302 (Schutzmann Kramer), reports from 29 March and 25 October 1905; 5298 (Schutzmann Noroschat), report from 6 December 1905 (with a characteristic comment by a worker: 'How many thousands of people have been slaughtered there [South-West Africa] and all really pointless. The colonies have already cost us millions and people's lives as well'); 5304 (Schutzmann Ramming), report from 4 January, 17 March, 27 March and 24 July 1905 (all unfoliated).

10 For example, political police reports of 20 February 1907, on meeting of the *Wahlverein*, or party branch, of the fourth Berlin *Wahlkreis* in February 1907. Landesarchiv Berlin (LAB), A Pr Br Rep. 030, No. 14146, Bl. 254–5, 260–1, 262–3; *Vorwärts*, no. 50, 28 February 1907 (report on meeting in fourth Berlin *Wahlkreis*).

11 LAB, A Pr Br Rep. 030, No. 14151, Bl. 270–1 (report dated 18 December 1907); No. 14152, Bl. 46–7 (report dated 26 February 1908).

12 Karl Kautsky, *Sozialismus und Kolonialpolitik* (Berlin: Buchhandlung Vorwärts, 1907). The debate at Essen proved to be an anticlimax, as it turned out (and Kautsky's book appeared too late for the occasion).

13 Standard works on the Germans in South-West Africa include Helmut Bley, trans. Hugh Ridley, *South-West Africa under German Rule, 1894–1914* (London: Heinemann, 1971); Hanno Drechsler, trans. Bernd Zöllner, *'Let Us Die Fighting'. The Struggle of the Herero and Nama against German Imperialism* (London: Zed Press, 1984; original German edn 1966); Jon M. Bridgman, *The Revolt of the Hereros* (Berkeley: University of California Press, 1981); Gesine Krüger, *Kriegsbewältigung und Geschichtsbewußtsein. Realität, Deutung und Verarbeitung des deutschen Kolonialkriegs in Namibia 1904 bis 1907* (Göttingen: Vandenhoeck & Ruprecht, 1999); Isabel V. Hull, *Absolute Destruction. Military Culture and the Practices of War in Imperial Germany* (Ithaca and London: Cornell University Press, 2005); Jürgen Zimmerer and Joachim Zeller (eds), *Völkermord in Deutsch-Südwestafrika. Der Kolonialkrieg (1904–1908) in Namibia und seine Folgen* (Berlin: Ch. Links, 2004). On the 1907 'Hottentot elections', see George Dunlap Crothers, *The German Elections of 1907* (New York: Columbia University Press, 1941; reprint edn 1968); Jonathan Sperber, *The Kaiser's Voters. Electors and Elections in Imperial Germany* (Cambridge: Cambridge University Press, 1997), pp. 240–54.

14 'Zur Reichstagswahl' (cover illustration), *Der wahre Jakob* (hereafter *WJ*), No. 534 (8 January 1907). *Der wahre Jakob* is now available in a complete digital edition through the website of the Heidelberg university library at http://digi.ub.uni-heidelberg.de/diglit/wj?sid=5894cc4556266c5419e8111221fe3c9b&ui_lang=eng. Also useful is the digital edition supported by the Herzogin Anna Amalia Bibliothek, Weimar, at www.der-wahre-jacob.de/. On the Knackfuss 'Yellow Peril' allegory designed by the Kaiser, see John C.G. Röhl, *Wilhelm II. Der Aufbau der persönlichen Monarchie 1888–1900* (Munich: C.H. Beck, 2001), pp. 840–1 (with illustrations), 1009–10. The Knackfuss picture is also reproduced online at https://upload.wikimedia.org/wikipedia/commons/f/fa/Voelker_Europas.jpg.

15 See Nicholas Stargardt, *The German Idea of Militarism. Radical and Socialist Critics, 1866–1914* (Cambridge: Cambridge University Press, 1994); Andrew G. Bonnell,

'Explaining Suicide in the Imperial German Army', *German Studies Review* 37:2 (May 2014), 275–95.

16  'Hobelspäne', *WJ*, No. 457 (16 January 1904), 4257. 'Das ist der Stamm der Bondelzwart / Der ist von ganz besonderer Art. / Nicht Steuern wollen zahlen sie / Und nicht durchdrücken ihre Knie. / Sie wollen leben in dieser Welt / Geradeso, wie es ihnen gefällt! / Wie bringt man solchem Gesindel nur / Bei einen Begriff von unsrer Kultur?'

17  H.Fl., 'Frechheit!', *WJ*, No. 465 (17 May 1904), 4356. For similar reflections on the 'blessings' of German culture in the colonies, see J.S., 'Kolonialprinzenlied', *WJ*, No. 462 (5 April 1904), 4319; Erich Mühsam, 'Weihnachtsbetrachtung', *WJ*, No. 480 (13 December 1904), 4557.

18  Erich Mühsam, 'Der friedliche Michel', *WJ*, No. 467 (14 June 1904), 4389.

19  'Der verkannte Heros', *WJ*, No. 478 (15 November 1904), 4525.

20  'Der neue Arminius', *WJ*, No. 480 (13 December 1904), 4546.

21  August Bebel, *Verhandlungen des Deutschen Reichstags* [=*VDRT*], 11th legis. per., 14th session, 19 January 1904, pp. 367–8.

22  'Vom Neger, der auszog, sein Recht zu suchen', *WJ*, No. 510 (6 February 1906), 4940.

23  'Bilder aus Puttkamerun' and 'Hererosang', *WJ*, No. 510 (6 February 1906), 4941.

24  A.S., 'Weil's gleich ist', *WJ*, No. 515 (17 April 1906), 5012.

25  A[lbert] Staehle, 'Bei den Hereros', *WJ*, No. 464 (3 May 1904), 4344.

26  H.G.J., 'Nach dem "Siege" ', *WJ*, No. 476 (18 October 1904), 4492. In this image, the Herero displays very much a cartoon stereotype of African physiognomy, but the main butt of the joke is the German military being outwitted.

27  'Die verletzte deutsche Waffenehre', *WJ*, No. 534 (8 January 1907), 5300.

28  'Hobelspäne', *WJ*, No. 499 (5 September 1905), 4792.

29  'Die neuen Transporte nach Südwestafrika', *WJ*, No. 467 (14 June 1904), 4383.

30  'Zarte Rücksicht', *WJ*, No. 481 (27 December 1904), 4570; 'Andenken', *WJ*, No. 478 (15 November 1904), 4524.

31  'Der Segen der Kolonialpolitik', *WJ*, No. 502 (17 October 1905), 4833. The commentary was a topical, if macabre, allusion to the controversy over high meat prices caused by protectionist policies in Germany at the time.

32  W. Lehmann, 'Aus unseren Kolonien', *WJ*, No. 511 (20 February 1906), 4959.

33  Klaus Epstein, *Matthias Erzberger and the Dilemma of German Democracy* (New York: Howard Fertig, 1971), pp. 52–6; a more detailed account is in Epstein, 'Erzberger and the German Colonial Scandals, 1905–1910', *English Historical Review* 74:293 (1959), 637–63.

34  For example, 'Hobelspäne', *WJ*, No. 474 (20 September 1904), 4467; 'Hobelspäne', *WJ*, No. 479 (29 November 1904), 4531; 'Hobelspäne', *WJ*, No. 489 (18 April 1905), 4667; 'Das ist ein Geschäft!', *WJ*, No. 514 (3 April 1906), 4988.

35  [Emil] Erk, '200 Million Mark für Kolonialzwecke', *WJ*, No. 479 (29 November 1904), 4534; for another cartoon on the same theme, G. Koch, 'Bülows Kummer', *WJ*, No. 499 (5 September 1905), 4792.

36  R.L., 'Vom Kolonialamt', *WJ*, No. 522 (24 July 1906), p. 5110. On the same theme, J.S., 'Des Kolonialamts Klage', *WJ*, No. 524 (21 August 1906), 5138; R.T., 'Die Lieferantenpresse in der Kolonialabteilung, Modell Fischer', *WJ*, No. 524 (21 August 1906), p. 5139; 'Im Kolonialamt stinkt's', *WJ*, No. 524 (21 August 1906), 5140; 'Hobelspäne' and poem 'Unser Krieg', *WJ*, No. 525 (4 September 1906), 5153; 'In der Kolonialabteilung', *WJ*, No. 525 (4 September 1906), 5163; 'Der Ramschbazar', *WJ*, No. 526 (18 September 1906), 5174; 'Fallobst' (cover illustration), *WJ*, No. 527 (2 October 1906), p5181; 'Pod's Blitzableiter bei dem herrschenden Kolonialgewitter', *WJ*, No. 527 (2 October 1906), 5185; E., 'Der Unbestechliche', *WJ*, No. 527 (2 October 1906), 5192.

37  W.L.. 'Im Kolonialsumpf', *WJ*, No. 525 (4 September 1906), 5155.

38  A.F., 'Die Abgeordneten auf der Studienreise in den Kolonien', *WJ*, No. 525 (4 September 1906), 5157.

39  Untitled cartoon, *WJ*, No. 525 (4 September 1906), 5160.

40  EE, 'Vorbereitung der parlamentarischen Studienkommission in Afrika', *WJ*, No. 527 (2 October 1906), 5187.

41  'Deutsche Kultur in Afrika', *WJ*, No. 534 (8 January 1907), 5302.
42  H.L., 'Kampflied für Südwestafrika', *WJ*, No. 466 (31 May 1904), 4368.
43  'Aus einem Kolonialbericht', *WJ*, No. 515 (17 April 1906), 5010.
44  [Emil] Erk, 'Befürchtung', *WJ*, No. 467 (14 June 1904), 4385.
45  [Emil] Erk, 'Pardon wird nicht gegeben', *WJ*, No. 483 (24 January 1905), 4591.
46  A. Staehle, 'System Trotha', *WJ*, No. 503 (31 October 1905), 4853.
47  'Deutsches Büchsenfleisch', *WJ*, No. 526 (18 September 1906), 5177.
48  Leo, 'Trotha in Nöten', *WJ*, No. 499 (5 September 1905), 4795 (cartoon of von Trotha forbidding a Windhoek rooster to crow, while grinning natives holding spears watch from behind a wall); and the poem 'Der Erste Sieg', *WJ*, No. 498 (22 August 1905), 4780.
49  August Bebel, *VDRT*, 11th legis. per., 60th session, 14 March, pp. 1891–2, and 17 March 1904, p. 1901.
50  Visual stereotypes: cf. David Ciarlo, *Advertising Empire: Race and Visual Culture in Imperial Germany* (Cambridge, MA: Harvard University Press, 2011), p. 269, 392 n. 21. See also Edward Graham Norris and Arnold Beuke, 'Kolonialkrieg und Karikatur in Deutschland: Die Aufstände der Herero und der Nama und die Zeichnungen der deutschen satirischen Zeitschriften', in Peter Heine and Ulrich von der Heyden (eds), *Studien zur Geschichte des deutschen Kolonialismus in Afrika: Festschrift zum 60. Geburtstag von Peter Sebald* (Pfaffenweiler: Centaurus, 1995) (also cited by Ciarlo, ibid.), who include a few references to *Der wahre Jakob*, pp. 393, 394, 397.
51  H.C.J., 'Die Schattenseite', *WJ*, No. 468 (28 June 1904), 4394.
52  'Der Landsmann', *WJ*, No. 460 (8 March 1904), 4298.
53  'Der Handel mit unseren Kolonien', *WJ*, No. 534 (8 January 1907), 5303.
54  A.R., 'Unser "Landsmann"', *WJ*, No. 462 (5 April 1904), 4324.
55  'Illustrierte Hofnachricht', *WJ*, No. 509 (23 January 1907), 4932.
56  'Aus den Kolonien', *WJ*, No. 515 (17 April 1906), 5011.
57  Bebel, *VDRT*, 11th legis. per., 60th session, 17 March 1904, p. 1902.
58  Bebel, *VDRT*, 11th legis per., 60th session, 14 March 1904, p. 1891.
59  Bebel, *VDRT*, 11th legis. per., 73rd session, 23 March 1906, p. 2246.
60  'Im Zeichen des Kreuzes', *Süddeutscher Postillon*, No. 11 (1904) (reprinted in Udo Achten (ed.), *Süddeutscher Postillon* (Berlin and Bonn J.H.W. Dietz Nachf., 1979), p. 206).
61  For example, 'Die Wahrheit über den Herero-Aufstand', *Vorwärts*, no. 69 (22 March 1904); 'Koloniale Schlachtopfer', *Vorwärts*, No. 98 (27 April 1904); 'Unser afrikanisches China', *Vorwärts*, No. 106 (6 May 1904).
62  'Die Vernichtung der Herero', *Vorwärts*, No. 287 (7 December 1904).
63  Short, *Magic Lantern Empire*, pp. 141–2.
64  Otto Bauer, 'Die Kolonialpolitik und die Arbeiter', *Die Neue Zeit* 23:2 (1904–5), 265.
65  'Rundschau', *Sozialistische Monatshefte*, 1904, 1:4 (April), 319. Surprisingly, perhaps, Fletcher, *Revisionism and Empire*, does not mention the war in South-West Africa or Social Democrats' responses to it.
66  Bebel, *VDRT*, 11th legis. per., 14th session, 19 January 1904, pp. 366–8. See the defence of this abstention in the report of the parliamentary caucus to the Social Democratic party congress: *Protokoll über die Verhandlungen des Parteitages der Sozialdemokratischen Partei Deutschlands. Abgehalten zu Bremen vom 18. Bis 24. September 1904* (= *Protokoll* 1904) (Berlin: Buchhandlung Vorwärts, 1904), pp. 89–91, and Bebel's own justification of the abstention in the face of arguments that the Social Democrats should always oppose colonial expenditure, indicative of the broader anti-colonial consensus in the party, pp. 211–12.
67  Bebel, *VDRT*, 11th legis. per., 129th session, 30 January 1905, pp. 4096–105.
68  Bebel, *VDRT*, 11th legis. per., 131st session, 1 December 1906, pp. 4059–60.
69  August Bebel, *VDRT*, 11th legis. per., 60th session, 17 March 1904, p. 1900.
70  Quoted in Krüger, *Kriegsbewältigung und Geschichtsbewußtsein*, p. 104.
71  *Protokoll* 1904, p. 206.

72  Schröder, *Sozialismus und Imperialismus*, p. 191. Karl Kautsky acknowledged this fact in his critique of colonial policy, but he doubted whether a short visit by visiting parliamentarians would have been of any great value, and he pointed out that the advocates of a 'positive' socialist colonial policy were equally lacking in first-hand knowledge. Kautsky, *Sozialismus und Kolonialpolitik*, pp. 14, 15.
73  Robbie Aitken and Eve Rosenhaft, *Black Germany* (Cambridge and New York: Cambridge University Press, 2013); see especially p. 26 on the experiences of the Cameroonian Alfred Bell and his contacts with Social Democrats.
74  See *Handbuch für Sozialdemokratische Wähler* (Berlin: Buchhandlung Vorwärts, 1911), pp. 63–118, on *Kolonialpolitik* in general, on risk of war, p. 64, oppression of other peoples, p. 67.
75  Guettel, 'Myth of the Pro-Colonialist SPD', pp. 471–2.
76  See Richard Saage, *Zwischen Darwin und Marx. Zur Rezeption der Evolutionstheorie in der deutschen und der österreichischen Sozialdemokratie vor 1933/34* (Vienna, Cologne and Weimar: Böhlau, 2012).

# SELECT BIBLIOGRAPHY

Abdelfettah, Ahcène, Messaoudi, Alain and Nordman, Daniel (eds), *Savoirs d'Allemagne en Afrique du Nord (XVIIIe–XXe siècle)* (Saint-Denis: Bouchène, 2012).

Abel, Richard, Bertellini, Giorgio and King, Rob (eds), *Early Cinema and the 'National'* (Bloomington: Indiana University Press, 2016).

Abinales, Patricio N. and Amoroso, Donna J., *State and Society in the Philippines* (Pasig: Anvil, 2005).

Abu-Lughod, Janet L., *Before European Hegemony: The World System AD 1250–1350* (New York: Oxford University Press, 1989).

Adler, Hans and Koepke, Wulf (eds), *A Companion to the Works of Johann Gottfried Herder* (Rochester, NY: Camden House, 2009).

Aitken, Robbie and Rosenhaft, Eve, *Black Germany* (Cambridge and New York: Cambridge University Press, 2013).

Alatas, Syed, *The Myth of the Lazy Native: A Study of the Image of the Malays, Filipinos and Javanese from the 16th to the 20th Century and Its Function in the Ideology of Colonial Capitalism* (London: Cass, 1977).

Alcoff, Linda Martín, *Visible Identities: Race, Gender, and the Self* (New York: Oxford University Press, 2006).

Aldinger, Paul, *Das Itajahy-Tal. Deutsche Siedlung im brasilianischen Urwald. Blumenau und Hansa* (Hamburg: H.O. Persiehl, 1910).

Almeida Demarquet, Sonia de, *Os Xokleng de Ibirama, uma comunidade indígena de Santa Catarina, Boletim do Museo do Índio: Documentação*, 3 (1983).

Ames, Eric, *Carl Hagenbeck's Empire of Entertainments* (Seattle: University of Washington Press, 2008).

Ames, Eric, Klotz, Marcia and Wildenthal, Lora (eds), *Germany's Colonial Pasts* (Lincoln: University of Nebraska Press, 2005).

Anderson, Benedict, *Spectre of Comparisons: Nationalism, Southeast Asia, and the World* (Quezon City: Ateneo de Manila University Press, 2004).

Anderson, Benedict, *Under Three Flags: Anarchism and the Anti-Colonial Imagination* (Pasig: Anvil, 2006).

Anderson, Gary Clayton, *Ethnic Cleansing and the Indian: The Crime that Should Haunt America* (Norman: University of Oklahoma Press, 2014).

Anderson, Jeffrey E. (ed.), *The Voodoo Encyclopedia: Magic, Ritual, and Religion* (Santa Barbara: ABC-CLIO, 2015).

Anderson, Kay and Perrin, Colin, ' "The Miserablest People in the World": Race, Humanism and the Australian Aborigine', *The Australian Journal of Anthropology* 18:1 (2007), 18–39.

Andreucci, Franco, *Socialdemocrazia e imperialismo. I marxisti tedeschi e la politica mondiale 1884–1914* (Rome: Editori Riuniti, 1988).

Arndt, Karl J.R., *Sämtliche Werke*, Vols 6–7 (Hildesheim: Olms Presse, 1972).

Asher, Michael, *Khartoum. The Ultimate Imperial Adventure* (London: Penguin, 2006).

Bachmann, Klaus, 'On the Margins of German *Vergangenheitsbewältigung*. Germany's Colonial Past Revisited', *Przegląd Zachodni* 1 (2014), 147–50.

Backhouse, Rofer and Fontaine, Phillipa (eds), *A Historiography of the Modern Social Sciences* (Cambridge: Cambridge University Press, 2014).

Ballantyne, Tony, *Entanglements of Empire: Missionaries, Maori, and the Question of the Body* (Durham, NC: Duke University Press, 2014).

Ballantyne, Tony and Burton, Antoinette, *Empires and the Reach of the Global, 1870–1945* (Cambridge, MA: Harvard University Press, 2012).

Baranowski, Shelley, *Nazi Empire: German Colonialism and Imperialism from Bismarck to Hitler* (Cambridge: Cambridge University Press, 2011).

Barth, Fredrick, Gingrich, Andre, Parkin, Robert and Silverman, Sydel. *One Discipline, Four Ways: British, German, French, and American Anthropology* (Chicago and London: University of Chicago Press, 2005).

Barth, Volker and Cvetkovski, Roland (eds), *Imperial Cooperation and Transfer, 1870–1930 Empires and Encounters* (London: Bloomsbury, 2015).

Bastian, Adolf, *Die Völker des östlichen Asien: Studien und Reisen, fünfter Band: Reisen im indischen Archipel: Singapore, Batavia, Manilla und Japan* (Jena: Hermann Costenoble, 1869).

Bateman, Fiona and Pilkington, Lionel (eds), *Studies in Settler Colonialism: Politics, Identity and Culture* (New York: Palgrave Macmillan, 2011).

Bauer, Friedrich, Deinzer, Johannes and Deinzer, Martin, *Christliche Ethik auf Lutherischer Grundlage* (Neuendettelsau: Selbstverlag der Missionsanstalt, 1904).

Bechhaus-Gerst, Marianne and Giesecke, Sunna (eds), *Koloniale und postkoloniale Konstruktionen von Afrika und Menschen afrikanischer Herkunft in der deutschen Alltagskultur* (Frankfurt am Main: Lang, 2006).

Bechhaus-Gerst, Marianne and Klein-Arendt, Richard (eds), *AfrikanerInnen in Deutschland und schwarze Deutsche – Geschichte und Gegenwart* (Münster: Lit, 2004).

Bechhaus-Gerst, Marianne and Klein-Arendt, Richard (eds), *Die (koloniale) Begegnung. AfrikanerInnen in Deutschland. Deutsche in Afrika 1880–1918* (Frankfurt: Lang, 2003).

Bechhaus-Gerst, Marianne and Leutner, Mechthild (eds), *Frauen in den deutschen Kolonien* (Berlin: Links, 2009).

Becker, Carl Heinrich, *Islamstudien. Vom Werden und Wesen der islamischen Welt*, 2 vols (Leipzig: Hildesheim, 1924–32).

Becker, Felicitas and Beez, Jigal (eds), *Der Maji Maji-Krieg gegen die deutsche Kolonialherrschaft in Tanzania, 1905–08* (Berlin: Christoph Links Verlag, 2005).

Becker, Ítala Irene Basile, *O índio Kaingáng no Rio Grande do Sul* (São Leopoldo: Instituto Anchietano de Pesquisas, Universidade do Vale do Rio dos Sinos, 1995).

Beckert, Sven, 'From Tuskegee to Togo: The Problem of Freedom in the Empire of Cotton', *Journal of American History* 92:2 (2005), 498–526.

SELECT BIBLIOGRAPHY

Behdad, Ali and Gartlan, Luke (eds), *Photography's Orientalism. New Essays on Colonial Representation* (Los Angeles: Getty Research Institute, 2013).

Beiser, Frederik, *The Genesis of Neo-Kantianism, 1796–1880* (Oxford: Oxford University Press, 2014).

Berghahn, Volker, 'German Colonialism and Imperialism from Bismarck to Hitler', *German Studies Review* 40:1 (2017), 147–62.

Berman, Nina, *Impossible Missions?: German Economic, Military, and Humanitarian Efforts in Africa* (Lincoln: University of Nebraska Press, 2004).

Berman, Nina, *Orientalismus, Kolonialismus und Moderne. Zum Bild des Orients in der deutschsprachigen Kultur um 1900* (Stuttgart: M&P, 1997).

Berman, Nina, Mühlhahn, Klaus and Nganang, Patrice Alain (eds), *German Colonialism Revisited: African, Asian, and Oceanic Experiences* (Ann Arbor: University of Michigan Press, 2014).

Berman, Russell, *Enlightenment or Empire: Colonial Discourse in German Culture* (Lincoln: University of Nebraska Press, 1998).

Bernhard, Robert, *Dona Francisca, Hansa und Blumenau, drei deutsche Mustersiedelungen im südbrasilianischen Staate Santa Catharina: Eine Festschrift zur Feier des 50jährigen Bestehens von Dona Francisca und Blumenau* (Breslau: S. Schottlaender, 1901).

Berzieri, Frank, *Sûra. Ecrivians, voyageurs et photographes en Egypte au XIXe siècle* (Paris: Phebus, 2012).

Birkett, D., *Spinsters Abroad: Victorian Lady Explorers* (Oxford: Blackwell, 1989).

Bischoff, Eva, '"Heimischwerden deutscher Art und Sitte": Power, Gender, and Diaspora in the Colonial Contest', *Itinerario* 37:1 (2013), 43–58.

Bischoff, Eva, *Kannibale-Werden: Eine postkoloniale Geschichte deutscher Männlichkeit um 1900* (Bielefeld: transcript, 2011).

Bitterli, Urs, *Die 'Wilden' und die 'Zivilisierten'. Grundzüge einer Geistes- und Kulturgeschichte der europäischen überseeischen Begegnungen* (Munich: CH Beck, 1991).

Blackbourn, David, *The Long Nineteenth Century* (Hammersmith: Fontana, 1997).

Bley, Helmut, trans. Hugh Ridley, *South-West Africa under German Rule, 1894–1914* (London: Heinemann, 1971).

Blumenbach, Johann Friedrich, *Über die natürlichen Verschiedenehiten im Menschengeschlechte* (Berlin: Humboldt Universität zu Berlin, 2011).

Bodi, Leslie, Jeffries, Stephen and Radvansky, Susan, *Image of a Continent. A Bibliography of German Australiana from the Beginnings to 1975 – Bild eines Kontinents. Eine Bibliographie deutscher Australiana von den Anfängen bis 1975* (Wiesbaden: O. Harrasowitz, 1990).

Bonnell, Andrew G., 'Explaining Suicide in the Imperial German Army', *German Studies Review* 37:2 (May 2014), 275–95.

Bonniot, Béatrice, *Homme de culture et républicain de raison. Carl Heinrich Becker, serviteur de l'Etat sous la République de Weimar (1918–1933)* (Frankfurt am Main: Lang, 2012).

Borgolte, Michael, and Tischler, Matthias M. (eds), *Transkulturelle Verflechtungen im mittelalterlichen Jahrtausend: Europa, Ostasien, Afrika* (Darmstadt: Wissenschaftliche Buchgesellschaft, 2012).

Boucher, Leigh and Russell, Lynette (eds), *Settler Colonial Governance in Nineteenth-Century Victoria* (Canberra: Australian National University Press, 2015).

Bowersox, Jeff, *Raising Germans in the Age of Empire: Youth and Colonial Culture, 1871–1914* (Oxford: Oxford University Press, 2013).

Bridgman, Jon M., *The Revolt of the Hereros* (Berkeley: University of California Press, 1981).

Broome, Richard, *Aboriginal Victorians. A History since 1800* (Crows Nest: Allen & Unwin, 2005).

Brown, B. Ricardo, *Until Darwin: Science, Human Variety and the Origins of Race* (London: Pickering and Chatto, 2010).

Brown, Hillary (ed.), *Landmarks in German Women's Writing* (Bern: Peter Lang, 2007).

Brunn, Gerhard, *Deutschland und Brasilien (1889–1914)* (Cologne: Böhlau Verlag, 1971).

Bunzl, Matti and Fabians, Johannes, ' "Time and the Other": Synthesen einer kritischen Anthropologie', *Historische Anthropologie* 6:3 (1998), 466–78.

Burke, Peter, *Augenzeugenschaft. Bilder als historische Quellen* (Berlin: Wagenbach, 2003).

Burton, Antoinette, *Burdens of History: British Feminists, Indian Women, and Imperial Culture, 1865–1915* (Chapel Hill: University of North Carolina Press, 2007).

Butler, Judith, *Gender Trouble: Feminism and the Subversion of Identity* (London: Routledge, 1990).

Camper, Petrus, trans. T. Cogan, *The works of the late Professor Petrus Camper on the connexion between the science of anatomy and the arts of drawing, painting, statuary* (London: C. Dilly, 1794).

Carini, Joel João, *Estado, índios e colonos: o conflito na reserve indgena de Serrinha norte do Rio Grande do Sul* (Passo Fundo: University of Passo Fundo, 2005).

Cassidy, Eugene S., 'Germanness, Civilisation, and Slavery: Southern Brazil as German Colonial Space (1819–1888)' (Unpublished Dissertation, University of Michigan, 2015).

Cazan-Simányi, Ildiko and Weiss, Gabriele (eds), *Aus dem Pazifik. Ein Sammler aus Leidenschaft – F.H. Otto Finsch (1839–1917)* (Vienna: Museum für Völkerkunde, 2012).

Chakrabarty, Dipesh, *Provincializing Europe: Postcolonial Thought and Historical Difference* (Princeton: Princeton University Press, 2007).

Chappell, David A., *Double Ghosts: Oceanian Voyagers on Euroamerican Ships* (Armonk: M.E. Sharpe, 1997).

Ciarlo, David, *Advertising Empire: Race and Visual Culture in Imperial Germany* (Cambridge, MA: Harvard University Press, 2011).

Clarence-Smith, William Gervase and Topik, Steven (eds), *The Global Coffee Economy in Africa, Asia, and Latin America, 1500–1989* (Cambridge: Cambridge University Press, 2003).

Clark, Ian D. and Cahir, Fred (eds), *The Aboriginal story of Burke and Wills: Forgotten Narratives* (Collingwood, VIC: CSIRO Publishing, 2013).

Coelho dos Santos, Silvio, *Indios e brancos no sul do Brasil: a dramática experiência dos Xokleng* (Florianópolis: Movimento, 1973).

Coelho dos Santos, Sílvio, *Os índios Xokleng: memoria visual* (Florianópolis: Editora da UFSC, 1997).

Conrad, Sebastian, 'Rethinking German Colonialism in a Global Age', *Journal of Imperial and Commonwealth History* 41:4 (2013), 543–66.

Conrad, Sebastian and Osterhammel, Jürgen (eds), *Das Kaiserreich transnational: Deutschland in der Welt, 1871–1914* (Göttingen: Vandenhoeck und Ruprecht, 2006).

Corkhill, Alan, *Antipodean Encounters: Australia and the German Literary Imagination 1754–1918* (Bern, Frankfurt am Main, New York and Paris: Peter Lang, 1990).

Corkhill, Alan, 'Space, Place and Identity in the Australian Fiction of Friedrich Gerstäcker', *Limbus Australisches Jahrbuch für germanistische Literatur- und Kulturwissenschaft* 6 (2013), 141–55.

Cullinane, Michael, *Arenas of Conspiracy and Rebellion in the Late Nineteenth-Century Philippines: The Case of the April 1898 Uprising in Cebu* (Quezon City: Ateneo de Manila University Press, 2014).

Czernin, Monika, *'Jenes herrliche Gefühl der Freiheit': Frieda von Bülow und die Sehnsucht nach Afrika* (Berlin: List, 2008).

Dampier, William, *A New Voyage Around the World* (New York: Dover Publications, 1968).

David, Bruno, Barker, Bryce and McNiven, Ian J., *The Social Archaeology of Australian Indigenous Societies* (Canberra: Aboriginal Studies Press, 2006).

Davis, Shelton H., *Victims of the Miracle: Development and the Indians of Brazil* (Cambridge: Cambridge University Press, 1977).

Deeke, José, *Das Munizip Blumenau und seine Entwicklungsgeschichte* (São Leopoldo: Rotermund, 1917).

Denby, David, 'Herder: Culture, Anthropology and the Enlightenment', *History of the Human Sciences* 18:1 (2005), 55–76.

Dernburg, B., *Zielpunkte des Deutschen Kolonialwesens: Zwei Vorträge* (Berlin: Mittler & Sohn, 1907).

Diacon, Todd A., *Stringing Together a Nation: Mariano da Silva Rondon and the Construction of a Modern Brazil, 1906–1930* (Durham: Duke University Press, 2004).

Dietrich, Anette, *Weiße Weiblichkeiten: Konstruktionen von 'Rasse' und Geschlecht im deutschen Kolonialismus* (Bielefeld: transcript, 2007).

Douglas, Bronwen, *Foreign Bodies in Oceania and the Science of Race 1750–1940* (Canberra: ANU E Press, 2008).

Dorson, Richard M. (ed.), *Folklore in the Modern World* (The Hague: Mouton Publishers, 1978).

Drechsler, Horst, trans. Bernd Zöllner, 'Let Us Die Fighting'. The Struggle of the Herero and Nama against German Imperialism (London: Zed Press, 1980).

Dreesbach, Anne, Gezähmte Wilde: Die Zurschaustellung 'exotischer' Menschen in Deutschland 1870–1940 (Frankfurt am Main: Campus, 2005).

Dreher, Martin N. et al. (eds), Imigração e relações interétnicas: XVII simpósio de história da imigração e colonização (São Leopoldo: Oikos Editora. 2008).

Dunker, Axel and Hofmann, Michael (eds), Morgenland und Moderne. Orient-Diskurse in der deutschsprachigen Literatur von 1980 bis zur Gegenwa: rt (Frankfurt am Main: Lang, 2014).

Ebers, Georg, Aegypten in Wort und Bild. Dargestellt von unseren ersten Künstlern, 2 vols (Stuttgart and Leipzig: Hallberger, 1879).

Ecker, Alexander, Hundert Jahre einer Freiburger Professoren-Familie. Biographische Aufzeichnungen (Freiburg im Breisgau, 1886).

Eckstein, Lars, 'Some Reflections on Entangled Knowledge and Decolonisation', Zeitschrift für Religions- und Geistesgeschichte 65:3 (2013), 283–88.

Eder, Franz X., Kühschelm, Oliver and Linsboth, Christina (eds), Bilder in historischen Diskursen (Wiesbaden: Springer, 2014).

Edwards, Elisabeth, 'Photography and the Material Performance of the Past', History and Theory 48:4 (2009), 130–50.

Eigen, Sara and Larrimore, Mark (eds), The German Invention of Race (Albany: State University of New York Press, 2006).

Ellis, Willis D. (ed.), A Source Book of Gestalt Psychology (Abingdon: Routledge, 1938).

Epstein, Arnold. L., Matupit: Land, Politics, and Change among the Tolai of New Britain (Canberra: Australian National University Press, 1969).

Erbar, Ralph, Ein 'Platz an der Sonne'? Die Verwaltungs- und Wirtschaftsgeschichte der deutschen Kolonie Togo, 1884–1914 (Stuttgart: Franz Steiner, 1991).

Evans, Andrew D., 'A Liberal Paradigm? Race and Ideology in Late-Nineteenth-Century German Physical Anthropology', Ab Imperio 8:1 (2007), 113–38.

Evans, Richard J., Kneipengespräche im Kaiserreich (Reinbek bei Hamburg: Rowohlt, 1989).

Eyre, Edward John, Journals of Expeditions of Discovery into Central Australia and Overland from Adelaide to King George's Sound in the Years 1840–1. Vol. II (London: T. & W. Boone, 1854).

Fabian, Ann, The Skull Collectors. Race, Science, and America's Unburied Dead (Chicago: University of Chicago Press, 2010).

Fabian, Johannes, Out of Our Minds: Reason and Madness in the Exploration of Central Africa (Berkeley: University of California Press, 2000).

Fabian, Johannes, Time and the Other. How Anthropology Makes Its Object (New York: Columbia University Press, 1983).

Favrod, Charles-Henri, Orient 1904–1930 (Heidelberg: Umschau, 1998).

Fforde, Cressida, Collecting the Dead: Archaeology and the Reburial Issue (London: Duckworth, 2004).

Finsch, Otto, Neu-Guinea und seine Bewohner (Bremen: C. Ed. Müller, 1865).

Finsch, Otto, *Samoafahrten. Reisen in Kaiser Wilhelms-Land und Englisch-Neu-Guinea in den Jahren 1884 u. 1885 an Bord des deutschen Dampfers 'Samoa'* (Leipzig: Ferdinand Hirt & Sohn, 1888).

Finsch, Otto, *Systematische Uebersicht der Ergebnisse seiner Reisen und schriftstellerischen Tätigkeit (1859–1899)* (Berlin: R. Friedländer & Sohn, 1899).

Finsch, Otto, *Tapinowanne Torondoluan, der erste Weltreisender Neupommerns (1882)* (Braunschweig: Julius Krampe, 1907).

Finzsch, Norbert, '"[...] Extirpate or remove that vermine": Genocide, Biological Warfare, and Settler Imperialism in the Eighteenth and Early Nineteenth Century', *Journal of Genocide Research* 10:2 (2008), 215–32.

Firth, Stewart, *New Guinea under the Germans* (Melbourne: Melbourne University Press, 1983).

Fischer, Bernd, 'Baumwolle und Indianer Zu Charles Sealsfields Der Legitime und die Republikaner', *Journal of German-American Studies* 19 (1984), 85–96.

Fischer-Kattner, Anke, *Spuren der Begegnung. Europäische Reiseberichte über Afrika 1760–1860* (Göttingen: Vandenhoeck & Ruprecht, 2015).

Fitzpatrick, Matthew P., *Liberal Imperialism in Germany: Expansionism and Nationalism, 1848–1884* (New York: Berghahn Books, 2008).

Fitzpatrick, Matthew P., 'The Pre-History of the Holocaust? The Sonderweg and Historikerstreit Debates and the Abject Colonial Past', *Central European History* 41:3 (2008), 477–503.

Fitzpatrick, Matthew P., 'The Samoan Women's Revolt: Race, Intermarriage and Imperial Hierarchy in German Samoa', *German History* 35:2 (2017), 206–28.

Fletcher, Roger, *Revisionism and Empire. Socialist Imperialism in Germany, 1897–1914* (London: Allen & Unwin, 1984).

Flierl, Johann, *Als Pioniermissionar in das ferne Neu Guinea: Johann Flierls Lebenserinnerungen* (Wiesbaden: Harrassowitz Verlag, 2015).

Förderer, Gabriele, *Koloniale Grüße aus Samoa: Eine Diskursanalyse von deutschen, englischen und US-amerikanischen Reisebeschreibungen aus Samoa von 1860–1916* (Bielefeld: Transcript, 2017).

Forster, Johann Reinhold, *Observations Made during a Voyage round the World* (Honolulu: University of Hawai'i Press, 1996).

Foster, Robert, 'An Imaginary Dominion. The Representation and Treatment of Aborigines in South Australia 1834–1911' (PhD Dissertation, University of Adelaide, 1993).

Foster, Robert, *Social Reproduction and History in Melanesia: Mortuary Ritual, Gift-Exchange, and Custom in the Tanga Islands* (Cambridge: Cambridge University Press, 1995).

Foster, Robert, Hosking, Rick and Nettelbeck, Amanda, *Fatal Collisions* (Adelaide: Wakefield Press, 2001).

Foucault, Michel, *The Archaeology of Knowledge* (New York: Routledge, 2002).

Foucault, Michel, *The Order of Things: An Archaeology of the Human Sciences* (New York: Routledge, 2002).

Fouquet, Carlos, *Der deutsche Einwanderer und seine Nachkommen in Brasilien, 1808–1824–1974* (São Paulo: Instituto Hans Staden, 1974).

Francis, Daniel, *The Imaginary Indian: The Image of the Indian in Canadian Culture* (Vancouver: Arsenal Pulp Press, 1992).

Freytag, Walter (ed.), *Die junge Christenheit im Umbruch des Ostens: Vom Gehorsam des Glaubens unter den Völkern* (Berlin: Furche-Verlag, 1938).

Fricke, Dieter, *Handbuchzur Geschichte der deutschen Arbeiterbewegung 1869 bis 1917* (Berlin: Dietz, 1987).

Friedrichsmeyer, Sara, Lennox, Sara and Zantop, Susanne (eds), *The Imperialist Imagination. German Colonialism and Its Legacy* (Ann Arbor: University of Michigan Press, 1998).

Fröschle, Hartmut (ed.), *Die Deutschen in Lateinamerika: Schicksal und Leistung* (Tübingen: Erdmann, 1979).

Fuhrmann, Wolfgang, *Imperial Projections: Screening the German Colonies* (New York: Berghahn, 2015).

Gammage, Bill, *The Biggest Estate on Earth. How Aborigines Made Australia* (Sydney: Allen & Unwin, 2011).

Gardner, Helen B., *Gathering for God: George Brown in Oceania* (Dunedin: Otago University Press, 2006).

Gascoigne, John, *The Enlightenment and the Origins of European Australia* (Cambridge: Cambridge University Press, 2002).

Gascoigne, John, *Joseph Banks and the English Enlightenment* (Cambridge: Cambridge University Press, 1994).

Gehrts, Meg, *A Camera Actress in the Wilds of Togoland: The Adventures, Observations & Experiences of a Cinematograph Actress in West African Forests whilst Collecting Films Depicting Native Life and when Posing as the White Woman in Anglo-African Cinematograph Dramas* (London and Philadelphia: Seeley, 1915).

Gehrts, Meg, *Weiße Göttin der Wangora: Eine Filmschauspielerin 1913 in Afrika* (Wuppertal: Hammer, 1999).

Gerstäcker, Friedrich, *Reisen*, Vol. IV (Stuttgart an Tübingen: Cotta, 1854).

Gerwarth, Robert and Malinowski, Stephan, 'Hannah Arendt's Ghosts: Reflections on the Disputable Path from Windhoek to Auschwitz', *Central European History*, 42:2 (2009), 279–300.

Giblin, James Leonard, and Monson, Jamie (eds), *Maji Maji: Lifting the Fog of War* (Leiden: Brill, 2010).

Gills, Barry K. and Frank, Andre G., *The World System: Five Hundred Years or Five Thousand?* (London: Routledge, 1993).

Gironière, Paul P e la, *Twenty Years in the Philippines* (Manila: Filipiniana Book Guild, 1962 [first published: Paris 1854]).

Gordon, Sophie, *Cairo to Constantinople. Francis Bedford's Photographs of the Middle East* (London: Royal Collection Trust, 2013).

Gould, Stephen J., *The Mismeasure of Man* (New York: Norton, 1996).

Gray, Alastair C., 'Trading Contacts in the Bismarck Archipelago during the Whaling Era, 1799–1884', *Journal of Pacific History* 34:1 (1999), 23–43.

Grosse, Pascal, *Kolonialismus, Eugenik und bürgerliche Gesellschaft in Deutschland, 1850–1918* (Frankfurt am Main: Campus, 2000).

Grove, Richard, Damodaran, V. and Sangwan, S. (eds), *Nature and the Orient: The Environmental History of South and Southeast Asia* (New Delhi: Oxford University Press, 1998).

Gründer, Horst, *Geschichte der deutschen Kolonien* (Paderborn: Schöningh, 2004).

Grünzweig, Walter, *Das demokratische Kanaan: Charles Sealsfields Amerika im Kontext amerikanischer Literatur und Ideologie* (Munich: Fink, 1987).

Guettel, Jens-Uwe, 'From the Frontier to German South-West Africa: German Colonialism, Indians and American Westward Expansion', *Modern Intellectual History* 7:3 (2010), 523–52.

Guettel, Jens-Uwe, *German Expansionism, Imperial Liberalism, and the United States, 1776–1945* (Cambridge: Cambridge University Press, 2012).

Guettel, Jens-Uwe, 'The Myth of the Pro-Colonialist SPD: German Social Democracy and Imperialism before World War I', *Central European History* 45 (2012), 452–84.

Guha, Ranajit, *History at the Limit of World History* (New York: Columbia University Press, 2003).

Habinger, Gabriele, *Ida Pfeiffer: Eine Forschungsreisende des Biedermeier* (Vienna: Milena, 2004).

Hagner, Michael, 'Skulls, Brains, and Memorial Culture: On Cerebral Biographies of Scientists in the Nineteenth Century', *Science in Context* 16:1–2 (June 2003), 195–218.

Hanemann, Emil F., *Keys to the Papuan's Soul: Some Practices and Legends Current among the Natives of the Madang Mission Field, New Guinea* (Ohio: Lutheran Book Concern, 1935).

Hanke, Christine, *Zwischen Auflösung und Fixierung. Zur Konstitution von 'Rasse' und 'Geschlecht' in der physischen Anthropologie um 1900* (Bielefeld: Transcript, 2007).

Haridi, Alexander, *Das Paradigma der islamischen Zivilisation – oder die Begründung der deutschen Islamwissenschaft durch Carl Heinrich Becker (1876–1933). Eine wissenschaftsgeschichtliche Untersuchung* (Würzburg: Ergon, 2005).

Hausen, Karin (ed.), *Frauengeschichte – Geschlechtergeschichte* (Frankfurt am Main: Campus, 1992).

Heine, Peter, and von der Heyden, Ulrich (eds), *Studien zur Geschichte des deutschen Kolonialismus in Afrika: Festschrift zum 60. Geburtstag von Peter Sebald* (Pfaffenweiler: Centaurus, 1995).

Hemming, John, *Amazon Frontier: The Defeat of the Brazilian Indians* (London: Harvard University Press, 1987).

Hempenstall, Peter J., *Pacific Islanders under German Rule: A Study in the Meaning of Colonial Resistance* (Canberra: Australian National University Press, 1978).

Herder, Johann Gottfried, trans. Marcia Bunge, *Against Pure Reason: Writings on Religion, Language and History* (Eugene, OR: Wipf & Stock, 1993).

Herder, Johann Gottfried, *Ausgewählte Werke in einem Band* (Stuttgart and Tübingen: J.G. Cotta'scher Verlag, 1844).

Herder, Johann Gottfried, *Ideen zur Philosophie der Geschichte der Menschheit* (Berlin: Holzinger, 2013).

Herder, Johann Gottfried, trans. Michael N. Forster, *Philosophical Writings* (Cambridge: Cambridge University Press, 2002).

Hermann, Elfriede (ed.), *Changing Contexts, Shifting Meanings: Transformations of Cultural Traditions in Oceania* (Honolulu: University of Hawai'i Press, 2011).

Hiery, Hermann J. (ed.), *Die deutsche Südsee 1884–1914. Ein Handbuch* (Paderborn, Munich, Vienna and Zürich: Ferdinand Schöningh, 2001).

Hiery, Hermann J., *The Neglected War: The German South Pacific and the Influence of World War I* (Honolulu: University of Hawai'i Press, 1995).

Hine, Robert V. and Faragher, John Mack, *The American West: A New Interpretive History* (New Haven: Yale University Press, 2000).

Hodkinson, James and Walker, John, with Muzamdar, Shaswati and Feichtinger, Johannes (eds), *Deploying Orientalism in Culture and History* (Rochester, NY: Camden House, 2013).

Holleuffer, Henriette von and Wimmer, Adi (eds), *Australien: Realität – Klischee – Vision* (Trier: Wissenschaftlicher Verlag Trier, 2012).

Honold, Alexander and Simons, Oliver (eds), *Kolonialismus als Kultur: Literatur, Medien, Wissenschaft in der deutschen Gründerzeit des Fremden* (Tübingen: Francke, 2002).

Howes, Hilary, 'Between Wealth and Poverty: Otto Finsch on Mabuyag, 1881', *Memoirs of the Queensland Museum – Culture* 8:1 (2015), 221–51.

Howes, Hilary S., *The Race Question in Oceania: A.B. Meyer and Otto Finsch between Metropolitan Theory and Field Experience, 1865–1914* (Frankfurt am Main: Peter Lang, 2013).

Huber, Valeska, *Channelling Mobilities: Migration and Globalisation in the Suez Canal Region and Beyond* (Cambridge: Cambridge University Press, 2013).

Hull, Isabel V., *Absolute Destruction. Military Culture and the Practices of War in Imperial Germany* (Ithaca and London: Cornell University Press, 2005).

Hulme, Peter and Youngs, Tim (eds), *The Cambridge Companion to Travel Writing* (Cambridge: Cambridge University Press, 2002).

Hunt, Shelley Leigh and Kelly, Alexander, *Tropical Trials. A Handbook for Women in the Tropics* (London: W.H. Allen, 1883).

Hyam, Ronald, *Understanding the British Empire* (Cambridge: Cambridge University Press, 2010).

Hyrkkänen, Markku, *Sozialistische Kolonialpolitik. Eduard Bernsteins Stellung zur Kolonialpolitik und zum Imperialismus 1882–1914* (Helsinki: SHS, 1986).

Ihering, Hermann von, 'Os Botocudos de Rio Doce', *Revista do Museu Paulista* 8 (1910), 38–51.

Inda, Jonathon Xavier, 'Performativity, Materiality and the Racial Body', *Latino Studies Journal* 11:3 (2000), 74–99.

Jacobson, Ken, *Odalisques & Arabesques. Orientalist Photography* (London: Quaritch, 2007).

Jagor, Fedor, *Reisen in den Philippinen* (Berlin: Weidmannsche Buchhandlung, 1873).

Janiewicz, Stephen, 'Orientalists in Love: Intimacy, Empire and Cross-Cultural Knowledge', *Journal of World History* 23:2 (2012), 345–73.

Jebens, Holger (ed.), *Cargo, Cult & Culture Critique* (Honolulu: University of Hawai'i Press, 2004).

Jedamski, Doris, Jehle, H. and Siebert, U. (eds), 'Und tät das Reisen wählen!': Frauenreisen, Reisefrauen (Zürich: EFeF, 1994).

Jensz, Felicity, German Moravian Missionaries in the British Colony of Victoria, Australia, 1848–1908. Influential Strangers (Leiden: Brill, 2010).

Keane, Webb, Christian Moderns: Freedom and Fetish in the Mission Encounter (Berkeley: University of California Press, 2007).

Keane, Webb, 'Semiotics and the Social Analysis of Material Things', Language & Communication 23 (2003), 409–25.

Kennedy, Paul M, The Samoan Triangle: A Study in Anglo-German-American Relations, 1878–1900 (Dublin: Irish University Press, 1974).

Kerber, Linda K. 'Separate Spheres, Female Worlds, Woman's Place: The Rhetoric of Women's History', Journal of American History 75:1 (1988), 9–39.

Keyßer, Christian, Eine Papuagemeinde (Kassel: Bärenreiter-Verlag, 1929).

King, Richard, 'The (Mis)uses of Cannibalism in Contemporary Cultural Critique', Diacritics 30:1 (2000), 106–23.

Kingsley, Mary H., Travels in West Africa: With an Introduction by Anthony Brandt (Washington: National Geographic Society, 2002).

Klein, Kerwin Lee, 'In Search of Narrative Mastery: Postmodernism and the People without History', History and Theory, 34:4 (1995), 275–98.

Klein-Arendt, Reinhardt, 'Kamina ruft Nauen!': Die Funkstellen in den deutschen Kolonien 1904–1918 (Cologne Herbst, 1996).

Knoll, Arthur J. and Gann, Lewis H. (eds), Germans in the Tropics: Essays in German Colonial History (New York: Greenwood Press, 1987).

Koepping, Klaus-Peter, Adolf Bastian and the Psychic Unity of Mankind (St Lucia: University of Queensland Press).

Kontje, Todd, German Orientalism (Ann Arbor: University of Michigan Press, 2004).

Kozma, Liat, Schayegh, Cyrus and Wishnitzer, Avner (eds), A Global Middle East: Mobility, Materiality and Culture in the Modern Age, 1880–1940 (London and New York: IB Tauris, 2015).

Kramer, Paul A., The Blood of Government: Race, Empire, the United States, and the Philippines (Quezon City: Ateneo de Manila University Press, 2006).

Kreimeier, Klaus and Ehmann, A. (eds), Geschichte des dokumentarischen Films in Deutschland: Band 2 Weimarer Republik (1918–1933) (Stuttgart: Reclam, 2005).

Kriegleder, Wynfrid, 'The American Indian in German Novels up to the 1850s', German Life and Letters 53:4 (2000), 487–98.

Kriegleder, Wynfrid, Vorwarts in der Vergangenheit. Das Bild der USA im deutschsprachigen Roman von 1776–1855 (Tübingen: Stauffenburg, 1999).

Kriegleder, Wynfrid and Pogatschnigg, Gustav-Adolf (eds), Literarische Narrationen der Migration Europa – Nordamerika im 19. Jahrhundert (Vienna: Praesens Verlag, 2012).

Krüger, Gesine, Kriegsbewältigung und Geschichtsbewußtsein. Realität, Deutung und Verarbeitung des deutschen Kolonialkriegs in Namibia 1904 bis 1907 (Göttingen: Vandenhoeck & Ruprecht, 1999).

Krumpelmann, John T., 'Tokeah, the First English-Language Novel in Our Southwest', The South Central Bulletin 28:4 (1968), 142–3.

Kuss, Susanne (ed.), *Carl Heinrich Becker in China. Reisebriefe des ehemaligen preußischen Kultusministers 1931/32* (Münster: Lit, 2004).

Kuss, Susanne, trans. Andrew Smith, *German Colonial Wars and the Context of Military Violence* (Cambridge, MA: Harvard University Press, 2017).

Laak, Dirk van, *Über Alles in der Welt: Deutscher Imperialismus im 19. Und 20. Jahrhundert* (Munich: Beck, 2005).

Lahti, Janne, 'German Colonialism and the Age of Global Empires', *Journal of Colonialism and Colonial History* 17:1 (2016), DOI: 10.1353/cch.2016.0015.

Langbehn, Volker, Mohammed Salama (eds). *German Colonialism. Race, the Holocaust and Postwar Germany* (New York: Columbia University Press, 2011).

Laroque, Luis Fernando, *Lideranças Kaingang no Brasil Meridional (1808–1889)* (São Leopoldo: Instituto Anchietano de Pesquisas, 2000).

Lazarus, Neil, 'What Postcolonial Theory Doesn't Say', *Race and Class* 53:3 (2011), 3–27.

Lee, Emily S., 'The Epistemology of the Question of Authenticity, in Place of Strategic Essentialism', *Hypatia* 26:2 (2011), 258–79.

Legarda, Benito J., *After the Galleons: Foreign Trade, Economic Change and Entrepreneurship in the Nineteenth-Century Philippines* (Quezon City: Ateneo de Manila University Press, 1999).

Lehner, Stephan, 'Märchen und Sagen des Melanesierstammes der Bukawac', *Baessler-Archiv Sonderabdruck aus Band XIV*, 2 (1931), 35–72.

Lenoir, Timothy, 'The Göttingen School and the Development of Transcendental *Naturphilosophie* in the Romantic Era', *Studies in the History of Biology* 5 (1981), 111–205.

Lepper, Verena M. (ed.), *Karl Richard Lepsius: der Begründer der deutschen Ägyptologie* (Berlin: Kadmos, 2012).

Lethen, Helmut, *Der Schatten des Fotografen. Bilder und ihre Wirklichkeit* (Reinbeck: Rowohlt, 2014).

Levene, Mark, 'The Chittagong Hill Tracts: A Case Study in the Political Economy of "Creeping" Genocide', *Third World Review* 20:2 (1999), 339–69.

Lewis, Alison, Anderson, Lara and Benbow, Heather Merle (eds), *Other Encounters: European Writers and Gender in Transnational Context* (St Ingbert: Röhrig Universitätsverlag, 2014).

Lewis, Albert, *Melanesian Shell Money in Field Museum Collections* (Chicago: Field Museum of Natural History, 1929).

Lindner, Ulrike, *Koloniale Begegnungen: Deutschland und Großbritannien als Imperialmächte in Afrika, 1880–1914* (Frankfurt am Main: Campus, 2011).

Lohmeyer, Julius (ed.), *Unter dem Dreizack. Neues Marine- und Kolonialbuch für Jung und Alt* (Bielefeld and Leipzig: Velhagen & Klasing, 1902).

Loosen, Livia, *Deutsche Frauen in den Südsee-Kolonien des Kaiserreichs: Alltag und Beziehungen zur indigenen Bevölkerung, 1884–1919* (Bielefeld: transcript, 2014).

Low, Rachael, *The History of British Film Vol. 2: The History of British Film, 1906–1914* (London: Routledge, 1997).

Lubrich, Oliver and Clark, Rex, 'German Studies Go Postcolonial', *Eighteenth-Century Studies* 35:4 (2002), 625–34.

Luttikhuis, Bart and Moses, Dirk, 'Mass Violence and the End of the Dutch Colonial Empire in Indonesia', *Journal of Genocide Research* 14:3–4 (2012), 257–76.

Lydon, Jane (ed.), *Calling the Shots. Aboriginal Photographies* (Canberra: Aboriginal Studies Press, 2014).

MacLeitch, Gail D., *Imperial Entanglements: Iroquois Change and Persistence on the Frontiers of Empire* (Philadelphia: University of Pennsylvania Press, 2011).

Madley, Benjamin, *An American Genocide: The United States and the California Indian Catastrophe* (New Haven: Yale University Press, 2016).

Madley, Benjamin, 'From Africa to Auschwitz: How German South West Africa Incubated Ideas and Methods Adopted and Developed by the Nazis in Eastern Europe', *European History Quarterly* 35:3 (2005), 429–64.

Malmkjær, Kirsten (ed.), *The Linguistics Encyclopaedia* (London: Routledge, 1991).

Mamozai, Martha, *Schwarze Frau, weiße Herrin: Frauenleben in den deutschen Kolonien* (Reinbek: Rowohlt, 1989).

Mangold, Sabine, *'Eine weltbürgerliche Wissenschaft': die deutsche Orientalistik im 19. Jahrhundert* (Stuttgart: Franz Steiner, 2004).

Mann, Günter and Dumont, F. (eds), *Die Natur des Menschen. Probleme der physischen Anthropologie und Rassenkunde (1750–1850)* (Stuttgart: Gustav Fischer Verlag, 1990).

Marchand, Suzanne, *German Orientalism in the Age of Empire: Religion, Race and Scholarship* (Cambridge: Cambridge University Press, 2009).

Marchand, Suzanne, 'Popularizing the Orient', *Intellectual History Review* 17 (2007), 175–202.

Martin, Laura (ed.), *Harmony in Discord: German Women Writers in the Eighteenth and Nineteenth Centuries* (Frankfurt am Main: Peter Lang, 2001).

Maxwell, Alexander and Davis, Sacha E., 'Germanness beyond Germany: Collective Identity in German Diaspora Communities', *German Studies Review* 39:1 (2016), 1–15.

Maxwell, Ann, *Colonial Photography and Exhibitions: Representations of the 'Native' People and the Making of European Identities* (London: Leicester University Press, 1999).

McClintock, Anne, *Imperial Leather: Race, Gender and Sexuality in the Colonial Contest* (New York: Routledge, 1995).

McClintock, Anne, Mufti, A. and Shohat, E. (eds), *Dangerous Liaisons: Gender, Nation, and Postcolonial Perspectives* (Minneapolis: University of Minnesota Press, 2004).

McCluer Stevens, C.L., *Famous Crimes and Criminals* (London: Stanley Pauls, 1924).

McFarland, Rob and James, Michelle Stott (eds), *Sophie Discovers Amerika: German Speaking Women Write the New World* (Rochester, NY: Camden House, 2014).

McGrath, Ann, *Illicit Love: Interracial Sex and Marriage in the United States and Australia* (Lincoln: University of Nebraska Press, 2015).

McGregor, William B., 'Missionary Linguistics in the Kimberley, Western Australia: A History of the First Seventy Years', *Historiographia Linguistica* 30:1 (2008), 121–62.

Meigs, J.A., *Catalogue of Human Crania in the Collection of the Academy of Natural Sciences of Philadelphia* (Philadelphia: J.B. Lippincott & Co., 1857).

Meijer, Miriam C., *Race and Aesthetics in the Anthropology of Petrus Camper (1722–1789)* (Amsterdam: Rodopi, 1999).

Michaelis, Kristina and Morgenstern, Ulf (eds), *Kaufleute, Kosmopoliten, Kunstmäzene: Die Gelnhäuser Großbürgerfamilien Becker und Schöffer* (Hamburg: Am Goldenen Fuss, 2013).

Midgley, Clare, *Feminism and Empire: Women Activists in Imperial Britain, 1790–1865* (London: Routledge, 2008).

Mojares, Resil B., *Brains of the Nation: Pedro Paterno, T.H. Pardo de Tavera, Isabelo de los Reyes and the Production of Modern Knowledge* (Quezon City: Ateneo de Manila University Press, 2006).

Möller, D., *Die Geschichte der Anthropologischen Sammlung Freiburg. Entstehung, Zusammenführung, Verlust* (Marburg: Tectum Verlag, 2015).

Monteath, Peter (ed.), *Australia. Friedrich Gerstäcker. A German Traveller in the Age of Gold* (Mile End: Wakefield Press, 2016).

Morgenroth, Matthias, *Nachrichten aus dem Land der Gegenfüßler: Untersuchungen zur deutschen Australienliteratur* (Tübingen: Stauffenberg, 2001).

Morlang, Thomas, *Askari und Fitafita: 'Farbige' Söldner in den deutschen Kolonien* (Berlin: Ch. Links, 2008).

Morlang, Thomas, *Rebellion in der Südsee: Der Aufstand auf Ponape gegen die deutschen Kolonialherren 1910/11* (Berlin: Ch. Links, 2010).

Moses, A. Dirk (ed.), *Empire, Colony, Genocide: Conquest, Occupation, and Subaltern Resistance in World History* (New York: Berghahn, 2008).

Moses, A. Dirk (ed.), *Genocide and Settler Society: Frontier Violence and Stolen Indigenous Children in Australian History* (New York: Berghahn, 2004).

Mosko, Mark, 'Partible Penitents: Dividual Personhood and Christian Practice in Melanesia and the West', *The Journal of the Royal Anthropological Institute* 16:2 (2010), 215–40.

Motadel, David (ed.), *Islam and the European Empires* (Oxford: Oxford University Press, 2014).

Mückler, Hermann, *Kolonialismus in Ozeanien* (Vienna: facultas.wuv, 2012).

Muijzenberg, Otto van den, *The Philippines through European Lenses: Late 19th Century Photographs from the Meerkamp van Embden Collection* (Quezon City: Ateneo de Manila University Press, 2008).

Müller, Guido, *Weltpolitische Bildung und Reform. Carl Heinrich Beckers Wissenschafts- und Hochschulpolitik 1908–1930* (Cologne: Böhlau Verlag, 1991).

Müller, Sven O. and Torp, Cornelius (eds), *Das deutsche Kaiserreich in der Kontroverse* (Göttingen: Vandenhoeck & Ruprecht, 2009).

Mundt, Theodor, *Geschichte der Literatur der Gegenwart* (Berlin: M. Simion, 1842).

Nacke, Aneliese, Renk, Arlene, Piovazana, Leonal and Sens Bloemer, Neusa Maria (eds), *Os kaingang no oeste catarinense: tradição e atualidade* (Chapecó: Argos, 2007).

Nagl, Tobias, *Die unheimliche Maschine: Rasse und Repräsentation im Weimarer Kino* (Munich: Edition Text + Kritik, 2009).

Namem, Alexandro Machado, *Indios botocudos: uma reconstituição histórica do contacto* (Florianópolis: Editora da UFSC, 1991).

Naranch, Bradley and Eley, Geoff (eds), *German Colonialism in a Global Age* (Durham, NC, and London: Duke University Press, 2014).

Nelson, Cary and Grossberg, L. (eds), *Marxism and the Interpretation of Culture* (Urbana: University of Illinois Press, 1988).

Nery, John, *Revolutionary Spirit: Jose Rizal in Southeast Asia* (Quezon City: Ateneo de Manila University Press, 2011).

Neuhauss, Richard, *Deutsch Neu-Guinea*, 3 vols (Berlin: Dietrich Reimer, 1911).

Neumann, K., *Not the Way It Really Was: Constructing the Tolai Past* (Honolulu: University of Hawai'i Press, 1992).

Noyes, John K., 'Commerce, Ccolonialism, and the Globalization of Action in Late Enlightenment Germany', *Postcolonial Studies* 9:1 (2006), 81–98.

O'Brien, Sean Michael, *In Bitterness and in Tears: Andrew Jackson's Destruction of the Creeks and Seminoles* (Westport: Praeger, 2003).

O'Donnell, Krista, Bridenthal, Renate and Reagin, Nancy (eds), *The Heimat Abroad: The Boundaries of Germanness* (Ann Arbor: University of Michigan Press, 2005).

Oermann, Nils Ole, *Mission, Church and State Relations in South West Africa under German Rule (1884–1915)* (Stuttgart: Franz Steiner Verlag, 1999).

Oguntoye, K., *Eine afro-deutsche Geschichte: Zur Lebenssituation von Afrikanern und Afro-Deutschen in Deutschland von 1884–1950* (Berlin: Hoho, 1997).

Olmos, Fernández M. and Paravisini-Gebert, L., *Creole Religions of the Caribbean: An Introduction from Vodou and Santería to Obeah and Espiritismo* (New York: New York University Press, 2011).

Oloukpona-Yinnon, A. P. (ed.), *Reiseliteratur und Wahrnehmung der Fremdheit am Beispiel Afrikas* (Lome: Presses de L'UL, 2011).

Orr, Deborah, McCalister, Linda Lopez, Kahl, Eileen and Earle, Kathleen, *Belief, Bodies, and Being: Feminist Reflections on Embodiment* (Oxford: Rowman & Littlefield, 2006).

Osborne, Myles and Kent, Susan Kngsley, *Africans and Britons in the Age of Empire, 1660–1980* (London and New York: Routledge, 2015).

Pahuja, Sundhya, *Decolonising International Law: Development, Economic Growth and the Politics of Universality* (Cambridge: Cambridge University Press, 2011).

Parkinson, Richard, *Dreißig Jahre in der Südsee. Land und Leute, Sitten und Gebräuche im Bismarckarchipel* (Stuttgart: Strecker & Schröder, 1907).

Parkinson, Richard, *Thirty Years in the South Seas: Land and People, Customs and Traditions in the Bismarck Archipelago* (Sydney: Sydney University Press, 2010).

Paul, Gerhard (ed.), *Visual History: Ein Studienbuch* (Göttingen: Vandenhoeck & Ruprecht, 2006).

Paula Souza, Geraldo H. de, 'Notas sobre uma visita a acampamentos de Índios Caingangs', *Revista do Museu Paulista* 10 (1918), 739–58.

Penny, H. Glenn, 'Elusive Authenticity: The Quest for the Authentic Indian in German Public Culture', *Comparative Studies in Society and History* 48:4 (2006), 798–819.

Penny, H. Glenn, 'German Polycentrism and the Writing of History', *German History* 30:2 (2012), 265–82.

Penny, H. Glenn, *Kindred by Choice: Germans and American Indians since 1800* (Chapel Hill: University of North Carolina Press, 2013).

Penny, H. Glenn, 'Latin American Connections: Recent Work on German Interactions with Latin America', *Central European History* 46:2 (2013), 362–94.

Penny, H. Glenn, 'The Politics of Anthropology in the Age of Empire: German Colonists, Brazilian Indians, and the Case of Alberto Vojtěch Frič', *Comparative Studies in Society and HIstory*, 45:2 (2003), 249–80.

Penny, H. Glenn and Bunzl, Matti (eds). *Worldly Provincialism* (Ann Arbor: University of Michigan Press, 2003).

Perras, Arne, *Carl Peters and German Imperialism, 1856–1918. A Political Biography* (Oxford: Oxford University Press, 2004).

Pesek, Michael, *Koloniale Herrschaft in Deutsch-Ostafrika: Expeditionen, Militär und Verwaltung seit 1880* (Frankfurt am Main: Campus, 2005).

Pilhofer, D. Georg, *Die Geschichte der Neuendettelsauer Mission in Neuguinea: Von den ersten Anfängen bis zum Kriegsausbruch 1914* (Neuendettelsau: Freimund, 1961).

Pratt, Marie Louise, *Imperial Eyes: Travel Writing and Transculturation* (New York: Routledge, 1992).

Presland, Gary, *The Land of the Kulin. Discovering the Lost Land-Scape and the First People of Port Phillip* (Fitzroy: McPhee Gribble Publishers, 1985).

Pugach, Sara, *Africa in Translation: A History of Colonial Linguistics in Germany and Beyond, 1814–1945* (Ann Arbor: University of Michigan Press, 2012).

Quibuyen, Floro C., *A Nation Aborted: Rizal, American Hegemony, and Philippine Nationalism* (Quezon City: Ateneo de Manila University Press, 2008).

Ratke, David C., *Confession and Mission, Word and Sacrament: The Ecclesial Theology of Wilhelm Löhe* (St Louis: Concordia, 1989).

Reagin, Nancy R., 'The Imagined Hausfrau: National Identity, Domesticity, and Colonialism in Imperial Germany', *Journal of Modern History* 73:1 (2001), 54–86.

Reagin, Nancy R., *Sweeping the German Nation: Domesticity and National Identity in Germany, 1870–1945* (Cambridge: Cambridge University Press, 2007).

Reinhard, Wolfgang (ed.), *Imperialistische Kontinuität und nationale Ungeduld im 19. Jahrhundert* (Frankfurt am Main: Fischer, 1991).

Reinkowski, Maurus and Thum, Gregor (eds), *Helpless Imperialists: Imperial Failure, Fear and Radicalization* (Göttingen: Vandenhoeck & Ruprecht, 2012).

Retzius, Anders, 'Ueber die Schädelformen der Nordbewohner', *Archiv für Anatomie, Physiologie und wissenschaftliche Medicin* (1845), 48–129.

SELECT BIBLIOGRAPHY

Reynolds, Henry, *Frontier. Aborigines, Settlers and Land* (St Leonards, NSW: Allen and Unwin, 1996).

Rischbieter, Laura Julia, *Mikro-Ökonomie der Globalisierung. Kaffee, Kaufleute und Konsumenten im Kaiserreich 1870 – 1914* (Cologne: Böhlau Verlag, 2011).

Ritz-Deutch, Ute, 'Alberto Vojtěch Frič, the German Diaspora, and Indian Protection in Southern Brazil, 1900–1920: A Transatlantic Ethno-Historical Case Study' (PhD Dissertation, Binghamton University, 2008).

Roche, Sophie von La, *Erscheinungen am See Oneida* (Eschborn: Dietmar Klotz, 1995).

Rockwell, Stephen J., *Indian Affairs and the Administrative State in the Nineteenth Century* (Cambridge, Cambridge University Press, 2010).

Roes, Aldwin, 'Towards a History of Mass Violence in the Etat Indépendant du Congo, 1885–1908', *South African Historical Journal* 62:4 (2010), 634–70.

Rottenburg, Richard, Schnepel, B. and Shimada, S. (eds), *The Making and Unmaking of Differences* (Bielefeld: transcript, 2006)

Ruppenthal, Jens, *Kolonialismus als Wissenschaft und Technik. Das Hamburgische Kolonialinstitut 1908 bis 1919* (Stuttgart: Steiner, 2007).

Russell, Lynette (ed.), *Colonial Frontiers: Indigenous-European Encounters in Settler Societies* (Manchester: Manchester University Press, 2001).

Saage, Richard, *Zwischen Darwin und Marx. Zur Rezeption der Evolutionstheorie in der deutschen und der österreichischen Sozialdemokratie vor 1933/34* (Vienna, Cologne and Weimar: Böhlau, 2012).

Sabrow, Martin (ed.), *ZeitRäume. Potsdamer Almanach* (Berlin: Transit, 2008).

Sack, P. and Clark, D. (ed. and trans.), *Eduard Hernsheim: South Sea Merchant* (Boroko: Institute of Papua New Guinea Island Studies, 1993).

Said, Edward W., *Culture and Imperialism* (New York: Knopf, 1994).

Saldanha, Arun, 'Reontologising Race: The Machinic Geography of Phenotype', *Environment and Planning D: Society and Space* 24 (2006), 9–24.

Sammons, Jeffrey L., *Ideology, Mimesis, Fantasy: Charles Sealsfield, Friedrich Gerstäcker, Karl May and Other German Novelists of America* (Chapel Hill: University of North Carolina Press, 1998).

Samson, Jane, *Imperial Benevolence: Making British Authority in the Pacific Islands* (Honolulu: University of Hawai'i Press, 1998).

Schaaffhausen, Hermann (ed.), *Die anthropologischen Sammlungen Deutschlands* Vol. 3 (Braunschweig: Vieweg & Sohn 1880).

Schaeder, Hans Heinrich, *C.H. Becker. Ein Gedenkbuch* (Göttingen: Vandenhoeck & Ruprecht, 1950).

Schaer, Bernhard C., *Tropenliebe. Schweizer Naturforscher und niederländischer Imperialismus in Südostasien um 1900* (Frankfurt am Main: Campus, 2015).

Schestokat, Karin U., 'German Women in Cameroon: Travelogues from Colonial Times' (PhD Dissertation, University of Southern California, 1995).

Schnee, Heinrich (ed.), *Deutsches Kolonial-Lexikon* (Leipzig: Quelle & Meyer, 1920), Vol. 3.

Schneider Nonnenmacher, Marisa, *Aldeamentos Kaingang no Rio Grande do Sul: Século XIX* (Porto Alegre: EDIPUCRS, 2000).

Schomburgk, Hans, *Bwakukama: Fahrten und Forschungen mit Büchse und Film im unbekannten Afrika* (Berlin: Deutsch-Literarisches Institut, 1922).

Schönig, Claus (ed.), *Türkisch-deutsche Beziehungen: Perspektiven aus Vergangenheit und Gegenwart* (Berlin: Klaus Schwarz Verlag, 2012).

Schröder, Hans-Christoph, *Gustav Noske und die Kolonialpolitik des Deutschen Kaiserreichs* (Berlin and Bonn: J.H.W. Dietz Nachf., 1979).

Schröder, Hans-Christoph, *Sozialismus und Imperialismus* (Hanover: Verlag für Literatur und Zeitgeschehen, 1968).

Schult, Volker, 'Sultans and Adventurers: German Blockade-runners in the Sulu Archipelago', *Philippine Studies* 50:3 (2002), 395–415.

Schulze, Frederik, *Auswanderung als nationalistisches Projekt: 'Deutschtum' und Kolonialdiskurse im südlichen Brasilien (1824–1941)* (Cologne: Böhlau, 2016).

Schwanitz, Wolfgang (ed.), *Germany and the Middle East 1871–1945* (Princeton: Wiener, 2004).

Scott, Michael W., 'Neither "New Melanesian History" nor "New Melanesian Ethnography": Recovering Emplaced Matrilineages in Southeast Solomon Islands', *Oceania* 77:3 (2007), 337–54.

Sebald, Peter, *Eine Geschichte der deutschen 'Musterkolonie' auf der Grundlage amtlicher Quellen* (Berlin: Akademie, 1988).

Segal, R., *Myth: A Very Short Introduction* (Oxford: Oxford University Press, 2004).

Semper, Carl, *Die Palau-Inseln im Stillen Ozean: Reiseerlebnisse* (Leipzig: Brockhaus, 1873).

Semper, Carl, *Die Philippinen und ihre Bewohner: Sechs Skizzen nach einem im Frankfurter geographischen Verein 1868 gehaltenen Cyclus von Vorträgen* (Würzburg: Stuber, 1869).

Semper, Carl, *Reisen im Archipel der Philippinen: Wissenschaftliche Resultate, Zweiter Theil: Ergänzungsheft* (Wiesbaden: Kreidel, 1895).

Semper, Carl, 'Reisen durch die nördlichen Provinzen der Insel Luzon', *Zeitschrift für allgemeine Erdkunde* 13 (1862), 81–96.

Semper, Karl, *Animal Life as Affected by the Natural Conditions of Existence* (New York: Appleton, 1881).

Shaw, A.G.L., *A History of the Port Phillip District. Victoria before Separation* (Carlton: Melbourne University Press, 2006).

Shell-Duncan, B. and Hernlund, Y. (eds), *Female 'Circumcision' in Africa: Culture, Controversy, and Change* (Boulder: Lynne Rienner, 2000).

Short, John Philip, *Magic Lantern Empire. Colonialism and Society in Germany* (Ithaca and London: Cornell University Press, 2012).

Sidebotham, Steven E., Hense, Martin and Nouwens, Hendrikje M., *The Red Land. The Illustrated Archeology of Egypt's Eastern Desert* (Cairo: American University in Cairo Press, 2008).

Silva, Simoens da, *A Tribu Caingang* (Rio de Janeiro: Alba, 1930).

Silva Selau, Mauricio da, 'A ocupação do território Xokleng pelos imigrantes italianos no Sul Catarinense (1875–1925): Resistência e Extermínio' (MA Thesis, Universidade Federal de Santa Catarina, Florianópolis, 2006).

Simet, Jacob L., Tabu: 'Analysis of a Tolai Ritual Object' (PhD Dissertation, The Australian National University, 1991).

Simons, Oliver, '"Amerika gibt es nicht": On the Semiotics of Literary America in the Twentieth Century', *German Quarterly* (2009), 196–211.

Smith, Bernard, *European Vision and the South Pacific* (Sydney: Harper and Row, 1985).

Smith, Woodruff, *The German Colonial Empire* (Chapel Hill: University of North Carolina Press, 1978).

Soemmering, S.T., *Über die körperliche Verschiedenheit des Mohren vom Europäer* (Mainz, 1784).

Sokolowsky, C., *Sprachenpolitik des deutschen Kolonialismus: Deutschunterricht als Mittel imperialer Herrschaftssicherung in Togo (1884–1914)* (Stuttgart: Ibidem, 2004).

Soodalter, Ron, 'On Removing Seminioles: Andrew Jackson's Policy of "Indian Removal" Ran in to Trouble in Florida – His Name was Osceola', *Military History* 29.2 (2012), 62–9.

Sperber, Jonathan, *The Kaiser's Voters. Electors and Elections in Imperial Germany* (Cambridge: Cambridge University Press, 1997).

Spieth, J. and Amoaku, W.K., *The Ewe People: A Study of the Ewe People in German Togo* (Accra: Sub-Saharan Publishers, 2011).

Spivak, Gayatri Chakravorty, *A Critique of Postcolonial Reason: Towards a History of the Vanishing Present* (Cambridge, MA: Harvard University Press, 1999), pp. 269–74.

Stadler, Jürgen, *Die Missionspraxis Christian Keyßers in Neuguinea 1899–1920: Erste Schritte auf dem Weg zu einer einheimischen Kirche* (Nuremberg: VTR, 2006).

Stargardt, Nicholas, *The German Idea of Militarism. Radical and Socialist Critics, 1866–1914* (Cambridge: Cambridge University Press, 1994).

Steevens, George W., *With Kitchener to Khartum* (London: Dodd, 1898).

Steffen, Paul, *Missionsbeginn in Neuguinea: Die Anfänge der Rheinischen, Neuendettelsauer und Steyler Missionsarbeit in Neuguinea* (Nettetal: Steyler Verlag, 1995).

Steindorff, Georg, *Die Blütezeit des Pharaonenreichs* (Bielefeld-Leipzig: Velhagen & Klasing, 1900).

Steinmetz, George, *The Devil's Handwriting. Precoloniality and the German Colonial State in Qingdao, Samoa, and Southwest Africa* (Chicago, London: University of Chicago Press, 2007).

Stern, Fritz, *Gold and Iron: Bismarck, Bleichröder, and the Building of the German Empire* (London: Allen & Unwin, 1977).

Steward, Julian H. (ed.), *Handbook of South American Indians, vol 1, The Marginal Tribes* (Washington: Cooper Square Publishers, 1946).

Stiegler, Bernd and Thürlemann, Felix (eds), *Orientbilder: Fotografien 1850–1910* (Frankfurt am Main: Weissbooks, 2015).

Stocking, George W., Jr, *Race, Culture and Evolution. Essays in the History of Anthropology* (New York: The Free Press, 1968).

Stocking, George W. (ed.). *Volksgeist as Method and Ethic: Essays on Boasian Ethnography and the German Anthropological Tradition* (Madison: University of Wisconsin Press, 1998).

Stoecker, Holger, Schnalke, T. and Winkelmann, A. (eds), *Sammeln, Forschen, Zurückgeben. Menschliche Gebeine aus der Kolonialzeit in akademischen und musealen Sammlungen* (Berlin: Ch. Links, 2013).

Stoler, Ann Laura, *Along the Archival Grain: Epistemic Anxieties and Colonial Common Sense* (Princeton: Princeton University Press, 2009).

Stoler, Ann Laura., 'Colonial Archives and the Arts of Governance', *Archival Science* 2:1 (2002), 103–9.

Stornig, Katharina, *Sisters Crossing Boundaries: German Missionary Nuns in Colonial Togo and New Guinea, 1897–1960* (Göttingen: Vandenhoek & Ruprecht, 2013).

Strathern, Marilyn, *The Gender of the Gift: Problems with Women and Problems with Society in Melanesia* (Berkeley: University of California Press, 1988).

Struck, Wolfgang, *Die Eroberung der Phantasie: Kolonialismus, Literatur und Film zwischen deutschem Kaiserreich und Weimarer Republik* (Göttingen: Vandenhoeck & Ruprecht, 2010).

Stuchtey, Benedikt and Wende, Peter (eds), *British and German Historiography 1750–1950* (Oxford: Oxford University Press, 2000).

El-Tayeb, F., *Schwarze Deutsche: Der Diskurs um 'Rasse' und nationale Identität 1890–1933* (Frankfurt am Main: Campus, 2001).

Teschauer, Carl, 'Die Caingang oder Coroados-Indianer im brasilianischen Staate Rio Grande do Sul', *Anthropos* 9 (1914), 16–35.

Theye, Thomas, *Wir und die Wilde. Einblicke in eine kannibalische Beziehung* (Reinbek: Rowohlt, 1985).

Thomas, Megan C., *Orientalists, Propagandists and Ilustrados: Filipino Scholarship and the End of Spanish Colonialism* (Minneapolis: University of Minnesota Press, 2012).

Thomas, Nicholas, *Discoveries: The Voyages of Captain Cook* (London: Penguin Books, 2004).

Thomas, Nicholas, *Entangled Objects: Exchange, Material Culture, and Colonialism in the Pacific* (Cambridge, MA: Harvard University Press, 1991).

Thompson, T. Jack, *Light on Darkness? Missionary Photography of Africa in the Nineteenth and Early Twentieth Century* (Grand Rapids and Cambridge: WB Eerdmans, 2012).

Tilley, Helen (ed.), *Ordering Africa. Anthropology, European Imperialism, and the Politics of Knowledge* (Manchester: Manchester University Press, 2007).

Tombini Wittmann, Luisa, *O vapor e o botoque: Imigrantes alemães e índios Xokleng no Vale do Itajaí/SC (1850–1926)* (Florianópolis: Letras Contemporâneas, 2007).

Torrence, Robin and Clarke, Anne (eds), *The Archaeology of Difference: Negotiating Cross-Cultural Engagements in Oceania* (London: Routledge, 2000).

Trotha, T. von, *Koloniale Herrschaft: Zur soziologischen Theorie der Staatsentstehung am Beispiel des 'Schutzgebietes' Togo* (Tübingen: J.C.B. Mohr, 1994).

Trümpler, Charlotte (ed.), *Das Große Spiel. Archäologie und Politik zur Zeit des Kolonialismus (1860–1940)* (Essen: DuMont, 2008).

Urban, Greg, 'Interpretations of Inter-Cultural Contact: The Shokleng and Brazilian National Society 1914–1916', *Ethnohistory* 32:3 (1985), 224–44.

Valledejuli, Galanes, 'Are We There Yet? The Tension between Nativism and Humanism in Fanon's Writings', *Human Architecture* 5 (2007), 59–70.

Vanfraechem, Inge, Pemberton, Antony and Ndahinda, Felix Mukwiza, *Justice for Victims: Perspectives on Rights, Transition and Reconciliation* (New York: Routledge, 2014).

Varisco, Daniel M., *Reading Orientalism: Said and the Unsaid* (Seattle: University of Washngton Press, 2007).

Veltzke, Veit (ed.), *Playing Lawrence on the Other Side. Die Expedition Klein und das Deutsch-osmanische Bündnis im Ersten Weltkrieg* (Berlin: Nicholai, 2014).

Veracini, Lorenzo, '"Settler Colonialism": Career of a Concept', *Journal of Imperial and Commonwealth History* 41:2 (2013), 313–33.

Veracini, Lorenzo, 'Settler Colonialism and Decolonisation', *Borderlands* 6:2 (2007), www.borderlands.net.au/vol6 no2_2007/veracini_settler.htm.

Vermeulen, Hans F., *Before Boas: The Genesis of Ethnography and Ethnology in the German Enlightenment* (Lincoln and London: University of Nebraska Press, 2015).

Viotti da Costa, Emilia, *The Brazilian Empire: Myths and Histories* (Chicago: University of Chicago Press, 1985).

Virchow, Rudolf, 'Über den Schädelbau der Bewohner der Philippinen, insbesondere der Negritos', *Zeitschrift für Ethnologie* 3 (1871), 33–42.

Vollmer, Renate, *Auswanderungspolitik und soziale Frage im 19. Jahrhundert. Staatlich geförderte Auswanderung aus der Berghauptmannschaft Clausthal nach Südaustralien, Nord- und Südamerika 1848–1854* (Frankfurt am Main, Berlin, Bern, New York, Paris and Vienna: Peter Lang, 1994).

Voss, Susanne, *Die Geschichte der Abteilung Kairo des DAI im Spannungsfeld deutscher politischer Interessen 1881–1929* (Rhaden/Westfalen: Verlag Marie Leidorf, 2013).

Wagner, Hewig and Reiner, Hermann (eds), *The Lutheran Church in Papua New Guinea: The First Hundred Years, 1886–1986* (Adelaide: Lutheran Publishing House, 1986).

Walter, Dierk, *Organisierte Gewalt in der europäischen Expansion. Gestalt und Logik des Imperialkrieges* (Hamburg: Hamburger Edition, 2014).

Walther, Thomas, *Focus Orient. Orientalist Photography from the Late 19th and Early 20th Centuries* (Cologne: König, 2010).

Wanhalla, Angela, '"One White Man I Like Very Much" Intermarriage and the Cultural Encounter in Southern New Zealand, 1829–1850', *Journal of Women's History* 20:2 (2008), 34–56.

Ware, Vron, *Beyond the Pale: White Women, Racism and History* (London: Verso, 1993).

Warmbold, Joachim, 'Germania in Afrika: Frieda Freiin von Bülow, "Schöpferin des deutschen Kolonialromans"', *Jahrbuch des Instituts für Deutsche Geschichte* 15 (1986), 309–36.

Warneck, Gustav, *Evangelische Missionslehre: Ein Missionstheoretischer Versuch*, 5 vols (Gotha: Frederich Andreas Perthes, 1887–1905).

Weller, Christiane, 'Das fremde Ich. Begegnungen im pazifischen Raum' (PhD Dissertation, Monash University, 1998).

Wende, Erich and Becker, C.H., *Mensch und Politiker. Ein biographischer Beitrag zur Kulturgeschichte der Weimarer Republik* (Stuttgart: Deutsche Verlags-Anstalt, 1959).

Wettstein, Karl Alexander, *Brasilien und die deutsch-brasilianische Kolonie Blumenau* (Leipzig: F. Engelmann, 1907).

Wettstein, Karl Alexander, 'Die Verkehrsverhältnisse der deutsch-brasilianischen Kolonie Blumenau' (PhD Dissertation, Universität Heidelberg, 1907).

Wiener, Michael, *Ikonographie des Wilden. Menschen-Bilder in Ethnographie und Photographie zwischen 1850 und 1918* (Munich: Trickster, 1990).

Wigger, Iris and Ritter, S. (eds), *Racism and Modernity* (Berlin: LIT Verlag, 2011).

Wildenthal, Lora, *German Women for Empire, 1884–1945* (Durham, NC: Duke University Press, 2001).

Wilson, Judith, 'Abjection, Subjection, Redemption: Georg Forster's and Therese Huber's Perspectives on the Penal Colony', *Georg-Forster-Studien* 14 (2009), 133–89.

Winter, Christine, *Looking after One's Own: The Rise of Nationalism and the Politics of the Neuendettelsauer Mission in Australia, New Guinea and Germany, 1921–1933* (Frankfurt am Main: Peter Lang, 2012).

Wiselius, J.A.B., *A Visit to Manila and Its Environs* (Quezon City: Ateneo de Manila University Press, 2016).

Wokoeck, Ursula, *German Orientalism. The Study of the Middle East and Islam from 1800 to 1945* (London: Routledge, 2009).

Wolfe, Patrick, 'Land, Labor and Difference: Elementary Structures of Race', *American Historical Review* 106:3 (2001).

Wolfe, Patrick, 'Settler Colonialism and the Elimination of the Native', *Journal of Genocide Research* 8:4 (2006), 387–409.

Wolff, Larry and Cipolloni, Marc (eds), *The Anthropology of the Enlightenment* (Stanford: Stanford University Press, 2007).

Wolter, Stefanie, *Die Vermarktung des Fremden. Exotismus und die Anfänge des Massenkonsums* (Frankfurt am Main and New York: Campus, 2005).

Zahn, Heinrich, trans. Philip W. Holzknecht, *Mission and Music: Jabêm Traditional Music and the Development of the Lutheran Hymnody* (Boroko: Institute of Papua New Guinea Studies, 1996).

Zantop, Susanne, *Colonial Fantasies: Conquest, Family and Nation in Precolonial Germany, 1770–1870* (Durham, NC: Duke University Press, 1997).

Zimmerer, Jürgen, *Deutsche Herrschaft über Afrikaner. Staatlicher Machtanspruch und Wirklichkeit im kolonialen Namibia.* (Münster: Lit Verlag, 2002).

Zimmerer, Jürgen, *Von Windhuk nach Auschwitz? Beiträge zum Verhältnis von Kolonialismus und Holocaust* (Berlin: LIT Verlag, 2011).

Zimmerer, Jürgen and Zeller, Joachim (eds), *Völkermord in Deutsch-Südwestafrika. Der Kolonialkrieg (1904–1908) in Namibia und seine Folgen* (Berlin: Ch. Links, 2004).

Zimmerman, Andrew, *Alabama in Africa: Booker T. Washington, the German Empire, and the Globalization of the New South* (Princeton: Princeton University Press, 2010).

Zimmerman, Andrew, *Anthropology and Antihumanism in Imperial Germany* (Chicago: University of Chicago Press, 2001).

Zurstrassen, Bettina, *'Ein Stück deutscher Erde schaffen': Koloniale Beamte in Togo 1884–1914* (Frankfurt am Main: Campus, 2008).

# INDEX

Note: page numbers in *italic* refer to illustrations. An 'n.' after a page reference indicates the number of a note on that page. Literary works can be found under authors' names.

# INDEX

Greenland natives 92
Grimm, Jacob and Wilhelm 92
Guettel, Jens Uwe 5, 170, 172, 176, 180–1,
    206–7, 225
Gunditjmara 112

Habsburg Empire 170
Haeckel, Ernst 3
Hagenauer, Friedrich August 108
Hagenbeck, Carl 65
Hamburg 25, 56, 58, 64, 68, 128, 140, 207–8
*Hamburger Echo* 207
*Hamburger Nachrichten* 48
Hansemann, Adolph von 46
Haridi, Alexander 128–9
Hawai'i 45
    Royal Hawaiian Army 57
Hawkesworth, John 151, 155
Hebrew 89
Hegel, Georg Wilhelm Friedrich 4
hegemony 5, 8, 201
Heidelberg 127, 137, 139
Heinse, Johann Jacob Wilhelm 118–19
Hellenes *see* Greeks
Henke, Alfred 224
Herder, Johann Gottfried 91–2, 148–51,
    154–6, 158, 160–1, 182
Herero 6, 15, 208–9, 211–12, *213*, *214*,
    215–18, 221–4
    *see also* Africans
Hermann (of the Cherusci) 211
Hernsheim, Eduard 56–7
Hesse 127
    Hessian woman 118
Hirschfeld, Alexander von 70
Hoerhan, Eduardo 35
Hoffmann, Albert 99
Holocaust 7, 16
Honke, Gudrun 63
Hottentot elections 216, 223
humanism 3, 63, 113, 122, 148
    anti- 163n.8
    liberal 3, 149, 162
human rights 206, 221, 224–5
Humboldt, Alexander von 3, 108, 122

Ibirama 35
Igorots 189, 191, 195
Ihering, Hermann von 21, 24, 26, 28, 34–5
*Illustrierte Zeitung* 49
immigration 24–5, 27, 198
    immigrants 21, 24–7, 29, 35, 187, 191
        German 21, 25, 34
Imperial Colonial Office 66
imperialism 1, 4–5, 7–11, 16, 21–2, 35, 136,
    139–40, 163, 166n.60, 169, 185, 187,
    196, 202n.24, 206–9
    anti-imperialism 222, 224
    settler imperialism 21–2
    *see also* European imperialism

India 74
    British colonial India 73
Indian Protection Service 35
Indian Removal Act (1830) 177–8
Indigenous Australians 105–6, 108
    Aboriginal Australians 13, 89, 105–11,
        113–22, 149–53, 155–63, 189
    Aboriginal linguistics 107
    Aboriginal protectors 157
    Australians 114, 117, 120–1
    *Australier* 115–17, 122
    *see also* race: Australian race; South
        Australia: native South Australians;
        Tasmania: Aboriginal Tasmanians;
        Victoria: Aboriginal Victorians
Indigenous North Americans 3, 89, 169–73,
    175–6, 178–82
    indigenous languages 174
    Native Americans 89
    North American Indians 170
    *see also* North America: Americans
Indigenous people of Brazil 21–37
    Indians 21–2, 24–5, 28–31, 33–5, 37, 38n.28
    *see also* Brazilians
Indigenous peoples 1, 3–10, 13, 15, 22, 29,
    31–2, 34–6, 72, 93, 105, 108–9, 136,
    162, 169–71, 176, 181, 188, 191, 207,
    217
International Congress of Americanists 26
Iroquois 172, 174
Islam 128–9, 132, 137, 139–40
Islamic East Africa 142
    *see also* Africa
Islamic Studies (*Islamwissenschaft*) 127–9
Istanbul *see* Constantinople
Itajaí 25, 27, 34
    river 24–5
Italy 31, 127
    Italians 25, 29, 36

Jabêm 94, 96
    language 15, 90, 96
Jackson, Andrew (General; President) 177–81
Jacksonianism 178
Jagor, Fedor 14, 185–201
Jakarta *see* Batavia
Jamaica 179
Japan 58, 146n.78, 192
Java 147
Jena 35
Jensz, Felicity 7
Jerusalem 137
Jesuits 35, 175
Jesus Martins, Marcelino de (Martinho) 30
Jomey 119
Junkers 207, 209, 215

Kaingang (*Coroado*) 21–4, 26–8, 30–3, 35, 37
Kaingang nation 21
*Kaiserreich see* German Empire

[ 257 ]

# INDEX

Tasmania 56
  Aboriginal Tasmanians 108–9
  *see also* Indigenous Australians
Tati Tati country 112
Taunay, Alfredo d'Escragnolle 34
Tauralome King 51
technology 65–6, 192
Teichelmann, Christian 157
Teschauer, Carl 35
Thomas, Megan 188
Thomas, Nicholas 7
Tierra del Fuego 92
Tietê River 22
Tilki (Jemmy) 111–13, 116–17, 122
Tipping, Marjorie 108, 111
Tocqueville, Alexis de 176
Togo 11, 63–7, 70–1, 73, 76–8
Togolese 68, 71
Tolai 10, 44, 49–55, 57
  *see also* New Britons
Torre, Carlos de la (Governor-General) 187
Torres Strait 51, 56
trade 10, 25, 44, 52, 65, 133, 147, 153,
    155–6, 160, 187, 189, 197, 219
  skin trade 163n.8, 186
transatlantic 2, 65, 169
travel literature 10–11, 14, 42, 63–4, 69–71,
    74–8, 105, 127, 134, 139, 141, 149,
    156–8, 162, 164n.11, 177, 185–6, 188,
    192, 194–5, 200
Trotha, Lothar von (General) 212–13, *214*,
    215, 217, 222–3
Tschopowa 70

United States 6, 74, 169–70, 172, 177–80, 199
  *see also* Americas, the; North America,
    America
universalism 88, 94, 97, 98, 148, 154
uprisings 5, 66, 223
  *see also* revolts
Uruguai River 22
Uruguay 32
utilitarianism 159
Utrecht Mission Society 51

Versailles Peace Treaty 95
Vetter, Konrad 94–5
Victoria 106–9, 116
  Aboriginal Victorians 110
  *see also* Indigenous Australians
Vienna 26, 34
violence 1, 2, 4–8, 10, 13, 15–16, 18n.18, 32–4,
    36–7, 48–9, 52, 66, 109, 157, 189
Virchow, Rudolf 3, 57–8, 186–7, 189
Visayas 185, 194
Visayans 196–8
Vodou 71
  Baron Samedi 71
  Maman Brigitte 71

Vogt, Anton 114–15
*Völkerschauen* 64
*Vorwärts* 222

*wahre Jakob, Der* 207–24
War of 1812 179–80
warfare 9, 29, 31, 36, 50, 222
Warmbrunn (now Cieplice) 44
Warnambool tribe 112
Warneck, Gustav 92
Weimar Republic 78, 127–8
*Weltgeist* 4
*Weltpolitik* 139
Wertheimer, Max 97–8
West Africa 65, 69, 74
  West African Slave Coast 71
  *see also* Africa; German South-West Africa
West, Benjamin 173
Western Isles 153
Wieland, Christoph Martin 171
Wilhelm II, Kaiser 44, 131, 209, 212, 223–4
Wilhelmine Germany *see* German Empire
Windhoek 42, 223
Witbooi, Hendrik (Nama chief) 211–12
Woersmann, Adolf 215
Wolfe, James (British Major-General) 173
Wolfe, Patrick 14
women 11, 23, 28, 30–1, 33–4, 37, 53, 56,
    64–5, 67–75, 77–8, 114, 118–19, 130,
    133, 171, 174, 181, 190, 196–7, 217,
    219, *220*, 221–2
  Aboriginal 108
  African 70–4, 209, 219
  British 73
  European 63, 70, 82n.62
  German 82n.63, 84n.92
  Herero 223
  Indian 73
  Nubian 136
  Sudanese 135
Wonga, Simon 108–9
World War I *see* First World War
World War II *see* Second World War
Wurundjeri 108, 124

Xokleng nation 21
Xokleng, the (Botocudo) 22–4, 26–8, 30–3,
    35–7

Yarra tribe 108
Youl, Richard 112

Zahn, Heinrich 92–7
Zantop, Susanne 3, 151, 164
Zimmerman, Andrew 3, 163n.8
zoology 108, 160, 185

CPSIA information can be obtained
at www.ICGtesting.com
Printed in the USA
BVHW041656271221
624946BV00006B/18

9 781526 151650